ISBN 978-1-330-87860-6
PIBN 10116137

For support please visit www.forgottenbooks.com

English
Français
Deutsche
Italiano
Español
Português

# www.forgottenbooks.com

**Mythology** Photography **Fiction**
Fishing Christianity **Art** Cooking
Essays Buddhism Freemasonry
Medicine **Biology** Music **Ancient**
**Egypt** Evolution Carpentry Physics
Dance Geology **Mathematics** Fitness
Shakespeare **Folklore** Yoga Marketing
**Confidence** Immortality Biographies
Poetry **Psychology** Witchcraft
Electronics Chemistry History **Law**
Accounting **Philosophy** Anthropology
Alchemy Drama Quantum Mechanics
Atheism Sexual Health **Ancient History**
**Entrepreneurship** Languages Sport
Paleontology Needlework Islam
**Metaphysics** Investment Archaeology
Parenting Statistics Criminology
**Motivational**

# FROM THE AUTHOR, TO THE AMERICAN EDITOR OF HIS WORKS.

[Published by JAMES R. OSGOOD & Co., successors to TICKNOR AND FIELDS.]

THESE papers I am anxious to put into the hands of your house, and, so far as regards the U. S., of *your* house exclusively; not with any view to further emolument, but as an acknowledgment of the services which you have already rendered me; namely, first, in having brought together so widely scattered a collection, — a difficulty which in my own hands by too painful an experience I had found from nervous depression to be absolutely insurmountable; secondly, in having made me a participator in the pecuniary profits of the American edition, without solicitation or the shadow of any expectation on my part, without any legal claim that I could plead, or equitable warrant in established usage, solely and merely upon your own spontaneous motion. Some of these new papers, I hope, will not be without their value in the eyes of those who have taken an interest in the original series. But at all events, good or bad, they are now tendered to the appropriation of your individual house, the MESSRS. TICKNOR AND FIELDS, according to the amplest extent of any power to make such a transfer that I may be found to possess by law or custom in America.

I wish this transfer were likely to be of more value. But the veriest trifle, interpreted by the spirit in which I offer it, may express my sense of the liberality manifested throughout this transaction by your honorable house.

Ever believe me, my dear sir,

Your faithful and obliged,

THOMAS DE QUINCEY.

De Quincey's Works.

*AUTHOR'S LIBRARY EDITION.*

# THE NOTE-BOOK

OF AN

# ENGLISH OPIUM-EATER,

AND

# MISCELLANEOUS ESSAYS.

BY

## THOMAS DE QUINCEY.

BOSTON:

JAMES R. OSGOOD AND COMPANY,

LATE TICKNOR & FIELDS, AND FIELDS, OSGOOD, & Co.

1873.

# THE NOTE-BOOK

OF AN

# ENGLISH OPIUM-EATER.

# CONTENTS.

# THREE MEMORABLE MURDERS.

A SEQUEL TO

'MURDER CONSIDERED AS ONE OF THE FINE ARTS.'*

[1854.]

It is impossible to conciliate readers of so saturnine and gloomy a class, that they cannot enter with genial sympathy into any gaiety whatever, but, least of all, when the gaiety trespasses a little into the province of the extravagant. In such a case, not to sympathize is not to understand; and the playfulness, which is not relished, becomes flat and insipid, or absolutely without meaning. Fortunately, after all such churls have withdrawn from my audience in high displeasure, there remains a large majority who are loud in acknowledging the amusement which they have derived from a former paper of mine, 'On Murder considered as one of the Fine Arts;' at the same time proving the sincerity of their praise by one hesitating expression of censure. Repeatedly they have suggested to me, that perhaps the extravagance, though clearly intentional, and forming one element in the general gaiety of the

* See 'Miscellaneous Essays,' p. 17.

conception, went too far. I am not myself of that opinion; and I beg to remind these friendly censors, that it is amongst the direct purposes and efforts of this *bagatelle* to graze the brink of horror, and of all that would in actual realization be most repulsive. The very excess of the extravagance, in fact, by suggesting to the reader continually the mere aeriality of the entire speculation, furnishes the surest means of disenchanting him from the horror which might else gather upon his feelings. Let me remind such objectors, once for all, of Dean Swift's proposal for turning to account the supernumerary infants of the three kingdoms, which, in those days, both at Dublin and at London, were provided for in foundling hospitals, by cooking and eating them. This was an extravaganza, though really bolder and more coarsely practical than mine, which did not provoke any reproaches even to a dignitary of the supreme Irish church; its own monstrosity was its excuse; mere extravagance was felt to license and accredit the little *jeu d'esprit,* precisely as the blank impossibilities of Lilliput, of Laputa, of the Yahoos, &c., had licensed those. If, therefore, any man thinks it worth his while to tilt against so mere a foam-bubble of gaiety as this lecture on the æsthetics of murder, I shelter myself for the moment under the Telamonian shield of the Dean. But, in reality, my own little paper may plead a privileged excuse for its extravagance, such as is altogether wanting to the Dean's. Nobody can pretend, for a moment, on behalf of the Dean, that there is any ordinary and natural tendency in human thoughts, which could ever turn to infants as articles of diet under any conceivable circumstances, this would be felt as the most aggravated form of cannibalism — cannibalism applying itself to the most defenceless part of the species. But, on the other hand, the tendency to a critical or æsthetic valuation of fires and murders is universal. If you are summoned to the spectacle of a great fire, undoubtedly the first impulse is — to assist in putting it out. But that field of exertion is very limited, and is soon filled by regular professional people, trained and equipped for the service. In the case of a fire which is operating upon *private* property, pity for a neighbor's calamity checks us at first in treating the affair as a scenic spectacle. But perhaps the fire may be confined to public buildings. And in any case, after we have paid our tribute of regret to the affair, considered as a calamity, inevitably, and without restraint, we go on to consider it as a stage spectacle. Exclamations of — How grand! how magnificent! arise in a sort of rapture from the crowd. For instance, when Drury Lane was burned down in the first decennium of this century, the falling in of the roof was signalized by a mimic suicide of the protecting Apollo that surmounted and crested the centre of this roof. The god was stationary with his lyre, and seemed looking down upon the fiery ruins that were so rapidly approaching him. Suddenly the supporting timbers below him gave way; a convulsive heave of the billowing flames seemed for a moment to raise the statue; and then, as if on some impulse of despair, the presiding deity appeared not to fall, but to throw himself into the fiery deluge, for he went down head foremost; and in all respects, the descent had the air of a voluntary act. What followed? From every one of the bridges over the river, and from other

open areas which commanded the spectacle, there
arose a sustained uproar of admiration and sympathy.
Some few years before this event, a prodigious fire
occurred at Liverpool; the *Goree*, a vast pile of ware-
houses close to one of the docks, was burned to the
ground. The huge edifice, eight or nine stories high,
and laden with most combustible goods, many thousand
bales of cotton, wheat and oats in thousands of quarters, tar, turpentine, rum, gunpowder, &c., continued
through many hours of darkness to feed this tremendous
fire. To aggravate the calamity, it blew a regular gale
of wind; luckily for the shipping, it blew inland, that
is, to the east; and all the way down to Warrington,
eighteen miles distant to the eastward, the whole air
was illuminated by flakes of cotton, often saturated
with rum, and by what seemed absolute worlds of
blazing sparks, that lighted up all the upper chambers
of the air. All the cattle lying abroad in the fields
through a breadth of eighteen miles, were thrown into
terror and agitation. Men, of course, read in this
hurrying overhead of scintillating and blazing vortices,
the annunciation of some gigantic calamity going on in
Liverpool; and the lamentation on that account was
universal. But that mood of public sympathy did not
at all interfere to suppress or even to check the
momentary bursts of rapturous admiration, as this
arrowy sleet of many-colored fire rode on the wings
of hurricane, alternately through open depths of air, or
through dark clouds overhead.

Precisely the same treatment is applied to murders
After the first tribute of sorrow to those who have
perished, but, at all events, after the personal interests
have been tranquillized by time, inevitably the scenical

features (what æsthetically may be called the comparative *advantages*) of the several murders are reviewed and valued. One murder is compared with
another; and the circumstances of superiority, as, for
example, in the incidence and effects of surprise, of
mystery, &c., are collated and appraised. I, therefore, for *my* extravagance, claim an inevitable and
perpetual ground in the spontaneous tendencies of the
human mind when left to itself. But no one will
pretend that any corresponding plea can be advanced
on behalf of Swift.

In this important distinction between myself and the
Dean, lies one reason which prompted the present writing. A second purpose of this paper is, to make the
reader acquainted circumstantially with three memorable cases of murder, which long ago the voice of
amateurs has crowned with laurel, but especially
with the two earliest of the three, viz., the immortal
Williams' murders of 1812. The act and the actor
are each separately in the highest degree interesting;
and, as forty-two years have elapsed since 1812, it cannot be supposed that either is known circumstantially to
the men of the current generation.

Never, throughout the annals of universal Christendom, has there indeed been any act of one solitary
insulated individual, armed with power so appalling
over the hearts of men, as that exterminating murder,
by which, during the winter of 1812, John Williams in
one hour, smote two houses with emptiness, exterminated all but two entire households, and asserted his own
supremacy above all the children of Cain. It would be
absolutely impossible adequately to describe the frenzy
of feelings which, throughout the next fortnight, mas

tered the popular heart; the mere delirium of indignant
horror in some, the mere delirium of panic in others.
For twelve succeeding days, under some groundless
notion that the unknown murderer had quitted London,
the panic which had convulsed the mighty metropolis
diffused itself all over the island. I was myself at that
time nearly three hundred miles from London; but
there, and everywhere, the panic was indescribable.
One lady, my next neighbor, whom personally I knew,
living at the moment, during the absence of her husband, with a few servants in a very solitary house,
never rested until she had placed eighteen doors (so she
told me, and, indeed, satisfied me by ocular proof), each
secured by ponderous bolts, and bars, and chains, between her own bedroom and any intruder of human
build. To reach her, even in her drawing-room, was
like going, as a flag of truce, into a beleaguered fortress; at every sixth step one was stopped by a sort of
portcullis. The panic was not confined to the rich,
women in the humblest ranks more than once died upon
the spot, from the shock attending some suspicious attempts at intrusion upon the part of vagrants, meditating
probably nothing worse than a robbery, but whom the
poor women, misled by the London newspapers, had
fancied to be the dreadful London murderer. Meantime, this solitary artist, that rested in the centre of
London, self-supported by his own conscious grandeur,
as a domestic Attila, or ' scourge of God ;' this man,
that walked in darkness, and relied upon murder (as
afterwards transpired) for bread, for clothes, for promotion in life, was silently preparing an effectual answer
to the public journals; and on the twelfth day after his
inaugural murder, he advertised his presence in Lon-

don, and published to all men the absurdity of ascribing
to *him* any ruralizing propensities, by striking a second
blow, and accomplishing a second family extermination.
Somewhat lightened was the *provincial* panic by this
proof that the murderer had not condescended to sneak
into the country, or to abandon for a moment, under
any motive of caution or fear, the great metropolitan
*castra stativa* of gigantic crime, seated for ever on the
Thames.  In fact, the great artist disdained a provincial
reputation ; and he must have felt, as a case of ludicrous
disproportion, the contrast between a country town or
village, on the one hand, and, on the other, a work
more lasting than brass — a κτῆμα ἐς αει — a murder such
in quality as any murder that *he* would condescend to
own for a work turned out from his own *studio*.

Coleridge, whom I saw some months after these
terrific murders, told me, that, for *his* part, though at
the time resident in London, he had not shared in the
prevailing panic ; *him* they effected only as a philosopher, and threw him into a profound reverie upon the
tremendous power which is laid open in a moment to
any man who can reconcile himself to the abjuration
of all conscientious restraints, if, at the same time,
thoroughly without fear.  Not sharing in the public
panic, however, Coleridge did not consider that panic
at all unreasonable ; for, as he said most truly in that
vast metropolis there are many thousands of households,
composed exclusively of women and children ; many
other thousands there are who necessarily confide their
safety, in the long evenings, to the discretion of a young
servant girl ; and if she suffers herself to be beguiled
by the pretence of a message from her mother, sister,
or sweetheart, into opening the door, there, in one

second of time, goes to wreck the security of the house
However, at that time, and for many months afterwards,
the practice of steadily putting the chain upon the door
before it was opened prevailed generally, and for a long
time served as a record of that deep impression left
upon London by Mr. Williams.   Southey, I may add,
entered deeply into the public feeling on this occasion,
and said to me, within a week or two of the first murder, that it was a private event of that order which rose
to the dignity of a national event.*   But now, having
prepared the reader to appreciate on its true scale this
dreadful tissue of murder (which as a record belonging
to an era that is now left forty-two years behind us, not
one person in four of this generation can be expected
to know correctly), let me pass to the circumstantial
details of the affair.

Yet, first of all, one word as to the local scene of the
murders.   Ratcliffe Highway is a public thoroughfare
in a most chaotic quarter of eastern or nautical London ;
and at this time (viz., in 1812), when no adequate
police existed except the *detective* police of Bow Street,
admirable for its own peculiar purposes, but utterly incommensurate to the general service of the capital, it
was a most dangerous quarter.   Every third man at
the least might be set down as a foreigner.   Lascars
Chinese, Moors, Negroes, were met at every step.
And apart from the manifold ruffianism, shrouded im-
penetrably under the mixed hats and turbans of men
whose past was untraceable to any European eye, it is

---

* I am not sure whether Southey held at this time his appointment to the editorship of the ' Edinburgh Annual Register.'   If
he did, no aoubt in the domestic section of that chronicle will be
found an excellent account of the whole.

well known that the navy (especially, in time of war,) the commercial navy) of Christendom is the sure receptacle of all the murderers and ruffians whose crimes have given them a motive for withdrawing themselves for a season from the public eye. It is true, that few of this class are qualified to act as ' able ' seamen: but at all times, and especially during war, only a small .proportion (or *nucleus*) of each ship's company consists of such men: the large majority being mere untutored landsmen. John Williams, however, who had been occasionally rated as a seaman on board of various Indiamen, &c., was probably a very accomplished seaman. Pretty generally, in fact, he was a ready and adroit man, fertile in resources under all sudden difficulties, and most flexibly adapting himself to all varieties of social life. Williams was a man of middle stature (five feet seven and a-half, to five feet eight inches high), slenderly built, rather thin, but wiry, tolerably muscular, and clear of all superfluous flesh. A lady, who saw him under examination (I think at the Thames Police Office), assured me that his hair was of the most extraordinary and vivid color, viz., bright yellow, something between an orange and lemon color. Williams had been in India; chiefly in Bengal and Madras: but he had also been upon the Indus. Now, it is notorious that, in the Punjaub, horses of a high caste are often painted — crimson, blue, green, purple; and it struck me that Williams might, for some casual purpose of disguise, have taken a hint from this practice of Scinde and Lahore, so that the color might not have been natural. In other respects, his appearance was natural enough; and, judging by a plaster cast of him, which I purchased in London, I should say mean, as regaraed his facial structure. One fact, however, was striking, and fell in with the impression of his natural tiger character, that his face wore at all times a bloodless ghastly pallor. 'You might imagine,' said my informant, 'that in his veins circulated not red life-blood, such as could kindle into the blush of shame, of wrath, of pity — but a green sap that welled from no human heart.' His eyes seemed frozen and glazed, as if their light were all converged upon some victim lurking in the far background. So far his appearance might have repelled; but, on the other hand, the concurrent testimony of many witnesses, and also the silent testimony of facts, showed that the oiliness and snaky insinuation of his demeanor counteracted the repulsiveness of his ghastly face, and amongst inexperienced young women won for him a very favorable reception. In particular, one gentle-mannered girl, whom Williams had undoubtedly designed to murder, gave in evidence — that once, when sitting alone with her, he had said, 'Now, Miss R., supposing that I should appear about midnight at your bedside, armed with a carving knife, what would you say?' To which the confiding girl had replied, 'Oh, Mr. Williams, if it was anybody else, I should be frightened. But, as soon as I heard *your* voice, I should be tranquil.' Poor girl! had this outline sketch of Mr. Williams been filled in and realized, she would have seen something in the corpse-like face, and heard something in the sinister voice, that would have unsettled her tranquillity for ever. But nothing short of such dreadful experiences could avail to unmask Mr. John Williams.

Into this perilous region it was that, on a Saturday night in December, Mr. Williams, whom we suppose to

have long since made his *coup d'essai,* forced his way
through the crowded streets, bound on business. To
say, was to do. And this night he had said to himself
secretly, that he would execute a design which he had
already sketched, and which, when finished, was destined on the following day to strike consternation into
' all that mighty heart' of London, from centre to circumference. It was afterwards remembered that he
had quitted his lodgings on this dark errand about
eleven o'clock P. M.; not that he meant to begin so
soon: but he needed to reconnoitre. He carried his
tools closely buttoned up under his loose roomy coat.
It was in harmony with the general subtlety of his
character, and his polished hatred of brutality, that by
universal agreement his manners were distinguished
for exquisite suavity : the tiger's heart was masked by
the most insinuating and snaky refinement. All his
acquaintances afterwards described his dissimulation as
so ready and so perfect, that if, in making his way
through the streets, always so crowded on a Saturday
night in neighborhoods so poor, he had accidentally
jostled any person, he would (as they were all satisfied)
have stopped to offer the most gentlemanly apologies.
with his devilish heart brooding over the most hellish
of purposes, he would yet have paused to express a
benign hope that the huge mallet, buttoned up under
his elegant surtout, with a view to the little business
that awaited him about ninety minutes further on, had
not inflicted any pain on the stranger with whom he
had come into collision. Titian, I believe, but certainly
Rubens, and perhaps Vandyke, made it a rule never to
practise his art but in full dress — point ruffles, bag
wig, and diamond-hilted sword; and Mr. Williams,

there is reason to believe, when he went out for a grand compound massacre (in another sense, one might have applied to it the Oxford phrase of *going out as Grand Compounder*), always assumed black silk stockings and pumps; nor would he on any account have degraded his position as an artist by wearing a morning gown. In his second great performance, it was particularly noticed and recorded by the one sole trembling man, who under killing agonies of fear was compelled (as the reader will find) from a secret stand to become the solitary spectator of his atrocities, that Mr. Williams wore a long blue frock, of the very finest cloth, and richly lined with silk. Amongst the anecdotes which circulated about him, it was also said at the time, that Mr. Williams employed the first of dentists, and also the first of chiropodists. On no account would he patronize any second-rate skill. And beyond a doubt, in that perilous little branch of business which was practised by himself, he might be regarded as the most aristocratic and fastidious of artists.

But who meantime was the victim, to whose abode he was hurrying? For surely he never could be so indiscreet as to be sailing about on a roving cruise in search of some chance person to murder? Oh, no: he had suited himself with a victim some time before, viz., an old and very intimate friend. For he seems to have laid it down as a maxim — that the best person to murder was a friend; and, in default of a friend, which is an article one cannot always command, an acquaintance: because, in either case, on first approaching his subject, suspicion would be disarmed: whereas a stranger might take alarm, and find in the very countenance of his murderer elect a warning

summons to place himself on guard. However, in
the present case, his destined victim was supposed to
unite both characters : originally he had been a friend ;
but subsequently, on good cause arising, he had become an enemy. Or more probably, as others said,
the feelings had long since languished which gave life
to either relation of friendship or of enmity. Marr
was the name of that unhappy man, who (whether in
the character of friend or enemy) had been selected
for the subject of this present Saturday night's performance. And the story current at that time about
the connection between Williams and Marr, having
(whether true or not true) never been contradicted
upon authority, was, that they sailed in the same India-
man to Calcutta ; that they had quarrelled when at
sea ; but another version of the story said — no : they
had quarrelled after returning from sea ; and the sub-
jcet of their quarrel was Mrs. Marr, a very pretty
young woman, for whose favor they had been rival
candidates, and at one time with most bitter enmity
towards each other. Some circumstances give a color
of probability to this story. Otherwise it has sometimes happened, on occasion of a murder not sufficiently accounted for, that, from pure goodness of
heart intolerant of a mere sordid motive for a striking
murder, some person has forged, and the public has
accredited, a story representing the murderer as having
moved under some loftier excitement : and in this
case the public, too much shocked at the idea of Williams having on the single motive of gain consummated
so complex a tragedy, welcomed the tale which represented him as governed by deadly malice, growing out
of the more impassioned and noble rivalry for the

favor of a woman. The case remains in some degree
doubtful; but, certainly, the probability is, that Mrs.
Marr had been the true cause, the *causa teterrima*, of
the feud between the men. Meantime, the minutes are
numbered, the sands of the hour-glass are running out,
that measure the duration of this feud upon earth.
This night it shall cease. To-morrow is the day which
in England they call Sunday, which in Scotland they
call by the Judaic name of 'Sabbath.' To both nations, under different names, the day has the same
functions; to both it is a day of rest. For thee also,
Marr, it shall be a day of rest; so is it written; thou,
too, young Marr, shalt find rest — thou, and thy household, and the stranger that is within thy gates. But
that rest must be in the world which lies beyond the
grave. On this side the grave ye have all slept your
final sleep.

The night was one of exceeding darkness; and in
this humble quarter of London, whatever the night
happened to be, light or dark, quiet or stormy, all shops
were kept open on Saturday nights until twelve o'clock,
at the least, and many for half an hour longer. There
was no rigorous and pedantic Jewish superstition about
the exact limits of Sunday. At the very worst, the
Sunday stretched over from one o'clock, A. M. of one
day, up to eight o'clock A. M. of the next, making a
clear circuit of thirty-one hours. This, surely, was
long enough. Marr, on this particular Saturday night,
would be content if it were even shorter, provided it
would come more quickly, for he has been toiling
through sixteen hours behind his counter. Marr's
position in life was this: he kept a little hosier's shop,
and had invested in his stock and the fittings of his

shop about £180. Like all men engaged in trade, he suffered some anxieties. He was a new beginner; but, already, bad debts had alarmed him; and bills were coming to maturity that were not likely to be met by commensurate sales. Yet, constitutionally, he was a sanguine hoper. At this time he was a stout, fresh-colored young man of twenty-seven; in some slight degree uneasy from his commercial prospects, but still cheerful, and anticipating — (how vainly!) — that for this night, and the next night, at least, he will rest his wearied head and his cares upon the faithful bosom of his sweet lovely young wife. The household of Marr, consisting of five persons, is as follows : First, there is himself, who, if he should happen to be ruined, in a limited commercial sense, has energy enough to jump up again, like a pyramid of fire, and soar high above ruin many times repeated. Yes, poor Marr, so it might be, if thou wert left to thy native energies unmolested ; but even now there stands on the other side of the street one born of hell, who puts his peremptory negative on all these flattering prospects. Second in the list of his household, stands his pretty and amiable wife, who is happy after the fashion of youthful wives, for she is only twenty-two, and anxious (if at all) only on account of her darling infant. For, thirdly, there is in a cradle, not quite nine feet below the street, viz., in a warm, cosy kitchen, and rocked at inter-vals by the young mother, a baby eight months old. Nineteen months have Marr and herself been married ; and this is their first-born child. Grieve not for this child, that it must keep the deep rest of Sunday in some other world; for wherefore should an orphan, steeped to the lips in poverty, when once bereaved

of father and mother, linger upon an alien and murderous earth? Fourthly, there is a stoutish boy, an
apprentice, say thirteen years old; a Devonshire boy,
with handsome features, such as most Devonshire
youths have;* satisfied with his place; not over-
worked; treated kindly, and aware that he was treated
kindly, by his master and mistress. Fifthly, and lastly,
bringing up the rear of this quiet household, is a servant girl, a grown-up young woman; and she, being
particularly kind-hearted, occupied (as often happens
in families of humble pretensions as to rank) a sort of
sisterly place in her relation to her mistress. A great
democratic change is at this very time (1854), and has
been for twenty years, passing over British society.
Multitudes of persons are becoming ashamed of saying, 'my master,' or 'my mistress:' the term now in
the slow process of superseding it is, 'my employer.'
Now, in the United States, such an expression of
democratic hauteur, though disagreeable as a needless
proclamation of independence which nobody is dis-
puting, leaves, however, no lasting bad effect. For
the domestic 'helps' are pretty generally in a state of
transition so sure and so rapid to the headship of
domestic establishments belonging to themselves, that
in effect they are but ignoring, for the present
moment, a relation which would at any rate dissolve
itself in a year or two. But in England, where no

---

* An artist told me in this year, 1812, that having accidentally
seen a native Devonshire regiment (either volunteers or militia),
nine hundred strong, marching past a station at which he had
posted himself, he did not observe a dozen men that would not
have been described in common parlance as 'good looking.'

such resources exist of everlasting surplus lands, the tendency of the change is painful. It carries with it a sullen and a coarse expresion of immunity from a yoke which was in any case a light one, and often a benign one. In some other place I will illustrate my meaning. Here, apparently, in Mrs. Marr's service, the principle concerned illustrated itself practically. Mary, the female servant, felt a sincere and unaffected respect for a mistress whom she saw so steadily occupied with her domestic duties, and who, though so young, and invested with some slight authority, never exerted it capriciously, or even showed it at all conspiciously. According to the testimony of all the neighbors, she treated her mistress with a shade of unobtrusive respect on the one hand, and yet was eager to relieve her, whenever that was possible, from the weight of her maternal duties, with the cheerful voluntary service of a sister.

To this young woman it was, that, suddenly, within three or four minutes of midnight, Marr called aloud from the head of the stairs — directing her to go out and purchase some oysters for the family supper. Upon what slender accidents hang oftentimes solemn lifelong results ! Marr occupied in the concerns of his shop, Mrs. Marr occupied with some little ailment and restlessness of her baby, had both forgotten the affair of supper; the time was now narrowing every moment, as regarded any variety of choice ; and oysters were perhaps ordered as the likeliest article to be had at all, after twelve o'clock should have struck. And yet, upon this trivial circumstance depended Mary's life. Had she been sent abroad for supper at the ordinary time of ten or eleven o'clock, it is almost

2

certain that she, the solitary member of the household who escaped from the exterminating tragedy, would *not* have escaped; too surely she would have shared the general fate. It had now become necessary to be quick. Hastily, therefore, receiving money from Marr with a basket in her hand, but unbonneted, Mary tripped out of the shop. It became afterwards, on recollection, a heart-chilling remembrance to herself— that, precisely as she emerged from the shop-door, she noticed, on the opposite side of the street, by the light of the lamps, a man's figure; stationary at the instant, but in the next instant slowly moving. This was Williams; as a little incident, either just before or just after (at present it is impossible to say which), sufficiently proved. Now, when one considers the inevitable hurry and trepidation of Mary under the circumstances stated, time barely sufficing for any chance of executing her errand, it becomes evident that she must have connected some deep feeling of mysterious uneasiness with the movements of this unknown man; else, assuredly, she would not have found her attention disposable for such a case. Thus far, she herself threw some little light upon what it might be that, semi-consciously, was then passing through her mind; she said, that, notwithstanding the darkness, which would not permit her to trace the man's features, or to ascertain the exact direction of his eyes, it yet struck her, that from his carriage when in motion, and from the apparent inclination of his person, he must be looking at No. 29.

The little incident which I have alluded to as confirming Mary's belief was, that, at some period not very far from midnight, the watchman had specially

noticed this stranger; he had observed him continually peeping into the window of Marr's shop; and
had thought this act, connected with the man's appearance, so suspicious, that he stepped into Marr's shop,
and communicated what he had seen. This fact he
afterwards stated before the magistrates; and he
added, that subsequently, viz., a few minutes after
twelve (eight or ten minutes, probably, after the departure of Mary), he (the watchman), when re-entering
upon his ordinary half-hourly beat, was requested by
Marr to assist him in closing the shutters. Here they
had a final communication with each other; and the
watchman mentioned to Marr that the mysterious
stranger had now apparently taken himself off; for
that he had not been visible since the first communication made to Marr by the watchman. There is little
doubt that Williams had observed the watchman's visit
to Marr, and had thus had his attention seasonably
drawn to the indiscretion of his own demeanor; so
that the warning, given unavailingly to Marr, had been
turned to account by Williams. There can be still
less doubt, that the bloodhound had commenced his
work within one minute of the watchman's assisting
Marr to put up his shutters. And on the following
consideration: — that which prevented Williams from
commencing even earlier, was the exposure of the
shop's whole interior to the gaze of street passengers.
It was indispensable that the shutters should be accurately closed before Williams could safely get to work.
But, as soon as ever this preliminary precaution had
been completed, once having secured that concealment
from the public eye it then became of still greater
importance not to lose a moment by delay, than pre-

viously it had been not to hazard any thing by precipitance. For all depended upon going in before Marr
should have locked the door. On any other mode of
effecting an entrance (as, for instance, by waiting for
the return of Mary, and making his entrance simultaneously with her), it will be seen that Williams must
have forfeited that particular advantage which mute
facts, when read into their true construction, will soon
show the reader that he must have employed. Williams
waited, of necessity, for the sound of the watchman's
retreating steps; waited, perhaps, for thirty seconds;
but when that danger was past, the next danger was,
lest Marr should lock the door; one turn of the key,
and the murderer would have been locked out. In,
therefore, he bolted, and by a dexterous movement of
his left hand, no doubt, turned the key, without letting
Marr perceive this fatal stratagem. It is really wonderful and most interesting to pursue the successive
steps of this monster, and to notice the absolute certainty with which the silent hieroglyphics of the case
betray to us the whole process and movements of the
bloody drama, not less surely and fully than if we
had been ourselves hidden in Marr's shop, or had
looked down from the heavens of mercy upon this
hell-kite, that knew not what mercy meant. That he
had concealed from Marr his trick, secret and rapid,
upon the lock, is evident; because else, Marr would
instantly have taken the alarm, especially after what
the watchman had communicated. But it will soon
be seen that Marr had *not* been alarmed. In reality,
towards the full success of Williams, it was important
in the last degree, to intercept and forestall any yell
or shout of agony from Marr. Such an outcry, and

in a situation so slenderly fenced off from the street, viz., by walls the very thinnest, makes itself heard outside pretty nearly as well as if it were uttered in the street. Such an outcry it was indispensable to stifle. It *was* stifled; and the reader will soon understand *how*. Meantime, at this point, let us leave the murderer alone with his victims. For fifty minutes let him work his pleasure. The front-door, as we know, is now fastened against all help. Help there is none. Let us, therefore, in vision, attach ourselves to Mary; and, when all is over, let us come back with *her*, again raise the curtain, and read the dreadful record of all that has passed in her absence.

The poor girl, uneasy in her mind to an extent that she could but half understand, roamed up and down in search of an oyster shop; and finding none that was still open, within any circuit that her ordinary experience had made her acquainted with, she fancied it best to try the chances of some remoter district. Lights she saw gleaming or twinkling at a distance, that still tempted her onwards; and thus, amongst unknown streets poorly lighted,* and on a night of peculiar darkness, and in a region of London where ferocious tumults were continually turning her out of what seemed to be the direct course, naturally she got bewildered. The purpose with which she started, had by this time become hopeless. Nothing remained for her now but to retrace

---

* I do not remember, chronologically, the history of gas-lights. But in London, long after Mr. Winsor had shown the value of gas-lighting, and its applicability to street purposes, various districts were prevented, for many years, from resorting to the new system, in consequence of old contracts with oil-dealers, subsisting through long terms of years.

her steps. But this was difficult; for she was afraid to ask directions from chance passengers, whose appearance the darkness prevented her from reconnoitring. At length by his lantern she recognized a watchman; through him she was guided into the right road; and in ten minutes more, she found herself back at the door of No. 29, in Ratcliffe Highway. But by this time she felt satisfied that she must have been absent for fifty or sixty minutes; indeed, she had heard, at a distance, the cry of *past one o'clock*, which, commencing a few seconds after one, lasted intermittingly for ten or thirteen minutes.

In the tumult of agonizing thoughts that very soon surprised her, naturally it became hard for her to recall distinctly the whole succession of doubts, and jealousies, and shadowy misgivings that soon opened upon her. But, so far as could be collected, she had not in the first moment of reaching home noticed anything decisively alarming. In very many cities bells are the main instruments for communicating between the street and the interior of houses: but in London knockers prevail. At Marr's there was both a knocker and a bell. Mary rang, and at the same time very gently knocked. She had no fear of disturbing her master or mistress; *them* she made sure of finding still up. Her anxiety was for the baby, who being disturbed, might again rob her mistress of a night's rest. And she well knew that, with three people all anxiously awaiting her return, and by this time, perhaps, seriously uneasy at her delay, the least audible whisper from herself would in a moment bring one of them to the door. Yet how is this? To her astonishment, but with the astonishment came creeping over her an icy horror, no stir nor murmur was heard ascending from the kitchen. At this moment came back upon her, with shuddering anguish, the indistinct image of the stranger in the loose dark coat, whom she had seen stealing along under the shadowy lamp-light, and too certainly watching her master's motions: keenly she now reproached herself that, under whatever stress of hurry, she had not ac-quainted Mr. Marr with the suspicious appearances. Poor girl! she did not then know that, if this commu-nication could have availed to put Marr upon his guard, it had reached him from another quarter; so that her own omission, which had in reality arisen under her hurry to execute her master's commission, could not be charged with any bad consequences. But all such reflections this way or that were swallowed up at this point in over-mastering panic. That her double. sum-mons *could* have been unnoticed — this solitary fact in one moment made a revelation of horror. One person might have fallen asleep, but two — but three — *that* was a mere impossibility. And even supposing all three together with the baby locked in sleep, still how unaccountable was this utter — utter silence! Most naturally at this moment something like hysterical horror overshadowed the poor girl, and now at last she rang the bell with the violence that belongs to sickening terror. This done, she paused: self-command enough she still retained, though fast and fast it was slipping away from her, to bethink herself — that, if any over-whelming accident *had* compelled both Marr and his apprentice-boy to leave the house in order to summon surgical aid from opposite quarters — a thing barely supposable — still, even in that case Mrs. Marr and her infant would be left; and some murmuring reply, under any extremity, would be elicited from the poor mother. To pause, therefore, to impose stern silence upon herself, so as to leave room for the possible answer to this final appeal, became a duty of spasmodic effort. Listen, therefore, poor trembling heart; listen, and for twenty seconds be still as death. Still as death she was: and during that dreadful stillness, when she hushed her breath that she might listen, occurred an incident of killing fear, that to her dying day would never cease to renew its echoes in her ear. She, Mary, the poor trembling girl, checking and overruling herself by a final effort, that she might leave full opening for her dear young mistress's answer to her own last frantic appeal, heard at last and most distinctly a sound within the house. Yes, now beyond a doubt there is coming an answer to her summons. What was it? On the stairs, not the stairs that led downwards to the kitchen, but the stairs that led upwards to the single story of bed-chambers above, was heard a creaking sound. Next was heard most distinctly a footfall: one, two, three, four, five stairs were slowly and distinctly descended. Then the dreadful footsteps were heard advancing along the little narrow passage to the door. The steps — oh heavens! *whose* steps? — have paused at the door. The very breathing can be heard of that dreadful being, who has silenced all breathing except his own in the house. There is but a door between him and Mary. What is he doing on the other side of the door? A cautious step, a stealthy step it was that came down the stairs, then paced along the little narrow passage — narrow as a coffin — till at last the step pauses at the door. How hard the fellow breathes! He, the solitary murderer, is on one side the door; Mary is on the other side. Now, suppose that he should suddenly open the door, and that incautiously in the dark Mary should rush in, and find herself in the arms of the murderer. Thus far the case is a possible one — that to a certainty, had this little trick been tried immediately upon Mary's return, it would have succeeded; had the door been opened suddenly upon her first tingle-tingle, headlong she would have tumbled in, and perished. But now Mary is upon her guard. The unknown murderer and she have both their lips upon the door, listening, breathing hard; but luckily they are on different sides of the door; and upon the least indication of unlocking or unlatching, she would have recoiled into the asylum of general darkness.

What was the murderer's meaning in coming along the passage to the front door? The meaning was this: separately, as an individual, Mary was worth nothing at all to him. But, considered as a member of a household, she had this value, viz., that she, if caught and murdered, perfected and rounded the desolation of the house. The case being reported, as reported it would be all over Christendom, led the imagination captive. The whole covey of victims was thus netted; the household ruin was thus full and orbicular; and in that proportion the tendency of men and women, flutter as they might, would be helplessly and hopelessly to sink into the all-conquering hands of the mighty murderer. He had but to say — my testimonials are dated from No. 29 Ratcliffe Highway, and the poor vanquished imagination sank powerless before the fascinating rattlesnake eye of the murderer. There is not a doubt that the motive of the murderer for standing on the inner side

3

of Marr's front-door, whilst Mary stood on the outside, was — a hope that, if he quietly opened the door whisperingly counterfeiting Marr's voice, and saying What made you stay so long? possibly she might have been inveigled. He was wrong; the time was past for that; Mary was now maniacally awake; she began now to ring the bell and to ply the knocker with unin- termitting violence. And the natural consequence was, that the next door neighbor, who had recently gone to bed and instantly fallen asleep, was roused; and by the incessant violence of the ringing and the knocking, which now obeyed a delirious and uncontrollable im- pulse in Mary, he became sensible that some very dreadful event must be at the root of so clamorous an uproar. To rise, to throw up the sash, to demand angrily the cause of this unseasonable tumult, was the work of a moment. The poor girl remained sufficiently mistress of herself rapidly to explain the circumstance of her own absence for an hour; her belief that Mr. and Mrs. Marr's family had all been murdered in the interval; and that at this very moment the murderer was in the house.

The person to whom she addressed this statement was a pawnbroker; and a thoroughly brave man he must have been; for it was a perilous undertaking, merely as a trial of physical strength, singly to face a mysterious assassin, who had apparently signalized his prowess by a triumph so comprehensive. But, again, for the imagination it required an effort of self-conquest to rush headlong into the presence of one invested with a cloud of mystery, whose nation, age, motives, were all alike unknown. Rarely on any field of battle has a soldier been called upon to face so complex a danger. For if the entire family of his neighbor Marr had been exterminated, were this indeed true, such a scale of bloodshed would seem to argue that there must have been two persons as the perpetrators; or if one singly had accomplished such a ruin, in that case how colossal must have been his audacity! probably, also, his skill and animal power! Moreover, the unknown enemy (whether single or double) would, doubtless, be elaborately armed. Yet, under all these disadvantages, did this fearless man rush at once to the field of butchery in his neighbor's house. Waiting only to draw on his trousers, and to arm himself with the kitchen poker, he went down into his own little back-yard. On this mode of approach, he would have a chance of intercepting the murderer; whereas from the front there would be no such chance; and there would also be considerable delay in the process of breaking open the door. A brick wall, nine or ten feet high, divided his own back premises from those of Marr. Over this he vaulted; and at the moment when he was recalling himself to the necessity of going back for a candle, he suddenly perceived a feeble ray of light already glimmering on some part of Marr's premises. Marr's back-door stood wide open. Probably the murderer had passed through it one half minute before. Rapidly the brave man passed onwards to the shop, and there beheld the carnage of the night stretched out on the floor, and the narrow premises so floated with gore, that it was hardly possible to escape the pollution of blood in picking out a path to the front-door. In the lock of the door still remained the

key which had given to the unknown murderer so
fatal an advantage over his victims.   By this time, the
heart-shaking news involved in the outcries of Mary
(to whom it occurred that by possibility some one ou
of so many victims might still be within the reach of
medical aid, but that all would depend upon speed)
had availed, even at that late hour, to gather a small
mob about the house.   The pawnbroker threw open
the door.   One or two watchmen headed the crowd;
but the soul-harrowing spectacle checked them, and
impressed sudden silence upon their voices, previously
so loud.   The tragic drama read aloud its own history
and the succession of its several steps — few and
summary.   The murderer was as yet altogether unknown; not even suspected.   But there were reasons
for thinking that he must have been a person familiarly
known to Marr.   He had entered the shop by opening
the door after it had been closed by Marr.   But it was
justly argued — that, after the caution conveyed to
Marr by the watchman, the appearance of any stranger
in the shop at that hour, and in so dangerous a neighborhood, and entering by so irregular and suspicious a
course, (*i. e.*, walking in after the door had been
closed, and after the closing of the shutters had cut
off all open communication with the street), would
naturally have roused Marr to an attitude of vigilance
and self-defence.   Any indication, therefore, that Marr
had *not* been so roused, would argue to a certainty
that *something* had occurred to neutralize this alarm,
and fatally to disarm the prudent jealousies of Marr.
But this 'something' could only have lain in one
simple fact, viz., that the person of the murderer was
familiarly known to Marr as that of an ordinary and

unsuspected acquaintance. This being presupposed as the key to all the rest, the whole course and evolution of the subsequent drama becomes clear as daylight. The murderer, it is evident, had opened gently, and again closed behind him with equal gentleness, the street-door. He had then advanced to the little counter, all the while exchanging the ordinary salutation of an old acquaintance with the unsuspecting Marr. Having reached the counter, he would then ask Marr for a pair of unbleached cotton socks. In a shop so small as Marr's, there could be no great latitude of choice for disposing of the different commodities. The arrangement of these had no doubt become familiar to the murderer; and he had already ascertained that, in order to reach down the particular parcel wanted at present, Marr would find it requisite to face round to the rear, and, at the same moment, to raise his eyes and his hands to a level eighteen inches above his own head. This movement placed him in the most disadvantageous possible position with regard to the murderer, who now, at the instant when Marr's hands and eyes were embarrassed, and the back of his head fully exposed, suddenly from below his large surtout, had unslung a heavy ship-carpenter's mallet, and, with one solitary blow, had so thoroughly stunned his victim, as to leave him incapable of resistance. The whole position of Marr told its own tale. He had collapsed naturally behind the counter, with his hands so occupied as to confirm the whole outline of the affair as I have here suggested it. Probable enough it is that the very first blow, the first indication of treachery that reached Marr, would also be the last blow as regarded the abolition of consciousness The

murderer's plan and *rationale* of murder started syste
matically from this infliction of apoplexy, or at least
of a stunning sufficient to insure a long loss of consciousness. This opening step placed the murderer at
his ease. But still, as returning sense might constantly
have led to the fullest exposures, it was his settled
practice, by way of consummation, to cut the throat.
To one invariable type all the murders on this occasion
conformed: the skull was first shattered; this step
secured the murderer from instant retaliation; and
then, by way of locking up all into eternal silence,
uniformly the throat was cut. The rest of the circumstances, as self-revealed, were these. The fall of
Marr might, probably enough, cause a dull, confused
sound of a scuffle, and the more so, as it could not
now be confounded with any street uproar — the shop-
door being shut. It is more probable, however, that
the signal for the alarm passing down to the kitchen,
would arise when the murderer proceeded to cut
Marr's throat. The very confined situation behind the
counter would render it impossible, under the critical
hurry of the case, to expose the throat broadly; the
horrid scene would proceed by partial and interrupted
cuts; deep groans would arise; and then would come
the rush up-stairs. Against this, as the only dangerous
stage in the transaction, the murderer would have
specially prepared. Mrs. Marr and the apprentice-
boy, both young and active, would make, of course,
for the street door; had Mary been at home, and three
persons at once had combined to distract the purposes
of the murderer, it is barely possible that one of them
would have succeeded in reaching the street. But the
**dreadful** swing of the heavy mallet intercepted both

the boy and his mistress before they could reach the door. Each of them lay stretched out on the centre of the shop floor; and the very moment that this disabling was accomplished, the accursed hound was down upon their throats with his razor. The fact is, that, in the mere blindness of pity for poor Marr, on hearing his groans, Mrs. Marr had lost sight of her obvious policy; she and the boy ought to have made for the back door; the alarm would thus have been given in the open air; which, of itself, was a great point; and several means of distracting the murderer's attention offered upon that course, which the extreme limitation of the shop denied to them upon the other.

Vain would be all attempts to convey the horror which thrilled the gathering spectators of this piteous tragedy. It was known to the crowd that one person had, by some accident, escaped the general massacre: but she was now speechless, and probably delirious; so that, in compassion for her pitiable situation, one female neighbor had carried her away, and put her to bed. Hence it had happened, for a longer space of time than could else have been possible, that no person present was sufficiently acquainted with the Marrs to be aware of the little infant; for the bold pawnbroker had gone off to make a communication to the coroner; and another neighbor to lodge some evidence which he thought urgent at a neighboring police-office. Suddenly some person appeared amongst the crowd who was aware that the murdered parents had a young infant; this would be found either below-stairs, or in one of the bedrooms above. Immediately a stream of people poured down into the kitchen, where at once they saw

the cradle — but with the bedclothes in a state of indescribable confusion.  On disentangling these, pools of
blood became visible ; and the next ominous sign was,
that the hood of the cradle had been smashed to pieces.
It became evident that the wretch had found himself
doubly embarrassed — first, by the arched hood at the
head of the cradle, which, accordingly, he had beat into
a ruin with his mallet, and secondly, by the gathering
of the blankets and pillows about the baby's head.
The free play of his blows had thus been baffled.
And he had therefore finished the scene by applying
his razor to the throat of the little innocent ; after
which, with no apparent purpose, as though he had
become confused by the spectacle of his own atrocities, he had busied himself in piling the clothes elaborately over the child's corpse.  This incident undeniably
gave the character of a vindictive proceeding to the
whole affair, and so far confirmed the current rumor
that the quarrel between Williams and Marr had
originated in rivalship.  One writer, indeed, alleged
that the murderer might have found it necessary for
his own safety to extinguish the crying of the child ;
but it was justly replied, that a child only eight months
old could not have cried under any sense of the tragedy proceeding, but simply in its ordinary way for the
absence of its mother ; and such a cry, even if audible
at all out of the house, must have been precisely what
the neighbors were hearing constantly, so that it could
have drawn no special attention, nor suggested any
reasonable alarm to the murderer.  No one incident,
indeed, throughout the whole tissue of atrocities, so
much envenomed the popular fury against the unknown ruffian, as this useless butchery of the infant.

Naturally, on the Sunday morning that dawned four or five hours later, the case was too full of horror not to diffuse itself in all directions; but I have no reason to think that it crept into any one of the numerous Sunday papers. In the regular course, any ordinary occurrence, not occurring, or not transpiring until fifteen minutes after 1 A. M. on a Sunday morning, would first reach the public ear through the Monday editions of the Sunday papers, and the regular morning papers of the Monday. But, if such were the course pursued on this occasion, never can there have been a more signal oversight. For it is certain, that to have met the public demand for details on the Sunday, which might so easily have been done by cancelling a couple of dull columns, and substituting a circumstantial narrative, for which the pawnbroker and the watchman could have furnished the materials, would have made a small fortune. By proper handbills dispersed through all quarters of the infinite metropolis, two hundred and fifty thousand extra copies might have been sold; that is, by any journal that should have collected *exclusive* materials, meeting the public excitement, everywhere stirred to the centre by flying rumors, and everywhere burning for ampler information. On the Sunday se'ennight (Sunday the *octave* from the event), took place the funeral of the Marrs; in the first coffin was placed Marr; in the second Mrs. Marr, and the baby in her arms; in the third the apprentice boy. They were buried side by side; and thirty thousand laboring people followed the funeral procession, with horror and grief written in their countenances.

As yet no whisper was astir that indicated, even conjecturally, the hideous author of these ruins — this patron of grave-diggers.   Had as much been known on this Sunday of the funeral concerning that person as became known universally six days later, the people would have gone right from the churchyard to the murderer's lodgings, and (brooking no delay) would have torn him limb from limb.   As yet, however, in mere default of any object on whom reasonable suspicion could settle, the public wrath was compelled to suspend itself.   Else, far indeed from showing any tendency to subside, the public emotion strengthened every day conspicuously, as the reverberation of the shock began to travel back from the provinces to the capital.   On every great road in the kingdom, continual arrests were made of vagrants and 'trampers,' who could give no satisfactory account of themselves, or whose appearance in any respect answered to the imperfect description of Williams furnished by the watchman.

With this mighty tide of pity and indignation pointing backwards to the dreadful past, there mingled also in the thoughts of reflecting persons an under-current of fearful expectation for the immediate future.   'The earthquake,' to quote a fragment from a striking passage in Wordsworth —

'The earthquake is not satisfied at once.'

All perils, specially malignant, are recurrent.   A murderer, who is such by passion and by a wolfish craving for bloodshed as a mode of unnatural luxury cannot relapse into *inertia*.   Such a man, even more than the Alpine chamois hunter, comes to crave the dangers and the hairbreadth escapes of his trade, as a condiment for seasoning the insipid monotonies of daily life.   But, apart from the hellish instincts that might too surely be relied on for renewed atrocities, it was clear that the murderer of the Marrs, wheresoever lurking, must be a needy man; and a needy man of that class least likely to seek or to find resources in honorable modes of industry; for which, equally by haughty disgust and by disuse of the appropriate habits, men of violence are specially disqualified. Were it, therefore, merely for a livelihood, the murderer whom all hearts were yearning to decipher, might be expected to make his resurrection on some stage of horror, after a reasonable interval. Even in the Marr murder, granting that it had been governed chiefly by cruel and vindictive impulses, it was still clear that the desire of booty had co-operated with such feelings. Equally clear it was that this desire must have been disappointed: excepting the trivial sum reserved by Marr for the week's expenditure, the murderer found, doubtless, little or nothing that he could turn to account. Two guineas, perhaps, would be the outside of what he had obtained in the way of booty. A week or so would see the end of that. The conviction, therefore, of all people was, that in a month or two, when the fever of excitement might a little have cooled down, or have been superseded by other topics of fresher interest, so that the newborn vigilance of household life would have had time to relax, some new murder, equally appalling, might be counted upon.

Such was the public expectation. Let the reader then figure to himself the pure frenzy of horror when in this hush of expectation, looking, indeed, and waiting for the unknown arm to strike once more, but not believing that any audacity could be equal to such an attempt as yet, whilst all eyes were watching, suddenly, on the twelfth night from the Marr murder, a second case of the same mysterious nature, a murder on the same exterminating plan was perpetrated in the very same neighborhood. It was on the Thursday next but one succeeding to the Marr murder that this second atrocity took place; and many people thought at the time, that in its dramatic features of thrilling interest, this second case even went beyond the first. The family which suffered in this instance was that of a Mr. Williamson; and the house was situated, if not absolutely *in* Ratcliffe Highway, at any rate immediately round the corner of some secondary street, running at right angles to this public thoroughfare. Mr. Williamson was a well-known and respectable man, long settled in that district; he was supposed to be rich; and more with a view to the employment furnished by such a calling, than with much anxiety for further accumulations, he kept a sort of tavern; which, in this respect, might be considered on an old patriarchal footing — that, although people of considerable property resorted to the house in the evenings, no kind of anxious separation was maintained between them and the other visiters from the class of artisans or common laborers. Anybody who conducted himself with propriety was free to take a seat, and call for any liquor that he might prefer. And thus the society was pretty miscellaneous; in part stationary, but in some proportion fluctuating. The household consisted of the following five persons : — 1. Mr. Williamson, its head, who was an old man above seventy, and was well fitted for his situation, being civil, and not at all morose, but, at the same time, firm in maintaining order; 2. Mrs. Williamson, his wife, about ten years younger than himself; 3. a

little grand-daughter, about nine years old; 4. a housemaid, who was nearly forty years old; 5. a young
journeyman, aged about twenty-six, belonging to some
manufacturing establishment (of what class I have forgotten); neither do I remember of what nation he
was. It was the established rule at Mr. Williamson's,
that, exactly as the clock struck eleven, all the company, without favor or exception, moved off. That
was one of the customs by which, in so stormy a district, Mr. Williamson had found it possible to keep his
house free from brawls. On the present Thursday
night everything had gone on as usual, except for one
slight shadow of suspicion, which had caught the attention of more persons than one. Perhaps at a less
agitating time it would hardly have been noticed; but
now, when the first question and the last in all social
meetings turned upon the Marrs, and their unknown
murderer, it was a circumstance naturally fitted to
cause some uneasiness, that a stranger, of sinister appearance, in a wide surtout, had flitted in and out of
the room at intervals during the evening; had sometimes retired from the light into obscure corners; and,
by more than one person, had been observed stealing
into the private passages of the house. It was presumed in general, that the man must be known to Williamson. And, in some slight degree, as an occasional
customer of the house, it is not impossible that he *was*.
But afterwards, this repulsive stranger, with his cadaverous ghastliness, extraordinary hair, and glazed
eyes showing himself intermittently through the hours
from 9 to 11 P. M., revolved upon the memory of all
who had steadily observed him with something of the
same freezing effect as belongs to the two assassins in

'Macbeth,' who present themselves reeking from the murder of Banquo, and gleaming dimly, with dreadful faces, from the misty background, athwart the pomps of the regal banquet.

Meantime the clock struck eleven; the company broke up; the door of entrance was nearly closed; and at this moment of general dispersion the situation of the five inmates left upon the premises was precisely this: the three elders, viz., Williamson, his wife, and his female servant, were all occupied on the ground floor — Williamson himself was drawing ale, porter, &c., for those neighbors, in whose favor the house-door had been left ajar, until the hour of twelve should strike; Mrs. Williamson and her servant were moving to and fro between the back-kitchen and a little parlor; the little grand-daughter, whose sleeping-room was on the *first* floor (which term in London means always the floor raised by one flight of stairs above the level of the street), had been fast asleep since nine o'clock; lastly, the journeyman artisan had retired to rest for some time. He was a regular lodger in the house; and his bedroom was on the second floor. For some time he had been undressed, and had lain down in bed. Being, as a working man, bound to habits of early rising, he was naturally anxious to fall asleep as soon as possible. But, on this particular night, his uneasiness, arising from the recent murders at No. 29, rose to a paroxysm of nervous excitement which kept him awake. It is possible, that from somebody he had heard of the suspicious-looking stranger, or might even personally observed him slinking about. But, were it otherwise, he was aware of several circumstances dangerously affecting this house; for instance, the ruffianism of this whole neighborhood, and the disagreeable fact that the Marrs nad lived within a few doors of this very house, which again argued that the murderer also lived at no great distance. These were matters of *general* alarm. But there were others peculiar to this house; in particular, the notoriety of Williamson's opulence; the belief, whether well or ill founded, that he accumulated, in desks and drawers, the money continually flowing into his hands; and lastly, the danger so ostentatiously courted by that habit of leaving the house-door ajar through one entire hour — and that hour loaded with extra danger, by the well-advertised assurance that no collision need be feared with chance convivial visiters, since all such people were banished at eleven. A regulation, which had hitherto operated beneficially for the character and comfort of the house, now, on the contrary, under altered circumstances, became a positive proclamation of exposure and defencelessness, through one entire period of an hour. Williamson himself, it was said generally, being a large unwieldy man, past seventy, and signally inactive, ought, in prudence, to make the locking of his door coincident with the dismissal of his evening party.

Upon these and other grounds of alarm (particularly this, that Mrs. Williamson was reported to possess a considerable quantity of plate), the journeyman was musing painfully, and the time might be within twenty-eight or twenty-five minutes of twelve, when all at once, with a crash, proclaiming some hand of hideous violence, the house-door was suddenly shut and locked. Here, then, beyond all doubt, was the diabolic man, clothed in mystery, from No. 29 Ratcliffe Highway.

Yes, that dreadful being, who for twelve days had employed all thoughts and all tongues, was now, too certainly, in this defenceless house, and would, in a few minutes, be face to face with every one of its inmates. A question still lingered in the public mind — whether at Marr's there might not have been *two* men at work. If so, there would be two at present; and one of the two would be immediately disposable for the up-stairs work; since no danger could obviously be more immediately fatal to such an attack than any alarm given from an upper window to the passengers in the street. Through one half-minute the poor panic-stricken man sat up motionless in bed. But then he rose, his first movement being towards the door of his room. Not for any purpose of securing it against intrusion — too well he knew that there was no fastening of any sort — neither lock, nor bolt; nor was there any such moveable furniture in the room as might have availed to barricade the door, even if time could be counted on for such an attempt. It was no effect of prudence, merely the fascination of killing fear it was, that drove him to open the door. One step brought him to the head of the stairs: he lowered his head over the balustrade in order to listen; and at that moment ascended, from the little parlor, this agonizing cry from the woman-servant, 'Lord Jesus Christ! we shall all be murdered!' What a Medusa's head must have lurked in those dreadful bloodless features, and those glazed rigid eyes, that seemed rightfully belonging to a corpse, when one glance at them sufficed to proclaim a death-warrant.

Three separate death-struggles were by this time over; and the poor petrified journeyman, quite uncon scious of what he was doing, in blind, passive, self-surrender to panic, absolutely descended both flights of stairs. Infinite, terror inspired him with the same impulse as might have been inspired by headlong courage. In his shirt, and upon old decaying stairs, that at times creaked under his feet, he continued to descend, until he had reached the lowest step but four. The situation was tremendous beyond any that is on record. A sneeze, a cough, almost a breathing, and the young man would be a corpse, without a chance or a struggle for his life. The murderer was at that time in the little parlor — the door of which parlor faced you in descending the stairs; and this door stood ajar; indeed, much more considerably open than what is understood by the term 'ajar.' Of that quadrant, or 90 degrees, which the door would describe in swinging so far open as to stand at right angles to the lobby, or to itself, in a closed position, 55 degrees at the least were exposed. Consequently, two out of three corpses were exposed to the young man's gaze. Where was the third? And the murderer — where was he? As to the murderer, he was walking rapidly backwards and forwards in the parlor, audible but not visible at first, being engaged with something or other in that part of the room which the door still concealed. What the something might be, the sound soon explained; he was applying keys tentatively to a cupboard, a closet, and a scrutoire, in the hidden part of the room. Very soon, however, he came into view; but, fortunately for the young man, at this critical moment, the murderer's purpose too entirely absorbed him to allow of his throwing a glance to the staircase, on which else the white figure of the journeyman, standing in motionless horror, would have

4

been detected in one instant, and seasoned for the grave in the second. As to the third corpse, the missing corpse, viz., Mr. Williamson's, *that* is in the cellar; and how its local position can be accounted for, remains a separate question much discussed at the time, but never satisfactorily cleared up. Meantime, that Williamson was dead, became evident to the young man; since else he would have been heard stirring or groaning. Three friends, therefore, out of four, whom the young man had parted with forty minutes ago, were now extinguished; remained, therefore, 40 per cent. (a large per centage for Williams to leave); remained, in fact, himself and his pretty young friend, the little grand-daughter, whose childish innocence was still slumbering without fear for herself, or grief for her aged grand-parents. If *they* are gone for ever, happily one friend (for such he will prove himself, indeed, if from such a danger he can save this child) is pretty near to her. But alas! he is still nearer to a murderer. At this moment he is unnerved for any exertion whatever; he has changed into a pillar of ice; for the objects before him, separated by just thirteen feet, are these: — The housemaid had been caught by the murderer on her knees; she was kneeling before the firegrate, which she had been polishing with black lead. That part of her task was finished; and she had passed on to another task, viz., the filling of the grate with wood and coals, not for kindling at this moment, but so as to have it ready for kindling on the next day. The appearances all showed that she must have been engaged in this labor at the very moment when the murderer entered; and perhaps the succession of the incidents arranged itself as follows: — From the awful

ejaculation and loud outcry to Christ, as overheard by
the journeyman, it was clear that then first she had
been alarmed; yet this was at least one and a-half or
even two minutes after the door-slamming.    Consequently the alarm which had so fearfully and seasonably alarmed the young man, must, in some unaccountable way, have been misinterpreted by the two women.
It was said, at the time, that Mrs. Williamson labored
under some dulness of hearing; and it was conjee-
tured that the servant, having her ears filled with the
noise of her own scrubbing, and her head half under
the grate, might have confounded it with the street
noises, or else might have imputed this violent closure
to some mischievous boys.    But, howsoever explained,
the fact was evident, that, until the words of appeal to
Christ, the servant had noticed nothing suspicious,
nothing which interrupted her labors.    If so, it followed
that neither had Mrs. Williamson noticed anything; for,
in that case, she would have communicated her own
alarm to the servant, since both were in the same small
room.    Apparently the course of things after the murderer had entered the room was this : — Mrs. Williamson
had probably not seen him, from the accident of standing with her back to the door.    Her, therefore, before
he was himself observed at all, he had stunned and
prostrated by a shattering blow on the back of her
head; this blow, inflicted by a crow-bar, had smashed
in the hinder part of the skull.    She fell; and by the
noise of her fall (for all was the work of a moment)
had first roused the attention of the servant; who then
uttered the cry which had reached the young man; but
before she could repeat it, the murderer had descended
with his uplifted instrument upon *her* head, crushing

the skull inwards upon the brain.    Both the women
were irrecoverably destroyed, so that further outrages
were needless ; and, moreover, the murderer was conscious of the imminent danger from delay ; and yet, in
spite of his hurry, so fully did he appreciate the fatal
consequences to himself, if any of his victims should so
far revive into consciousness as to make circumstantial
depositions, that, by way of making this impossible, he
had proceeded instantly to cut the throats of each.    All
this tallied with the appearances as now presenting
themselves.    Mrs. Williamson had fallen backwards
with her head to the door ; the servant, from her kneeling posture, had been incapable of rising, and had
presented her head passively to blows ; after which, the
miscreant had but to bend her head backwards so as to
expose her throat, and the murder was finished.

It is remarkable that the young artisan, paralyzed
as he had been by fear, and evidently fascinated for a
time so as to walk right towards the lion's mouth, yet
found himself able to notice everything important.
The reader must suppose him at this point watching
the murderer whilst hanging over the body of Mrs.
Williamson, and whilst renewing his search for certain
important keys.    Doubtless it was an anxious situation
for the murderer ; for, unless he speedily found the
keys wanted, all this hideous tragedy would end in
nothing but a prodigious increase of the public horror,
in tenfold precautions therefore, and redoubled obstacles interposed between himself and his future game.
Nay, there was even a nearer interest at stake ; his
own immediate safety might, by a probable accident,
be compromised.    Most of those who came to the
house for liquor were giddy girls or children, who, on

finding this house closed, would go off carelessly to some other; but, let any thoughtful woman or man come to the door now, a full quarter of an hour before the established time of closing, in that case suspicion would arise too powerful to be checked. There would be a sudden alarm given; after which, mere luck would decide the event. For it is a remarkable fact, and one that illustrates the singular inconsistency of this villain, who, being often so superfluously subtle, was in other directions so reckless and improvident, that at this very moment, standing amongst corpses that had deluged the little parlor with blood, Williams must have been in considerable doubt whether he had any sure means of egress. There were windows, he knew, to the back; but upon what ground they opened, he seems to have had no certain information; and in a neighborhood so dangerous, the windows of the lower story would not improbably be nailed down; those in the upper might be free, but then came the necessity of a leap too formidable. From all this, however, the sole practical inference was to hurry forward with the trial of further keys, and to detect the hidden treasure. This it was, this intense absorption in one overmastering pursuit, that dulled the murderer's perceptions as to all around him; otherwise, he must have heard the breathing of the young man, which to himself at times became fearfully audible. As the murderer stood once more over the body of Mrs. Williamson, and searched her pockets more narrowly, he pulled out various clusters of keys, one of which dropping, gave a harsh gingling sound upon the floor. At this time it was that the secret witness, from his secret stand, noticed the fact of Williams's surtout being lined with silk of the

finest quality.   One other fact he noticed, which eventually became more immediately important than many
stronger circumstances of incrimination ; this was, that
the shoes of the murderer, apparently new, and bought,
probably, with poor Marr's money, creaked as he
walked, harshly and frequently.   With the new clusters
of keys, the murderer walked off to the hidden section
of the parlor.   And here, at last, was suggested to the
journeyman the sudden opening for an escape.   Some
minutes would be lost to a certainty trying all these
keys ; and subsequently in searching the drawers, supposing that the keys answered — or in violently forcing
them, supposing that they did *not*.   He might thus
count upon a brief interval of leisure, whilst the rattling of the keys might obscure to the murderer the
creaking of the stairs under the re-ascending journeyman.   His plan was now formed : on regaining his
bedroom, he placed the bed against the door by way
of a transient retardation to the enemy, that might give
him a short warning, and in the worst extremity, might
give him a chance for life by means of a desperate
leap.   This change made as quietly as possible, he
tore the sheets, pillow-cases, and blankets into broad
ribbons ; and after plaiting them into ropes, spliced
the different lengths together.   But at the very first he
descries this ugly addition to his labors.   Where shall
he look for any staple, hook, bar, or other fixture,
from which his rope, when twisted, may safely depend ?
Measured from the window-*sill* — *i. e.*, the lowest part
of the window architrave — there count but twenty-two
or twenty-three feet to the ground.   Of this length
ten or twelve feet may be looked upon as cancelled,
because to that extent he might drop without danger.

So much being deducted, there would remain, say, a dozen feet of rope to prepare. But, unhappily, there is no stout iron fixture anywhere about his window. The nearest, indeed the sole fixture of that sort, is not near to the window at all; it is a spike fixed (for no reason at all that is apparent) in the bed-tester; now, the bed being shifted, the spike is shifted; and its distance from the window, having been always four feet, is now seven. Seven entire feet, therefore, must be added to that which would have sufficed if measured from the window. But courage! God, by the proverb of all nations in Christendom, helps those that help themselves. This our young man thankfully acknowledges; he reads already, in the very fact of any spike at all being found where hitherto it has been useless, an earnest of providential aid. Were it only for himself that he worked, he could not feel himself meritoriously employed; but this is not so; in deep sincerity, he is now agitated for the poor child, whom he knows and loves; every minute, he feels, brings ruin nearer to *her;* and, as he passed her door, his first thought had been to take her out of bed in his arms, and to carry her where she might share his chances. But, on consideration, he felt that this sudden awaking of her, and the impossibility of even whispering any explanation, would cause her to cry audibly; and the inevitable indiscretion of one would be fatal to the two. As the Alpine avalanches, when suspended above the traveller's head, oftentimes (we are told) come down through the stirring of the air by a simple whisper, precisely on such a tenure of a whisper was now suspended the murderous malice of the man below. No; there is but one way to save the child; towards *her* deliverance, the first step is through his own. And he has made an excellent beginning; for the spike, which too fearfully he had expected to see torn away by any strain upon the half-carious wood, stands firmly when tried against the pressure of his own weight. He has rapidly fastened on to it three lengths of his new rope, measuring eleven feet. He plaits it roughly; so that only three feet have been lost in the intertwisting; he has spliced on a second length equal to the first; so that, already, sixteen feet are ready to throw out of the window; and thus, let the worst come to the worst, it will not be absolute ruin to swarm down the rope so far as it will reach, and then to drop boldly. All this has been accomplished in about six minutes; and the hot contest between above and below is steadily but fervently proceeding. Murderer is working hard in the parlor; journeyman is working hard in the bedroom. Miscreant is getting on famously down-stairs; one batch of bank-notes he has already bagged; and is hard upon the scent of a second. He has also sprung a covey of golden coins. Sovereigns as yet were not; but guineas at this period fetched thirty shillings a-piece; and he has worked his way into a little quarry of these. Murderer is almost joyous; and if any creature is still living in this house, as shrewdly he suspects, and very soon means to know, with that creature he would be happy, before cutting the creature's throat, to drink a glass of something. Instead of the glass, might he not make a present to the poor creature of its throat? Oh no! impossible! Throats are a sort of thing that he never makes presents of; business — business must be attended to. Really the two men, considered simply as men of business, are both meritorious. Like chorus and semi-chorus, strophe and antistrophe, they work each against the other. Pull journeyman, pull murderer! Pull baker, pull devil! As regards the journeyman, he is now safe. To his sixteen feet, of which seven are neutralized by the distance of the bed, he has at last added six feet more, which will be short of reaching the ground by perhaps ten feet — a trifle which man or boy may drop without injury. All is safe, therefore, for him : which is more than one can be sure of for miscreant in the parlor. Miscreant, however, takes it coolly enough : the reason being, that, with all his cleverness, for once in his life miscreant has been over-reached. The reader and I know, but miscreant does not in the least suspect, a little fact of some importance, viz., that just now through a space of full three minutes he has been overlooked and studied by one, who (though reading in a dreadful book, and suffering under mortal panic) took accurate notes of so much as his limited opportunities allowed him to see, and will assuredly report the creaking shoes and the silk-mounted surtout in quarters where such little facts will tell very little to his advantage. But, although it is true that Mr. Wil-liams, unaware of the journeyman's having 'assisted' at the examination of Mrs. Williamson's pockets, could not connect any anxiety with that person's subsequent proceedings, nor specially, therefore, with his having embarked in the rope-weaving line, assuredly he knew of reasons enough for not loitering. And yet he *did* loiter. Reading his acts by the light of such mute traces as he left behind him, the police became aware that latterly he must have loitered. And the reason

5

which governed him is striking; because at once it
records — that murder was not pursued by him simply
as a means to an end, but also as an end for itself.
Mr. Williams had now been upon the premises for
perhaps fifteen or twenty minutes; and in that space
of time he had dispatched, in a style satisfactory to
himself, a considerable amount of business. He had
done, in commercial language, 'a good stroke of business.' Upon two floors, viz., the cellar-floor and the
ground-floor, he has 'accounted for' all the population.
But there remained at least two floors more; and it
now occurred to Mr. Williams that, although the landlord's somewhat chilling manner had shut him out from
any familiar knowledge of the household arrangements, too probably on one or other of those floors
there must be some throats. As to plunder, he has
already bagged the whole. And it was next to impossible that any arrear the most trivial should still remain
for a gleaner. But the throats — the throats — there
it was that arrears and gleanings might perhaps be
counted on. And thus it appeared that, in his wolfish
thirst for blood, Mr. Williams put to hazard the whole
fruits of his night's work, and his life into the bargain.
At this moment, if the murderer knew all, could he
see the open window above stairs ready for the descent
of the journeyman, could he witness the life-and-death
rapidity with which that journeyman is working, could
he guess at the almighty uproar which within ninety
seconds will be maddening the population of this populous district — no picture of a maniac in flight of
panic or in pursuit of vengeance would adequately
represent the agony of haste with which he would
himself be hurrying to the street-door for final evasion.

That mode of escape was still free. Even at this moment, there yet remained time sufficient for a successful flight, and, therefore, for the following revolution in the romance of his own abominable life. He had in his pockets above a hundred pounds of booty; means, therefore, for a full disguise. This very night, if he will shave off his yellow hair, and blacken his eyebrows, buying, when morning light returns, a dark-colored wig, and clothes such as may co-operate in personating the character of a grave professional man, he may elude all suspicions of impertinent policemen; may sail by any one of a hundred vessels bound for any port along the huge line of sea-board (stretching through twenty-four hundred miles) of the American United States; may enjoy fifty years for leisurely repentance; and may even die in the odor of sanctity. On the other hand, if he prefer active life, it is not impossible that, with *his* subtlety, hardihood, and unscrupulousness, in a land where the simple process of naturalization converts the alien at once into a child of the family, he might rise to the president's chair; might have a statue at his death; and afterwards a life in three volumes quarto, with no hint glancing towards No. 29 Ratcliffe Highway. But all depends on the next ninety seconds. Within that time there is a sharp turn to be taken; there is a wrong turn, and a right turn. Should his better angel guide him to the right one, all may yet go well as regards this world's prosperity. But behold! in two minutes from this point we shall see him take the wrong one: and then Nemesis will be at his heels with ruin perfect and sudden.

Meantime, if the murderer allows himself to loiter, the ropemaker overhead does *not*. Well he knows

that tne poor child's fate is on the edge of a razor : for
all turns upon the alarm being raised before the murderer reaches her bedside.    And at this very moment,
whilst desperate agitation is nearly paralyzing his
fingers, he hears the sullen stealthy step of the murderer creeping up through the darkness.    It had been
the expectation of the journeyman (founded on the
clamorous uproar with which the street-door was slam-
med) that Williams, when disposable for his up-stairs
work, would come racing at a long jubilant gallop, and
with a tiger roar; and perhaps, on his natural instincts,
he would have done so.    But this mode of approach,
which was of dreadful effect when applied to a case
of surprise, became dangerous in the case of people
who might by this time have been placed fully upon
their guard.    The step which he had heard was on the
staircase — but upon which stair?    He fancied upon
the lowest: and in a movement so slow and cautious,
even this might make all the difference; yet might it
not have been the tenth, twelfth, or fourteenth stair?
Never, perhaps, in this world did any man feel his own
responsibility so cruelly loaded and strained, as at this
moment did the poor journeyman on behalf of the
slumbering child.    Lose but two seconds, through
awkwardness or through the self-counteractions of
panic, and for *her* the total difference arose between
life and death.    Still there is a hope : and nothing can
so frightfully expound the hellish nature of him whose
baleful shadow, to speak astrologically, at this moment
darkens the house of life, than the simple expression
of the ground on which this hope rested.    The journeyman felt sure that the murderer would not be satisfied
to kill the poor child whilst unconscious.    This would

be to defeat his whole purpose in murdering ner at all.
To an epicure in murder such as Williams, it would be
taking away the very sting of the enjoyment, if the
poor child should be suffered to drink off the bitter cup
of death without fully apprehending the misery of the
situation. But this luckily would require time: the
double confusion of mind, first, from being roused up
at so unusual an hour, and, secondly, from the horror
of the occasion when explained to her, would at first
produce fainting, or some mode of insensibility or distraction, such as must occupy a considerable time.
The logic of the case, in short, all rested upon the *ultra*
fiendishness of Williams. Were he likely to be content with the mere fact of the child's death, apart from
the process and leisurely expansion of its mental
agony — in that case there would be no hope. But,
because our present murderer is fastidiously finical in
his exactions — a sort of martinet in the scenical grouping and draping of the circumstances in his murders —
therefore it is that hope becomes reasonable, since all
such refinements of preparation demand time. Murders of mere necessity Williams was obliged to hurry;
but, in a murder of pure voluptuousness, entirely disinterested, where no hostile witness was to be removed,
no extra booty to be gained, and no revenge to be grat-
ified, it is clear that to hurry would be altogether to
ruin. If this child, therefore, is to be saved, it will be
on pure æsthetical considerations.*

* Let the reader, who is disposed to regard as exaggerated or
romantic the pure fiendishness imputed to Williams, recollect that,
except for the luxurious purpose of basking and revelling in the
anguish of dying despair, he had no motive at all, small or great,
for attempting the murder of this young girl. She had seen

But all considerations whatever are at this moment suddenly cut short. A second step is heard on the stairs, but still stealthy and cautious; a third — and then the child's doom seems fixed. But just at that moment all is ready. The window is wide open; the rope is swinging free; the journeyman has launched himself; and already he is in the first stage of his descent. Simply by the weight of his person he descended, and by the resistance of his hands he retarded the descent. The danger was, that the rope should run too smoothly through his hands, and that by too rapid an acceleration of pace he should come violently to the ground. Happily he was able to resist the descending impetus: the knots of the splicings furnished a succession of retardations. But the rope proved shorter by four or five feet than he had calculated: ten or eleven feet from the ground he hung suspended in the air; speechless for the present, through long-continued agitation; and not daring to drop boldly on the rough carriage pavement, lest he should fracture his legs. But the night was not dark, as it had been on occasion of the Marr murders. And yet, for purposes of criminal police, it was by accident worse than the darkest night that ever hid a murder or baffled a pursuit. London, from east to west, was covered with a deep pall (rising from the river) of universal fog. Hence it happened, that for twenty or thirty seconds the young man hanging in the air was not observed. His white shirt at

nothing, heard nothing — was fast asleep, and her door was closed; so that, as a witness against him, he knew that she was as. useless as any one of the three corpses. And yet he *was* making preparations for her murder, when the alarm in the street interrupted him.

length attracted notice. Three or four people ran up, and received him in their arms, all anticipating some dreadful annunciation. To what house did he belong? Even *that* was not instantly apparent; but he pointed with his finger to Williamson's door, and said in a half-choking whisper — '*Marr's murderer, now at work!*'

All explained itself in a moment: the silent language of the fact made its own eloquent revelation. The mysterious exterminator of No. 29 Ratcliffe Highway had visited another house; and, behold! one man only had escaped through the air, and in his night-dress, to tell the tale. Superstitiously, there was something to check the pursuit of this unintelligible criminal. Morally, and in the interests of vindictive justice, there was everything to rouse, quicken, and sustain it.

Yes, Marr's murderer — the man of mystery — was again at work; at this moment perhaps extinguishing some lamp of life, and not at any remote place, but here — in the very house which the listeners to this dreadful announcement were actually touching. The chaos and blind uproar of the scene which followed, measured by the crowded reports in the journals of many subsequent days, and in one feature of that case, has never to my knowledge had its parallel; or, if a parallel, only in one case — what followed, I mean, on the acquittal of the seven bishops at Westminster in 1688. At present there was more than passionate enthusiasm. The frenzied movement of mixed horror and exultation — the ululation of vengeance which ascended instantaneously from the individual street, and then by a sublime sort of magnetic contagion from all

the adjacent streets, can be adequately expressed only
by a rapturous passage in Shelley: —

> 'The transport of a fierce and monstrous gladness
>   Spread through the multitudinous streets, fast flying
> Upon the wings of fear : — From his dull madness
>   The starveling waked, and died in joy : the dying,
>   Among the corpses in stark agony lying,
>   Just heard the happy tidings, and in hope
> Closed their faint eyes : from house to house replying
>   With loud acclaim the living shook heaven's cope,
> And fill'd the startled earth with echoes.'*

There was something, indeed, half inexplicable in the
instantaneous interpretation of the gathering shout according to its true meaning. In fact, the deadly roar
of vengeance, and its sublime unity, *could* point in this
district only to the one demon whose idea had brooded
and tyrannized, for twelve days, over the general
heart : every door, every window in the neighborhood,
flew open as if at a word of command ; multitudes,
without waiting for the regular means of egress, leaped
down at once from the windows on the lower story ;
sick men rose from their beds ; in one instance, as if
expressly to verify the image of Shelley (in v. 4, 5, 6, 7),
a man whose death had been looked for through some
days, and who actually *did* die on the following day,
rose, armed himself with a sword, and descended in
his shirt into the street. The chance was a good one,
and the mob were made aware of it, for catching the
wolfish dog in the high noon and carnival of his bloody
revels — in the very centre of his own shambles. For

---

* 'Revolt of Islam,' canto xii.

a moment the mob was self-baffled by its own numbers
and its own fury.  But even that fury felt the call for
self-control.  It was evident that the massy street-door
must be driven in, since there was no longer any living
person to co-operate with their efforts from within, excepting only a female child.  Crowbars dexterously
applied in one minute tnrew the door out of hangings,
and the people entered like a torrent.  It may be
guessed with what fret and irritation to their consuming
fury, a signal of pause and absolute silence was made
by a person of local importance.  In the hope of receiving some useful communication, the mob became
silent.  'Now listen,' said the man of authority, 'and
we shall learn whether he is above-stairs or below.'
Immediately a noise was heard as if of some one
forcing windows, and clearly the sound came from a
bedroom above.  Yes, the fact was apparent that the
murderer was even yet in the house: he had been
caught in a trap.  Not having made himself familiar
with the details of Williamson's house, to all appearance he had suddenly become a prisoner in one of the
upper rooms.  Towards this the crowd now rushed
impetuously.  The door, however, was found to be
slightly fastened; and, at the moment when this was
forced, a loud crash of the window, both glass and
frame, announced that the wretch had made his escape.
He had leaped down; and several persons in the
crowd, who burned with the general fury, leaped after
him.  These persons had not troubled themselves about
the nature of the ground; but now, on making an examination of it with torches, they reported it to be an
inclined plane, or embankment of clay, very wet and
adhesive.  The prints of the man's footsteps were

deeply impressed upon the clay, and therefore easily
traced up to the summit of the embankment; but it was
perceived at once that pursuit would be useless, from
the density of the mist. Two feet ahead of you, a man
was entirely withdrawn from your power of identification; and, on overtaking him, you could not venture
to challenge him as the same whom you had lost sight
of. Never, through the course of a whole century,
could there be a night expected more propitious to an
escaping criminal: means of disguise Williams now
had in excess; and the dens were innumerable in the
neighborhood of the river that could have sheltered him
for years from troublesome inquiries. But favors are
thrown away upon the reckless and the thankless.
That night, when the turning-point offered itself for his
whole future career, Williams took the wrong turn;
for, out of mere indolence, he took the turn to his old
lodgings — that place which, in all England, he had
just now the most reason to shun.

Meantime the crowd had thoroughly searched the
premises of Williamson. The first inquiry was for the
young grand-daughter. Williams, it was evident, had
gone into her room: but in this room apparently it was
that the sudden uproar in the streets had surprised him;
after which his undivided attention had been directed
to the windows, since through these only any retreat
had been left open to him. Even this retreat he owed
only to the fog and to the hurry of the moment, and to
the difficulty of approaching the premises by the rear.
The little girl was naturally agitated by the influx of
strangers at that hour; but otherwise, through the hu-
mane precautions of the neighbors, she was preserved
from all knowledge of the dreadful events that had oc-

curred whilst she herself was sleeping. Her poor old grandfather was still missing, until the crowd descended into the cellar; he was then found lying prostrate on the cellar floor: apparently he had been thrown down from the top of the cellar stairs, and with so much violence, that one leg was broken. After he had been thus disabled, Williams had gone down to him, and cut his throat. There was much discussion at the time, in some of the public journals, upon the possibility of reconciling these incidents with other circumstantialities of the case, supposing that only one man had been concerned in the affair. That there *was* only one man concerned, seems to be certain. One only was seen or heard at Marr's: one only, and beyond all doubt the same man, was seen by the young journeyman in Mrs. Williamson's parlor; and one only was traced by his footmarks on the clay embankment. Apparently the course which he had pursued was this: he had introduced himself to Williamson by ordering some beer. This order would oblige the old man to go down into the cellar; Williams would wait until he had reached it, and would then 'slam' and lock the street-door in the violent way described. Williamson would come up in agitation upon hearing this violence. The murderer, aware that he would do so, met him, no doubt, at the head of the cellar stairs, and threw him down; after which he would go down to consummate the murder in his ordinary way. All this would occupy a minute, or a minute and a half; and in that way the interval would be accounted for that elapsed between the alarming sound of the street-door as heard by the journeyman, and the lamentable outcry of the female servant. It is evident also, that the reason why no cry whatsoever

had been heard from the lips of Mrs. Williamson, is
due to the positions of the parties as I have sketched
them.   Coming behind Mrs. Williamson, unseen therefore, and from her deafness unheard, the murderer
would inflict entire abolition of consciousness while she
was yet unaware of his presence.   But with the servant,
who had unavoidably witnessed the attack upon her
mistress, the murderer could not obtain the same fulness of advantage ; and *she* therefore had time for
making an agonizing ejaculation.

It has been mentioned, that the murderer of the Marrs
was not for nearly a fortnight so much as suspected ;
meaning that, previously to the Williamson murder, no
vestige of any ground for suspicion in any direction
whatever had occurred either to the general public or to
the police.   But there were two very limited exceptions
to this state of absolute ignorance.   Some of the magistrates had in their possession something which, when
closely examined, offered a very probable means for
tracing the criminal.   But as yet they had *not* traced
him.   Until the Friday morning next after the destruction of the Williamsons, they had not published the important fact, that upon the ship-carpenter's mallet (with
which, as regarded the stunning or disabling process,
the murders had been achieved) were inscribed the letters ' J. P.'   This mallet had, by a strange oversight
on the part of the murderer, been left behind in Marr's
shop ; and it is an interesting fact, therefore, that, had
the villain been intercepted by the brave pawnbroker,
he would have been met virtually disarmed.   This public notification was made officially on the Friday, viz.,
on the thirteenth day after the first murder.   And it
was instantly followed (as will be seen) by a most im

portant result.  Meantime, within the secrecy of one
single bedroom in all London, it is a fact that Williams
had been whisperingly the object of very deep suspicion
from the very first — that is, within that same hour
which witnessed the Marr tragedy.  And singular it is,
that the suspicion was due entirely to his own folly.
Williams lodged, in company with other men of various
nations, at a public-house.  In a large dormitory there
were arranged five or six beds; these were occupied
by artisans, generally of respectable character.  One
or two Englishmen there were, one or two Scotchmen,
three or four Germans, and Williams, whose birth-place
was not certainly known.  On the fatal Saturday night,
about half-past one o'clock, when Williams returned
from his dreadful labors, he found the English and
Scotch party asleep, but the Germans awake : one of
them was sitting up with a lighted candle in his hands,
and reading aloud to the other two.  Upon this, Williams said, in an angry and very peremptory tone, ' Oh,
put that candle out; put it out directly; we shall all be
burned in our beds.'  Had the British party in the room
been awake, Mr. Williams would have roused a mutinous protest against this arrogant mandate.  But Germans are generally mild and facile in their tempers ;
so the light was complaisantly extinguished.  Yet, as
there were no curtains, it struck the Germans that the
danger was really none at all; for bed-clothes, massed
upon each other, will no more burn than the leaves of
a closed book.  Privately, therefore, the Germans drew
an inference, that Mr. Williams must have had some
urgent motive for withdrawing his own person and dress
from observation.  What this motive might be, the next
day's news diffused all over London, and of course at

this house, not two furlongs from Marr's shop, made awfully evident; and, as may well be supposed, the suspicion was communicated to the other members of the dormitory. All of them, however, were aware of the legal danger attaching, under English law, to insinuations against a man, even if true, which might not admit of proof. In reality, had Williams used the most obvious precautions, had he simply walked down to the Thames (not a stone's-throw distant), and flung two of his implements into the river, no conclusive proof could have been adduced against him. And he might have realized the scheme of Courvoisier (the murderer of Lord William Russell) — viz., have sought each separate month's support in a separate well-concerted murder. The party in the dormitory, meantime, were satisfied themselves, but waited for evidences that might satisfy others. No sooner, therefore, had the official notice been published as to the initials J. P. on the mallet, than every man in the house recognized at once the well-known initials of an honest Norwegian ship-carpenter, John Petersen, who had worked in the English dockyards until the present year; but, having occasion to revisit his native land, had left his box of tools in the garrets of this inn. These garrets were now searched. Petersen's tool-chest was found, but wanting the mallet; and, on further -examination, another overwhelming discovery was made. The surgeon, who examined the corpses at Williamson's had given it as his opinion that the throats were not cut by means of a razor, but of some implement differently shaped. It was now remembered that Williams had recently borrowed a large French knife of peculiar construction; and accordingly, from a heap of old lumber and rags, there was soon extricated a waistcoat, which the whole house could swear to as recently worn by Williams. In this waistcoat, and glued by gore to the lining of its pockets, was found the French knife. Next, it was matter of notoriety to everybody in the inn, that Williams ordinarily wore at present a pair of creaking shoes, and a brown surtout lined with silk. Many other presumptions seemed scarcely called for. Williams was immediately apprehended, and briefly examined. This was on the Friday. On the Saturday morning (viz., fourteen days from the Marr murders) he was again brought up. The circumstantial evidence was overwhelming; Williams watched its course, but said very little. At the close, he was fully committed for trial at the next sessions; and it is needless to say, that, on his road to prison, he was pursued by mobs so fierce, that, under ordinary circumstances, there would have been small hope of escaping summary vengeance. But upon this occasion a powerful escort had been provided; so that he was safely lodged in jail. In this particular jail at this time, the regulation was, that at five o'clock, P. M. all the prisoners on the criminal side should be finally locked up for the night, and without candles. For fourteen hours (that is, until seven o'clock on the next morning) they were left unvisited, and in total darkness. Time, therefore, Williams had for committing suicide. The means in other respects were small. One iron bar there was, meant (if I remember) for the suspension of a lamp; upon this he had hanged himself by his braces. At what hour was uncertain : some people fancied at midnight. And in that case, precisely at the hour when, fourteen days before, he had been spreading horror and desolation through the quiet family of poor Marr, now was **he** forced into drinking of the same cup, presented to his lips by the same accursed hands.

.    .    .    .    .    .

The case of the M'Keans, which has been specially alluded to, merits also a slight rehearsal for the dreadful picturesqueness of some two or three amongst its circumstances. The scene of this murder was at a rustic inn, some few miles (I think) from Manchester; and the advantageous situation of this inn it was, out of which arose the two fold temptations of the case. Generally speaking, an inn argues, of course, a close cincture of neighbors — as the original motive for opening such an establishment. But, in this case, the house individually was solitary, so that no interruption was to be looked for from any persons living within reach of screams; and yet, on the other hand, the circumjacent vicinity was eminently populous; as one consequence of which, a benefit club had established its weekly rendezvous in this inn, and left the peculiar accumulations in their club-room, under the custody of the landlord. This fund arose often to a considerable amount, fifty or seventy pounds, before it was transferred to the hands of a banker. Here, therefore, was a treasure worth some little risk, and a situation that promised next to none. These attractive circumstances had, by accident, become accurately known to one or both of the two M'Keans; and, unfortunately, at a moment of overwhelming misfortune to themselves. They were hawkers; and, until lately, had borne most respectable characters : but some mercantile crash had overtaken them with utter ruin, in which their joint capital had been swallowed up to the last shilling.

This sudden prostration had made them desperate :: their own little property had been swallowed up in a large *social* catastrophe, and society at large they looked upon as accountable to them for a robbery. In preying, therefore, upon society, they considered themselves as pursuing a wild natural justice of retaliation. The money aimed at did certainly assume the character of public money, being the product of many separate subscriptions. They forgot, however, that in the murderous acts, which too certainly they meditated as preliminaries to the robbery, they could plead no such imaginary social precedent. In dealing with a family that seemed almost helpless, if all went smoothly, they relied entirely upon their own bodily strength. They were stout young men, twenty-eight to thirty-two years old; somewhat undersized as to height; but squarely built, deep-chested, broad-shouldered, and so beautifully formed, as regarded the symmetry of their limbs and their articulations, that, after their execution, the bodies were privately exhibited by the surgeons of the Manchester Infirmary, as objects of statuesque interest. On the other hand, the household which they proposed to attack consisted of the following four persons : — 1. the landlord, a stoutish farmer — but *him* they intended to disable by a trick then newly introduced amongst robbers, and termed *hocussing, i. e.,* clandestinely drugging the liquor of the victim with laudanum ; 2. the landlord's wife ; 3. a young servant woman ; 4. a boy, twelve or fourteen years old. The danger was, that out of four persons, scattered by possibility over a house which had two separate exits, one at least might escape, and by better acquaintance with the adjacent paths, might succeed in giving an alarm to some of the

6

houses a furlong distant. Their final resolution was, to be guided by circumstances as to the mode of conducting the affair; and yet, as it seemed essential to success that they should assume the air of strangers to each other, it was necessary that they should preconcert some general outline of their plan; since it would on this scheme be impossible, without awaking violent suspicions, to make any communications under the eyes of the family. This outline included, at the least, one murder: so much was settled; but, otherwise, their subsequent proceedings make it evident that they wished to have as little bloodshed as was consistent with their final object. On the appointed day, they presented themselves separately at the rustic inn, and at different hours. One came as early as four o'clock in the afternoon; the other not until half-past seven. They saluted each other distantly and shyly; and, though occasionally exchanging a few words in the character of strangers, did not seem disposed to any familiar intercourse. With the landlord, however, on his return about eight o'clock from Manchester, one of the brothers entered into a lively conversation; invited him to take a tumbler of punch; and, at a moment when the landlord's absence from the room allowed it, poured into the punch a spoonful of laudanum. Some time after this, the clock struck ten; upon which the elder M'Kean, professing to be weary, asked to be shown up to his bedroom: for each brother, immediately on arriving, had engaged a bed. On this, the poor servant girl had presented herself with a bed-candle to light him upstairs. At this critical moment the family were distributed thus:—the landlord, stupefied with the horrid narcotic which he had drunk, had retired to a private

room adjoining the public room, for the purpose of re-
clining upon a sofa : and he, luckily for his own safety,
was looked upon as entirely incapacitated for action.
The landlady was occupied with her husband. And
thus the younger M'Kean was left alone in the public
room. He rose, therefore, softly, and placed himself
at the foot of the stairs which his brother had just
ascended, so as to be sure of intercepting any fugitive
from the bed-room above. Into that room the elder
M'Kean was ushered by the servant, who pointed to two
beds — one of which was already half occupied by the
boy, and the other empty : in these, she intimated that
the two strangers must dispose of themselves for the
night, according to any arrangement that they might
agree upon. Saying this, she presented him with the
candle, which he in a moment placed upon the table ;
and, intercepting her retreat from the room threw his
arm round her neck with a gesture as though he meant
to kiss her. This was evidently what she herself an-
ticipated, and endeavored to prevent. Her horror may
be imagined, when she felt the perfidious hand that
clasped her neck armed with a razor, and violently cutting her throat. She was hardly able to utter one
scream, before she sank powerless upon the floor. This
dreadful spectacle was witnessed by the boy, who was
not asleep, but had presence of mind enough instantly
to close his eyes. The murderer advanced hastily to
the bed, and anxiously examined the expression of the
boy's features : satisfied he was not, and he then placed
his hand upon the boy's heart, in order to judge by its
beatings whether he were agitated or not. This was a
dreadful trial : and no doubt the counterfeit sleep would
immediately have been detected, when suddenly a

dreadful spectacle drew off the attention of the murderer.
Solemnly, and in ghostly silence, uprose in her dying
delirium the murderèd girl; she stood upright, she
walked steadily for a moment or two, she bent her steps
towards the door.  The murderer turned away to pursue her; and at that moment the boy, feeling that his
one solitary chance was to fly while this scene was in
progress, bounded out of bed.  On the landing at the
head of the stairs was one murderer, at the foot of the
stairs was the other: who could believe that the boy had
the shadow of a chance for escaping?  And yet, in the
most natural way, he surmounted all hindrances.  In
the boy's horror, he laid his left hand on the balustrade,
and took a flying leap over it, which landed him at the
bottom of the stairs, without having touched a single
stair.  He had thùs effectually passed one of the murderers: the other, it is true, was still to be passed;
and this would have been impossible but for a sudden
accident.  The landlady had been alarmed by the faint
scream of the young woman; had hurried from her private room to the girl's assistance; but at the foot of
the stairs had been intercepted by the younger brother,
and was at this moment struggling with *him*.  The
confusion of this life-and-death conflict had allowed the
boy to whirl past them.  Luckily he took a turn into a
kitchen, out of which was a back-door, fastened by a
single bolt, that ran freely at a touch; and through this
door he rushed into the open fields.  But at this moment
the elder brother was set free for pursuit by the death
of the poor girl.  There is no doubt, that in her deli-
riun the image moving through her thoughts was that
of the club, which met once a-week.  She fancied it
no doubt sitting; and to this room, for help and for

safety she staggered along ; she entered it, and within the doorway once more she dropped down, and instantly expired. Her murderer, who had followed her closely, now saw himself set at liberty for the pursuit of the boy. At this critical moment, all was at stake ; unless the boy were caught, the enterprise was ruined. He passed his brother, therefore, and the landlady without pausing, and rushed through the open door into the fields. By a single second, perhaps, he was too late. The boy was keenly aware, that if he continued in sight, he would have no chance of escaping from a powerful young man. He made, therefore, at once for a ditch, into which he tumbled headlong. Had the murderer ventured to make a leisurely examination of the nearest ditch, he would easily have found the boy — made so conspicuous by his white shirt. But he lost all heart, upon failing at once to arrest the boy's flight. And every succeeding second made his despair the greater. If the boy had really effected his escape to the neigh- boring farm-house, a party of men might be gathered within five minutes ; and already it might have become difficult for himself and his brother, unacquainted with the field paths, to evade being intercepted. Nothing remained, therefore, but to summon his brother away. Thus it happened that the landlady, though mangled, escaped with life, and eventually recovered. The land- lord owed his safety to the stupefying potion. And the baffled murderers had the misery of knowing that their dreadful crime had been altogether profitless. The road, indeed, was now open to the club-room ; and, probably, forty seconds would have sufficed to carry off the box of treasure, which afterwards might have been burst open and pillaged at leisure. But the fear of intercepting enemies was too strongly upon them ; and they fled rapidly by a road which carried them actually within six feet of the lurking boy. That night they passed through Manchester. When daylight returned, they slept in a thicket twenty miles distant from the scene of their guilty attempt. On the second and third nights, they pursued their march on foot, resting again during the day. About sunrise on the fourth morning, they were entering some village near Kirby Lonsdale, in Westmoreland. They must have designedly quitted the direct line of route ; for their object was Ayrshire, of which county they were natives ; and the regular road would have led them through Shap, Penrith, Carlisle. Probably they were seeking to elude the persecution of the stage-coaches, which, for the last thirty hours, had been scattering at all the inns and road-side *cabarets* hand-bills describing their persons and dress. It happened (perhaps through design) that on this fourth morning they had separated, so as to enter the village ten minutes apart from each other. They were exhausted and footsore. In this condition it was easy to stop them. A blacksmith had silently reconnoitred them, and compared their appearance with the description of the hand-bills. They were then easily overtaken, and separately arrested. Their trial and condemnation speedily followed at Lancaster ; and in those days it followed, of course, that they were executed. Otherwise their case fell so far within the sheltering limits of what would *now* be regarded as extenuating circumstances — that, whilst a murder more or less was not to repel them from their object, very evidently they were anxious to economize the bloodshed as much as possible. Immeasurable, therefore, was the interval which divided them from the monster Williams. They perished on the scaffold: Williams, as I have said, by his own hand; and, in obedience to the law as it then stood, he was buried in the centre of a *quadrivium*, or conflux of four roads (in this case four streets), with a stake driven through nis heart. And over him drives for ever the uproar of unresting London!

# THE TRUE RELATIONS OF THE BIBLE TO MERELY HUMAN SCIENCE.

It is sometimes said, that a religious messenger from God does not come amongst men for the sake of teaching truths in science, or of correcting errors in science. Most justly is this said: but often in terms far too feeble. For generally these terms are such as to imply, that, although no direct and imperative function of his mission, it was yet open to him, as a permissible function — that, although not pressing with the force of an obligation upon the missionary, it was yet at his discretion — if not to correct other men's errors, yet at least in his own person to speak with scientific precision. I contend that it was *not*. I contend, that to have uttered the truths of astronomy, of geology, &c., at the era of new-born Christianity, was not only *below* and *beside* the purposes of a religion, but would have been *against* them. Even upon errors of a far more important class than errors in science can ever be — superstitions, for instance, that degraded the very idea of God; prejudices and false usages, that laid waste human happiness (such as slavery, and many hundreds of other abuses that might be mentioned), the rule evidently acted upon by the Founder of Christianity was this — Given the purification of the well-head, once assumed that the fountains of truth are

[72]

cleansed, all these derivative currents of evil will cleanse themselves. As a general rule, the branches of error were disregarded, and the roots only attacked. If, then, so lofty a station was taken with regard even to such errors as really *had* moral and spiritual relations, how much more with regard to the comparative trifles (as in the ultimate relations of human nature they are) of merely human science! But, for my part, I go further, and assert, that upon three reasons it was impossible for any messenger from God (or offering himself in that character) to have descended into the communication of truth merely scientific, or economic, or worldly. And the three reasons are these: — *First*, Because such a descent would have degraded his mission, by lowering it to the base level of a collusion with human curiosity, or (in the most favorable case) of a collusion with petty and transitory interests. *Secondly*, Because it would have ruined his mission, by disturbing its free agency, and misdirecting its energies, in two separate modes: first, by destroying the spiritual *auctoritas* (the prestige and consideration) of the missionary; secondly, by vitiating the spiritual atmosphere of his audience — that is, corrupting and misdirecting the character of their thoughts and expectations. He that in the early days of Christianity should have proclaimed the true theory of the solar system, or that by any chance word or allusion should then, in a condition of man so little prepared to receive such truths, have asserted or assumed the daily motion of the earth on its own axis, or its annual motion round the sun, would have found himself entangled at once and irretrievably in the following unmanageable consequences: — First of all, and in-

stantaneously, he would have been roused to the alarm
ing fact, that, by this dreadful indiscretion he himself,
the professed deliverer of a new and spiritual religion,
had in a moment untuned the spirituality of his audience.   He would find that he had awakened within
them the passion of curiosity — the most unspiritual
of passions, and of curiosity in a fierce polemic shape.
The very safest step in so deplorable a situation would
be, instantly to recant.   Already by this one may
estimate the evil, when such would be its readiest
palliation.   For in what condition would the reputation
of the teacher be left for discretion and wisdom as an
intellectual guide, when his first act must be to recant
— and to recant what to the whole body of his hearers
would wear the character of a lunatic proposition.
Such considerations might possibly induce him *not* to
recant.   But in that case the consequences are far
worse.   Having once allowed himself to sanction what
nis hearers regard as the most monstrous of paradoxes,
he has no liberty of retreat open to him.   He must
stand to the promises of his own acts.   Uttering the
first truth of a science, he is pledged to the second ;
taking the main step, he is committed to all which
follow.   He is thrown at once upon the endless con-
troversies which science in every stage provokes, and
in none more than in the earliest.   Starting, besides,
from the authority of a divine mission, he could not
(as others might) have the privilege of selecting arbi-
trarily or partially.   If upon one science, then upon
all ; if upon science, then upon art ; if upon art and
science, then upon *every* branch of social economy
his reformations and advances are equally due — due
**as to all, if** due as to any.   To move in one direction,

is constructively to undertake for all. Without power
to retreat, he has thus thrown the intellectual interests
of his followers into a channel utterly alien to the
purposes of a spiritual mission.

The spiritual mission, therefore, the purpose for
which only the religious teacher was sent, has now
perished altogether — overlaid and confounded by the
merely scientific wranglings to which his own inconsiderate precipitance has opened the door. But suppose at this point that the teacher, aware at length of
the mischief which he has caused, and seeing that the
fatal error of uttering one solitary novel truth upon a
matter of mere science is by inevitable consequence
to throw him upon a road leading altogether away
from the proper field of his mission, takes the laudable
course of confessing his error, and of attempting a
return into his proper spiritual province. This may be
his best course ; yet, after all, it will not retrieve his
lost ground. He returns with a character confessedly
damaged. His very excuse rests upon the blindness
and shortsightedness which forbade his anticipating the
true and natural consequences. Neither will his own
account of the case be generally accepted. He will
not be supposed to retreat from further controversy, as
inconsistent with spiritual purposes, but because he
finds nimself unequal to the dispute. And, in the
very best case, he is, by his own acknowledgment,
tainted with human infirmity. He has been ruined for
a servant of inspiration ; and how ? By a process, let
it be remembered, of which all the steps are inevitable
under the same agency : that is, in the case of any
primitive Christian teacher having attempted to speak
the language of scientific truth in dealing with the

phenomena of astronomy, geology, or of any merely
h1man knowledge.

. Now, thirdly and lastly, in order to try the question
in an extreme form, let it be supposed that, aided by
powers of working miracles, some early apostle of
Christianity should actually have succeeded in carrying
through the Copernican system of astronomy, as an
article of blind belief, sixteen centuries before the progress of man's intellect had qualified him for naturally
developing that system. What, in such a case, would
be the true estimate and valuation of the achievement?
Simply this, that he had thus succeeded in cancelling
and counteracting a determinate scheme of divine dis-
cipline and training for man. Wherefore did God
give to man the powers for contending with scientific
difficulties? Wherefore did he lay a secret train of
continual occasions, that should rise, by relays, through
scores of generations, for provoking and developing
those activities in man's intellect, if, after all, he is to
send a messenger of his own, more than human, to
intercept and strangle all these great purposes? This
is to mistake the very meaning and purposes of a revelation. A revelation is not made for the purpose of
showing to indolent men that which, by faculties already given to them, they may show to themselves;
no: but for the purpose of showing *that* which the
moral darkness of man will not, without supernatural
light, allow him to perceive. With disdain, therefore,
must every thoughtful person regard the notion, that
God could wilfully interfere with his own plans, by
accrediting ambassadors to reveal astronomy, or any
other science, which he has commanded men, by
qualifying men, to reveal for themselves.

Even as regards astronomy — a science so nearly allying itself to religion by the loftiness and by the purity of its contemplations — Scripture is nowhere the *parent* of any doctrine, nor so much as the silent sanctioner of any doctrine. It is made impossible for Scripture to teach falsely, by the simple fact that Scripture, on such subjects, will not condescend to teach at all. The Bible adopts the erroneous language of men (which at any rate it must do, in order to make itself understood), not by way of sanctioning a theory, but by way of using a fact. The Bible, for instance, *uses* (postulates) the phenomena of day and night, of summer and winter; and, in relation to their causes, speaks by the same popular and inaccurate language which is current for ordinary purposes, even amongst the most scientific of astronomers. For the man of science, equally with the populace, talks of the sun as rising and setting, as having finished half his day's journey, &c., and, without pedantry, could not in many cases talk otherwise. But the results, which are all that concern Scripture, are equally true, whether accounted for by one hypothesis which is philosophically just, or by another which is popular and erring.

Now, on the other hand, in geology and cosmology, the case is stronger. *Here* there is no opening for a compliance even with a *language* that is erroneous; for no language at all is current upon subjects that have never engaged the popular attention. *Here,* where there is no such stream of apparent phenomena running counter (as in astronomy there is) to the real phenomena, neither is there any popular language opposed to the scientific. The whole are abtruse speculations, even as regards their objects, nor dreamed of as possibilities, either in their true aspects or their false aspects, till modern times.  The Scriptures, therefore, nowhere allude to such sciences, either as taking the shape of histories, applied to processes current and in movement, or as taking the shape of theories applied to processes past and accomplished.  The Mosaic cos· mogony, indeed, gives the succession of natural births , and probably the general outline of such a succession will be more and more confirmed as geology ad- vances.  But as to the time, the duration, of this suc- cessive evolution, it is the idlest of notions that the Scriptures either have, or could have, condescended to human curiosity upon so awful a prologue to the drama of this world.  Genesis would no more have indulged so mean a passion with respect to the myste- rions inauguration of the world, than the Apocalypse with respect to its mysterious close.  ' Yet the six *days* of Moses !'  Days!  But is it possible that human folly should go the length of understanding by the Mosaical *day*, the mysterious *day* of that awful agency which moulded the heavens and the heavenly host, no more than the ordinary *nychthemeron* or cycle of twenty-four hours ?  The period implied in a *day*, when used in relation to the inaugural manifestation of creative power in that vast drama which introduces God to man in the character of a demiurgus or creator of the world, indicated one stage amongst six ; in- volving probably many millions of years.  The silliest of nurses, in her nursery babble, could hardly suppose that the mighty process began on a Monday morning, and ended on Saturday night.  If we are seriously to study the value and scriptural acceptation of scriptural words and phrases, I presume that our first business will be to collate the use of these words in one part of Scripture, with their use in other parts, holding the same spiritual relations. The creation, for instance, does not belong to the earthly or merely historical records, but to the spiritual records of the Bible; to the same category, therefore, as the prophetic sections of the Bible. Now, in those, and in the Psalms, how do we understand the word *day*? Is any man so little versed in biblical language as not to know, that (except in the merely historical parts of the Jewish records) every section of time has a secret and separate acceptation in the Scriptures? Does an *æon*, though a Grecian word, bear scripturally (either in Daniel or in St. John) any sense known to Grecian ears? Do the seventy *weeks* of the prophet mean weeks in the sense of human calendars? Already the Psalms (xc.), already St. Peter (2d Epist.), warn us of a peculiar sense attached to the word *day* in divine ears. And who of the innumerable interpreters understands the twelve hundred and sixty days in Daniel, or his two thousand and odd days, to mean, by possibility, periods of twenty-four hours? Surely the theme of Moses was as mystical, and as much entitled to the benefit of mystical language, as that of the prophets.

The sum of this matter is this: — God, by a Hebrew prophet, is sublimely described as *the Revealer;* and, in variation of his own expression, the same prophet describes him as the Being 'that knoweth the darkness.' Under no idea can the relations of God to man be more grandly expressed. But of what is he the revealer? Not surely of those things which he has enabled man to reveal for himself, but of those things which, were it not through special light from heaven, must eternally remain sealed up in inaccessible darkness.  On this principle we should all laugh at a revealed cookery.  But essentially the same ridicule, not more, and not less, applies to a revealed astronomy, or a revealed geology.  ·As a fact, there *is* no such astronomy or geology : as a possibility, by the *à priori* argument which I have used (viz., that a revelation on such fields would counteract *other* machineries of providence), there *can* be no such astronomy or geology in the Bible.  Consequently there *is* none.  Consequently there can be no schism or feud upon *these* subjects between the Bible and the philosophies outside.

# SCHLOSSER'S LITERARY HISTORY OF THE EIGHTEENTH CENTURY.

In the person of this Mr. Schlosser is exemplified a common abuse, not confined to literature. An artist from the Italian opera of London and Paris, making a professional excursion to our provinces, is received according to the tariff of the metropolis; no one being bold enough to dispute decisions coming down from the courts above. In that particular case there is seldom any reason to complain — since really out of Germany and Italy there is no city, if you except Paris and London, possessing *materials*, in that field of art, for the composition of an audience large enough to act as a court of revision. It would be presumption in the provincial audience, so slightly trained to good music and dancing, if it should affect to reverse a judgment ratified in the supreme capital. The result, therefore, is practically just, if the original verdict was just; what was right from the first cannot be made wrong by iteration. Yet, even in such a case, there is something not satisfactory to a delicate sense of equity; for the artist returns from the tour as if from some new and independent triumph, whereas, all is but the reverberation of an old one; it seems a new access of sunlight, whereas it is but a reflex illumination from satellites.

In literature the corresponding case is worse. **An** author, passing by means of translation before a foreign people, ought *de jure* to find himself before a new tribunal; but *de facto*, he does not. Like the opera artist, but not with the same propriety, he comes before a court that never interferes to disturb a judgment, but only to re-affirm it. And he returns to his native country, quartering in his armorial bearings these new trophies, as though won by new trials, when, in fact they are due to servile ratifications of old ones. When Sue, or Balzac, Hugo, or George Sand, comes before an English audience — the opportunity is invariably lost for estimating them at a new angle of sight. All who dislike them lay them aside — whilst those only apply themselves seriously to their study, who are predisposed to the particular key of feeling, through which originally these authors had prospered. And thus a new set of judges, that might usefully have modified the narrow views of the old ones, fall by mere *inertia* into the humble character of echoes and sounding-boards to swell the uproar of the original mob.

In this way is thrown away the opportunity, not only of applying corrections to false national tastes, but oftentimes even to the unfair accidents of *luck* that befall books. For it is well known to all who watch literature with vigilance, that books and authors have their fortunes, which travel upon a far different scale of proportions from those that measure their merits. Not even the caprice or the folly of the reading public is required to account for this. Very often, indeed, the whole difference between an extensive circulation fhr one book, and none at all for another of about equal merit, belongs to no particular blindness in men, but to the simple fact, that the one *has*, whilst the other has *not*, been brought effectually under the eyes of the public. By far the greater part of books are lost, not because they are rejected, but because they are never introduced. In any proper sense of the word, very few books are published. Technically they are published; which means, that for six or ten times they are *advertised*, but they are not made known to *attentive* ears, or to ears *prepared* for attention. And amongst the causes which account for this difference in the fortune of books, although there are many, we may reckon, as foremost, *personal* accidents of position in the authors. For instance, with us in England it will do a bad book no *ultimate* service, that it is written by a lord, or a bishop, or a privy counsellor, or a member of Parliament — though, undoubtedly, it will do an *instant* service — it will sell an edition or so. This being the case, it being certain that no rank will reprieve a bad writer from *final* condemnation, the sycophantic glorifier of the public fancies his idol justified; but not so. A bad book, it is true, will not be saved by advantages of position in the author; but a book moderately good will be extravagantly aided by such advantages. Lectures on *Christianity*, that happened to be respectably written and delivered, had prodigious success in my young days, because, also, they happened to be lectures of a prelate; three times the ability would not have procured them any attention had they been the lectures of an obscure curate. Yet, on the other hand, it is but justice to say, that, if written with three times *less* ability, lawn-sleeves would not have given them buoyancy, but, on the contrary

they would have sunk the bishop irrecoverably; whilst
the curate, favored by obscurity, would have survived
for another chance.   So again, and indeed, more than
so, as to poetry.   Lord Carlisle, of the last generation,
wrote tolerable verses.   They were better than Lord
Roscommon's, which, for one hundred and fifty years,
the judicious public has allowed the booksellers to
incorporate, along with other refuse of the seventeenth
and eighteenth century, into the costly collections of
the 'British Poets.'   And really, if you *will* insist on
odious comparisons, they were not so very much
below the verses of an amiable prime minister known
to us all.   Yet, because they wanted vital *stamina*, not
only they fell, but, in falling, they caused the earl to
reel much more than any commoner would have done.
Now, on the other hand, a kinsman of Lord Carlisle,
viz., Lord Byron, because he brought real genius and
power to the effort, found a vast auxiliary advantage
in a peerage and a very ancient descent.   On these
double wings he soared into a region of public interest,
far higher than ever he *would* have reached by poetic
power alone.   Not only all his rubbish — which in
quantity is great — passed for jewels, but also what *are*
incontestably jewels have been, and will be, valued at
a far higher rate than if they had been raised from
less aristocratic mines.   So fatal for mediocrity, so
gracious for real power, is any adventitious distinction
from birth, station, or circumstances of brilliant notoriety.   In reality, the public, our never-sufficiently-to-
be-respected mother, is the most unutterable sycophant
that ever the clouds dropped their rheum upon.   She
is always ready for jacobinical scoffs at a man for
being a lord, if he happens to fail; she is always

ready for toadying a lord, if he happens to make a hit. Ah, dear sycophantic old lady, I kiss your sycophantic hands, and wish heartily that I were a duke for your sake!

It would be a mistake to fancy that this tendency to confound real merit and its accidents of position is at all peculiar to us or to our age. Dr. Sacheverell, by embarking his small capital of talent on the spring-tide of a furious political collision, brought back an ampler return for his little investment than ever did Wickliffe or Luther. Such was his popularity in the heart of love and the heart of hatred, that he would have been assassinated by the Whigs, on his triumphal progresses through England, had he not been canon-ized by the Tories. He was a dead man if he had not been suddenly gilt and lacquered as an idol. Neither is the case peculiar at all to England. Ronge, the *ci-devant* Romish priest (whose name pronounce as you would the English word *wrong*, supposing that it had for a second syllable the final *a* of 'sopha,' *i. e.*, *Wronguh*), has been found a wrong-headed man by *all* parties, and in a venial degree is, perhaps, a stupid man; but he moves about with more *eclat* by far than the ablest man in Germany. And, in days of old, the man that burned down a miracle of beauty, viz., the temple of Ephesus, protesting, with tears in his eyes, that he had no other way of getting himself a name, *has* got it in spite of us all. He's booked for a ride down all history, whether you and I like it or not. Every pocket dictionary knows that Erostratus was that scamp. So of Martin, the man that parboiled, or par-roasted York Minster some ten or twelve years back; that fellow will float down to posterity with the annals of the glorious cathedral: he will

'Pursue the triumph and partake the gale,'

whilst the founders and benefactors of the Minster are practically forgotten.

These incendiaries, in short, are as well known as Ephesus or York; but not one of us can tell, without humming and hawing, who it was that rebuilt the Ephesian wonder of the world, or that repaired the time-honored Minster. Equally in literature, not the weight of service done, or the power exerted, is sometimes considered chiefly — either of these must be very conspicuous before it will be considered at all — but the splendor, or the notoriety, or the absurdity, or even the scandalousness of the circumstances[1] surrounding the author.

Schlosser must have benefitted in some such adventitious way before he ever *could* have risen to his German celebrity. What was it that raised him to his momentary distinction? Was it something very wicked that he did, or something very brilliant that he said? I should rather conjecture that it must have been something inconceivably absurd which he proposed. Any one of the three achievements stands good in Germany for a reputation. But, however it were that Mr. Schlosser first gained his reputation, mark what now follows. On the wings of this equivocal reputation he flies abroad to Paris and London. There he thrives, not by any approving experience or knowledge of his works, but through blind faith in his original German public. And back he flies afterwards to Germany, as if carrying with him new and independent testimonies to his merit, and from two nations that are directly concerned in his violent judgments · whereas (which is the simple truth) he carries back a careless reverberation of his first German character, from those who have far too much to read for declining aid from vicarious criticism when it will spare that effort to themselves. Thus it is that German critics become audacious and libellous. Kohl, Von Raumer, Dr. Carus, physician to the King of Saxony, by means of introductory letters floating them into circles far above any they had seen in homely Germany, are qualified by our own negligence and indulgence for mounting a European tribunal, from which they pronounce malicious edicts against ourselves. Sentinels present arms to Von Raumer at Windsor, because he rides in a carriage of Queen Adelaide's; and Von Raumer immediately conceives himself the Chancellor of all Christendom, keeper of the conscience to universal Europe, upon all questions of art, manners, politics, or any conceivable intellectual relations of England. Schlosser meditates the same career.

But have I any right to quote Schlosser's words from an English translation? I do so only because this happens to be at hand, and the German not. German books are still rare in this country, though more (by one thousand to one) than they were thirty years ago. But I have a full right to rely on the English of Mr. Davison. 'I hold in my hand,' as gentlemen so often say at public meetings, 'a certificate from Herr Schlosser, that to quote Mr. Davison is to quote *him.*' The English translation is one which Mr. Schlosser '*durchgelesen hat, und für deren genauigkeit und richtigkeit er bürgt* [has read through, and for the accuracy and propriety of which he pledges himself]. Mr. Schossler was so anxious for the spiritual welfare of us poor islanders, that he not only read it

through, but he has even *aufmerksam durchgelesen* it
[read it through wide awake] *und geprüft* [and care
fully examined it] ; nay, he has done all this in company with the translator. ' Oh ye Athenians ! how
hard do I labor to earn your applause ! ' And, as the
result of such herculean labors, a second time he
makes himself surety for its precision ; ' *er bürgt also
dafür wie für seine eigne arbeit* ' [he guarantees it
accordingly as he would his own workmanship]. Were
it not for this unlimited certificate, I should have sent
for the book to Germany.   As it is, I need not wait ;
and all complaints on this score I defy, above all from
Herr Schlosser.[2]

In dealing with an author so desultory as Mr.
Schlosser, the critic has a right to an *extra* allowance
of desultoriness for his own share ; so excuse me,
reader, for rushing at once *in medias res*.

Of Swift, Mr. Schlosser selects for notice three
works — the ' Drapier's Letters,' ' Gulliver's Travels,'
and the ' Tale of a Tub.'   With respect to the first, as
it is a necessity of Mr. S. to be forever wrong in
his substratum of facts, he adopts the old erroneous
account of Wood's contract as to the copper coinage,
and of the imaginary wrong which it inflicted on Ireland.   Of all Swift's villainies for the sake of popularity, and still more for the sake of wielding this
popularity vindictively, none is so scandalous as this.
In any new life of Swift the case must be stated *de
novo*.   Even Sir Walter Scott is not impartial ; and
for the same reason as now forces me to blink it, viz.,
the difficulty of presenting the details in a readable
shape.   ' Gulliver's Travels ' Schlosser strangely considers ' spun out to an intolerable extent.'   Many evil

things might be said of Gulliver; but not this. The captain is anything but tedious. And, indeed, it becomes a question of mere mensuration, that can be settled in a moment. A year or two since I had in my hands a pocket edition, comprehending all the four parts of the worthy skipper's adventures within a single volume of 420 pages. Some part of the space was a'so wasted on notes, often very idle. Now the 1st part contains *two* separate voyages (Lilliput and Blefuscu), the 2d, *one*, the 3d, *five*, and the 4th, *one;* so that, in all, this active navigator, who has enriched geography, I hope, with something of a higher quality than your old muffs that thought much of doubling Cape Horn, here gives us *nine* great discoveries, far more surprising than the pretended discoveries of Sinbad (which are known to be fabulous), averaging *quam proximè*, forty-seven small 16mo pages each. Oh you unconscionable German, built round in your own country with circumvallations of impregnable 4tos, oftentimes dark and dull as Avernus — that you will have the face to describe dear excellent Captain Lemuel Gulliver of Redriff, and subsequently of Newark, that 'darling of children and men,' as tedious. It is exactly because he is *not* tedious, because he does not shoot into German foliosity, that Schlosser finds him '*intolerable.*' I have justly transferred to Gulliver's use the words originally applied by the poet to the robin-redbreast, for it is remarkable that *Gulliver* and the *Arabian Nights* are amongst the few books where children and men find themselves meeting and jostling each other. This was the case from its first publication, just one hundred and twenty years since. 'It was received,' says Dr. Johnson, 'with such avidity, that the price of the first edition was raised before the second could be made — it was read by the high and the low, the learned and the illiterate. Criticism was lost in wonder. Now, on the contrary, Schlosser wonders not at all, but simply criticises; which we could bear, if the criticism were even ingenious. Whereas, he utterly misunderstands Swift, and is a malicious calumniator of the captain who, luckily, roaming in Sherwood, and thinking, often with a sigh, of his little nurse,[3] Glumdalclitch, would trouble himself slightly about what Heidelberg might say in the next century. There is but one example on our earth of a novel received with such indiscriminate applause as ' Gulliver ; ' and *that* was ' Don Quixote.' Many have been welcomed joyfully by a class — these two by a people. Now, could that have happened had it been characterized by dulness ? Of all faults, it could least have had *that*. As to the ' Tale of a Tub,' Schlosser is in such Cimmerian vapors that no system of bellows could blow open a shaft or tube through which he might gain a glimpse of the English truth and daylight. It is useless talking to such a man on such a subject. I consign him to the attentions of some patriotic Irishman.

Schlosser, however, is right in a graver reflection which he makes upon the prevailing philosophy of Swift, viz., that ' all his views were directed towards what was *immediately* beneficial, which is the characteristic of savages.' This is undeniable. The meanness of Swift's nature, and his rigid incapacity for dealing with the grandeurs of the human spirit, with religion, with poetry, or even with science, when it rose above the mercenary practical, is absolutely ap-

palling. His own *yahoo* is not a more abominable
one-sided degradation of humanity, than is he himself
under this aspect. And, perhaps, it places this incapacity of his in its strongest light, when we recur to
the fact of his *astonishment* at a religious princess refusing to confer a bishoprick upon one that had treated
the Trinity, and all the profoundest mysteries of Christianity, not with mere scepticism, or casual sneer, but
with set pompous merriment and farcical buffoonery.
This dignitary of the church, Dean of the most conspicuous cathedral in Ireland, had, in full canonicals,
made himself into a regular mountebank, for the sake
of giving fuller effect, by the force of contrast, to the
silliest of jests directed against all that was most
inalienable from Christianity. Ridiculing such things,
could he, in any just sense, be thought a Christian?
But, as Schlosser justly remarks, even ridiculing the
peculiarities of Luther and Calvin as he *did* ridicule
them, Swift could not be thought other than constitutionally incapable of religion. Even a Pagan philosopher, if made to understand the case, would be inca-
pahle of scoffing at any *form*, natural or casual, simple
or distorted, which might be assumed by the most
solemn of problems — problems that rest with the
weight of worlds upon the human spirit —

    ' Fix'd fate, free-will, fore-knowledge absolute.'

the destiny of man, or the relations of man to God.
Anger, therefore, Swift *might* feel, and he felt it* to
the end of his most wretched life; but what reasonable
ground had a man of sense for *astonishment* — that a
princess, who (according to her knowledge) was sin-

---

* See his bitter letters to Lady Suffolk.

cerely pious, should decline to place such a man upon
an Episcopal throne? This argues, beyond a doubt,
that Swift was in that state of constitutional irreligion,
irreligion from a vulgar temperament, which imputes
to everybody else its own plebeian feelings. People
differed, he fancied, not by more and less religion, but
by more and less dissimulations. And, therefore, it
seemed to him scandalous that a princess, who must,
of course, in her heart regard (in common with himself) all mysteries as solemn masques and mummeries,
should pretend in a case of downright serious business,
to pump up, out of dry conventional hoaxes, any solid
objection to a man of his shining merit. ' The Trinity,'
for instance, *that* he viewed as the password, which
the knowing ones gave in answer to the challenge of
the sentinel; but, as soon as it had obtained admission
for the party within the gates of the camp, it was
rightly dismissed to oblivion or to laughter. No case
so much illustrates Swift's essential irreligion; since,
if he had shared in ordinary human feelings on such
subjects, not only he could not have been surprised at
his own exclusion from the bench of bishops, *after*
such ribaldries, but originally he would have abstained
from them as inevitable bars to clerical promotion,
even upon principles of public decorum.

As to the *style* of Swift, Mr. Schlosser shows himself without sensibility in his objections, as the often
hackneyed English reader shows himself without philosophic knowledge of style in his applause. Schlosser
thinks the style of Gulliver ' somewhat dull.' This
shows Schlosser's presumption in speaking upon a
point where he wanted, 1st, original delicacy of tact;
and, 2dly, familiar knowledge of English. Gulliver's

style is *purposely* touched slightly with that dulness of circumstantiality which besets the excellent, but 'somewhat dull' race of men — old sea captains. Yet it wears only an aërial tint of dulness; the felicity of this coloring in Swift's management is, that it never goes the length of wearying, but only of giving a comic air of downright Wapping and Rotherhithe verisimilitude. All men grow dull, and ought to be dull, that live under a solemn sense of eternal danger, one inch only of plank (often worm-eaten) between themselves and the grave; and, also, that see for ever one wilderness of waters — sublime, but (like the wilderness on shore) monotonous. All sublime people, being monotonous, have a tendency to be dull, and sublime things also. Milton and Æschylus, the sublimest of men, are crossed at times by a shade of dulness. It is their weak side. But as to a sea captain, a regular nor'-nor'-wester, and sou'-sou'-easter, he ought to be kicked out of the room if he is *not* dull. It is not 'ship-shape,' or barely tolerable, that he should be otherwise. Yet, after all, considering what I have stated about Captain Gulliver's nine voyages crowding into one pocket volume, he cannot really have much abused his professional license for being dull. Indeed, one has to look out an excuse for his being so little dull; which excuse is found in the fact that he had studied three years at a learned university. Captain Gulliver, though a sailor, I would have you to know, was a gownsman of Cambridge: so says Swift, who knew more about the Captain than anybody nowa-days. Cantabs are all horsemen, *ergo*, Gulliver was fit for any thing, from the *wooden shoon* of Cambridge up to the Horse Marines.

Now, on the other hand, you, common-place reader, that (as an old tradition) believe Swift's style to be a model of excellence, hereafter I shall say a word to you, drawn from deeper principles. At present I con-tent myself with these three propositions, which over-throw if you can ; —

1. That the merit, which justly you ascribe to Swift, is *vernacularity ;* he never forgets his mother-tongue in exotic forms, unless we may call Irish exotic ; for Hibernicisms he certainly has. This merit, however, is exhibited—not, as *you* fancy, in a graceful artless-ness, but in a coarse inartificiality. To be artless, and to be inartificial, are very different things ; as different as being natural and being gross ; as different as being simple and being homely.

2. That whatever, meantime, be the particular sort of excellence, or the value of the excellence, in the style of Swift, he had it in common with multitudes beside of that age. De Foe wrote a style for all the world the same as to kind and degree of excellence, only pure from Hibernicisms. So did every honest skipper [Dampier was something more] who had occa-sion to record his voyages in this world of storms. So did many a hundred of religious writers. And what wonder should there be in this, when the main qualifi-cation for such a style was plain good sense, natural feeling, unpretendingness, some little scholarly practice in putting together the clockwork of sentences, so as to avoid mechanical awkwardness of construction, but above all the advantage of a *subject,* such in its nature as instinctively to reject ornament, lest it should draw off attention from itself ? Such subjects are common ; but grand impassioned subjects insist upon a different

treatment; and *there* it is that the true difficulties of style commence.

3. [Which partly is suggested by the last remark.] That nearly all the blockheads with whom I have at any time had the pleasure of conversing upon the subject of style (and pardon me for saying that men of the most sense are apt, upon two subjects, viz., poetry and style, to talk *most* like blockheads), have invariably regarded Swift's style not as if *relatively* good [*i. e. given* a proper subject], but as if *absolutely* good—good unconditionally, no matter what the subject. Now, my friend, suppose the case, that the Dean had been required to write a pendant for Sir Walter Raleigh's immortal apostrophe to Death, or to many passages that I will select in Sir Thomas Brown's 'Religio Medici,' and his 'Urn-burial,' or to Jeremy Taylor's inaugural sections of his 'Holy Living and Dying,' do you know what would have happened? Are you aware what sort of ridiculous figure your poor bald Jonathan would have cut? About the same that would be cut by a forlorn scullion or waiter from a greasy eating-house at Rotterdam, if suddenly called away in vision to act as seneschal to the festival of Belshazzar the king, before a thousand of his lords.

Schlosser, after saying any thing right and true (and he really did say the true thing about Swift's *essential* irreligion), usually becomes exhausted, like a boa-constrictor after eating his half-yearly dinner. The boa gathers himself up, it is to be hoped for a long fit of dyspepsy, in which the horns and hoofs that he has swallowed may chance to avenge the poor goat that owned them. Schlosser, on the other hand, retires into a corner, for the purpose of obstinately talking

nonsense, until the gong sounds again for a slight refection of sense.    Accordingly he likens Swift, before
he has done with him, to whom ?   I might safely allow
the reader three years for guessing, if the greatest of
wagers were depending between us.   He likens him to
Kotzebue, in the first place.   How faithful the resemblance !   How exactly Swift reminds you of Count
Benyowski in Siberia, and of Mrs. Haller moping her
eyes in the 'Stranger !'   One really is puzzled to say,
according to the negro's logic, whether Mrs. Haller is
more like the Dean of St. Patrick's, or the Dean more
like Mrs. Haller.   Anyhow, the likeness is prodigious,
if it is not quite reciprocal.   The other *terminus* of the
comparison is Wieland.   Now there *is* some shadow
of a resemblance there.   For Wieland had a touch of
the comico-cynical in his nature ; and it is notorious
that he was often called the German Voltaire, which
argues some tiger-monkey grin that traversed his features at intervals.   Wieland's malice, however, was
far more playful and genial than Swift's ; something of
this is shown in his romance of ' Idris,' and oftentimes
in his prose.   But what the world knows Wieland by is
his ' Oberon.'   Now in this gay, musical romance of
Sir Huon and his enchanted horn, with its gleams of
voluptuousness, is there a possibility that any suggestion of a scowling face like Swift's should cross the
festal scenes ?

From Swift the scene changes to Addison and
Steele.   Steele is of less importance ; for, though a
man of greater intellectual activity [4] than Addison, he
had far less of genius.   So I turn him out, as one would
turn out upon a heath a ram that had missed his way

into one's tulip preserve; requesting him to fight for himself against Schlosser, or others that may molest him.   But, so far as concerns Addison, I am happy to support the character of Schlosser for consistency, by assuring the reader that, of all the monstrosities uttered by any man upon Addison, and of all the monstrosities uttered by Schlosser upon any man, a thing which he says about Addison is the worst.   But this I reserve for a climax at the end.   Schlosser really puts his best leg foremost at starting, and one thinks he's going to mend; for he catches a truth, viz., the following — that all the brilliances of the Queen Anne period (which so many inconsiderate people have called the Augustan age of our literature) 'point to this — that the reading public wished to be entertained, not roused to think; to be gently moved, not deeply excited.'   Undoubtedly what strikes a man in Addison, or *will* strike him when indicated, is the coyness and timidity, almost the girlish shame, which he betrays in the presence of all the elementary majesties belonging to impassioned or idealized nature.   Like one bred in crowded cities, when first left alone in forests or amongst mountains, he is frightened at their silence, their solitude, their magnitude of form, or their frowning glooms.   It has been remarked by others that Addison and his companions never rise to the idea of addressing the 'nation' or the 'people;' it is always the 'town.'   Even their audience was conceived of by *them* under a limited form.   Yet for this they had some excuse in the state of facts.   A man would like at this moment to assume that Europe and Asia were listening to him; and as some few copies of his book do really go to Paris and Naples, some to Calcutta, there is a sort of legal fiction that such an

9

assumption is steadily taking root. Yet, unhappily, that ugly barrier of languages interferes. Schamyl, the Circassian chief, though much of a savage, is not so wanting in taste and discernment as to be backward in reading any book of yours or mine. Doubtless he yearns to read it. But then, you see, that infernal *Tchirkass* language steps between our book, the darling, and *him*, the discerning reader. Now, just such a barrier existed for the Spectator in the travelling arrangements of England. The very few old heavies that had begun to creep along three or four main roads, depended so much on wind and weather, their chances of foundering were so uncalculated, their periods of revolution were so cometary and uncertain, that no body of scientific observations had yet been collected to warrant a prudent man in risking a heavy bale of goods; and, on the whole, even for York, Norwich, or Winchester, a consignment of ' *Specs* ' was not quite a safe spec. Still, I could have told the Spectator who was anxious to make money, where he might have been sure of a distant sale, though returns would have been slow, viz., at Oxford and Cambridge. We know from Milton that old Hobson delivered his parcels pretty regularly eighty years before 1710. And, one generation before *that*, it is plain, by the interesting (though somewhat Jacobinical) letters [5] of Joseph Mede, the commenter on the Apocalypse, that news and politics of one kind or other (and scandal of *every* kind) found out for themselves a sort of contraband lungs to breathe through between London and Cambridge ; not quite so regular in their *systole* and *diastole* as the tides of ebb and flood, but better than nothing. If you consigned a packet into the proper hands on the 1st **of**

May, 'as sure as death' to speak *Scottice*) it would be
delivered within sixty miles of the capital before mid-
summer. Still there were delays; and these forced a
man into carving his world out of London. That
excuses the word *town*.

Inexcusable, however, were many other forms of expression in those days, which argued cowardly feelings. One would like to see a searching investigation
into the state of society in Anne's days — its extreme
artificiality, its sheepish reserve upon all the impassioned grandeurs, its shameless outrages upon all the
decencies of human nature. Certain it is, that Addison (because everybody) was in that meanest of conditions which blushes at any expression of sympathy with
the lovely, the noble, or the impassioned. The wretches
were ashamed of their own nature, and perhaps with
reason; for in their own denaturalized hearts they read
only a degraded nature. Addison, in particular, shrank
from every bold and every profound expression as from
an offence against good taste. He durst not for his life
have used the word 'passion' except in the vulgar sense
of an angry paroxysm. He durst as soon have danced
a hornpipe on the top of the 'monument' as have
talked of a 'rapturous emotion.' What *would* he have
said? Why, 'sentiments that were of a nature to prove
agreeable after an unusual rate.' In their odious
verses, the creatures of that age talk of love as something that 'burns' them. You suppose at first that
they are discoursing of tallow candles, though you can
not imagine by what impertinence they address *you*
that are no tallow-chandler, upon such painful subjects
And, when they apostrophize the woman of their heart
(for you are to understand that they pretend to such an

organ), they beseech her to 'ease their pain.' Can human meanness descend lower? As if the man, being ill from pleurisy, therefore had a right to take a lady for one of the dressers in an hospital, whose duty it would be to fix a burgundy-pitch plaster between his shoulders. Ah, the monsters! Then to read of their Phillises and Strephons, and Chloes, and Corydons — names that, by their very non-reality amongst names of flesh and blood proclaim the fantasticalness of the life with which they are poetically connected — it throws me into such convulsions of rage, that I move to the window, and (without thinking what I am about) throwing it up, calling, '*Police! police!*' What's *that* for? What can the police do in the business? Why, certainly nothing. What I meant in my dream was, perhaps [but one forgets *what* one meant upon recovering one's temper], that the police should take Strephon and Corydon into custody, whom I fancied at the other end of the room. And really the justifiable fury, that arises upon recalling such abominable attempts at bucolic sentiments in such abominable language, sometimes transports me into a luxurious vision sinking back through one hundred and thirty years, in which I see Addison, Phillips, both John and Ambrose, Tickell, Fickell, Budgell, and Cudgell, with many others beside, all cudgelled in a round robin, none claiming precedency of another, none able to shrink from his own dividend, until a voice seems to recall me to milder thoughts by saying, ' But surely, my friend, you never could wish to see Addison cudgelled? Let Strephon and Corydon be cudgelled without end, if the police can show any warrant for doing it But Addison was a man of great genius.' True, he was so. I recollect it suddenly, and will back out of any angry things that I have been misled into saying by Schlosser, who, by-the-bye, was right, after all, for a wonder.

But now I will turn my whole fury in vengeance upon Schlosser. And, looking round for a stone to throw at him, I observe this. Addison could not be so entirely careless of exciting the public to think and feel, as Schlosser pretends, when he took so much pains to inoculate that public with a sense of the Miltonic grandeur. The 'Paradise Lost' had then been published barely forty years, which was nothing in an age without reviews; the editions were still scanty; and though no Addison could eventually promote, for the instant he quickened, the circulation. If I recollect, Tonson's accurate revision of the text followed immediately upon Addison's papers. And it is certain that Addison[6] must have diffused the knowledge of Milton upon the continent, from signs that soon followed. But does not this prove that I myself have been in the wrong as well as Schlosser? No: that's impossible. Schlosser's always in the wrong; but it's the next thing to an impossibility that I should be detected in an error: philosophically speaking, it is supposed to involve a contradiction. 'But surely I said the very same thing as Schlosser by assenting to what he said.' Maybe I did: but then I have time to make a distinction, because my article is not yet finished; we are only at page six or seven; whereas Schlosser can't make any distinction now, because his book's printed; and his list of *errata* (which is shocking though he does not confess to the thousandth part), is actually published. My distinction is — that, though Addison generally hated the impassioned, and shrank

from it as from a fearful thing, yet this was when it
combined with forms of life and fleshy realities (as
in dramatic works), but not when it combined with
elder forms of eternal abstractions.  Hence, he did
not read, and did not like Shakspeare ; the music was
here too rapid and life-like : but he sympathized profoundly with the solemn cathedral chanting of Milton.
An appeal to his sympathies which exacted quick
changes in those sympathies he could not meet, but a
more stationary *key* of solemnity he *could*.  Indeed,
this difference is illustrated daily.  A long list can be
cited of passages in Shakspeare, which have been
solemnly denounced by many eminent men (all blockheads) as ridiculous : and if a man *does* find a passage
in a tragedy that displeases him, it is sure to seem
ludicrous : witness the indecent exposures of themselves made by Voltaire, La Harpe, and many billions
beside of bilious people.  Whereas, of all the shameful
people (equally billions and not less bilious) that have
presumed to quarrel with Milton, not one has thought
him ludicrous, but only dull and somnolent.  In ' Lear '
and in ' Hamlet,' as in a human face agitated by
passion, are many things that tremble on the brink
of the ludicrous to an observer endowed with small
range of sympathy or intellect.  But no man ever
found the starry heavens ludicrous, though many find
them dull, and prefer a near view of a brandy flask.
So in the solemn wheelings of the Miltonic movement,
Addison could find a sincere delight.  But the sub-
limities of earthly misery and of human frenzy were
for him a book sealed.  Beside all which, Milton renewed the types of Grecian beauty as to *form*, whilst
Shakspeare, without designing at all to contradict these

types, did so, in effect, by his fidelity to a new nature, radiating from a Gothic centre.

In the midst, however, of much just feeling, which one could only wish a little deeper, in the Addisonian papers on 'Paradise Lost,' there are some gross blunders of criticism, as there are in Dr. Johnson, and from the self-same cause — an understanding suddenly palsied from defective passion. A feeble capacity of passion must, upon a question of passion, constitute a feeble range of intellect. But, after all, the worst thing uttered by Addison in these papers is, not *against* Milton, but meant to be complimentary. Towards enhancing the splendor of the great poem, he tells us that it is a Grecian palace as to amplitude, symmetry, and architectural skill: but being in the English language, it is to be regarded as if built in brick; whereas, had it been so happy as to be written in Greek, then it would have been a palace built in Parian marble. Indeed! that's smart — 'that's handsome, I calculate.' Yet, before a man undertakes to sell his mother-tongue, as old pewter trucked against gold, he should be quite sure of his own metallurgic skill; because else, the gold may happen to be copper, and the pewter to be silver. Are you quite sure, my Addison, that you have understood the powers of this language which you toss away so lightly, as an old tea-kettle? Is it a ruled case that you have exhausted its resources? Nobody doubts your grace in a certain line of composition, but it is only one line among many, and it is far from being amongst the highest. It is dangerous, without examination, to sell even old kettles; misers conceal old stockings filled with guineas in old tea-kettles; and we all know that

Aladdin's servant, by exchanging an old lamp for a
new one, caused an Iliad of calamities : his master's
palace jumped from Bagdad to some place on the road
to Ashantee; Mrs. Aladdin and the piccaninies were
carried off as inside passengers; and Aladdin himself
only escaped being lagged, for a rogue and a conjuror,
by a flying jump after his palace.  Now, mark the
folly of man.  Most of the people I am going to mention subscribed, generally, to the supreme excellence
of Milton ; but each wished for a little change to be
made — which, and which only was wanted to perfection.  Dr. Johnson, though he pretended to be
satisfied with the ' Paradise Lost,' even in what he regarded as the undress of blank verse, still secretly
wished it in rhyme.  That's No. 1.  Addison, though
quite content with it in English, still could have wished
it in Greek.  That's No. 2.  Bentley, though admiring
the blind old poet in the highest degree, still observed,
smilingly, that after all he *was* blind; he, therefore,
slashing Dick, could have wished that the great man
had always been surrounded by honest people ; but,
as that was not to be, he could have wished that his
amanuensis has been hanged ; but, as that also had
become impossible, he could wish to do execution upon
him in effigy, by sinking, burning, and destroying his
handywork — upon which basis of posthumous justice,
he proceeded to amputate all the finest passages in the
poem.  Slashing Dick was No. 3.  Payne Knight was
a severer man even than slashing Dick ; he professed
to look upon the first book of ' Paradise Lost ' as the
finest thing that earth had to show ; but, for that very
reason, he could have wished, by your leave, to see
the other eleven books sawed off, and sent overboard ;

because, though tolerable perhaps in another situation, they really were a national disgrace, when standing behind that unrivalled portico of book 1. There goes No. 4. Then came a fellow, whose name was either not on his title page, or I have forgotten it, that pronounced the poem to be laudable, and full of good materials; but still he could have wished that the materials had been put together in a more workmanlike manner; which kind office he set about himself. He made a general clearance of all lumber: the expression of every thought he entirely re-cast: and he fitted up the metre with beautiful patent rhymes; not, I believe, out of any consideration for Dr. Johnson's comfort, but on principles of mere abstract decency: as it was, the poem seemed naked, and yet was not ashamed. There went No. 5. *Him* succeeded a droller fellow than any of the rest. A French bookseller had caused a prose French translation to be made of the 'Paradise Lóst,' without particularly noticing its English origin, or at least not in the title page. Our friend, No. 6, getting hold of this as an original French romance, translated it back into English prose, as a satisfactory novel for the season. His little mistake was at length discovered, and communicated to him with shouts of laughter; on which, after considerable kicking and plunging (for a man cannot but turn restive when he finds that he has not only got the wrong sow by the ear, but actually sold the sow to a bookseller), the poor translator was tamed into sulkiness; in which state he observed that he could have wished his own work, being evidently so much superior to the earliest form of the romance, might be admitted by the courtesy of England to take the pre-

cedency as the original ' Paradise Lost,' and to super-
sede the very rude performance of ' Milton, Mr.
John.' [7]

Schlosser makes the astounding assertion, that a compliment of Boileau to Addison, and a pure compliment
of ceremony upon Addison's early Latin verses, was
(*credite posteri !*) the making of Addison in England.
Understand, Schlosser, that Addison's Latin verses
were never heard of by England, until long after his
English prose had fixed the public attention upon him ;
his Latin reputation was a slight reaction from his
English reputation : and, secondly, understand that
Boileau had at no time any such authority in England
as to *make* anybody's reputation ; he had first of all to
make his own.   A sure proof of this is, that Boileau's
name was first published to London, by Prior's burlesque of what the Frenchman had called an ode.
This gasconading ode celebrated the passage of the
Rhine in 1672, and the capture of that famous fortress
called *Skink* (' le fameux fort de '), by Louis XIV.,
known to London at the time of Prior's parody by the
name of ' Louis Baboon.' [8]   *That* was not likely to
recommend Master Boileau to any of the allies against
the said Baboon, had it ever been heard of out of France.
Nor was it likely to make him popular in England,
that his name was first mentioned amongst shouts of
laughter and mockery.   It is another argument of the
slight notoriety possessed by Boileau in England —
that no attempt was ever made to translate even his
satires, epistles, or ' Lutrin,' except by booksellers'
hacks; and that no such version ever took the slightest
root amongst ourselves, from Addison's day to this
very summer of 1847.   Boileau was essentially, and

in two senses, viz., both as to mind and as to influence, *un homme borné.*

Addison's 'Blenheim' is poor enough; one might think it a translation from some German original of those times. Gottsched's aunt, or Bodmer's wet-nurse, might have written it; but still no fibs even as to 'Blenheim.' His 'enemies' did not say this thing against 'Blenheim' 'aloud,' nor his friends that thing against it 'softly.' And why? Because at that time (1704–5) he had made no particular enemies, nor any particular friends; unless by friends you mean his Whig patrons, and by enemies his tailor and co.

As to 'Cato,' Schlosser, as usual, wanders in the shadow of ancient night. The English 'people,' it seems, so 'extravagantly applauded' this wretched drama, that you might suppose them to have 'altogether changed their nature,' and to have forgotten Shakspeare. That man must have forgotten Shakspeare, indeed, and from *ramollissement* of the brain, who could admire 'Cato.' 'But,' says Schlosser, 'it was only a 'fashion;' and the English soon repented.' The English could not repent of a crime which they had never committed. Cato was not popular for a moment, nor tolerated for a moment, upon any literary ground, or as a work of art. It was an apple of temptation and strife thrown by the goddess of faction between two infuriated parties. 'Cato,' coming from a man without Parliamentary connections, would have dropped lifeless to the ground. The Whigs have always affected a special love and favor for popular counsels: they have never ceased to give themselves the best of characters as regards public freedom. The Tories, as contradistinguished to the

Jacobites, knowing that without *their* aid, the Revolution could not have been carried, most justly contended that the national liberties had been at least as much indebted to themselves.  When, therefore, the Whigs put forth *their* man Cato to mouth speeches about liberty, as exclusively *their* pet, and about patriotism and all that sort of thing, saying insultingly to the Tories, ' How do you like *that* ?  Does *that* sting ? '  ' Sting, indeed! ' replied the Tories ; ' not at all ; it's quite refreshing to us, that the Whigs have not utterly disowned such sentiments, which, by their public acts, we really thought they *had*.'  And, accordingly, as the popular anecdote tells us, a Tory leader, Lord Bolingbroke, sent for Booth who performed Cato, and presented him (*populo spectante*) with fifty guineas ' for defending so well the cause of the people against a perpetual dictator.'  In which words, observe, Lord Bolingbroke at once asserted the cause of his own party, and launched a sarcasm against a great individual opponent, viz., Marlborough.  Now, Mr. Schlosser, I have mended your harness : all right ahead ; so drive on once more.

But, oh Castor and Pollux, whither — in what direction is it, that the man is driving us ?  Positively, Schlosser, you must stop and let *me* get out.  I 'll go no further with such a drunken coachman.  Many another absurd thing I was going to have noticed, such as his utter perversion of what Mandeville said about Addison (viz., by suppressing one word, and misapprehending all the rest).  Such, again, as his point-blank misstatement of Addison's infirmity in his official character, which was *not* that ' he could not prepare despatches in a good style,' but diametrically the opposite case — that he insisted too much on style, to the serious retardation of public business. But all these things are as nothing to what Schlosser says elsewhere. He actually describes Addison, on the whole, as a ' dull prosaist,' and the patron of pedantry ! Addison, the man of all that ever lived most hostile even to what was good in pedantry, to its tendencies towards the profound in erudition and the non-popular ; Addison, the champion of all that is easy, natural, superficial, a pedant and a master of pedantry ! Get down, Schlosser, this moment; or let *me* get out.

Pope, by far the most important writer, English or Continental, of his own age, is treated with more extensive ignorance by Mr. Schlosser than any other, and (excepting Addison) with more ambitious injustice. A false abstract is given, or a false impression, of any one amongst his brilliant works, that is noticed at all ; and a false sneer, a sneer irrelevant to the case, at any work dismissed by name as unworthy of notice. The three works, selected as the gems of Pope's collection, are the ' Essay on Criticism,' the ' Rape of the Lock,' and the ' Essay on Man.' On the first, which (with Dr. Johnson's leave) is the feeblest and least interesting of Pope's writings, being substantially a mere versification, like a metrical multiplication-table, of commonplaces the most mouldy with which criticism has baited its rat-traps ; since nothing is said worth answering, it is sufficient to answer nothing. The ' Rape of the Lock' is treated with the same delicate sensibility that we might have looked for in Brennns, if consulted on the picturesque, or in Attila the Hun, if adjured to decide æsthetically, between two rival cameos. Attila is

said (though no doubt falsely) to have described himself as not properly a man so much as the Divine wrath
incarnate. This would be fine in a melodrama, with
Bengal lights burning on the stage. But, if ever he
said such a naughty thing, he forgot to tell us what it
was that had made him angry; by what *title* did *he*
come into alliance with the Divine wrath, which was
not likely to consult a savage? And why did his
wrath hurry, by forced marches, to the Adriatic? Now
so much do people differ in opinion, that, to us, who
look at him through a telescope from an eminence,
fourteen centuries distant, he takes the shape rather of
a Mahratta trooper, painfully gathering *chout*, or a
cateran levying black-mail, or a decent tax-gatherer
with an inkhorn at his button-hole, and supported by a
select party of constabulary friends. The very natural
instinct which Attila always showed for following the
trail of the wealthiest footsteps, seems to argue a most
commercial coolness in the dispensation of his wrath.
Mr. Schlosser burns with the wrath of Attila against all
aristocracies, and especially that of England. He
governs his fury, also, with an Atilla discretion in many
cases; but not here. Imagine this Hun coming down,
sword in hand, upon Pope and his Rosicrucian light
troops, levying *chout* upon Sir Plume, and fluttering the
dove-cot of the Sylphs. Pope's 'duty it was,' says this
demoniac, to 'scourge the follies of good society,' and
also 'to break with the aristocracy.' No, surely?
something short of a total rupture would have satisfied
the claims of duty? Possibly; but it would not have
satisfied Schlosser. And Pope's guilt consists in having
made his poem an idol or succession of pictures representing the gayer aspects of society as it really was,

and supported by a comic interest of the mock-heroic derived from a playful machinery, instead of converting it into a bloody satire. Pope, however, did not shrink from such assaults on the aristocracy, if these made any part of his duties. Such assaults he made twice at least too often for his own peace, and perhaps for his credit at this day. It is useless, however, to talk of the poem as a work of art, with one who sees none of its exquisite graces, and can imagine his countryman Zachariä equal to a competition with Pope. But this it may be right to add, that the 'Rape of the Lock' was *not* borrowed from the 'Lutrin' of Boileau. That was impossible. Neither was it suggested by the 'Lutrin.' The story in Herodotus of the wars between cranes and pigmies, or the *Batrachomyomachia* (so absurdly ascribed to Homer) might have suggested the idea more naturally. Both these, there is proof that Pope had read: there is none that he had read the 'Lutrin,' nor did he read French with ease to himself. The 'Lutrin,' meantime, is as much below the 'Rape of the Lock' in brilliancy of treatment, as it is dissimilar in plan or the quality of its pictures.

The 'Essay on Man' is a more thorny subject. When a man finds himself attacked and defended from all quarters, and on all varieties of principle, he is bewildered. Friends are as dangerous as enemies. He must not defy a bristling enemy, if he cares for repose; he must not disown a zealous defender, though making concessions on his own behalf not agreeable to himself; he must not explain away ugly phrases in one direction, or perhaps he is recanting the very words of his 'guide, philosopher, and friend,' who cannot safely be taxed with having first led him into tempta-

tion; he must not explain them away in another direction, or he runs full tilt into the wrath of motner
Church — who will soon bring him to his senses by
penance. Long lents, and no lampreys allowed, would
soon cauterize the proud flesh of heretical ethics. Pope
did wisely, situated as he was, in a decorous nation,
and closely connected, upon principles of fidelity under
political suffering, with the Roman Catholics, to say
little in his own defence. That defence, and any reversionary cudgelling which it might entail upon the
Quixote undertaker, he left — meekly but also slyly,
humbly but cunningly — to those whom he professed
to regard as greater philosophers than himself. All
parties found their account in the affair. Pope slept in
peace; several pugnacious gentlemen up and down
Europe expectorated much fiery wrath in dusting each
other's jackets; and Warburton, the attorney, finally
earned his bishoprick in the service of whitewashing a
writer, who was aghast at finding himself first trampled
on as a deist, and then exalted as a defender of the
faith. Meantime, Mr. Schlosser mistakes Pope's courtesy, when he supposes his acknowledgments to Lord
Bolingbroke sincere in their whole extent.

Of Pope's 'Homer' Schlosser think fit to say, amongst
other evil things, which it really *does* deserve (though
hardly in comparison with the German 'Homer' of the
ear-splitting Voss), 'that Pope pocketed the subscription
of the " Odyssey," and left the work to be done by his
understrappers.' Don't tell fibs, Schlosser. Never do
*that* any more. True it is, and disgraceful enough,
that Pope (like modern contractors for a railway
or a loan) let off to sub-contractors several portions of
the undertaking. He was perhaps not illiberal in the

terms of his contracts. At least I know of people now-a-days (much better artists) that would execute such contracts, and enter into any penalties for keeping time at thirty per cent. less. But *navies* and bill-brokers, that are in excess now, then were scarce. Still the affair, though not mercenary, was illiberal in a higher sense of art; and no anecdote shows more pointedly Pope's sense of the mechanic fashion, in which his own previous share of the Homeric labor had been executed. It was disgraceful enough, and needs no exaggeration. Let it, therefore, be reported truly: Pope personally translated one-half of the 'Odyssey'—a dozen books he turned out of his own oven: and, if you add the *Batrachomyomachia*, his dozen was a baker's dozen. The journeyman did the other twelve; were regularly paid; regularly turned off when the job was out of hand; and never once had to 'strike for wages.' How much beer was allowed, I cannot say. This is the truth of the matter. So no more fibbing, Schlosser, if you please.

But there remains behind all these labors of Pope, the 'Dunciad,' which is by far his greatest. I shall not, within the narrow bounds assigned to me, enter upon a theme so exacting; for, in this instance, I should have to fight not against Schlosser only, but against Dr. Johnson, who has thoroughly misrepresented the nature of the 'Dunciad,' and, consequently, could not measure its merits. Neither he, nor Schlosser, in fact, ever read more than a few passages of this admirable poem. But the villany is too great for a brief exposure. One thing only I will notice of Schlosser's misrepresentations. He asserts (not when directly speaking of Pope, but after-wards, under the head of Voltaire) that the French

10

author's trivial and random *Temple de Gout* ' shows the
superiority in this species of poetry to have been greatly
on the side of the Frenchman.' Let's hear a reason,
though but a Schlosser reason, for this opinion : know,
then, all men whom it concerns, that ' the Englishman's
satire only hit such people as would never have been
known without his mention of them, whilst Voltaire
selected those who were still called great, and their re-
spective schools.' Pope's men, it seems, never *had*
been famous — Voltaire's might cease to be so, but as
yet they had *not* ceased ; as yet they commanded interest. Now mark how I will put three bullets into
that plank, riddle it so that the leak shall not be stopped
by all the old hats in Heidelberg, and Schlosser will
have to swim for his life. First, he is forgetting that,
by his own previous confession, Voltaire, not less than
Pope, had ' immortalized a great many *insignificant*
persons ;' consequently, had it been any fault to do so,
each alike was caught in that fault ; and insignificant
as the people might be, if they *could* be ' immortalized,'
then we have Schlosser himself confessing to the possibility that poetic splendor should create a secondary
interest where originally there had been none. Sec·
ondly, the question of merit does not arise from the
object of the archer, but from the style of his archery.
Not the choice of victims, but the execution done is
what counts. Even for continued failures it would
plead advantageously, much more for continued and
brilliant successes, that Pope fired at an object offering
no sufficient breadth of mark. Thirdly, it is the
grossest of blunders to say that Pope's objects of satire
were obscure ·by comparison with Voltaire's. True,
the Frenchman's example of a scholar, viz., the French

Salmasius, was most accomplished.  But so was the Englishman's scholar, viz., the English Bentley.  Each was absolutely without a rival in his own day.  But the day of Bentley was the very day of Pope.  Pope's man had not even faded; whereas the day of Salmasius, as respected Voltaire had gone by for more than half a century.  As to Dacier, '*which* Dacier, Bezonian?' The husband was a passable scholar — but madame was a poor sneaking fellow, fit only for the usher of a boarding-school.  All this, however, argues Schlosser's two-fold ignorance — first, of English authors ; second, of the ' Dunciad ;' — else he would have known that even Dennis, mad John Dennis, was a much cleverer man than most of those alluded to by Voltaire.  Cibber, though slightly a coxcomb, was born a brilliant man. Aaron Hill was so lustrous, that even Pope's venom fell off spontaneously, like rain from the plumage of a pheasant, leaving him to ' mount far upwards with the swans of Thames ' — and, finally, let it not be forgotten, that Samuel Clarke Burnet, of the Charterhouse, and Sir Isaac Newton, did not wholly escape tasting the knout; if *that* rather impeaches the equity, and sometimes the judgment of Pope, at least it contributes to show the groundlessness of Schlosser's objection — that the population of the Dunciad, the characters that filled its stage, were inconsiderable.

### FOX AND BURKE.

It is, or it *would* be, if Mr. Schlosser were himself more interesting, luxurious to pursue his ignorance as to facts, and the craziness of his judgment as to the valuation of minds, throughout his comparison of Burke with Fox.  The force of antithesis brings out into a

feeble life of meaning, what, in its own insulation, had
been languishing mortally into nonsense.   The darkness of his ' Burke ' becomes *visible* darkness under the
glimmering that steals upon it from the desperate commonplaces of this ' Fox.'   Fox is painted exactly as
he *would* have been painted fifty years ago by any pet
subaltern of the Whig club, enjoying free pasture in
Devonshire House.   The practised reader knows well
what is coming.   Fox is ' formed after the model of the
ancients ' — Fox is ' simple ' — Fox is ' natural ' — Fox
is ' chaste ' — Fox is ' forcible ; '   why yes, in a sense,
Fox is even ' forcible : '   but then, to feel that he was
so, you must have *heard* him ; whereas, for forty years
he has been silent.   We of 1847, that can only *read*
him, hearing Fox described as *forcible,* are disposed to
recollect Shakspeare's Mr. Feeble amongst Falstaff's
recruits, who also is described as *forcible,* viz., as the
' most forcible Feeble.'   And, perhaps, a better description could not be devised for Fox himself — so
feeble was he in matter, so forcible in manner ; so powerful for instant effect, so impotent for posterity.   In the
Pythian fury of his gestures — in his screaming voice —·
in his directness of purpose, Fox would now remind
you of some demon steam-engine on a railroad, some
Fire-king or Salmoneus, that had counterfeited, because
he could not steal, Jove's thunderbolts ; hissing, bubbling, snorting, fuming ; demoniac gas, you think —
gas from Acheron must feed that dreadful system of
convulsions.   But pump out the imaginary gas, and
behold ! it is ditch-water.   Fox, as Mr. Schlosser rightly
thinks, was all of a piece — simple in his manners,
simple in his style, simple in his thoughts.   No waters
in *him* turbid with new crystalizations ; everywhere **the**

eye can see to the bottom. No music in *him* dark with
Cassandra meanings. Fox, indeed, disturb decent gentlemen by ' allusions to all the sciences, from the in-
tegral calculus and metaphysics to navigation ! ' Fox
would have seen you hanged first. Burke, on the other
hand, did all that, and other wickedness besides, which
fills an 8vo page in Schlosser; and Schlosser crowns
his enormities by charging him, the said Burke (p. 99),
with ' *wearisome tediousness.*' Among my own acquaintances are several old women, who think on this
point precisely as Schlosser thinks ; and they go further,
for they even charge Burke with ' tedious wearisome-
ness.' Oh, sorrowful woe, and also woeful sorrow,
when an Edmund Burke arises, like a *cheeta* or hunting
leopard coupled in a tiger-chase with a German poodle.
To think, in a merciful spirit, of the jungle — barely to
contemplate, in a temper of humanity, the incompre-
hensible cane-thickets, dark and bristly, into which that
bloody *cheeta* will drag that unoffending poodle !

But surely the least philosophic of readers, who hates
philosophy ' as toad or asp, ' must yet be aware, that,
where new growths are not germinating, it is no sort
of praise to be free from the throes of growth. Where
expansion is hopeless, it is little glory to have escaped
distortion. Nor is it any blame that the rich fermenta-
tion of grapes should disturb the transparency of their
golden fluids. Fox had nothing new to tell us, nor did
he hold a position amongst men that required or would
even have allowed him to tell anything new. He was
helmsman to a party ; what he had to do, though
seeming to *give* orders, was simply to repeat *their*
orders — ' Port your helm,' said the party ; ' Port it is,'
replied the helmsman. But Burke was no steersman;

he was the Orpheus that sailed with the Argonauts; he was their *seer*, seeing more in his visions than he always understood himself; he was their watcher through the hours of night; he was their astrological interpreter. Who complains of a prophet for being a little darker of speech than a post-office directory? or of him that reads the stars for being sometimes perplexed?

But, even as to facts, Schlosser is always blundering. Post-office directories would be of no use to *him;* nor link-boys; nor blazing tar-barrels. He wanders in a fog such as sits upon the banks of Cocytus. He fancies that Burke, in his lifetime, was *popular*. Of course, it is so natural to be popular by means of '*wearisome tediousness*,' that Schlosser, above all people, should credit such a tale. Burke has been dead just fifty years, come next autumn. I remember the time from this accident — that my own nearest relative stepped on a day of October, 1797, into that same suite of rooms at Bath (North Parade) from which, six hours before, the great man had been carried out to die at Beaconsfield. It is, therefore, you see, fifty years. Now, ever since then, his *collective* works have been growing in bulk by the incorporation of juvenile essays (such as his 'European Settlements,' his 'Essay on the Sublime,' on 'Lord Bolingbroke,' &c.), or (as more recently) by the posthumous publication of his MSS.;[9] and yet, ever since then, in spite of growing age and growing bulk, are more in demand. At this time, half a century after his last sigh, Burke *is* popular; a thing, let me tell you, Schlosser, which never happened before to a writer steeped to his lips in *personal* politics. What a tilth of intellectual lava must that man have interfused amongst the refuse and scoria of such mouldering party rubbish, to force up a new verdure and laughing harvests, annually increasing for new generations! Popular he *is* now, but popular he was not in his own generation. And how could Schlosser have the face to say that he was? Did he never hear the notorious anecdote, that at one period Burke obtained the *sobriquet* of ' dinner-bell?' And why? Not as one who invited men to a banquet by his gorgeous eloquence, but as one that gave a signal to shoals in the House of Commons, for seeking refuge in a *literal* dinner from the oppression of his philosophy. This was, perhaps, in part a scoff of his opponents. Yet there must have been some foundation for the scoff, since, at an earlier stage of Burke's career, Goldsmith had independently said, that this great orator

——————' went on refining,
And thought of convincing, whilst *they* thought of dining.'

I blame neither party. It ought not to be expected of any *popular* body that it should be patient of abstractions amongst the intensities of party-strife, and the immediate necessities of voting. No deliberative body would less have tolerated such philosophic exorbitations from public business than the *agora* of Athens, or the Roman senate. So far the error was in Burke, not in the House of Commons. Yet, also, on the other side, it must be remembered, that an intellect of Burke's combining power and enormous compass, could not, from necessity of nature, abstain from such speculations. For a man to reach a remote posterity, it is sometimes necessary that he should throw his

voice over to them in a vast arch — it must sweep
a parabola — which, therefore, rises high above the
heads of those next to him, and is heard by the bystanders but indistinctly, like bees swarming in the
upper air before they settle on the spot fit for hiving.

See, therefore, the immeasurableness of misconception.  Of all public men, that stand confessedly in
the first rank as to splendor of intellect, Burke was the
*least* popular at the time when our blind friend
Schlosser assumes him to have run off with the lion's
share of popularity.  Fox, on the other hand, as the
leader of opposition, was at that time a household term
of love or reproach, from one end of the island to the
other.  To the very children playing in the streets,
Pitt and Fox, throughout Burke's generation, were
pretty nearly as broad distinctions, and as much a
war-cry, as English and French, Roman and Punic.
Now, however, all this is altered.  As regards the
relations between the two Whigs whom Schlosser so
steadfastly delighteth to misrepresent,

> ' Now is the winter of our discontent
> Made glorious summer '

for that intellectual potentate, Edmund Burke, the man
whose true mode of power has never yet been truly
investigated; whilst Charles Fox is known only as an
echo is known, and for any real *effect* of intellect upon
this generation, for anything but the ' whistling of a
name,' the Fox of 1780 – 1807 sleeps where the
carols of the larks are sleeping, that gladdened the
spring-tides of those years — sleeps with the roses that
glorified the beauty of their summers.[10]

JUNIUS.

Schlosser talks of Junius, who is to him, as to many people, more than entirely the enigma of an enigma, Hermes Trismegistus, or the mediæval Prester John. Not only are most people unable to solve the enigma, but they have no idea of what it is that they are to solve. I have to inform Schlosser that there are three separate questions about Junius, of which he has evidently no distinct knowledge, and cannot, therefore, have many chances to spare for settling them. The three questions are these : — A. Who *was* Junius? B. What was it that armed Junius with a power so unaccountable at this day over the public mind? C. Why, having actually exercised this power, and gained under his masque far more than he ever hoped to gain, did this Junius not come forward *in his own person*, when all the legal danger had long passed away, to claim a distinction that for *him* (among the vainest of men) must have been more precious than his heart's blood? The two questions, B and C, I have examined in past times, and I will not here repeat my explanations further than to say, with respect to the last, that the reason for the author not claiming his own property was this, because he *dared* not; because it would have been *infamy* for him to avow himself as Junius; because it would have revealed a crime and published a crime in his own earlier life, for which many a man is transported in our days, and for less than which many a man has been in past days hanged, broken on the wheel, burned, gibbeted, or impaled. To say that he watched and listened at his master's key-holes, is nothing. It was not key-holes only that he made free

11

with, but keys; he tampered with his master's seals .
he committed larcenies; not, like a brave man, risking his life on the highway, but petty larcenies — larcenies in a dwelling-house — larcenies under the opportunities of a confidential situation — crimes which
formerly, in the days of Junius, our bloody code never
pardoned in villains of low degree.   Junius was in the
situation of Lord Byron's Lara, or, because Lara is a
plagiarism, of Harriet Lee's Kraitzrer.   But this man,
because he had money, friends, and talents, instead of
going to prison, took himself off for a jaunt to the
continent.   From the continent, in full security and in
possession of the *otium cum dignitate*, he negotiated
with the government, whom he had alarmed by publishing the secrets which he had stolen.   He succeeded.   He sold himself to great advantage.   Bought
and sold he was; and of course it is understood that,
if you buy a knave, and expressly in consideration of
his knaveries, you secretly undertake not to hang him.
'Honor bright!'   Lord Barrington might certainly
have indicted Junius at the Old Bailey, and had a reason for wishing to do so; but George III., who was a
party to the negotiation, and all his ministers, would
have said, with fits of laughter —'Oh, come now, my
lord, you must *not* do that.   For, since we have bar-
gained for a price to send him out as a member of
council to Bengal, you see clearly that we could not
possibly hang him *before* we had fulfilled our bargain.
Then it is true we might hang him after he comes
back.   But, since the man (being a clever man) has a
fair chance in the interim of rising to be Governor-
General, we put it to your candor, Lord Barrington,
whether it would be for the public service to hang his

excellency?' In fact, he might probably have been Governor-General, had his bad temper not over-mastered him. Had he not quarrelled so viciously with Mr. Hastings, it is ten to one that he might, by playing his cards well, have succeeded him. As it was, after enjoying an enormous salary, he returned to England — not Governor-General, certainly, but still in no fear of being hanged. Instead of hanging him, on second thoughts, Government gave him a red ribbon. He represented a borough in Parliament. He was an authority upon Indian affairs. He was caressed by the Whig party. He sat at good men's tables. He gave for toasts — *Joseph Surface* sentiments at dinner parties — 'The man that betrays' [something or other] — 'the man that sneaks into' [other men's portfolios, perhaps] — 'is' — ay, *what* is he? Why he is, perhaps, a Knight of the Bath, has a sumptuous mansion in St. James's Square, dies full of years and honor, has a pompous funeral, and fears only some such epitaph as this — 'Here lies, in a red ribbon, the man who built a great prosperity on the basis of a great knavery.' I complain heavily of Mr. Taylor, the very able unmasker of Junius, for blinking the whole questions B and C. He it is that has settled the question A, so that it will never be re-opened by a man of sense. A man who doubts, after *really* reading Mr. Taylor's work, is not only a blockhead, but an irreclaimable blockhead. It is true that several men, among them Lord Brougham, whom Schlosser (though hating him, and kicking him) cites, still profess scepticism. But the reason is evident: they have not *read* the book, they have only heard of it. They are unacquainted with the strongest arguments, and even with

the nature of the evidence.[11]   Lord Brougham, indeed,
is generally reputed to have reviewed Mr. Taylor's
book.  *That* may be : it is probable enough : what I
am denying is not at all that Lord Brougham *reviewed*
Mr. Taylor, but that Lord Brougham *read* Mr. Taylor.
And there is not much wonder in *that*, when we see
professed writers on the subject — bulky writers —
writers of Answers and Refutations, dispensing with
the whole of Mr. Taylor's book, single paragraphs of
which would have forced them to cancel their own.
The possibility of scepticism, after really *reading* Mr.
Taylor's book, would be the strongest exemplification
upon record of Sancho's proverbial reproach, that a
man ' wanted better bread than was made of wheat —'
would be the old case renewed from the scholastic
grumblers ' that some men do not know when they are
answered.'  They have got their *quietus*, and they still
continue to ' maunder ' on with objections long since
disposed of.   In fact, it is not too strong a thing to
say — and Chief Justice Dallas *did* say something like
it — that if Mr. Taylor is not right, if Sir Philip Francis is *not* Junius, then was no man ever yet hanged on
sufficient evidence.   Even confession is no absolute
proof.   Even confessing to a crime, the man may be
mad.   Well, but at least seeing is believing : if the
court sees a man commit an assault, will not *that*
suffice ?   Not at all : ocular delusions on the largest
scale are common.   What 's a court ?  Lawyers have
no better eyes than other people.   Their physics are
often out of repair, and whole cities have been known
to see things that could have no existence.   Now, all
other evidence is held to be short of this blank seeing
or blank confessing.   But I am not at all sure of *that.*

Circumstantial evidence, that multiplies indefinitely its points of *internexus* with known admitted facts, is more impressive than direct testimony. If you detect a fellow with a large sheet of lead that by many (to wit seventy) salient angles, that by tedious (to wit thirty) reëntrant angles, fits into and owns its sisterly relationship to all that is left of the lead upon your roof — this tight fit will weigh more with a jury than even if my lord chief justice should jump into the witness-box, swearing that, with judicial eyes, he saw the vagabond cutting the lead whilst he himself sat at breakfast; or even than if the vagabond should protest before this honorable court that he *did* cut the lead, in order that he (the said vagabond) might have hot rolls and coffee as well as my lord, the witness. If Mr. Taylor's body of evidence does *not* hold water, then is there no evidence extant upon any question, judicial or not judicial, that *will*.

But I blame Mr. Taylor heavily for throwing away the whole argument applicable to B and C; not as any debt that rested particularly upon *him* to public justice; but as a debt to the integrity of his own book. That book is now a fragment; admirable as regards A; but (by omitting B and C) not sweeping the whole area of the problem. There yet remains, therefore, the dissatisfaction which is always likely to arise — not from the smallest *allegatio falsi*, but from the large *suppressio veri*. B, which, on any other solution than the one I have proposed, is perfectly unintelligible, now becomes plain enough. To imagine a heavy, coarse, hard-working government, seriously affected by such a bauble as *they* would consider performances on the tight rope of style, is mere midsum-

mer madness. ' Hold your absurd tongue,' would any
of the ministers have said to a friend descanting on
Junius as a powerful artist of style — ' do you dream,
dotard, that this baby's rattle is the thing that keeps
us from sleeping? Our eyes are fixed on something
else : that fellow, whoever he is, knows what he ought
*not* to know; he has had his hand in some of our
pockets : he 's a good locksmith, is that Junius; and
before he reaches Tyburn, who knows what amount
of mischief he may do to self and partners?' The
rumor that ministers were themselves alarmed (which
was the naked truth) travelled downwards; but the
*why* did not travel; and the innumerable blockheads
of lower circles, not understanding the real cause of
fear, sought a false one in the supposed thunderbolts
of the rhetoric. Opera-house thunderbolts they were :
and strange it is, that grave men should fancy newspapers, teeming, (as they have always done) with
*Publicolas*, with *Catos*, with *Algernon Sidneys*, able
by such trivial small shot to gain a moment's attention
from the potentates of Downing Street. Those who
have despatches to write, councils to attend, and votes
of the Commons to manage, think little of Junius
Brutus. A Junius Brutus, that dares not sign by his
own honest name, is presumably skulking from his
creditors. A Timoleon, who hints at assassination in
a newspaper, one may take it for granted, is a manu-
facturer of begging letters. And it is a conceivable
case that a twenty pound note, enclosed to Timoleon's
address, through the newspaper office, might go far to
soothe that great patriot's feelings, and even to turn
aside his avenging dagger. These sort of people were
not the sort to frighten a British Ministry. One laughs

at the probable conversation between an old hunting squire coming up to comfort the First Lord of the Treasury, on the rumor that he was panic-struck. 'What, surely, my dear old friend, you're not afraid of Timoleon?' First Lord. — 'Yes, I am.' C. Gent. — 'What, afraid of an anonymous fellow in the papers?' F. L. — 'Yes, dreadfully.' C. Gent. — 'Why, I always understood that these people were a sort of shams — living in Grub Street — or where was it that Pope used to tell us they lived? Surely you're not afraid of Timoleon, because some people think he's a patriot?' F. L. — 'No, not at all; but I am afraid because some people think he's a housebreaker!' In that character only could Timoleon become formidable to a Cabinet Minister; and in some such character must our friend, Junius Brutus, have made himself alarming to Government. From the moment that B is properly explained, it throws light upon C. The Government was alarmed — not at such moonshine as patriotism, or at a soap-bubble of rhetoric — but because treachery was lurking amongst their own households: and, if the thing went on, the consequences might be appalling. But this domestic treachery, which accounts for B, accounts at the same time for C. The very same treachery that frightened its objects at the time by the consequences it might breed, would frighten its author afterwards from claiming its literary honors by the remembrances it might awaken. The mysterious disclosures of official secrets, which had once roused so much consternation within a limited circle, and (like the French affair of the diamond necklace) had sunk into neglect only when all clue seemed lost for *perfectly* unravelling it, would revive in all its interest when a discovery came before the public, viz., a claim on the part of Francis to have written the famous letters, which must at the same time point a strong light upon the true origin of the treacherous disclosures. Some astonishment had always existed as to Francis — how he rose so suddenly into rank and station : some astonishment always existed as to Junius, how he should so suddenly have fallen asleep as a writer in the journals. The coincidence of this sudden and unaccountable silence with the sudden and unaccountable Indian appointment of Francis ; the extraordinary familiarity of Junius, which had *not altogether escaped notice*, with the secrets of one particular office, viz., the War Office ; the sudden recollection, sure to flash upon all who remembered Francis, if again he should become revived into suspicion, that he had held a situation of trust in that particular War Office ; all these little recollections would begin to take up their places in a connected story : *this* and *that*, laid together, would become clear as day-light ; and to the keen eyes of still surviving enemies — Horne Tooke, 'little Chamier,' Ellis, the Fitzroy, Russell, and Murray houses — the whole progress and catastrophe of the scoundrelism, the perfidy and the profits of the perfidy, would soon become as intelligible as any tale of midnight burglary from without, in concert with a wicked butler within, that was ever sifted by judge and jury at the Old Bailey, or critically reviewed by Mr. John Ketch at Tyburn.

Francis was the man. Francis was the wicked butler within, whom Pharaoh ought to have hanged, but whom he clothed in royal apparel, and mounted upon a horse that carried him to a curule chair of honor. So far his burglary prospered. But, as generally happens in such cases, this prosperous crime subsequently avenged itself. By a just retribution, the success of Junius, in two senses so monstrously exaggerated — exaggerated by a romantic over-estimate of its intellectual power through an error of the public, not admitted to the secret — and equally exaggerated as to its political power by the government in the hush-money for its future suppression, became the heaviest curse of the successful criminal. This criminal thirsted for literary distinction above all other distinction, with a childish eagerness, as for the *amrecta* cup of immortality. And, behold! there the brilliant bauble lay, glittering in the sands of a solitude, unclaimed by any man; disputed with him (if he chose to claim it) by nobody; and yet for his life he durst not touch it. He stood — he knew that he stood — in the situation of a murderer who has dropt an inestimable jewel upon the murdered body in the death-struggle with his victim. The jewel is his! Nobody will deny it. He may have it for asking. But to ask is his death-warrant. 'Oh yes!' would be the answer, 'here's your jewel, wrapt up safely in tissue paper. But here's another lot that goes along with it — no bidder can take them apart — viz. a halter, also wrapt up in tissue paper.' Francis, in relation to Junius, was in that exact predicament. 'You are Junius? You are that famous man who has been missing since 1772? And you can prove it? God bless me! sir; what a long time you've been sleeping: every body's gone to bed. Well, then, you are an exceedingly clever fellow, that have had the luck to be thought ten times more clever than really you were. And also, you are the greatest scoundrel that at this hour rests in Europe unhanged!'—Francis died, and made no sign. Peace of mind he had parted with for a peacock's feather, which feather, living or dying, he durst not mount in the plumage of his cap.

# NOTES.

## Note 1. Page 86.

EVEN Pope, with all his natural and reasonable interest in aristocratic society, could not shut his eyes to the fact that a jest in *his* mouth became twice a jest in a lord's. But still he failed to perceive what I am here contending for, that if the jest happened to miss fire, through the misfortune of bursting its barrel, the consequences would be far worse for the lord than the commoner. There *is*, you see, a blind sort of compensation.

## Note 2. Page 88.

Mr. Schlosser, who speaks English, who has read rather too much English for any good that he has turned it to, and who ought to have a keen eye for the English version of his own book, after so much reading and study of it, has, however, overlooked several manifest errors. I do not mean to tax Mr. Davison with general inaccuracy. On the contrary, he seems wary, and in most cases successful as a dealer with the peculiarities of the German. But several cases of error I detect without needing the original: they tell their own story. And one of these I here notice, not only for its own importance, but out of love to Schlosser, and by way of nailing his guarantee to the counter — not altogether as a bad shilling, but as a light one. At p. 5 of vol. 2, in a foot-note, which is speaking of Kant, we read of his *attempt to introduce the notion of negative greatness into Philosophy. Negative greatness!* What strange bird may *that* be? Is it the *ornithorynchus paradoxus?* Mr. Schlosser was not wide awake *there*. The reference is evidently to Kant's essay upon the advantages of introducing into philosophy the algebraic

idea of *negative quantities*. It is one of Kant's grandest gleams
into hidden truth. Were it only for the merits of this most
masterly essáy in reconstituting the algebraic meaning of a
*negative quantity* [so generally misunderstood as a *negation*
of quantity, and which even Sir Isaac Newton misconstrued as
regarded its metaphysics], great would have been the service
rendered to logic by Kant. But there is a greater. From this
little *brochure* I am satisfied was derived originally the German
regeneration of the Dynamic philosophy, its expansion through
the idea of polarity, indifference, &c. Oh, Mr. Schlosser, you
had not *geprüft* p. 5 of vol. 2. You skipped the notes.

### Note 3.  Page 90.

'*Little nurse:*'—the word *Glumdalclitch*, in Brobding-
nagian, absolutely *means little nurse*, and nothing else. It may
seem odd that the captain should call any nurse of Brobdingnag,
however kind to him, by such an epithet as *little;* and the
reader may fancy that Sherwood forest had put it into his head,
where Robin Hood always called his right hand man ' Little
John,' not *although*, but expressly *because* John stood seven feet
high in his stockings. But the truth is—that Glumdalclitch
*was* little; and literally so; she was only nine years old, and
(says the captain) ' little of her age,' being barely forty feet
high. She had time to grow certainly, but as she had so much
to do before she could overtake other women, it is probable that
she would turn out what, in Westmoreland, they call a *little
stiffenger* — very little, if at all, higher than a common English
church steeple.

### Note 4.  Page 96.

'*Activity.*'—It is some sign of this, as well as of the more
thoroughly English taste in literature which distinguished Steele,
that hardly twice throughout the ' Spectator ' is Shakspeare
quoted or alluded to by Addison. Even these quotations he had
from the theatre, or the breath of popular talk. Generally, if
you see a line from Shakspeare, it is safe to bet largely that the
paper is Steele's; sometimes, indeed, of casual contributors ; but,
almost to a certainty, *not* a paper of Addison's. Another mark
of Steele's superiority in vigor of intellect is, that much oftener

in *him* than in other contributors strong thoughts came forward; harsh and disproportioned, perhaps, to the case, and never harmoniously developed with the genial grace of Addison, but original, and pregnant with promise and suggestion.

### NOTE 5.   Page 98.

'Letters of Joseph Mede,' published more than twenty years ago by Sir Henry Ellis.

### NOTE 6.   Page 101.

It is an idea of many people, and erroneously sanctioned by Wordsworth, that Lord Somers gave a powerful lift to the 'Paradise Lost.' He was a subscriber to the sixth edition, the first that had plates ; but this was some years before the Revolution of 1688, and when he was simply Mr. Somers, a barrister, with no effectual power of patronage.

### NOTE 7.   Page 106.

'*Milton, Mr. John :* ' — Dr. Johnson expressed his wrath, in an amusing way, at some bookseller's hack who, when employed to make an index, introduced Milton's name among the M's, under the civil title of — 'Milton, Mr. John.'

### NOTE 8.   Page 106.

'*Louis Baboon :* ' — As people read nothing in these days that is more than forty-eight hours old, I am daily admonished that allusions the most obvious to anything in the rear of our own time, needs explanation. *Louis Baboon* is Swift's jesting name for *Louis Bourbon, i. e.,* Louis XIV.

### NOTE 9.   Page 118.

'Of his MSS. : ' — And, if all that I have heard be true, much has somebody to answer for, that so little has been yet published. The two executors of Burke were Dr. Lawrence, of Doctors' Commons, a well-known M. P. in forgotten days, and Windham, a man too like Burke in elasticity of mind ever to be spoken of in connection with forgotten things. Which of them was to blame, I know not. But Mr. R. Sharpe, M. P. twenty-five years ago, well known as *River* Sharpe, from the ἀπεραντολογια of his conversation, used to say, that one or both of the executors had offered *him* (the river) a huge travelling trunk, perhaps an Imperial or a Salisbury boot (equal to the wardrobe of a family), filled with Burke's MSS., on the simple condition of editing them with proper annotations. An Oxford man, and also the celebrated Mr. Christian Curwen, then member for Cumberland, made, in my hearing, the same report. The Oxford man, in particular, being questioned as to the probable amount of MS., deposed, that he could not speak upon oath to the cubical contents; but this he could say, that, having stripped up his coat sleeve, he had endeavored, by such poor machinery as nature had allowed him, to take the soundings of the trunk, but apparently there were none; with his middle finger he could find no bottom; for it was stopped by a dense stratum of MS.; below which, you know, other strata might lie *ad infinitum*. For anything proved to the contrary, the trunk might be bottomless.

NOTE 10.   Page 120.

A man in Fox's situation is sure, whilst living, to draw after him trains of sycophants; and it is the evil necessity of newspapers the most independent, that they *must* swell the mob of sycophants. The public compels them to exaggerate the true proportions of such people as we see every hour in our own day. Those who, for the moment, modify, or *may* modify the national condition, become preposterous idols in the eyes of the gaping public; but with the sad necessity of being too utterly trodden under foot after they are shelved, unless they live in men's memory by something better than speeches in Parliament. Having the usual fate, Fox was complimented, *whilst living*, on his knowledge of Homeric Greek, which was a jest: he knew neither more nor less of Homer, than, fortunately, most English gentlemen of his rank; quite enough that is to read the 'Iliad' with unaffected pleasure, far too little to revise the text of any three lines, without making himself ridiculous. The excessive slenderness of his general literature, English and French, may be seen in the letters published by his Secretary, Trotter. But his fragment of a History, published by Lord Holland, at two guineas, and currently sold for two shillings (not two *pence*, or else I have been defrauded of 1*s.* 10*d.*), most of all proclaims the tenuity of his knowledge. He looks upon Malcolm Laing as a huge oracle ; and, having read even less than Hume, a thing not very easy, with great *naiveté*, cannot guess where Hume picked up his facts.

### NOTE 11.  Page 124.

Even in Dr. Francis's Translation of Select Speeches from Demosthenes, which Lord Brougham naturally used a little in his own labors on that theme, there may be traced several peculiarities of diction that startle us in Junius. Sir P. had them from his father. And Lord Brougham ought not to have overlooked them. The same thing may be seen in the notes to Dr. Francis's translation of Horace. These points, though not *independently* of much importance, become far more so in combination with others. The reply made to me once by a publisher of some eminence upon this question, was the best fitted to lower Mr. Taylor's investigation with a *stranger* to the long history of the dispute. ' I feel,' he said, ' the impregnability of the case made out by Mr. Taylor. But the misfortune is, that I have seen so many previous impregnable cases made out for other claimants.' Ay, that *would* be unfortunate. But the misfortune for this repartee was, that I, for whose use it was intended, not being in the predicament of a *stranger* to the dispute, having seen every page of the pleadings, knew all (except Mr. Taylor's) to be false in their statements ; after which their arguments signified nothing.

# THE ANTIGONE OF SOPHOCLES,

## AS REPRESENTED ON THE EDINBURGH STAGE.

EVERY thing in our days is new. *Roads*, for instance, which, being formerly 'of the earth earthy,'
and therefore perishable, are now iron, and next door
to being immortal; *tragedies*, which are so entirely
new, that neither we nor our fathers, through eighteen
hundred and ninety odd years, gone by, since Cæsar
did our little island the honor to sit upon its skirts,
have ever seen the like to this 'Antigone;' and, finally,
even more new are *readers*, who, being once an obedient race of men, most humble and deferential in the
presence of a Greek scholar, are now become intrac-
tably mutinous; keep their hats on whilst he is addressing them; and listen to him or not, as he seems
to talk sense or nonsense. Some there are, however,
who look upon all these new things as being intensely
old. Yet, surely the railroads are new? No; not at
all. Talus, the iron man in Spenser, who continually
ran round the island of Crete, administering gentle
warning and correction to offenders, by flooring them
with an iron flail, was a very ancient personage in
Greek fable; and the received opinion is, that he must
have been a Cretan railroad, called The Great Circular
Coast-Line, that carried my lords the judges on their
circuits of jail-delivery. The 'Antigone,' again, that

12                                          [137]

wears the freshness of morning dew, and is so fresh
and dewy in the beautiful person of Miss Faucit, had
really begun to look faded on the Athenian stage, and
even ' of a certain age,' about the death of Pericles,
whose meridian year was the year 444 before Christ.
Lastly, these modern *readers*, that are so obstinately
rebellious to the once Papal authority of Greek, they —
No; on consideration, they *are* new.  Antiquity produced many monsters, but none like *them*.

The truth is, that this vast multiplication of readers,
within the last twenty-five years, has changed the
prevailing character of readers.  The minority has
become the overwhelming majority : the quantity has
disturbed the quality.  Formerly, out of every five
readers, at least four were, in some degree, classical
scholars : or, if *that* would be saying too much, if two
of the four had ' small Latin and less Greek,' they
were generally connected with those who had more, or
at the worst, who had much reverence for Latin, and
more reverence for Greek.  If they did not all share
in the services of the temple, all, at least, shared in
the superstition.  But, now-a-days, the readers come
chiefly from a class of busy people who care very
little for ancestral crazes.  Latin they have heard of,
and some of them know it as a good sort of industrious
language, that even, in modern times, has turned out
many useful books, astronomical, medical, philosophical, and (as Mrs. Malaprop observes) diabolical; but,
as to Greek, they think of it as of an ancient mummy :
you spend an infinity of time in unswathing it from its
old dusty wrappers, and, when you have come to the
end, what do you find for your pains ?  A woman's
face, or a baby's, that certainly is not the better for

being three thousand years old; and perhaps a few
ears of wheat, stolen from Pharaoh's granary; which
wheat, when sown [1] in Norfolk or Mid-Lothian, reaped,
thrashed, ground, baked, and hunted through all sorts
of tortures, yields a breakfast roll that (as a Scottish
baker observed to me) is 'not just *that* bad.' Certainly not: not exactly '*that* bad;' not worse than the
worst of our own; but still, much fitter for Pharaoh's
breakfast-table than for ours.

I, for my own part, stand upon an isthmus, connecting me, at one terminus, with the rebels against
Greek, and, at the other, with those against whom they
are in rebellion. On the one hand, it seems shocking
to me, who am steeped to the lips in antique prejudices,
that Greek, in unlimited quantities, should not secure a
limited privilege of talking nonsense. Is all reverence
extinct for old, and ivy-mantled, and worm-eaten
things? Surely, if your own grandmother lectures on
morals, which perhaps now and then she does, she will
command that reverence from you, by means of her
grandmotherhood, which by means of her ethics she
might *not*. To be a good Grecian, is now to be a
faded potentate; a sort of phantom Mogul, sitting at
Delhi, with an English sepoy bestriding his shoulders.
Matched against the master of *ologies*, in our days,
the most accomplished of Grecians is becoming what
the 'master of sentences' had become long since, in
competition with the political economist. Yet, be
assured, reader, that all the 'ologies' hitherto christened oölogy, ichthyology, ornithology, conchology,
palæodontology, &c., do not furnish such mines of
labor as does the Greek language when thoroughly
searched. The 'Mithridates' of Adelung, improved

by the commentaries of Vater and of subsequent authors, numbers up about four thousand languages and
jargons on our polyglot earth; not including the
chuckling of poultry, nor caterwauling, nor barking,
howling, braying, lowing, nor other respectable and
ancient dialects, that perhaps have their elegant and
their vulgar varieties, as well as prouder forms of communication. But my impression is, that the Greek,
taken by itself, this one exquisite language, considered
as a quarry of *intellectual* labor, has more work in it,
is more truly a *pièce de resistance*, than all the remaining three thousand nine hundred and ninety-nine,
with caterwauling thrown into the bargain. So far I
side with the Grecian, and think that he ought to be
honored with a little genuflexion. Yet, on the other
hand, the finest sound on this earth, and which rises
like an orchestra above all the uproars of earth, and
the Babels of earthly languages, is truth    absolute
truth; and the hatefulest is conscious falsehood. Now,
there *is* falsehood, nay (which seems strange), even
sycophancy, in the old undistinguishing homage to all
that is called classical. Yet why should men be sycophants in cases where they *must* be disinterested?
Sycophancy grows out of fear, or out of mercenary
self-interest. But what can there exist of either pointing to an old Greek poet? Cannot a man give his
free opinion upon Homer, without fearing to be waylaid by his ghost? But it is not *that* which startles
him from publishing the secret demur which his heart
prompts, upon hearing false praises of a Greek poet,
or praises which, if not false, are extravagant. What
he fears, is the scorn of his contemporaries. Let
once a party have formed itself considerable enough to

protect a man from the charge of presumption in
throwing off the yoke of *servile* allegiance to all that
is called classical, — let it be a party ever so small
numerically, and the rebels will soon be many.   What
a man fears is, to affront the whole storm of indignation, real and affected, in his own solitary person.
'Goth!' 'Vandal!' he hears from every side.   Break
that storm by dividing it, and he will face its anger.
' Let me be a Goth,' he mutters to himself, ' but let me
not dishonor myself by affecting an enthusiasm which
my heart rejects ! '

Ever since the restoration of letters there has been a
cabal, an academic interest, a factious league amongst
universities, and learned bodies, and individual scholars,
for exalting as something superterrestrial, and quite
unapproachable by moderns, the monuments of Greek
literature.   France, in the time of Louis XIV., England, in the latter part of that time; in fact, each
country as it grew polished at some cost of strength,
carried this craze to a dangerous excess — dangerous
as all things false are dangerous, and depressing to
the aspirations of genius.   Boileau, for instance, and
Addison, though neither[2] of them accomplished in
scholarship, nor either of them extensively read in *any*
department of the classic literature, speak every where
of the classics as having notoriously, and by the
general confession of polished nations, carried the
functions of poetry and eloquence to that sort of faultless beauty which probably does *really* exist in the
Greek sculpture.   There are few things perfect in
this world of frailty.   Even lightning is sometimes a
failure: Niagara has horrible faults ; and Mont Blanc
might be improved by a century of chiselling from

judicious artists. Such are the works of blind elements, which (poor things!) cannot improve by experience. As to man who *does*, the sculpture of the
Greeks in their marbles and sometimes in their gems,
seems the only act of *his* workmanship which has hit
the bull's eye in the target at which we are all aiming.
Not so, with permission from Messrs. Boileau and Addison, the Greek literature. The faults in this are
often conspicuous; nor are they likely to be hidden
for the coming century, as they have been for the
three last. The idolatry will be shaken: as *idols*,
some of the classic models are destined to totter: and
I foresee, without gifts of prophecy, that many laborers
will soon be in this field — many idoloclasts, who will
expose the signs of disease, which zealots had interpreted as power; and of weakness, which is not the
less real because scholars had fancied it health, nor the
less injurious to the total effect because it was inevitable under the accidents of the Grecian position.

Meantime, I repeat, that to disparage any thing
whatever, or to turn the eye upon blemishes, is no part
of my present purpose. Nor could it be: since the
one sole section of the Greek literature, as to which I
profess myself an enthusiast, happens to be the tragic
drama; and here, only, I myself am liable to be challenged as an idolater. As regards the Antigone in
particular, so profoundly do I feel the impassioned
beauty of her situation in connection with her character, that long ago, in a work of my own (yet unpub-
lished), having occasion (by way of overture introducing one of the sections) to cite before the reader's
eye the chief pomps of the Grecian theatre, after
invoking ' the magnificent witch' Medea, I call up

Antigone to this shadowy stage by the apostrophe,
'Holy heathen, daughter of God, before God was
known,[3] flower from Paradise after Paradise was
closed; that quitting all things for which flesh lan-
guishes, safety and honor, a palace and a home, didst
make thyself a houseless pariah, lest the poor pariah
king, thy outcast father, should want a hand to lead
him in his darkness, or a voice to whisper comfort in
his misery; angel, that badst depart for ever the
glories of thy own bridal day, lest he that had shared
thy nursery in childhood, should want the honors of a
funeral; idolatrous, yet Christian Lady, that in the
spirit of martyrdom trodst alone the yawning billows
of the grave, flying from earthly hopes, lest everlasting despair should settle upon the grave of thy brother,'
&c.   In fact, though all the groupings, and what I
would call permanent attitudes of the Grecian stage,
are majestic, there is none that, to my mind, towers
into such affecting grandeur, as this final revelation,
through Antigone herself, and through her own dreadful death, of the tremendous wo that destiny had suspended over her house.  If therefore my business had
been chiefly with the individual drama, I should have
found little room for any sentiment but that of profound admiration.  But my present business is different: it concerns the Greek drama generally, and the
attempt to revive it; and its object is to elucidate,
rather than to praise or to blame.  To explain this
better, I will describe two things: — 1st, The sort
of audience that I suppose myself to be addressing;
and, 2dly, As growing out of *that*, the particular
quality of the explanations which I wish to make.

1st, As to the audience: in order to excuse the tone

(which occasionally I may be obliged to assume) of
one speaking as from a station of knowledge, to others
having no knowledge, I beg it to be understood, that I
take that station deliberately, on no conceit of superiority to my readers, but as a companion adapting my
services to the wants of those who need them. I am
not addressing those already familiar with the Greek
drama, but those who frankly confess, and (according
to their conjectural appreciation of it) who regret their
non-familiarity with that drama. It is a thing well
known to publishers, through remarkable results, and
is now showing itself on a scale continually widening,
that a new literary public has arisen, very different
from any which existed at the beginning of this century. The aristocracy of the land have always been,
in a moderate degree, literary; less, however, in connection with the *current* literature, than with literature
generally — past as well as present. And this is a
tendency naturally favored and strengthened in *them*,
by the fine collections of books, carried forward through
successive generations, which are so often found as a
sort of hereditary foundation in the country mansions
of our nobility. But a class of readers, prodigiously
more extensive, has formed itself within the commercial orders of our great cities and manufacturing
districts. These orders range through a large scale.
The highest classes amongst them were always literary.
But the interest of literature has now swept downwards
through a vast compass of descents: and this large
body, though the busiest in the nation, yet, by having
under their undisturbed command such leisure time as
they have *at all* under their command, are eventually
able to read more than those even who seem to have

nothing else but leisure.   In justice, however, to the
nobility of our land, it should be remembered, that
their stations in society, and their wealth, their terri-
torial duties, and their various public duties in London,
as at court, at public meetings, in parliament, &c.,
bring crowded claims upon their time; whilst even
sacrifices of time to the graceful courtesies of life, are in
reference to *their* stations, a sort of secondary duties.
These allowances made, it still remains true that the
busier classes are the main reading classes; whilst
from their immense numbers, they are becoming effectually the body that will more and more impress
upon the moving literature its main impulse and direction.   One other feature of difference there is
amongst this commercial class of readers: amongst
the aristocracy all are thoroughly educated, excepting
those who go at an early age into the army; of the
commercial body, none receive an elaborate, and what
is meant by a liberal education, except those standing
by their connections in the richest classes.   Thus it
happens that, amongst those who have not inherited
but achieved their stations, many men of fine and
powerful understandings, accomplished in manners,
and admirably informed, not having had the benefits when young of a regular classical education, find
(upon any accident bringing up such subjects) a deficiency which they do not find on other subjects.
They are too honorable to undervalue advantages,
which they feel to be considerable, simply because
they were denied to themselves.   They regret their
loss.   And yet it seems hardly worth while, on a
simple prospect of contingencies that may never be
realized, to undertake an entirely new course of study

13

for redressing this loss. But they would be glad to avail themselves of any useful information not exacting study. These are the persons, this is the class, to which I address my remarks on the 'Antigone;' and out of *their* particular situation, suggesting upon all elevated subjects a corresponding tone of liberal curiosity, will arise the particular nature and direction of these remarks.

Accordingly, I presume, secondly, that this curiosity will take the following course : — these persons will naturally wish to know, at starting, what there is *differentially* interesting in a Grecian tragedy, as contrasted with one of Shakspeare's or of Schiller's : in what respect, and by what agencies, a Greek tragedy affects us, or is meant to affect us, otherwise than as *they* do ; and how far the Antigone of Sophocles was judiciously chosen as the particular medium for conveying to British minds a first impression, and a representative impression, of Greek tragedy. So far, in relation to the ends proposed, and the means selected. Finally, these persons will be curious to know the issue of such an experiment. Let the purposes and the means have been bad or good, what was the actual success ? And not merely success, in the sense of the momentary acceptance by half a dozen audiences, whom the mere decencies of justice must have compelled to acknowledge the manager's trouble and expense on their behalf; but what was the degree of satisfaction felt by students of the Athenian[4] tragedy, in relation to their long-cherished ideal ? Did the representation succeed in realizing, for a moment, the awful pageant of the Athenian stage ? Did **Tragedy** in Milton's immortal expression,

——— come sweeping by
In sceptred pall ?

Or was the whole, though successful in relation to the thing attempted, a failure in relation to what ought to have been attempted ?  Such are the questions to be answered.

The first elementary idea of a Greek tragedy, is to be sought in a serious Italian opera.  The Greek dialogue is represented by the recitative, and the tumultuous lyrical parts assigned chiefly, though not exclusively, to the chorus on the Greek stage, are represented by the impassioned airs, duos, trios, choruses, &c. on the Italian.  And here, at the very outset, occurs a question which lies at the threshold of a Fine Art, — that is, of *any* Fine Art: for had the views of Addison upon the Italian opera had the least foundation in truth, there could have been no room or opening for any mode of imitation except such as belongs to a *mechanic* art.

The reason for at all connecting Addison with this case is, that *he* chiefly was the person occupied in assailing the Italian opera; and this hostility arose, probably, in his want of sensibility to good (that is, to Italian) music.  But whatever might be his motive for the hostility, the single argument by which he supported it was this, — that a hero ought not to sing upon the stage, because no hero known to history ever summoned a garrison in a song, or charged a battery in a semichorus.  In this argument lies an ignorance of the very first principle concerned in *every* Fine Art.  In all alike, more or less directly, the object is to reproduce in the mind some great effect, through

the agency of *idem in alio*.   The *idem*, the same im
pression, is to be restored; but *in alio*, in a different
material, — by means of some different instrument.
For instance, on the Roman stage there was an art,
now entirely lost, of narrating, and, in part of dramatically representing an impassioned tale, by means of
dancing, of musical accompaniment in the orchestra,
and of elaborate pantomime in the performer.  *Saltavit
Hypermnestram*, he danced (that is, he represented by
dancing and pantomime the story of) Hypermnestra.
Now, suppose a man to object, that young ladies,
when saving their youthful husbands at midnight from
assassination, could not be capable of waltzing or
quadrilling, how wide is this of the whole problem!
This is still seeking for the *mechanic* imitation, some
imitation founded in the very fact; whereas the object
is to seek the imitation in the sameness of the impression drawn from a different, or even from an
impossible fact.   If a man, taking a hint from the
Roman ' Saltatio' (*saltavit Andromachen*), should say
that he would ' whistle Waterloo,' that is, by whistling
connected with pantomime, would express the passion
and the changes of Waterloo, it would be monstrous to
refuse him his postulate on the pretence that ' people
did not whistle at Waterloo.'   Precisely so: neither
are most people made of marble, but of a material as
different as can well be imagined, viz. of elastic flesh,
with warm blood coursing along its tubes; and yet,
for all *that*, a sculptor will draw tears from you, by
exhibiting, in pure statuary marble, on a sepulchral
monument, two young children with their little heads
on a pillow, sleeping in each other's arms; whereas,
if he had presented them in wax-work, which yet is

far more like to flesh, you would have felt little more pathos in the scene than if they had been shown baked in gilt gingerbread. He has expressed the *idem*, the identical thing expressed in the real children; the sleep that masks death, the rest, the peace, the purity, the innocence; but *in alio*, in a substance the most different; rigid, non-elastic, and as unlike to flesh, if tried by touch, or eye, or by experience of life, as can well be imagined. So of the whistling. It is the very worst objection in the world to say, that the strife of Waterloo did not reveal itself through whistling: undoubtedly it did not; but that is the very ground of the man's art. He will reproduce the fury and the movement as to the only point which concerns you, viz. the effect, upon your own sympathies, through a language that seems without any relation to it: he will set before you what *was* at Waterloo through that which was *not* at Waterloo. Whereas any direct factual imitation, resting upon painted figures drest up in regimentals, and worked by watchwork through the whole movements of the battle, would have been no art whatsoever in the sense of a Fine Art, but a base *mechanic* mimicry.

This principle of the *idem in alio*, so widely diffused through all the higher revelations of art, it is peculiarly requisite to bear in mind when looking at Grecian tragedy, because no form of human composition employs it in so much complexity. How confounding it would have been to Addison, if somebody had told him, that, substantially, he had himself committed the offence (as he fancied it) which he charged so bitterly upon the Italian opera; and that, if the opera had gone farther upon that road than himself, the Greek tragedy,

which he presumed to be so prodigiously exalted beyond modern approaches, had gone farther even than
the opera.    Addison himself, when writing a tragedy,
made this violation (as he would have said) of nature,
made this concession (as *I* should say) to a higher
nature, that he compelled his characters to talk in
metre.    It is true this metre was the common iambic,
which (as Aristotle remarks) is the most natural and
spontaneous of all metres; and, for a sufficient reason,
in all languages.    Certainly; but Aristotle never
meant to say that it was natural for a gentleman in a
passion to talk threescore and ten iambics *consecu-
tively:* a chance line might escape him once and
away; as we know that Tacitus opened one of his
works by a regular dactylic hexameter in full curl,
without ever discovering it to his dying day (a fact
which is clear from his never having corrected it);
and this being a very artificial metre, *à fortiori* Tacitus
might have slipped into a simple iambic.    But that
was an accident, whilst Addison had deliberately and
uniformly made his characters talk in verse.    According to the common and false meaning [which was his
own meaning] of the word nature, he had as undeniably
violated the principle of the *natural*, by this metrical
dialogue, as the Italian opera by musical dialogue.    If
it is hard and trying for men to sing their emotions,
not less so it must be to deliver them in verse.

But, if this were shocking, how much more shocking
would it have seemed to Addison, had he been introduced to parts which really exist in the Grecian drama?
Even Sophocles, who, of the three tragic poets surviving from the wrecks of the Athenian stage, is
reputed the supreme *artist*,[5] if not the most impas-

sioned poet, with what horror he would have over-whelmed Addison, when read by the light of those principles which he had himself so scornfully applied to the opera! In the very monsoon of his raving misery, from calamities as sudden as they were irredeemable, a king is introduced, not only conversing, but conversing in metre; not only in metre, but in the most elaborate of choral metres; not only under the torture of these lyric difficulties, but also chanting; not only chanting, but also in all probability dancing. What do you think of *that*, Mr. Addison?

There is, in fact, a scale of graduated ascents in these artifices for unrealizing the effects of dramatic situations:

1. We may see, even in novels and prose comedies, a keen attention paid to the inspiriting and *dressing* of the dialogue: it is meant to be life-like, but still it is a little raised, pointed, colored, and idealized.

2. In comedy of a higher and more poetic cast, we find the dialogue *metrical*.

3. In comedy or in tragedy alike, which is meant to be still further removed from ordinary life, we find the dialogue fettered not only by metre, but by *rhyme*. We need not go to Dryden, and others, of our own middle stage, or to the French stage for this: even in Shakspeare, as for example, in parts of Romeo and Juliet (and for no capricious purpose), we may see effects sought from the use of rhyme. There is another illustration of the idealizing effect to be obtained from a particular treatment of the dialogue, seen in the Hamlet of Shakspeare. In that drama there arises a necessity for exhibiting a play within a play. This interior drama is to be further removed from the

spectator than the principal drama; it is a deep below a deep; and, to produce that effect, the poet relies chiefly upon the stiffening the dialogue, and removing it still farther, than the general dialogue of the *including* or *outside* drama, from the standard of ordinary life.

4. We find, superadded to these artifices for idealizing the situations, even music of an intermitting character, sometimes less, sometimes more impassioned — recitatives, airs, choruses. Here we have reached the Italian opera.

5. And, finally, besides all these resources of art we find dancing introduced; but dancing of a solemn, mystical, and symbolic character. Here, at last, we have reached the Greek tragedy. Probably the best exemplification cf a Grecian tragedy that ever *will* be given to a modern reader is found in the Samson Agonistes of Milton. Now, in the choral or lyric parts of this fine drama, Samson not only talks, 1st, metrically (as he does every where, and in the most level parts of the scenic business), but, 2d, in very intricate metres, and, 3d, occasionally in *rhymed* metres (though the rhymes are too sparingly and too capriciously scattered by Milton), and, 4th, *singing* or chanting these metres (for, as the chorus sang, it was impossible that *he* could be allowed to talk in his ordinary voice, else he would have put them out, and ruined the music). Finally, 5th, I am satisfied that Milton meant him to *dance*. The office of the *chorus* was imperfectly defined upon the Greek stage. They are generally understood to be the *moralizers* of the scene. But this is liable to exceptions. Some of them have been known to do very bad things on the stage, and to come

within a trifle of felony : as to misprision of felony,
if there *is* such a crime, a Greek chorus thinks nothing
of it.    But that is no business of mine.    What I was
going to say is, that, as the chorus sometimes inter-
mingles too much in the action, so the actors sometimes intermingle in the business of the chorus.    Now,
when you are at Rome, you must do as they do at
Rome.    And that the actor, who mixed with the
chorus, was compelled to sing, is a clear case ; for *his*
part in the choral ode is always in the nature of an
echo, or answer, or like an *antiphony* in cathedral services.    But nothing could be more absurd than that
one of these antiphonies should be sung, and another
said.    That he was also compelled to dance, I am
satisfied.    The chorus only *sometimes* moralized, but it
*always* danced : and any actor, mingling with the
chorus, must dance also.    A little incident occurs to
my remembrance, from the Moscow expedition of 1812,
which may here be used as an illustration : One day
King Murat, flourishing his plumage as usual, made a
gesture of invitation to some squadrons of cavalry that
they should charge the enemy : upon which the cavalry
advanced, but maliciously contrived to envelope the
king of dandies, before he had time to execute his
ordinary manœuvre of riding off to the left and becoming a spectator of their prowess.    The cavalry
resolved that his majesty should for once ride down at
their head to the melée, and taste what fighting was
like ; and he, finding that the thing must be, though
horribly vexed, made a merit of his necessity, and
afterwards pretended that he liked it very much.
Sometimes, in the darkness, in default of other mis-
anthropic visions, the wickedness of this cavalry, their

*méchanceté*, causes me to laugh immoderately. **Now**
I conceive that any interloper into the Greek chorus
must have danced when *they* danced, or he would have
been swept away by their impetus : *nolens volens*, he
must have rode along with the orchestral charge, he
must have rode on the crest of the choral billows, **or**
he would have been rode down by their impassioned
sweep.   Samson, and Œdipus, and others, must have
danced, if they sang ; and they certainly *did* sing, by
notoriously intermingling in the choral business.[6]

'But now,' says the plain English reader, 'what was
the object of all these elaborate devices?   And how
came it that the English tragedy, which surely is **as**
good as the Greek,' (and at this point a devil of defiance whispers to him, like the quarrelsome servant
of the Capulets or the Montagus, 'say *better*,') 'that
the English tragedy contented itself with fewer of these
artful resources than the Athenian?'   I reply, that
-the object of all these things was — to unrealize the
scene.   The English drama, by its metrical dress, and
by other arts more disguised, unrealized itself, liberated
itself from the oppression of life in its ordinary standards, up to a certain height.   Why it did not rise still
higher, and why the Grecian *did*, I will endeavor to
explain.   It was not that the English tragedy was less
impassioned ; on the contrary, it was far more so ; the
Greek being awful rather than impassioned ; but the
passion of each is in a different key.   It is not again
that the Greek drama sought a lower object than the
English : it sought a different object.   It is not im-
parity, but disparity, that divides the two magnificent
theatres.

Suffer me, reader  at this point, to borrow from **my**

self, and do not betray me to the authorities that rule in
this journal, if you happen to know [which is not
likely] that I am taking an idea from a paper which
years ago I wrote for an eminent literary journal. As
I have no copy of that paper before me, it is impossible that I should save myself any labor of writing.
The words at any rate I must invent afresh: and as
to the idea, you never *can* be such a churlish man as,
by insisting on a new one, in effect to insist upon my
writing a false one. In the following paragraph, therefore, I give the substance of a thought suggested by
myself some years ago.

That kind of feeling, which broods over the Grecian
tragedy, and to court which feeling the tragic poets
of Greece naturally spread all their canvas, was more
nearly allied to the atmosphere of death than that of
life. This expresses rudely the character of awe and
religious horror investing the Greek theatre. But to
my own feeling the different principle of passion which
governs the Grecian conception of tragedy, as compared with the English, is best conveyed by saying
that the Grecian is a breathing from the world of
sculpture, the English a breathing from the world
of painting. What we read in sculpture is not absolutely death, but still less is it the fulness of life. We
read there the abstraction of a life that reposes, the
sublimity of a life that aspires, the solemnity of a life
that is thrown to an infinite distance. This last is the
feature of sculpture which seems most characteristic:
the form which presides in the most commanding
groups, ' is not dead but sleepeth : ' true, but it is the
sleep of a life sequestrated, solemn, liberated from the
bonds of space and time, and (as to both alike) thrown

(I repeat the words) to a distance which is infinite.    It affects us profoundly, but not by agitation.    Now, on the other hand, the breathing life — life kindling, trembling, palpitating — that life which speaks to us in painting, this is also the life that speaks to us in English tragedy.    Into an English tragedy e ren festivals of joy may enter ; marriages, and baptisms, or commemorations of national trophies : which, or any thing *like* which, is incompatible with the very being of the Greek.    In that tragedy what uniformity of gloom ; in the English what light alternating with depths of darkness !    The Greek, how mournful ; the English, how tumultuous !    Even the catastrophes how different !    In the Greek we see a breathless waiting for a doom that cannot be evaded ; a waiting, as it were, for the last shock of an earthquake, or the inexorable rising of a deluge : in the English it is like a midnight of shipwreck, from which up to the last and till the final ruin comes, there still survives the sort of hope that clings to human energies.

Connected with this original awfulness of the Greek tragedy, and possibly in part its cause, or at least lending strength to its cause, we may next remark the grand dimensions of the ancient theatres.    Every citizen had a right to accommodation.    *There* at once was a pledge of grandeur.    Out of this original standard grew the magnificence of many a future amphitheatre, circus, hippodrome.    Had the original theatre been merely a speculation of private interest, then, exactly as demand arose, a corresponding supply would have provided for it through its ordinary vulgar channels ; and this supply would have taken place through rival theatres.    But the crushing exaction of ' room for *every* citizen,' put an end to that process of subdivision. Drury Lane, as 1 read (or think that I read) thirty years ago, allowed sitting room for three thousand eight hundred people. Multiply *that* by ten; imagine thirty-eight thousand instead of thirty-eight hundred, and then you have an idea of the Athenian theatre.[7]

Next, out of that grandeur in the architectural proportions arose, as by necessity, other grandeurs. You are aware of the *cothurnus*, or buskin, which raised the actor's heel by two and a half inches; and you think that this must have caused a deformity in the general figure as incommensurate to this height. Not at all. The flowing dress of Greece healed all *that*.

But, besides the *cothurnus*, you have heard of the mask. So far as it was fitted to swell the intonations of the voice, you are of opinion that this mask would be a happy contrivance; for what, you say, could a common human voice avail against the vast radiation from the actor's centre of more than three myriads? If, indeed (like the Homeric Stentor), an actor spoke in point of loudness, ὅσον ἄλλοι πεντήκοντα, as much as other fifty, then he might become audible to the assembled Athenians without aid. But this being impossible, art must be invoked; and well if the mask, together with contrivances of another class, could correct it. Yet if it could, still you think that this mask would bring along with it an overbalancing evil. For the expression, the fluctuating expression, of the features, the play of the muscles, the music of the eye and of the lips, — aids to acting that, in our times, have given immortality to scores, whither would those have vanished? Reader, it mortifies me that all which I said to you upon the peculiar and separate

grandeur investing the Greek theatre is forgotten.
For, you must consider, that where a theatre is built
for receiving upwards of thirty thousand spectators, the
curve described by what in modern times you would
call the tiers of boxes, must be so vast as to make the
ordinary scale of human features almost ridiculous by
disproportion.   Seat yourself at this day in the amphitheatre at Verona, and judge for yourself.   In an
amphitheatre, the stage, or properly the arena, occupying, in fact, the place of our modern pit, was much
nearer than in a scenic theatre to the surrounding
spectators.   Allow for this, and placing some adult in
a station expressing the distance of the Athenian stage,
then judge by his appearance if the delicate pencilling
of Grecian features could have told at the Grecian distance.   But even if it could, then I say that this circumstantiality would have been hostile to the general
tendencies (as already indicated) of the Grecian
drama.   The sweeping movement of the Attic tragedy
*ought* not to admit of interruption from *distinct* human
features; the expression of an eye, the loveliness of a
smile, *ought* to be lost amongst effects so colossal.
The mask aggrandized the features : even so far it
acted favorably.   Then figure to yourself this mask
presenting an idealized face of the noblest Grecian
outline, moulded by some skilful artist *Phidiacâ manu*,
so as to have the effect of a marble bust ; this accorded
with the aspiring *cothurnus ;* and the motionless character impressed upon the features, the marble tranquillity, would (I contend) suit the solemn processional
character of Athenian tragedy, far better than the most
expressive and flexible countenance on its natural
scale.   'Yes,' you say, on considering the character

of the Greek drama, 'generally it might; in forty-
nine cases suppose out of fifty : but what shall be done
in the fiftieth, where some dreadful discovery or *anag-
norisis* (*i. e.* recognition of identity) takes place within
the compass of a single line or two; as, for instance,
in the Œdipus Tyrannus, at the moment when Œdipus
by a final question of his own, extorts his first fatal
discovery, viz. that he had been himself unconsciously
the murderer of Laius?' True, he has no reason as
yet to suspect that Laius was his own father; which
discovery, when made further on, will draw with it
another still more dreadful, viz. that by this parricide
he had opened his road to a throne, and to a marriage
with his father's widow, who was also his own natural
mother. He does not yet know the worst : and to
have killed an arrogant prince, would not in those days
have seemed a very deep offence : but then he believes
that the pestilence had been sent as a secret vengeance
for this assassination, which is thus invested with a
mysterious character of horror. Just at this point,
Jocasta, his mother and his wife, says,[8] on witnessing
the sudden revulsion of feeling in his face, 'I shudder,
oh king, when looking on thy countenance.' Now, in
what way could this passing spasm of horror be reconciled with the unchanging expression in the marble-
looking mask? This, and similar cases to this,
must surely be felt to argue a defect in the scenic
apparatus. But I say, no : first, Because the general
indistinctiveness from distance is a benefit that applies
equally to the fugitive changes of the features and to
their permanent expression. You need not regret the
loss through *absence*, of an appearance that would
equally, though present, have been lost through *dis-*

*tance.* Secondly, The Greek actor had always the resource, under such difficulties, of averting his face; a resource sanctioned in similar cases by the greatest of the Greek painters.    Thirdly, The voluminous draperies of the scenic dresses, and generally of the Greek costume, made it an easy thing to muffle the features altogether by a gesture most natural to sudden horror.    Fourthly, We must consider that there were no stage lights : but, on the contrary that the general light of day was specially mitigated for that particular part of the theatre ; just as various architectural devices were employed to swell the volume of sound.  Finally, I repeat my sincere opinion, that the general indistinctness of the expression was, on principles of taste, an advantage, as harmonizing with the stately and sullen monotony of the Greek tragedy.    Grandeur in the attitudes, in the gestures, in the groups, in the processions — all this was indispensable : but, on so vast a scale as the mighty cartoons of the Greek stage, an Attic artist as little regarded the details of physiognomy, as a great architect would regard, on the frontispiece of a temple, the miniature enrichments that might be suitable in a drawing-room.

With these views upon the Grecian theatre, and other views that it might oppress the reader to dwell upon in this place, suddenly in December last an opportunity dawned — a golden opportunity, gleaming for a moment amongst thick clouds of impossibility that had gathered through three-and-twenty centuries — for seeing a Grecian tragedy presented on a British stage, and with the nearest approach possible to the beauty of those Athenian pomps which Sophocles, which Phidias, which Pericles created, beautified, pro moted. I protest, when seeing the Edinburgh theatre's *programme*, that a note dated from the Vatican would not have startled me more, though sealed with the seal of the fisherman, and requesting the favor of my company to take coffee with the Pope. Nay, less: for channels there were through which I might have compassed a presentation to his Holiness; but the daughter of Œdipus, the holy Antigone, could I have hoped to see *her* ' in the flesh?' This tragedy in an English version,[9] and with German music, had first been placed before the eyes and ears of our countrymen at Convent Garden during the winter of 1844–5. It was said to have succeeded. And soon after a report sprang up, from nobody knew where, that Mr. Murray meant to reproduce it in Edinburgh.

What more natural? Connected so nearly with the noblest house of scenic artists that ever shook the hearts of nations, nobler than ever raised undying echoes amidst the mighty walls of Athens, of Rome, of Paris, of London, — himself a man of talents almost unparalleled for versatility, — why should not Mr. Murray, always so liberal in an age so ungrateful to *his* profession, have sacrificed something to this occasion? He, that sacrifices so much, why not sacrifice to the grandeur of the Antique? I was then in Edinburgh, or in its neighborhood; and one morning, at a casual assembly of some literary friends, present Professor Wilson, Messrs. J. F., C. N., L. C., and others, advocates, scholars, lovers of classical literature, we proposed two resolutions, of which the first was, that the news was too good to be true. That passed *nem. con.;* and the second resolution was *nearly* passing, viz. that a judgment would certainly fall upon Mr.

14

Murray, had a second report proved true, viz. that not
the Antigone, but a burlesque on the Antigone, was
what he meditated to introduce.    This turned out
false ; [10] the original·report was suddenly revived eight
or ten months after.    Immediately on the heels of the
promise the execution followed ; and on the last (which
I believe was the seventh) representation of the Antigone, I prepared myself to attend.

It had been generally reported as characteristic of
myself, that in respect to all coaches, steamboats, railroads, wedding-parties, baptisms, and so forth, there
was a fatal necessity of my being a trifle too late.
Some malicious fairy, not invited to my own baptism,
was supposed to have endowed me with this infirmity.
It occurred to me that for once in my life I would show
the scandalousness of such a belief by being a trifle
too soon, say, three minutes.    And no name more
lovely for inaugurating such a change, no memory
with which I could more willingly connect any reformation, than thine, dear, noble Antigone !    Accordingly, because a certain man (whose name is down in
my pocket-book for no good) had told me that the
doors of the theatre opened at half-past six, whereas,
in fact, they opened at seven, there was I, if you
please, freezing in the little colonnade of the theatre
precisely as it wanted six-and-a-half minutes to seven,—
six-and-a-half minutes observe too soon.    Upon which
this son of absurdity coolly remarked, that, if he had
not set me half-an-hour forward, by my own showing,
I should have been twenty-three-and-a-half minutes too
late.    What sophistry !    But thus it happened (namely,
through the wickedness of this man), that, upon entering the theatre, I found myself like Alexander Selkirk,

ın a frightful solitude, or like a single family of Arabs
gathering at sunset about a solitary coffee-pot in the
boundless desert. Was there an echo raised? it was
from my own steps. Did any body cough? it was
too evidently myself. I was the audience; I was the
public. And, if any accident happened to the theatre,
such as being burned down, Mr. Murray would certainly lay the blame upon me. My business meantime,
as a critic, was — to find out the most malicious seat,
*i. e.* the seat from which all things would take the most
unfavorable aspect. I could not suit myself in this
respect; however bad a situation might seem, I still
fancied some other as promising to be worse. And I
was not sorry when an audience, by mustering in
strength through all parts of the house, began to divide
my responsibility as to burning down the building, and,
at the same time, to limit the caprices of my distracted
choice. At last, and precisely at half-past seven, the
curtain drew up; a thing not strictly correct on a
Grecian stage. But in theatres, as in other places,
one must forget and forgive. Then the music began,
of which in a moment. The overture slipped out at
one ear, as it entered the other, which, with submission
to Mr. Mendelssohn, is a proof that it must be horribly
bad; for, if ever there lived a man that in music can
neither forget nor forgive, that man is myself. Whatever is very good never perishes from my remembrance, — that is, sounds in my ears by intervals for
ever, — and for whatever is bad, I consign the author,
in my wrath, to his own consience, and to the tortures
of his own discords. The most villanous things, however, have one merit; they are transitory as the best
things; and *that* was true of the overture: it perished

Then, suddenly,—oh, heavens! what a revelation of beauty!—forth stepped, walking in brightness, the most faultless of Grecian marbles, Miss Helen Faucit as Antigone.   What perfection of Athenian sculpture! the noble figure, the lovely arms, the fluent drapery! What an unveiling of the ideal statuesque!  Is it Hebe? is it Aurora?  is it a goddess that moves before us? Perfect she is in form; perfect in attitude;

> 'Beautiful exceedingly,
> Like a ladie from a far countrie.'

Here was the redeeming jewel of the performance.   It flattered one's patriotic feelings, to see this noble young countrywoman realizing so exquisitely, and restoring to our imaginations, the noblest of Grecian girls.   We critics, dispersed through the house, in the very teeth of duty and conscience, all at one moment unanimously fell in love with Miss Faucit.   We felt in our remorse, and did not pretend to deny, that our duty was — to be savage.   But when was the voice of duty listened to in the first uproars of passion?   One thing I regretted, viz. that from the indistinctness of my sight for distant faces, I could not accurately discriminate Miss Faucit's features; but I was told by my next neighbor that they were as true to the antique as her figure.  Miss Faucit's voice is fine and impassioned, being deep for a female voice: but in this organ lay also the only blemish of her personation.   In her last scene, which is injudiciously managed by the Greek poet, — too long by much, and perhaps misconceived in the modern way of understanding it, — her voice grew too husky to execute the cadences of the intonations: yet, even in this scene, her fall to the ground, under the burden of

her farewell anguish, was in a high degree sculptur-
esque through the whole succession of its stages.

Antigone in the written drama, and still more in the
personated drama, draws all thoughts so entirely to
herself, as to leave little leisure for examining the
other parts; and, under such circumstances, the first
impulse of a critic's mind is, that he ought to massacre
all the rest indiscriminately; it being clearly his duty
to presume every thing bad which he is not unwillingly
forced to confess good, or concerning which he retains
no distinct recollection. But I, after the first glory of
Antigone's *avatar* had subsided, applied myself to consider the general 'setting' of this Theban jewel.
Creon, whom the Greek tragic poets take delight in
describing as a villain, has very little more to do (until
his own turn comes for grieving), than to tell Antigone,
by minute-guns, that die she must. 'Well, uncle,
don't say that so often,' is the answer which, secretly,
the audience whispers to Antigone. Our uncle grows
tedious; and one wishes at last that he himself could
be 'put up the spout.' Mr. Glover, from the sepulchral
depth of his voice, gave effect to the odious Creontic
menaces; and, in the final lamentations over the dead
body of Hæmon, being a man of considerable intellectual power, Mr. Glover drew the part into a promi
nence which it is the fault of Sophocles to have
authorized in that situation; for the closing sympathies
of the spectator ought not to be diverted, for a moment,
from Antigone.

But the chorus, how did *they* play their part? Mainly
*their* part must have always depended on the character
of the music: even at Athens, that must have been
very much the case, and at Edinburgh altogether, be-

cause dancing on the Edinburgh stage there was none.
How came *that* about? For the very word, ' orchestral,'
suggests to a Greek ear *dancing*, as the leading element in the choral functions.    Was it because dancing
with us is never used mystically and symbolically,
never used in our religious services?    Still it would
have been possible to invent solemn and intricate
dances, that might have appeared abundantly significant, if expounded by impassioned music.    But that
music of Mendelssohn! — like it I cannot.    Say not
that Mendelssohn is a great composer.    He *is* so.    But
here he was voluntarily abandoning the resources of
his own genius, and the support of his divine art, in
quest of a chimera: that is, in quest of a thing called
Greek music, which for *us* seems far more irrecover-
able than the ' Greek fire.'    I myself, from an early
date, was a student of this subject.    I read book after
book upon it; and each successive book sank me
lower into darkness, until I had so vastly improved in
ignorance, that I could myself have written a quarto
upon it, which all the world should not have found it
possible to understand.    It should have taken three
men to construe one sentence.    I confess, however, to
not having yet seen the writings upon this impractica-
ble theme of Colonel Perronet Thompson.    To write
experimental music for choruses that are to support the
else meagre outline of a Greek tragedy, will not do.
Let experiments be tried upon worthless subjects; and
if this of Mendelssohn's be Greek music, the sooner it
takes itself off the better.    Sophocles will be delivered
from an incubus, and we from an affliction of the audi-
tory nerves.

It strikes me that I see the source of this music.

We, that were learning German some thirty years ago,
must remember the noise made at that time about
Mendelssohn, the Platonic philosopher. And why?
Was there any thing particular in 'Der Phædon,' on
the immortality of the soul? Not at all; it left us
quite as mortal as it found us; and it has long since
been found mortal itself. Its venerable remains are
still to be met with in many worm-eaten trunks, pasted
on the lids of which I have myself perused a matter
of thirty pages, except for a part that had been too
closely perused by worms. But the key to all the
popularity of the Platonic Mendelssohn, is to be sought
in the whimsical nature of German liberality, which,
in those days, forced Jews into paying toll at the gates
of cities, under the title of ' swine,' but caressed their
infidel philosophers. Now, in this category of Jew
and infidel, stood the author of ' Phædon.' He was
certainly liable to toll as a hog; but, on the other
hand, he was much admired as one who despised the
Pentateuch. Now *that* Mendelssohn, whose learned
labors lined our trunks, was the father of *this* Mendelssohn, whose Greek music afflicts our ears. Naturally, then, it strikes me, that as ' papa' Mendelssohn
attended the synagogue to save appearances, the filial
Mendelssohn would also attend it. I likewise attended
the synagogue now and then at Liverpool, and elsewhere. We all three have been cruising in the same
latitudes; and, trusting to my own remembrances, I
should pronounce that Mendelssohn has stolen his
Greek music from the synagogue. There was, in the
first chorus of the ' Antigone,' one sublime ascent (and
once repeated) that rang to heaven: it might have
entered into the music of Jubal's lyre, or have glorified

the timbrel of Miriam.   All the rest, tried by the deep
standard of my own feeling, that clamors for the impassioned in music, even as the daughter of the horse-
leech says, ' Give, give,' is as much without meaning as
most of the Hebrew chanting that I heard at the Liverpool synagogue.   I advise Mr. Murray, in the event
of his ever reviving the ' Antigone,' to make the chorus
sing the Hundredth Psalm, rather than Mendelssohn's
music ; or, which would be better still, to import from
Lancashire the Handel chorus-singers.

But then, again, whatever change in the music were
made, so as to ' better the condition ' of the poor audience, something should really be done to ' better the
condition ' of the poor chorus.   Think of these worthy
men, in their white and skyblue liveries, kept standing
the whole evening ; no seats allowed, no dancing ; no
tobacco ; nothing to console them but Antigone's beauty ;
and all this in our climate, latitude fifty-five degrees,
30th of December, and Fahrenheit groping about, I
don't pretend to know where, but clearly on his road
down to the wine cellar.   Mr. Murray, I am perfectly
sure, is too liberal to have grudged the expense, if he
could have found any classic precedent for treating the
chorus to a barrel of ale.   Ale, he may object, is an
unclassical tipple ; but perhaps not.   Xenophon, the
most Attic of prose writers, mentions pointedly in his
*Anabasis*, that the Ten Thousand, when retreating
through snowy mountains, and in circumstances very
like our General Elphinstone's retreat from Cabul,
came upon a considerable stock of bottled ale.   To be
sure, the poor ignorant · man calls it *barley wine*,
[δίνος κρίθινος :] but the flavor was found so perfectly
classical that not one man of the ten thousand, not

even the Attic bee himself, is reported to have left any protest against it, or indeed to have left much of the ale.

But stop : perhaps I am intruding upon other men's space. Speaking, therefore, now finally to the principal question, How far did this memorable experiment succeed ? I reply, that, in the sense of realizing all that the joint revivers proposed to realize, it succeeded; and failed only where these revivers had themselves failed to comprehend the magnificent tendencies of Greek tragedy, or where the limitations of our theatres, arising out of our habits and social differences, had made it impossible to succeed. In London, I believe that there are nearly thirty theatres, and many more, if every place of amusement (not bearing the technical name of *theatre*) were included. All these must be united to compose a building such as that which received the vast audiences, and consequently the vast spectacles, of some ancient cities. And yet, from a great mistake in our London and Edinburgh attempts to imitate the stage of the Greek theatres, little use was made of such advantages as really *were* at our disposal. The possible depth of the Edinburgh stage was not laid open. Instead of a regal hall in Thebes, I protest I took it for the boudoir of Antigone. It was painted in light colors, an error which was abominable, though possibly meant by the artist (but quite unnecessarily) as a proper ground for relieving the sumptuous dresses of the leading performers. The doors of entrance and exit were most unhappily managed. As to the dresses, those of Creon, of his queen, and of the two loyal sisters, were good : chaste, and yet princely. The dress of the chorus was as bad as bad as bad could be : a few

surplices borrowed from Episcopal chapels, or rather
the ornamented *albes*, &c. from any rich Roman
Catholic establishment, would have been more effective.   The *Coryphæus* himself seemed, to my eyes, no
better than a railway laborer, fresh from tunnelling or
boring, and wearing a *blouse* to hide his working dress.
These ill-used men ought to ' strike ' for better clothes,
in case Antigone should again revisit the glimpses
of an Edinburgh moon ; and at the same time they
might mutter a hint about the ale.   But the great hindrances to a perfect restoration of a Greek tragedy,
lie in peculiarities of our theatres that cannot be removed, because bound up with their purposes.   I
suppose that Salisbury Plain would seem too vast a
theatre : but at least a cathedral would be required in
dimensions, York Minster or Cologne.   Lamp-light
gives to us some advantages which the ancients had
not.   But much art would be required to train and
organize the lights and the masses of superincumbent
gloom, that should be such as to allow no calculation
of the dimensions overhead.   Aboriginal night should
brood over the scene, and the sweeping movements of
the scenic groups : bodily expression should be given
to the obscure feeling of that dark power which moved
in ancient tragedy : and we should be made to know
why it is that, with the one exception of the *Persæ*,
founded on the second Persian invasion,[11] in which
Æschylus, the author, was personally a combatant, and
therefore a *contemporary*, not one of the thirty-four
Greek tragedies surviving, but recedes into the dusky
shades of the heroic, or even fabulous times.

A failure, therefore, I think the ' Antigone,' in relation to an object that for us is unattainable ; but a

failure worth more than many ordinary successes. We are all deeply indebted to Mr. Murray's liberality, in two senses; to his liberal interest in the noblest section of ancient literature, and to his liberal disregard of expense. To have seen a Grecian play is a great remembrance. To have seen Miss Helen Faucit's Antigone, were *that* all, with her bust, ὡς ἀγαλματος,[12] and her uplifted arm 'pleading against unjust tribunals,' is worth —— what is it worth? Worth the money? How mean a thought! To see *Helen*, to see Helen of Greece, was the chief prayer of Marlow's Dr. Faustus; the chief gift which he exacted from the fiend. To see Helen of Greece? Dr. Faustus, we *have* seen her: Mr. Murray is the Mephistopheles that showed her to us. It was cheap at the price of a journey to Siberia, and is the next best thing to having seen Waterloo at sunset on the 18th of June, 1815.[13]

# NOTES.

## NOTE 1. Page 139.

' *When sown ;* ' as it has been repeatedly ; a fact which some readers may not be aware of.

## NOTE 2. Page 141.

Boileau, it is true, translated Longinus. But there goes little Greek to *that.* It is in dealing with Attic Greek, and Attic *poets,* that a man can manifest his Grecian skill.

## NOTE 3. Page 143.

' Before God was known ; ' — *i. e.* known in Greece.

## NOTE 4. Page 146.

At times, I say pointedly, the *Athenian* rather than the *Grecian* tragedy, in order to keep the reader's attention awake to a remark made by Paterculus, — viz. That although Greece coquettishly welcomed homage to herself, as generally concerned in the Greek literature, in reality Athens only had any original share in the drama, or in the oratory of Greece.

## NOTE 5. Page 150.

' *The supreme artist :* ' — It is chiefly by comparison with Euripides, that Sophocles is usually crowned with the laurels of *art.* But there is some danger of doing wrong to the truth in too blindly adhering to these old rulings of critical courts. The judgments would sometimes be reversed, if the pleadings were before us. There were blockheads in those days. Undoubtedly

[173]

it is past denying that Euripides at times betrays marks of care-lessness in the structure of his plots, as if writing too much in a hurry : the original cast of the fable is sometimes not happy, and the evolution or disentangling is too precipitate. It is easy to see that he would have remoulded them in a revised edition, or *diaskeue* [διασκϑυη.] On the other hand, I remember nothing in the Greek drama more worthy of a great artist than parts in his Phœnissæ. Neither is he the effeminately tender, or merely pathetic poet that some people imagine. He was able to sweep *all* the chords of the impassioned spirit. But the whole of this subject is in arrear : it is in fact *rés integra,* almost unbroken ground.

### Note 6.    Page 154.

I see a possible screw loose at this point : if *you* see it, reader, have the goodness to hold your tongue.

### Note 7.    Page 157.

'*Athenian Theatre :* ' — Many corrections remain to be made Athens, in her bloom, was about as big as Calcutta, which con tained, forty years ago, more than half a million of people ; or as Naples, which (being long rated at three hundred thousand), is now known to contain at least two hundred thousand more. The well known census of Demetrius Phalereus gave twenty-one thousand citizens. Multiply this by 5, or 4¾, and you have their families. Add ten thousand, multiplied by 4½, for the *Inquilini.* Then add four hundred thousand for the slaves : total, about five hundred and fifty thousand. But upon the fluctuations of the Athenian population there is much room for speculation. And, quære, was not the population of Athens greater two centuries before Demetrius, in the days of Pericles ?

### Note 8.    Page 159.

Having no Sophocles at hand, I quote from memory, not pre-tending therefore to exactness : but the sense is what I state.

## NOTE 9.   Page 161

*Whose* version, I do not know.   But one unaccountable error was forced on one's notice.   *Thebes,* which by Milton and by every scholar is made a monosyllable, is here made a dissyllable. But *Thebez,* the dissyllable, is a *Syrian* city.   It is true that Causabon deduces from a Syriac word meaning a case or enclosure (a *theca*), the name of Thebes, whether Bœotian or Egyptian.   It is probable, therefore, that Thebes the hundred-gated of Upper Egypt, Thebes the seven-gated of Greece, and Thebes of Syria, had all one origin as regards the name.   But this matters not ; it is the *English* name that we are concerned with.

## NOTE 10.   Page 162.

' *False:* ' or rather inaccurate.   The burlesque was not on the Antigone, but on the Medea of Euripides ; and very amusing.

## NOTE 11.   Page 170.

But in this instance, perhaps, distance of space, combined with the unrivalled grandeur of the war, was felt to equiponderate the distance of time, Susa, the Persian capital, being fourteen hundred miles from Athens.

## NOTE 12.   Page 171.

Στερνα θ'ως αγαλματος, *her bosom as the bosom of a statue;* an expression of Euripides, and applied, I think, to Polyxena at the moment of her sacrifice on the tomb of Achilles, as the bride that was being married to him at the moment of his death.

## NOTE 13.   Page 171.

Amongst the questions which occurred to me as requiring an answer, in connection with this revival, was one with regard to the comparative fitness of the Antigone for giving a representative idea of the Greek stage.   I am of opinion that it was the worst choice which could have been made ; and for the very reason which no doubt governed that choice, viz. — because the austerity of the tragic passion is disfigured by a love episode.

Rousseau in his letter to D'Alembert upon his article *Genève*, in the French Encyclopédie, asks, — ' *Qui est-ce qui doute que, sur nos théatres, la meilleure pièce de Sophocle ne tombât tout-à-plat?*' And his reason (as collected from other passages) is — because an interest derived from the passion of sexual love can rarely be found on the Greek stage, and yet cannot be dispensed with on that of Paris. But why was it so rare on the Greek stage? Not from accident, but because it did not harmonize with the principle of that stage, and its vast overhanging gloom. It is the great infirmity of the French, and connected constitutionally with the gayety of their temperament, that they cannot sympathize with this terrific mode of grandeur. We can. And for *us* the choice should have been more purely and severely Grecian ; whilst the slenderness of the plot in any Greek tragedy, would require a far more effective support from tumultuous movement in the chorus. Even the French are not uniformly insensible to this Grecian grandeur. I remember that Voltaire, amongst many just remarks on the Electra of Sophocles, mixed with others that are *not* just, bitterly condemns this demand for a love fable on the French stage, and illustrates its extravagance by the French tragedy on the same subject, of Crebillon. He (in default of any more suitable resource) has actually made Electra, whose character on the Greek stage is painfully vindictive, in love with an imaginary son of Ægisthus, her father's murderer. Something should also have been said of Mrs. Leigh Murray's Ismene, which was very effective in supporting and in relieving the magnificent impression of Antigone. I ought also to have added a note on the scenic mask, and the common notion (not authorized, I am satisfied, by the practice in the *supreme* era of Pericles), that it exhibited a Janus face, the windward side expressing grief or horror, the leeward expressing tranquillity. Believe it not, reader. But on this and other points, it will be better to speak circumstantially, in a separate paper on the Greek drama, as a majestic but very exclusive and almost, if one may say so, bigoted form of the scenic art.

# THE MARQUESS WELLESLEY.*

IT sounds like the tolling of funeral bells, as the annunciation is made of one death after another amongst those who supported our canopy of empire through the last most memorable generation. The eldest of the Wellesleys is gone: he is gathered to his fathers; and here we have his life circumstantially written.

Who, and of what origin are the Wellesleys? There is an impression current amongst the public, or there *was* an impression, that the true name of the Wellesley family is Wesley. This is a case very much resembling some of those imagined by the old scholastic logicians, where it was impossible either to deny or to affirm: saying *yes*, or saying *no*, equally you told a falsehood. The facts are these: the family was originally English; and in England, at the earliest era, there is no doubt at all that its name was De Welles leigh, which was pronounced in the eldest times just as it is now, viz. as a dissyllable,† the first syllable sounding exactly like the cathedral city *Wells*, in

* Memoirs and Correspondence.

† '*As a dissyllable:*' —just as the *Annesley* family, of which Lord Valentia is the present head, do not pronounce their name trisyllabically (as strangers often suppose), but as the two syllables *Anns lea*, accent on the first.

Somersetshire, and the second like *lea*, (a field lying
fallow.) It is plain enough, from various records, that
the true historical *genesis* of the name, was precisely
through that composition of words, which here, for the
moment, I had imagined merely to illustrate its pronunciation. Lands in the diocese of Bath and Wells,
lying by the pleasant river Perret, and almost up to
the gates of Bristol, constituted the earliest possessions
of the De Wellesleighs. They, seven centuries before
Assay, and Waterloo, were ' seised ' of certain rich *leas*
belonging to *Wells*. And from these Saxon elements
of the name, some have supposed the Wellesleys a
Saxon race. They could not possibly have better
blood : but still the thing does not follow from the
premises. Neither does it follow from the *de* that
they were Norman. The first De Wellesley known to
history, the very tip-top man of the pedigree, is Ave-
nant de Wellesleigh. About a hundred years nearer
to our own times, viz. in 1239, came Michael de Wellesleigh ; of whom the important fact is recorded, that
he was the father of Wellerand de Wellesley. And
what did young Mr. Wellerand perform in this wicked
world, that the proud muse of history should condescend to notice his rather singular name ? Reader,
he was — ' killed : ' that is all ; and in company with
Sir Robert de Percival ; which again argues his Somersetshire descent : for the family of Lord Egmont, the
head of all Percivals, ever was, and ever will be, in
Somersetshire. But *how* was he killed ? The time
*when*, viz. 1303, the place *where*, are known : but the
manner *how*, is not exactly stated ; it was in skirmish
with rascally Irish ' kernes,' fellows that (when presented at the font of Christ for baptism) had their right

arms covered up from the baptismal waters, in order that, still remaining consecrated to the devil, those arms might inflict a devilish blow. Such a blow, with such an unbaptized arm, the Irish villain struck; and there was an end of Wellerand de Wellesleigh. Strange that history should make an end of a man, before it had made a beginning of him. These, however, are the *facts;* which, in writing a romance about Sir Wellerand and Sir Percival, I shall have great pleasure in falsifying. But how, says the too curious reader, did the De Wellesleighs find themselves amongst Irish kernes? Had these scamps the presumption to invade Somersetshire? Did they dare to intrude into Wells? Not at all: but the pugnacious De Wellesleys had dared to intrude into Ireland. Some say in the train of Henry II. Some say — but no matter: *there* they were: and *there* they stuck like limpets. They soon engrafted themselves into the county of Kildare; from which, by means of a fortunate marriage, they leaped into the county of Meath; and in that county, as if to refute the pretended mutability of human things, they have roosted ever since. There was once a famous copy of verses floating about Europe, which asserted that, whilst other princes were destined to fight for thrones, Austria — the handsome house of Hapsburgh — should obtain them by marriage:

'Pugnabunt alii: tu, felix Austria, nube.'

So of the Wellesleys: Sir Wellerand took quite the wrong way: not cudgelling, but courting, was the correct way for succeeding in Kildare. Two great estates, by two separate marriages, the De Wellesleighs obtained in Kildare; and, by a third marriage in a third generation, they obtained in the county of Meath, Castle Dengan (otherwise Dangan) with lordships as plentiful as blackberries.    Castle Dangan came to them in the year of our Lord, 1411, *i. e.* before Agincourt: and, in Castle Dangan did Field-marshal, the man of Waterloo, draw his first breath, shed his first tears, and perpetrate his earliest trespasses.    That is what one might call a pretty long spell for one family: four hundred and thirty-five years has Castle Dangan furnished a nursery for the Wellesley piccaninnies. Amongst the lordships attached to Castle Dangan was *Mornington*, which more than three centuries afterwards supplied an earldom for the grandfather of Waterloo.    Any further memorabilia of the Castle Dangan family are not recorded, except that in 1485 (which sure was the year of Bosworth field?) they began to omit the *de* and to write themselves Wellesley *tout court*.    From indolence, I presume: for a certain lady Di. le Fl., whom once I knew, a Howard by birth, of the house of Suffolk, told me as her reason for omitting the *Le*, that it caused her too much additional trouble.

So far the evidence seems in favor of Wellesley and against Wesley.    But, on the other hand, during the last three centuries the Wellesleys wrote the name Wesley.    They, however, were only the *maternal* ancestors of the present Wellesleys.    Garret Wellesley, the last male heir of the direct line, in the year 1745, left his whole estate to one of the Cowleys, a Staffordshire family who had emigrated to Ireland in Queen Elizabeth's time, but who were, however, descended from the Wellesleys.    This Cowley or Colley, taking, in 1745, the name of Wesley, received from George

II. the title of Earl Mornington: and Colley's grand-
son, the Marquess Wellesley of our age, was recorded
in the Irish peerage as *Wesley*, Earl of Mornington;
was uniformly so described up to the end of the eighteenth century; and even Arthur of Waterloo, whom
most of us Europeans know pretty well, on going to
India a little before his brother, was thus introduced by
Lord Cornwallis to Sir John Shore (Lord Teignmouth,
the Governor-general), 'Dear sir, I beg leave to introduce to you Colonel Wesley, who is a lieutenant-colonel
of my regiment. He is a sensible man, and a good
officer.' Posterity, for *we* are posterity in respect of
Lord Cornwallis, have been very much of *his* opinion.
Colonel Wesley really *is* a sensible man; and the
sensible man, soon after his arrival in Bengal,
under the instigation of his brother, resumed the old
name of Wellesley. In reality, the name of Wesley
was merely the abbreviation of indolence, as Chumley
for Cholmondeley, Pomfret for Pontefract, Cicester for
Cirencester; or, in Scotland, Marchbanks for Majori-
banks, Chatorow for the Duke of Hamilton's French
title of Chatelherault. I remember myself, in childhood, to have met a niece of John Wesley the Proto-
Methodist, who always spoke of the second Lord
Mornington (author of the well-known glees) as a
cousin, and as intimately connected with her brother
the great *foudroyant* performer on the organ. Southey,
in his Life of John Wesley, tells us that Charles
Wesley, the brother of John, and father of the great
organist, had the offer from Garret Wellesley of those
same estates which eventually were left to Richard
Cowley. This argues a recognition of near consan-
guinity. Why the offer was declined, is not distinctly

explained. But if it had been accepted, Southey thinks that then we should have had no storming of Seringapatam, no Waterloo, and no Arminian Methodists. All that is not quite clear. Tippoo was booked for a desperate British vengeance by his own desperate enmity to our name, though no Lord Wellesley had been Governor-General. Napoleon, by the same fury of hatred to us, was booked for the same fate, though the scene of it might not have been Waterloo. And, as to John Wesley, why should he not have made the same schism with the English Church, because his brother Charles had become unexpectedly rich?

The Marquess Wellesley was of the same standing, as to age, or nearly so, as Mr. Pitt; though he outlived Pitt by almost forty years. Born in 1760, three or four months before the accession of George III., he was sent to Eton, at the age of eleven; and from Eton, in his eighteenth year, he was sent to Christ Church, Oxford, where he matriculated as a nobleman. He then bore the courtesy title of Viscount Wellesley; but in 1781, when he had reached his twenty-first year, he was summoned away from Oxford by the death of his father, the second Earl of Mornington. It is interesting, at this moment, to look back on the family group of children collected at Dangan Castle. The young earl was within a month of his majority: his younger brothers and sisters were, William Wellesley Pole (since dead, under the title of Lord Maryborough), then aged eighteen; Anne, since married to Henry, son of Lord Southampton, aged thirteen; *Arthur*, aged twelve; Gerald Valerian, now in the church, aged ten; Mary Elizabeth (since Lady Culling Smith), aged nine; Henry, since Lord Cowley, and British ambassador to Spain, France, &c. aged eight. The new Lord Mornington showed his conscientious nature, by assuming his father's debts, and by superintending the education of his brothers. He had distinguished himself at Oxford as a scholar; but he returned thither no more, and took no degree. As Earl of Mornington, he sat in the Irish House of Lords; but not being a British peer, he was able to sit also in the English House of Commons; and of this opening for a more national career, he availed himself at the age of twenty-four. Except that he favored the claims of the Irish Catholics, his policy was pretty uniformly that of Mr. Pitt. He supported that minister throughout the contests on the French Revolution; and a little earlier, on the Regency question. This came forward in 1788, on occasion of the first insanity which attacked George III. The reader, who is likely to have been born since that era, will perhaps not be acquainted with the constitutional question then at issue. It was this: Mr. Fox held that, upon any incapacity arising in the sovereign, the regency would then settle (*ipso facto* of that incapacity) upon the Prince of Wales; overlooking altogether the case in which there should *be* no Prince of Wales, and the case in which such a Prince might be as incapable, from youth, of exercising the powers attached to the office, as his father from disease. Mr. Pitt denied that a Prince of Wales simply *as* such, and apart from any moral fitness which he might possess, had more title to the office of regent than any lamp-lighter or scavenger. It was the province of Parliament exclusively to legislate for the particular case. The practical decision of the question was not called for, from the accident of the king's sudden recovery : but in Ireland, from the independence asserted by the two houses of the British councils, the question grew still more complex. The Lord Lieutenant refused to transmit their address,[*] and Lord Mornington supported him powerfully in his refusal.

Ten years after this hot collision of parties, Lord Mornington was appointed Governor-General of India ; and now first he entered upon a stage worthy of his powers. I cannot myself agree with Mr. Pearce, that 'the wisdom of his policy is now universally recognized ; ' because the same false views of our Indian position, which at that time caused his splendid services to be slighted in many quarters, still preponderates. All administrations alike have been intensely ignorant of Indian politics ; and for the natural reason, that the business of home politics leaves them no disposable energies for affairs so distant, and with which each man's chance of any durable connection is so exceedingly small. What Lord Mornington did was this : he looked our prospects in the face. Two great enemies were then looming upon the horizon, both ignorant of our real resources, and both deluded by our imperfect use of such resources, as, even in a previous war, we had possessed. One of these enemies was Tippoo, the Sultan of Mysore : him, by the crushing energy of his arrangements, Lord Mornington was able utterly to destroy, and to distribute his dominions with equity and moderation, yet so as to prevent any

---

[*] Which adopted neither view ; for by *offering* the regency of Ireland to the Prince of Wales, they negatived Mr. Fox's view, who held it to be the Prince's by inherent right ; and, on the other hand, they still more openly opposed Mr. Pitt.

new coalition arising in that quarter against the British power. There is a portrait of Tippoo, of this very tiger, in the second volume of Mr. Pearce's work, which expresses sufficiently the unparalleled ferocity of his nature; and it is guaranteed, by its origin, as authentic. Tippoo, from the personal interest investing him, has more fixed the attention of Europe than a much more formidable enemy: that enemy was the Mahratta confederacy, chiefly existing in the persons of the Peishwah, of Scindia, of Holkar, and the Rajah of Berar. Had these four princes been less profoundly ignorant, had they been less inveterately treacherous, they would have cost us the only dreadful struggle. which in India we have stood. As it was, Lord Mornington's government reduced and crippled the Mahrattas to such an extent, that in 1817, Lord Hastings found it possible to crush them for ever. Three services of a profounder nature, Lord Wellesley was enabled to do for India; first, to pave the way for the propagation of Christianity, — mighty service, stretching to the clouds, and which, in the hour of death, must have given him consolation; secondly, to enter upon the abolition of such Hindoo superstitions as are most shocking to humanity, particularly the practice of Suttee, and the barbarous exposure of dying persons, or of first-born infants at Sangor on the Ganges; finally, to promote an enlarged system of education, which (if his splendid scheme had been adopted) would have diffused its benefits all over India. It ought also to be mentioned that the expedition by way of the Red Sea against the French in Egypt, was so entirely of his suggestion and his preparation; that, to the great dishonor of Messrs. Pitt and Dundas, whose administration was the worst, as a *war* administration, that ever misapplied, or non-applied, the resources of a mighty empire, it languished for eighteen months purely through *their* neglect.

In 1805, having staid about seven years in India, Lord Mornington was recalled, was created Marquess of Wellesley, was sent, in 1821, as Viceroy to Ireland, where there was little to do; having previously, in 1809, been sent Ambassador to the Spanish Cortes, where there was an affinity to do, but no means of doing it. The last great political act of Lord Welles-ley, was the smashing of the Peel ministry in 1834; viz. by the famous resolution (which he personally drew up) for appropriating to general education in Ireland any surplus arising from the revenues of the Irish Church. Full of honors, he retired from public life at the age of seventy-five, and, for seven years more of life, dedicated his time to such literary pur-suits as he had found most interesting in early youth.

Mr. Pearce, who is so capable of writing vigorously and sagaciously, has too much allowed himself to rely upon public journals. For example, he reprints the whole of the attorney-general's official information against eleven obscure persons, who, from the gallery of the Dublin theatre, did 'wickedly, riotously, and routously' hiss, groan, insult, and assault (to say nothing of their having caused and procured to be hissed, groaned, &c.) the Marquess Wellesley, Lord-Lieutenant General, and General Governor of Ireland. This document covers more than nine pages, and, after all, omits the only fact of the least consequence, viz., that several missiles were thrown by the rioters into the vice-regal box, and amongst them a quart-

bottle, which barely missed his excellency s temples.
Considering the impetus acquired by the descent from
the gallery, there is little doubt that such a weapon
would have killed Lord Wellesley on the spot.   In default however, of this weighty fact, the attorney-general
favors us with memorializing the very best piece of
doggerel that I remember to have read; viz., that upon
divers, to wit, three thousand papers, the rioters had
wickedly and maliciously written and printed, besides,
observe, *causing* to be written and printed, ' No
Popery,' as also the following traitorous couplet —

> ' The Protestants want Talbot,
>   As the Papists have got *all but;* '

Meaning ' all but ' that which they got some years
·ater by means of the Clare election.   Yet if, in some
instances like this, Mr. Pearce has too largely drawn
upon official papers, which he should rather have ab-
stracted and condensed, on the other hand, his work
has a specific value in bringing forward private documents, to which his opportunities have gained him
a confidential access.   Two portraits of Lord Wellesley, one in middle life, and one in old age, from
a sketch by the Comte d'Orsay, are felicitously executed.

Something remains to be said of Lord Wellesley as a
literary man; and towards such a judgment Mr. Pearce
has contributed some very pleasing materials.   As a
public speaker, Lord Wellesley had that degree of
brilliancy and effectual vigor, which might have been
expected in a man of great talents, possessing much
native sensibility to the charms of style, but not led by
any personal accidents of life into a separate cultiva·

vation of oratory, or into any profound investigation
of its duties and its powers on the arena of a British
senate.   There is less call for speaking of Lord Wellesley in this character, where he did not seek for any
eminent distinction, than in the more general character
of an elegant *litterateur*, which furnished to him much
of his recreation in all stages of his life, and much of
his consolation in the last.   It is interesting to see this
accomplished nobleman, in advanced age, when other
resources were one by one decaying, and the lights of
life were successively fading into darkness, still cheer-
ing his languid hours by the culture of classical literature, and in his eighty-second year drawing solace
from those same pursuits which had given grace and
distinction to his twentieth.

One or two remarks I will make upon Lord Wellesley's verses — Greek as well as Latin.   The Latin
lines upon Chantrey's success at Holkham in killing
two woodcocks at the first shot, which subsequently he
sculptured in marble and presented to Lord Leicester,
are perhaps the most felicitous amongst the whole.
Masquerading, in Lord Wellesley's verses, as Praxi-
teles, who could not well be represented with a Manon
having a percussion lock, Chantrey is armed with a
bow and arrows:

‘ En !  trajecit aves una sagitta duas.’

In the Greek translation of *Parthenopæus*, there are as
few faults as could reasonably be expected.   But, first,
one word as to the original Latin poem: to whom does
it belong?   It is traced first to Lord Grenville, who
received it from his tutor (afterwards Bishop of London), who had taken it as an anonymous poem from

the ' Censor's book ; ' and with very little probability,
it is doubtfully assigned to ' Lewis of the War Office,'
meaning, no doubt, the father of Monk Lewis.  By this
anxiety in tracing its pedigree, the reader is led to exaggerate the pretensions of the little poem; these are
inconsiderable : and there is a conspicuous fault, which
it is worth while noticing, because it is one peculiarly
besetting those who write modern verses with the help
of a gradus, viz. that the Pentameter is often a mere
reverberation of the preceding Hexameter.  Thus, for
instance —

> ' Parthenios inter saltus non amplius erro,
> Non repeto Dryadum pascua læta choris ; '

and so of others, where the second line is but a variation of the first.  Even Ovid, with all his fertility, and
partly in consequence of his fertility, too often commits
this fault.  Where indeed the thought is effectually
varied, so that the second line acts as a musical *minor*,
succeeding to the *major*, in the first, there may happen
to arise a peculiar beauty.  But I speak of the ordinary
case, where the second is merely the rebound of the
first, presenting the same thought in a diluted form.
This is the commonest resource of feeble thinking, and
is also a standing temptation or snare for feeble thinking.  Lord Wellesley, however, is not answerable for
these faults in the original, which indeed he notices
slightly as ' repetitions ; ' and his own Greek version is
spirited and good.  There, are, however, some mistakes.
The second line is altogether faulty ;

> Χωρια Μαιναλιω παντ' ερατεινα θεω
> 'Αχνυμενος λειπων

does not express the sense intended.  Construed cor-

rectly, this clause of the sentence would mean—'*I
sorrowfully leaving all places gracious to the Mæna-
lian god :*' but *that* is not what Lord Wellesley designed: '*I leaving the woods of Cyllene, and the
snowy summits of Pholoe, places that are all of them
dear to Pan*'—*that* is what was meant: that is to
say, not *leaving all places dear to Pan,* far from it;
but *leaving a few places, every one of which is dear to
Pan.* In the line beginning

*Καν ἰθ ὐφ' ἡλικιας*

where the meaning is—*and if as yet, by reason of my
immature age,* there is a metrical error; and *ηλικια* will
not express immaturity of age. I doubt whether in the
next line,

*Μηδ' ἀλκη θαλλοι γουνασιν ἠθεος*

*γουνασιν* could convey the meaning without the preposi-
tion *ἰν.* And in

*Σπερχομαι οὐ καλεουσι θεοι.*

*I hasten whither the gods summon me* — *οὐ* is not the
right word. It is, however, almost impossible to write
Greek verses which shall be liable to no verbal objections; and the fluent movement of these verses sufficiently argues the off-hand ease with which Lord
Wellesley must have *read* Greek, writing it so ele-
gantly and with so little of apparent constraint.

Meantime the most interesting (from its circumstances) of Lord Wellesley's verses, is one to which
his own English interpretation of it has done less than
justice. It is a Latin epitaph on the daughter (an only
child) of Lord and Lady Brougham. She died, and
(as was generally known at the time) of an organic
affection disturbing the action of the heart, at the early

age of eighteen. And the peculiar interest of the case lies in the suppression by this pious daughter (so far as it was possible) of her own bodily anguish, in order to beguile the mental anguish of her parents. The Latin epitaph is this :

> ' Blanda anima, e cunis heu ! longo exercita morbo, .
>   Inter maternas heu lachrymasque patris,
> Quas risu lenire tuo jucunda solebas,
>   Et levis, et proprii vix memor ipsa mali ;
> I, pete calestes, ubi nulla est cura, recessus :
>   Et tibi sit nullo mista dolore quies ! '

The English version is this :

> ' Doom'd to long suffering from earliest years,
>   Amidst your parents' grief and pain alone
> Cheerful and gay, you smiled to soothe their tears ;
>   And in *their* agonies forgot your own.
> Go, gentle spirit ; and among the blest
>   From grief and pain eternal be thy rest ! '

In the Latin, the phrase *e cunis* does not express *from your cradle upwards.* The second line is faulty in the opposition of *maternas* to *patris.* And in the fourth line *levis* conveys a false meaning : *levis* must mean either *physically light, i. e.* not heavy, which is not the sense, or else *tainted with levity,* which is still less the sense. What Lord Wellesley wished to say — was *light-hearted :* this he has *not* said : but neither is it easy to say it in good Latin.

I complain, however, of the whole as not bringing out Lord Weslesley's own feeling — which feeling is partly expressed in his verses, and partly in his accompanying prose note on Miss Brougham's mournful destiny (' her life was a continual illness ') contrasted with her fortitude, her innocent gaiety, and the pious motives with which she supported this gaiety to the

last. Not as a direct version, but as filling up the outline of Lord Wellesley, sufficiently indicated by himself, I propose this : —

'Child, that for thirteen years hast fought with pain,
  Prompted by joy and depth of natural love, —
Rest now at God's command : oh ! not in vain
  His angel ofttimes watch'd thee, — oft, above
All pangs, that else had dimm'd thy parents' eyes,
Saw thy young heart victoriously rise.
Rise now for ever, self-forgetting child,
  Rise to those choirs, where love like thine is blest,
From pains of flesh — from filial tears assoil'd,
  Love which God's hand shall crown with God's own rest '

# MILTON *VERSUS* SOUTHEY AND LANDOR.

THIS conversation is doubly interesting: interesting by its subject, interesting by its interlocutors; for the subject is Milton, whilst the interlocutors are *Southey* and *Landor*. If a British gentleman, when taking his pleasure in his well-armed yacht, descries, in some foreign waters, a noble vessel, from the Thames or the Clyde, riding peaceably at anchor — and soon after, two smart-looking clippers, with rakish masts, bearing down upon her in company — he slackens sail: his suspicions are slightly raised; they have not shown their teeth as yet, and perhaps all is right; but there can be no harm in looking a little closer; and, assuredly, if he finds any mischief in the wind against his countryman, he will show *his* teeth also; and, please the wind, will take up such a position as to rake both of these pirates by turns. The two dialogists are introduced walking out after breakfast, 'each his Milton in his pocket;' and says Southey, 'Let us collect all the graver faults we can lay our hands upon, without a too minute and troublesome research;' — just so; there would be danger in *that* — help might put off from shore; — 'not,' says he, 'in the spirit of Johnson, but in our own.' Johnson we may suppose, is some old ruffian well known upon that coast; and '*faults*' may be a flash term for what the Americans

call 'notions.' A part of the cargo it clearly is; and
one is not surprised to hear Landor, whilst assenting
to the general plan of attack, suggesting in a whisper,
' that they should abase their eyes in reverence to so
great a man, without absolutely closing them;' which
I take to mean — that, without trusting entirely to their
boarders, or absolutely closing their ports, they should
depress their guns and fire down into the hold, in respect of the vessel attacked standing so high out of the
water.  After such plain speaking, nobody can wonder
much at the junior pirate (Landor) muttering, 'It will
be difficult for us always to refrain.'  Of course it will:
*refraining* was no part of the business, I should fancy,
taught by that same buccaneer, Johnson.   There is
mischief, you see, reader, singing in the air — ' miching
malhecho' — and it is our business to watch it.

   But, before coming to the main attack, I must suffer
myself to be detained for a few moments by what Mr.
L. premises upon the ' moral' of any great fable,
and the relation which it bears, or *should* bear, to the
solution of such a fable.   Philosophic criticism is so
far improved, that, at this day, few people, who have
reflected at all upon such subjects, but are agreed as
to one point: viz., that in metaphysical language the
moral of an epos or a drama should be *immanent*, not
*transient;* or, otherwise, that it should be vitally distributed through the whole organization of the tree, not
gathered or secreted into a sort of red berry or *race-
mus*, pendent at the end of its boughs.   This view Mr.
Landor himself takes, as a general view; but, strange
to say, by some Landorian perverseness, where there
occurs a memorable exception to this rule (as in the
' Paradise Lost'), in that case he insists upon the rule

ın its rigor — the rule, and nothing *but* the rule.
Where, on the contrary, the rule does really and obviously take effect (as in the 'Iliad' and 'Odyssey'),
there he insists upon an exceptional case.   There *is*
a moral, in *his* opinion, hanging like a tassel of gold
bullion from the 'Iliad;' — and what is it?   Something so fantastic, that I decline to repeat it.   As well
might he have said, that the moral of 'Othello' was —
'*Try Warren's Blacking!*'   There is no moral,
little or big, foul or fair, to the 'Iliad.'   Up to the 17th
book, the moral might seem dimly to be this — 'Gentlemen, keep the peace: you see what comes of quarrelling.'   But *there* this moral ceases; — there is now
a break of guage: the narrow guage takes place after
this; whilst up to this point, the broad guage — viz.,
the wrath of Achilles, growing out of his turn-up with
Agamemnon — had carried us smoothly along without
need to shift our luggage.   There is no more quarrelling after Book 17, how then can there be any more
moral from quarrelling?   If you insist on *my* telling
*you* what is the moral of the 'Iliad,' I insist upon *your*
telling *me* what is the moral of a rattlesnake or the
moral of a Niagara.   I suppose the moral is — that
you must get out of their way, if you mean to moralize
much longer.   The going-up (or anabasis) of the
Greeks against Troy, was a *fact;* and a pretty dense
fact; and, by accident, the very first in which all
Greece had a common interest.   It was a joint-stock
concern — a representative expedition — whereas, previously there had been none; for even the Argonautic
expedition, which is rather of the darkest, implied no
confederation except amongst individuals.   How could
it?   For the Argo is supposed to have measured only

twenty-seven tons: how she would have been classed at Lloyd's is hard to say, but certainly not as A 1. There was no state-cabin; everybody, demi-gods and all, pigged in the steerage amongst beans and bacon. Greece was naturally proud of having crossed the herring-pond, small as it was, in search of an entrenched enemy; proud also of having licked him 'into Almighty smash;' this was sufficient; or if an impertinent moralist sought for something more, doubtless the moral must have lain in the booty. A peach is the moral of a peach, and moral enough; but if a man *will* have something better — a moral within a moral — why, there is the peach-stone, and its kernel, out of which he may make ratafia, which seems to be the ultimate morality that *can* be extracted from a peach. Mr. Archdeacon Williams, indeed, of the Edinburgh Academy, has published an *octavo* opinion upon the case, which asserts that the moral of the Trojan war was (to borrow a phrase from children) *tit for tat.* It was a case of retaliation for crimes against Hellas, committed by Troy in an earlier generation. It may be so; Nemesis knows best. But this moral, if it concerns the total expedition to the Troad, cannot concern the 'Iliad,' which does not take up matters from so early a period, nor go on to the final catastrophe of Ilium.

Now, as to the 'Paradise Lost,' it happens that there is — whether there ought to be or not — a pure golden moral, distinctly announced, separately contemplated, and the very weightiest ever uttered by man or realized by fable. It is a moral rather for the drama of a world than for a human poem. And this moral is made the more prominent and memorable by the grandeur of its annunciation.   The jewel is not more splendid in itself than in its setting.   Excepting the well-known passage on Athenian oratory in the ' Paradise Regained,' there is none even in Milton where the metrical pomp is made so effectually to aid the pomp of the sentiment.   Hearken to the way in which a roll of dactyles is made to settle, like the swell of the advancing tide, into the long thunder of billows breaking for leagues against the shore :

> ' That to the height of this great argument
> I may assert eternal Providence.' ——

Hear what a motion, what a tumult, is given by the dactylic close to each of the introductory lines !   And how massily is the whole locked up into the peace of heaven, as the aerial arch of a viaduct is locked up into tranquil stability by its key-stone, through the deep spondaic close,

> ' And justify the ways of God to man.'

That is the moral of the Miltonic epos ; and as much grander than any other moral *formally* illustrated by poets, as heaven is higher than earth.

But the most singular moral, which Mr. Landor anywhere discovers, is in his own poem of ' *Gebir.*' Whether he still adheres to it, does not appear from the present edition.   But I remember distinctly, in the original edition, a Preface (now withdrawn) in which he made his acknowledgments to some book read at a Welsh Inn for the outline of the story ; and as to the moral, he declared it to be an exposition of that most mysterious offence, *Over-Colonization.*   Much I mused, in my youthful simplicity, upon this criminal novelty. What might it be ?   Could I, by mistake, have committed it myself? Was it a felony, or a misde-meanor?—liable to transportation, or only to fine and imprisonment? Neither in the Decemviral Tables, nor in the Code of Justinian, nor the maritime Code of Oleron, nor in the Canon Law, nor the Code Napo-leon, nor our own Statutes at large, nor in Jeremy Bentham, had I read of such a crime as a possibility. Undoubted'y the vermin, locally called *Squatters*,\* both in the wilds of America and Australia, who pre-occupy other men's estates, have latterly illustrated the logical possibility of such an offence; but they were quite unknown at the era of Gebir. Even Dalica, who knew as much wickedness as most people, would have stared at this unheard of villany, and have asked, as eagerly as *I* did—'What is it now? Let's have a shy at it in Egypt.' I, indeed, knew a case, but Dalica did *not*, of shocking over-colonization. It was the case, which even yet occurs on out-of-the-way roads, where a man, unjustly big, mounts into the in-side of a stage-coach already sufficiently crowded. In streets and squares, where men could give him a wide berth, they had tolerated the injustice of his person; but now, in a chamber so confined, the length and breadth of his wickedness shines revealed to every eye. And if the coach should upset, which it would

---

\* *Squatters:*—They are a sort of self-elected warming-pans. What we in England mean by the political term '*warming-pans*,' are men who occupy, by consent, some official place, or Par-liamentary seat, until the proper claimant is old enough in law to assume his rights. When the true man comes to bed, the warming-pan respectfully turns out. But these ultra-marine warming-pans *wouldn't* turn out. They showed fight, and wouldn't hear of the true man, even as a bed-fellow.

not be the less likely to do for having *him* on board, somebody or other (perhaps myself) must lie beneath this monster, like Enceladus under Mount Etna, calling upon Jove to come quickly with a few thunderbolts and destroy both man and mountain, both *succubus* and *incubus*, if no other relief offered. Meantime, the only case of over-colonization notorious to all Europe, is that which some German traveller (Riedesel, I think) has reported so eagerly, in ridicule of our supposed English credulity; viz.— the case of the foreign swindler, who advertised that he would get into a quart bottle, filled Drury Lane, pocketed the admission money, and decamped, protesting (in his adieus to the spectators) that ' it lacerated his heart to disappoint so many noble islanders; but that on his next visit he would make full reparation by getting into a vinegar cruet.' Now, here certainly was a case of over-colonization, not perpetrated, but meditated. Yet, when one examines this case, the crime consisted by no means in doing it, but in *not* doing it; by no means in getting into the bottle, but in *not* getting into it. The foreign contractor would have been probably a very unhappy man, had he fulfilled his contract by over-colonizing the bottle, but he would have been decidedly a more virtuous man. He would have redeemed his pledge; and, if he had even died in the bottle, we should have honored him as a ' *vir bonus, cum malâ fortunâ compositus;* ' as a man of honor matched in single duel with calamity, and also as the best of conjurers. Over-colonization, therefore, except in the one case of the stage-coach, is apparently no crime; and the offence of King Gebir, in my eyes, remains a mystery to this day.

What next solicits notice is in the nature of a digression: it is a kind of parenthesis on Wordsworth.

'*Landor.* — When it was a matter of wonder how Keats, who was ignorant of Greek, could have written his " Hyperion," Shelley, whom envy never touched, gave as a reason — " because he *was* a Greek." Wordsworth, being asked his opinion of the same poem, called it, scoffingly, " a pretty piece of paganism ; " yet he himself, in the best verses he ever wrote — and beautiful ones they are — reverts to the powerful influence of the " pagan creed." '

Here are nine lines exactly in the original type. Now, nine tailors are ranked, by great masters of algebra, as $=$ one man; such is the received equation ; or, as it is expressed, with more liveliness, in an old English drama, by a man who meets and quarrels with eighteen tailors — ' Come, hang it! I'll fight you *both*.' But, whatever be the algebraic ratio of tailors to men, it is clear that nine Landorian lines are not always equal to the delivery of one accurate truth, or to a successful conflict with three or four signal errors. Firstly — Shelley's reason, if it ever was assigned, is irrelevant as regards any question that must have been intended. It could not have been meant to ask — Why was the ' Hyperion ' so Grecian in its spirit ? for it is anything but Grecian. We should praise it falsely to call it so ; for the feeble, though elegant, mythology of Greece was incapable of breeding anything so deep as the mysterious portents that, in the ' Hyperion,' run before and accompany the passing away of divine immemorial dynasties. Nothing can be more impressive than the picture of Saturn in his palsy of affliction, and

of the mighty goddess his grand-daughter, or than the
secret signs of coming woe in the palace of Hyperion.
These things grew from darker creeds than Greece
had ever known since the elder traditions of Pro-
metheus — creeds that sent down their sounding plum-
mets into far deeper wells within the human spirit.
What had been meant, by the question proposed to
Shelley, was no doubt — How so young a man as Keats,
not having had the advantage of a regular classical
education, could have been so much at home in the
details of the *elder* mythology ?    Tooke's 'Pantheon'
might have been obtained by favor of any English
schoolboy, and Dumoustier's ' *Lettres à Emile sur la
Mythologie* ' by favor of very many young ladies; but
these, according to my recollection of them, would
hardly have sufficed.    Spence's ' *Polymetis*,' however,
might have been had by favor of any good library;
and the ' *Bibliotheca* ' of Apollodorus, who is the cock
of the walk on this subject, might have been read by
favor of a Latin translation, supposing Keats really
unequal to the easy Greek text.    There is no wonder
in the case; nor, if there had been, would Shelley's
kind remark have solved it.    The *treatment* of the
facts must, in any case, have been due to Keats's
genius, so as to be the same whether he had studied
Greek or not : the *facts*, apart from the treatment,
must in any case have been had from a book.    Secondly — Let Mr. Landor rely upon it — that Wordsworth never said the thing ascribed to him here as any
formal judgment, or what Scottish law would call
*deliverance,* upon the 'Hyperion.'    As to what he
might have said incidentally and collaterally ;  the
meaning of words is so entirely affected by their posi-

tion in a conversation — what followed, what went before — that five words dislocated from their context
never would be received as evidence in the Queen's
Bench.   The court which, of all others, least strictly
weighs its rules of evidence, is the female tea-table;
yet even that tribunal would require the deponent to
strengthen his evidence, if he had only five detached
words to produce.   Wordsworth is a very proud man,
as he has good reason to be; and perhaps it was I,
myself, who once said in print of him — that it is not
the correct way of speaking, to say that Wordsworth
is as proud as Lucifer; but, inversely, to say of Lucifer
that some people have conceived him to be as proud
as Wordsworth.   But, if proud, Wordsworth is not
haughty, is not ostentatious, is not anxious for display,
is not arrogant, and, least of all, is he capable of descending to envy.   Who or what is it that *he* should be
envious of?   Does anybody suppose that Wordsworth
would be jealous of Archimedes if he now walked
upon earth, or Michael Angelo, or Milton?   Nature
does not repeat herself.   Be assured she will never
make a second Wordsworth.   Any of us would be
jealous of his own duplicate; and, if I had a *doppelganger*, who went about personating me, copying me,
and pirating me, philosopher as I am, I might (if the
Court of Chancery would not grant an injunction
against him) be so far carried away by jealousy as to
attempt the crime of murder upon his carcass; and no
great matter as regards HIM.   But it would be a sad
thing for *me* to find myself hanged; and for what, 1
beseech you? for murdering a sham, that was either
nobody at all, or oneself repeated once too often.   But
if you show to Wordsworth a man as great as himself

still that great man will not be much *like* Words-worth — the great man will not be Wordsworth's *doppelganger.* If not *impar* (as you say) he will be *dispar;* and why, then, should Wordsworth be jealous of him, unless he is jealous of the sun, and of Abd el Kāder, and of Mr. Waghorn — all of whom carry off a great deal of any spare admiration which Europe has to dispose of. But suddenly it strikes me that we are all proud, every man of us; and I daresay with some reason for it, ' be the same more or less.' For I never came to know any man in my whole life intimately, who could not do something or other better than any-body else. The only man amongst us that is thoroughly free from pride, that you may at all seasons rely on as a pattern of humility, is the pickpocket. That man is so admirable in his temper, and so used to pocketing anything whatever which Providence sends in his way, that he will even pocket a kicking, or anything in that line of favors which you are pleased to bestow. The smallest donations are by him thankfully received, provided only that you, whilst half-blind with anger in kicking him round a figure of eight, like a dexterous skater, will but allow *him* (which is no more than fair) to have a second ' shy' at your pretty Indian pocket-handkerchief, so as to convince you, on cooler reflec-tion, that he does not *always* miss. Thirdly — Mr. Landor leaves it doubtful what verses those are of Wordsworth's which celebrate the power ' of the Pagan creed;' whether that sonnet in which Wordsworth wishes to exchange for glimpses of human life, *then and in those circumstances,* ' forlorn,' the sight

'—— Of Proteus coming from the sea,
And hear old Triton wind his wreathed horn;'

whether this, or the passage on the Greek mythology
in 'The Excursion.' Whichever he means, I am the
last man to deny that it is beautiful, and especially if
he means the latter. But it is no presumption to deny
firmly Mr. Landor's assertion, that these are ' the best
verses Wordsworth ever wrote.' Bless the man !

> ' There are a thousand such elsewhere,
>     As worthy of your wonder : ' —

Elsewhere, I mean, in Wordsworth's poems. In reality
it is *impossible* that these should be the best; for even
if, in the executive part, they were so, which is not the
case, the very nature of the thought, of the feeling,
and of the relation, which binds it to the general
theme, and the nature of that theme itself, forbid the
possibility of merits so high. The whole movement
of the feeling is fanciful : it neither appeals to what is
deepest in human sensibilities, nor is meant to do so.
The result, indeed, serves only to show Mr. Landor's
slender acquaintance with Wordsworth. And what is
worse than being slenderly acquainted, he is erroneously acquainted even with these two short breathings
from the Wordsworthian shell. He mistakes the logic.
Wordsworth does not celebrate any power at all in
Paganism. Old Triton indeed! he's little better, in
respect of the terrific, than a mail-coach guard, nor
half as good, if you allow the guard his official seat, a
coal-black night, lamps blazing back upon his royal
scarlet, and his blunderbuss correctly slung. Triton
would not stay, I engage, for a second look at the old
Portsmouth mail, as once I knew it. But, alas ! better
things than ever stood on Triton's pins are now as little
able to stand up for themselves, or to startle the silent

fields in darkness, with the sudden flash of their
glory — gone before it had full come — as Triton is to
play the Freyschütz chorus on his humbug of a horn.
But the logic of Wordsworth is this — not that the
Greek mythology is potent; on the contrary, that it
is weaker than cowslip tea, and would not agitate
the nerves of a hen sparrow; but that, weak as it is —
nay, by means of that very weakness — it does but the
better serve to measure the weakness of something
which *he* thinks yet weaker — viz. the death-like torpor
of London society in 1808, benumbed by conventional
apathy and worldliness —

> ' Heavy as frost, and deep almost as life.'

This seems a digression from Milton, who is properly the subject of this colloquy. But, luckily, it is
not one of *my* sins. Mr. Landor is lord within the
house of his own book; he pays all accounts whatever; and readers that have either a bill, or bill of exceptions, to tender against the concern, must draw
upon *him.* To Milton he returns upon a very dangerous
topic indeed — viz. the structure of his blank verse.
I know of none that is so trying to a wary man's
nerves. You might as well tax Mozart with harshness
in the divinest passages of ' Don Giovanni,' as Milton
with any such offence against metrical science. Be
assured, it is yourself that do not read with understanding, not Milton that by possibility can be found deaf to
the demands of perfect harmony. You are tempted,
after walking round a line threescore times, to exclaim
at last — ' Well, if the Fiend himself should rise up
before me at this very moment, in this very study of
mine, and say that no screw was loose in that line,

then would I reply — ' Sir, with submission, you
are ———.' 'What!' suppose the Fiend suddenly to
demand in thunder; ' what am I ? ' ' Horribly wrong,'
you wish exceedingly to say; but, recollecting that
some people are choleric in argument, you confine
yourself to the polite answer — ' That, with deference
to his better education, you conceive him to lie ; ' —
that's a bad word to drop your voice upon in talking
with a fiend, and you hasten to add — under a slight, a
*very* slight mistake.' Ay, you might venture on that
opinion with a fiend. But how if an angel should
undertake the case ? And angelic was the ear of Milton. Many are the *primâ facie* anomalous lines in
Milton; many are the suspicious lines, which in many
a book I have seen many a critic peering into, with
eyes made up for mischief, yet with a misgiving that
all was not quite safe, very much like an old raven
looking down a marrow-bone. In fact, such is the
metrical skill of the man, and such the perfection of
his metrical sensibility, that, on any attempt to take
liberties with a passage of his, you feel as when
coming, in a forest, upon what seems a dead lion;
perhaps he may *not* be dead, but only sleeping; nay,
perhaps he may *not* be sleeping, but only shamming.
And you have a jealousy, as to Milton, even in the
most flagrant case of almost palpable error, that, after
all, there may be a plot in it. You may be put down
with shame by some man reading the line otherwise,
reading it with a different emphasis, a different cæsura,
or perhaps a different suspension of the voice, so as to
bring out a new and self-justifying effect. It must be
added, that, in reviewing Milton's metre, it is quite
necessary to have such books as ' Nare's English

Orthoēpy' (*in a late edition*), and others of that class, lying on the table; because the accentuation of Milton's age was, in many words, entirely different from ours. And Mr. Landor is not free from some suspicion of inattention as to this point. Over and above this accentual difference, the practice of our elder dramatists in the resolution of the final *tion* (which now is uniformly pronounced *shon*), will be found exceedingly important to the appreciation of a writer's verse. *Contribution*, which now is necessarily pronounced as a word of four syllables, would then, in verse, have five, being read into *con-tri-bu-ce-on*. Many readers will recollect another word, which for years brought John Kemble into hot water with the pit of Drury Lane. It was the plural of the word ache. This is generally made a dissyllable by the Elizabethan dramatists; it occurs in the ' Tempest.' Prospero says —

> ' I 'll fill thy bones with aches.'

What follows, which I do not remember *literatim*, is such metrically as to *require* two syllables for aches. But how, then, was this to be pronounced? Kemble thought *akies* would sound ludicrous; *aitches* therefore he called it: and always the pit howled like a famished *menagerie*, as they did also when he chose (and he constantly chose) to pronounce *beard* like *bird*. Many of these niceties must be known, before a critic can ever allow *himself* to believe that he is right in *obelizing*, or in marking with so much as a ? any verse whatever of Milton's. And there are some of these niceties, I am satisfied, not even yet fully investigated.

It is, however, to be borne in mind, after all allow-

ances and provisional reservations have been made,
that Bentley's hypothesis (injudiciously as it was
managed by that great scholar) has really a truth of
fact to stand upon.   Not only must Milton have composed his three greatest poems, the two 'Paradises'
and the 'Samson,' in a state of blindness — but subsequently, in the correction of the proofs, he must have
suffered still more from this conflict with darkness,
and, consequently, from this dependence upon careless readers.   This is Bentley's *case:* as lawyers say,
'My lord, that is my case.'   It is possible enough to
*write* correctly in the dark, as I myself often do, when
losing or missing my lucifers — which, like some elder
lucifers, are always rebelliously straying into places
where they *can* have no business.   But it is quite impossible to *correct a proof* in the dark.   At least, if
there *is* such an art, it must be a section of the black
art.   Bentley gained from Pope that admirable epithet
of *slashing,* ['*the ribbalds — from slashing Bentley
down to piddling Theobalds,*' i. e. *Tibbalds* as it was
pronounced], altogether from his edition of the 'Paradise Lost.'   This the doctor founded on his own
hypothesis as to the advantage taken of Milton's blindness; and corresponding was the havoc which he
made of the text.   In fact, on the really just allegation
that Milton must have used the services of an amanuensis; and the plausible one that this amanuensis,
being often weary of his task, would be likely to neglect punctilious accuracy; and the most improbable
allegation that this weary person would also be very
conceited, and add much rubbish of his own; Bentley
resigned himself luxuriously, without the whisper of a
scruple, to his own sense of what was or was not

poetic, which sense happened to be that of the adder for music. The deaf adder heareth not though the musician charm ever so wisely. No scholarship, which so far beyond other men Bentley had, could gain him the imaginative sensibility which, in a degree so far beyond average men, he wanted. Consequently the world never before beheld such a scene of massacre as his ' Paradise Lost' exhibited. He laid himself down to his work of extermination like the brawniest of reapers going in steadily with his sickle, coat stripped off, and shirt sleeves tucked up, to deal with an acre of barley. One duty, and no other, rested upon *his* conscience; one voice he heard — Slash away, and hew down the rotten growths of this abominable amanuensis. The carnage was like that after a pitched battle. The very finest passages in every book of the poem were marked by italics, as dedicated to fire and slaughter. 'Slashing Dick' went through the whole forest, like a woodman marking with white paint the giant trees that must all come down in a month or so. And one naturally reverts to a passage in the poem itself, where God the Father is supposed to say to his Filial assessor on the heavenly throne, when marking the desolating progress of Sin and Death, —

> ' See with what havoc these fell dogs advance
> To ravage this fair world.'

But still this inhuman extravagance of Bentley, in following out his hypothesis, does not exonerate *us* from bearing in mind so much truth as that hypothesis really must have had, from the pitiable difficulties of the great poet's situation.

18

My own opinion, therefore, upon the line, for instance, from 'Paradise Regained,' which Mr. Landor
appears to have indicated for the reader's amazement, viz. : —

> ' As well might recommend
> *Such solitude before choicest society,*'

is — that it escaped revision from some accident calling off the ear of Milton whilst in the act of having the
proof read ꞏto him.   Mr. Landor silently prints it in
italics, without assigning his objection ; but, of course,
that objection must be — that the line has one foot too
much.   It is an Alexandrine, such as Dryden scattered so profusely, without asking himself why ; but
which Milton never tolerates except in the choruses
of the Samson.

> ' *Not difficult, if thou hearken to me* ' —

is one of the lines which Mr. Landor thinks that ' no
authority will reconcile' to our ears.   I think otherwise.   The cæsura is meant to fall not with the comma
after *difficult*, but after *thou ;* and there is a most
effective and grand suspension intended.   It is Satan
who speaks — Satan in the wilderness ; and he marks,
as he wishes to mark, the tremendous opposition of
attitude between the two parties to the temptation.ꞏ

> ' Not difficult if *thou* —— '

there let the reader pause, as if pulling up suddenly
four horses in harness, and throwing them on their
haunches — not difficult if thou (in some mysterious
sense the son of God) ; and then, as with a burst of
thunder, again giving the reins to your *quadriga*,

> ' —— hearken to me ꞏ '

that is, to me, that am the Prince of the Air, and able
to perform all my promises for those that hearken to
my temptations.

Two lines are cited under the same ban of irrecon-
cilability to our ears, but on a very different plea.
The first of these lines is —

> ‘ *Launcelot, or Pellias, or Pellinore;* ’

The other

> ‘ *Quintius, Fabricius, Curius, Regulus.*’

The reader will readily suppose that both are objected
to as ‘ roll-calls of proper names.’   Now, it is very
true that nothing is more offensive to the mind than
the practice of mechanically packing into metrical
successions, as if packing a portmanteau, names without meaning or significance to the feelings.   No man
ever carried that atrocity so far as Boileau, a fact of
which Mr. Landor is well aware; and slight is the
sanction or excuse that can be drawn from *him*.   But
it must not be forgotten that Virgil, so scrupulous in
finish of composition, committed this fault.   I remember a passage ending

> ‘——— Noëmonaque Prytaninque ; ’

but, having no Virgil within reach, I cannot at this
moment quote it accurately.   Homer, with more excuse, however, from the rudeness of his age, is a
deadly offender in this way.   But the cases from Milton are very different.   Milton was incapable of the
Homeric or Virgilian blemish.   The objection to such
rolling musketry of names is, that unless interspersed
with epithets, or broken into irregular groups by brief
circumstances of parentage, country, or romantic inci-

dent, they stand audaciously perking up their heads
like lots in a catalogue, arrow-headed palisades, or
young larches in a nursery ground, all occupying the
same space, all drawn up in line, all mere iterations
of each other.   But in

> ' *Quintius, Fabricius, Curius, Regulus,*'

though certainly not a good line *when insulated,*
(better, however, in its connection with the entire succession of which it forms part), the apology is, that the
massy weight of the separate characters enables them
to stand like granite pillars or pyramids, proud of their
self-supporting independency.

Mr. Landor makes one correction by a simple improvement in the punctuation, which has a very fine
effect.   Rarely has so large a result been distributed
through a sentence by so slight a change.   It is in the
' Samson.'   Samson says, speaking of himself (as
elsewhere) with that profound pathos, which to all
hearts invests Milton's own situation in the days of his
old age, when he was composing that drama —

> ' Ask for this great deliverer now, and find him
> *Eyeless in Gaza at the mill with slaves.*'

Thus it is usually printed ; that is, without a comma in
the latter 'ine ; but, says Landor, ' there ought to be
commas after *eyeless,* after *Gaza,* after *mill.*'   And
why ?  because thus ' the grief of Samson is aggravated
at every member of the sentence.'   He (like Milton)
was — 1. blind ; 2. in a city of triumphant enemies ;
3. working for daily bread ; 4. herding with slaves ;
Samson literally, and Milton with those whom politi-
cally he regarded as such.

Mr. Landor is perfectly wrong, I must take the

liberty of saying, when he demurs to the line in
' Paradise Regained : '

> ' *From that placid aspéct and meek regard,*'

on the ground that ' *meek regard* conveys no new idea
to *placid aspéct.*' But *aspéct* is the countenance of
Christ when passive to the gaze of others : *regard* is
the same countenance in active contemplation of those
others whom he loves or pities. The *placid aspéct*
expresses, therefore, the divine rest; the *meek regard*
expresses the divine benignity : the one is the self-
absorption of the total Godhead, the other the eternal
emanation of the Filial Godhead.

' By what ingenuity,' says Landor, ' can we erect
into a verse —

> " *In the bosom of bliss, and light of light ?* " '

Now really it is by my watch exactly three minutes
too late for *him* to make that objection. The court
cannot receive it now ; for the line just this moment
cited, the ink being hardly yet dry, is of the same
identical structure. The usual iambic flow is disturbed
in both lines by the very same ripple, viz., a trochee
in the second foot, *placid* in the one line, *bosom* in the
other. They are a sort of *snags*, such as lie in the
current of the Mississippi. *There* they do nothing but
mischief. Here, when the lines are read in their
entire *nexus*, the disturbance stretches forwards and
backwards with good effect on the music. Besides, if
it did *not*, one is willing to take a *snag* from Milton,
but one does not altogether like being *snagged* by the
Mississippi. One sees no particular reason for bearing
it, if one only knew how to be revenged on a river.

But, of these metrical skirmishes, though full of

importance to the impassioned text of a great poet
(for mysterious is the life that connects all modes
of passion with rhythmus), let us suppose the casual
reader to have had enough.   And now at closing for
the sake of change, let us treat him to a harlequin
trick upon another theme.   Did the reader ever happen
to see a sheriff's officer arresting an honest gentleman, who was doing no manner of harm to gentle or
simple, and immediately afterwards a second sheriff's
officer   arresting   the   first — by   which   means   that
second officer merits for himself a place in history;
for at the same moment he liberates a deserving
creature (since an arrested officer cannot possibly bag
his prisoner), and he also avenges the insult put upon
that worthy man?   Perhaps the reader did *not* ever
see such a sight; and, growing personal, he asks *me*,
in return, if *I* ever saw it.   To say the truth, I never
*did;* except once, in a too-flattering dream; and
though I applauded so loudly as even to waken myself,
and shouted ' *encore*,' yet all went for nothing; and I
am still waiting for that splendid exemplification of
retributive justice.   But why?   Why should it be a
spectacle so uncommon?   For surely those official
arresters of men must want arresting at times as well
as better people.   At least, however, *en attendant* one
may luxuriate in the vision of such a thing; and the
reader shall now see such a vision rehearsed.   He
shall see Mr. Landor arresting Milton — Milton, of all
men! — for a flaw in his Roman erudition; and then
he shall see me instantly stepping up, tapping Mr.
Landor on the shoulder, and saying, ' Officer, you're
wanted;' whilst to Milton I say, touching my hat,
'"Now, sir, be off; run for your life, whilst I hold

this man in custody, lest he should fasten on you again.'

What Milton had said, speaking of the '*watchful cherubim*,' was —

> ' Four faces each
> Had, *like a double Janus;* '

Upon which Southey — but, of course, Landor, ventriloquizing through Southey — says, 'Better left this to the imagination: double Januses are queer figures.' Not at all. On the contrary, they became so common, that finally there were no other. Rome, in her days of childhood, contented herself with a two-faced Janus; but, about the time of the first or second Cæsar, a very ancient statue of Janus was exhumed, which had four faces. Ever afterwards, this sacred resurgent statue became the model for any possible Janus that could show himself in good company. The *quadrifrons Janus* was now the orthodox Janus; and it would have been as much a sacrilege to rob him of any single face as to rob a king's statue * of its horse. One thing may recall this to Mr. Landor's memory. I think it was Nero, but certainly it was one of the first six Cæsars, that built, or that finished, a magnificent temple to Janus; and each face was so managed as to point down an avenue leading to a separate market-place. Now, that there were *four* market-places, I

---

* *A king's statue :* — Till very lately the etiquette of Europe was, that none but royal persons could have equestrian statues. Lord Hopetoun, the reader will object, is allowed to have a horse, in St. Andrew's Square, Edinburgh. True, but observe that he is not allowed to mount him. The first person, so far as I remember, that, not being royal, has, in our island, seated himself comfortably in the saddle, is the Duke of Wellington.

will make oath before any Justice of the Peace.   One was called the *Forum Julium*, one the *Forum Augustum*, a third the *Forum Transitorium*: what the fourth was called is best known to itself, for really I forget.   But if anybody says that perhaps it was called the *Forum Landorium*, I am not the man to object; for few names have deserved such an honor more, whether from those that then looked forward into futurity with one face, or from our posterity that will look back into the vanishing past with another.

I AM myself, and always have been, a member of the Church of England, and am grieved to hear the many attacks against the Church [frequently most illiberal attacks], which not so much religion as political rancor gives birth to in every third journal that I take up. This I say to acquit myself of all dishonorable feelings, such as I would abhor to co-operate with, in bringing a very heavy charge against that great body in its literary capacity. Whosoever has reflected on the history of the English constitution — must be aware that the most important stage of its development lies within the reign of Charles I. It is true that the judicial execution of that prince has been allowed by many persons to vitiate all that was done by the heroic parliament of November, 1640: and the ordinary histories of England assume as a matter of course that the whole period of parliamentary history through those times is to be regarded as a period of confusion. Our constitution, say they, was formed in 1688 – 9. Meantime it is evident to any reflecting man that the revolution simply re-affirmed the principles developed in the strife between the two great parties which had arisen in the reign of James I., and had ripened and

19                               [217]

come to issue with each other in the reign of his son.
Our constitution was not a birth of a single instant, as
they would represent it, but a gradual growth and
development through a long tract of time. In particular the doctrine of the king's vicarious responsibility in the person of his ministers, which first gave
a sane and salutary meaning to the doctrine of the
king's personal irresponsibility ['The king can do no
wrong'], arose undeniably between 1640 and 1648.
This doctrine is the main pillar of our constitution, and
perhaps the finest discovery that was ever made in the
theory of government. Hitherto the doctrine *that the
King can do no wrong* had been used not to protect
the indispensable sanctity of the king's constitutional
character, but to protect the wrong. Used in this way,
it was a maxim of Oriental despotism, and fit only for
a nation where law had no empire. Many of the
illustrious patriots of the Great Parliament saw this;
and felt the necessity of abolishing a maxim so fatal to
the just liberties of the people. But some of them fell
into the opposite error of supposing that this abolition
could be effected only by the direct negation of it;
*their* maxim accordingly was — 'The king *can* do
wrong,' *i. e.* is responsible in his own person. In this
great error even the illustrious wife of Colonel Hutchinson participated; [1] and accordingly she taxes those of
her own party who scrupled to accede to the new
maxim, and still adhered to the old one, with uncon-
scientious dealing. But she misapprehended their
meaning, and failed to see where they laid the emphasis: the emphasis was not laid, as it was by the
royal party, on the words 'can do no *wrong*' — but
on 'The king:' that is, wrong may be done; and in

the king's name; but it cannot be the king who did it [the king cannot constitutionally be supposed the person who did it]. By this exquisite political refinement, the old tyrannical maxim was disarmed of its sting; and the entire redress of all wrong, so indispensable to the popular liberty, was brought into perfect reconciliation with the entire inviolability of the sovereign, which is no less indispensable to the popular liberty. There is moreover a double wisdom in the new sense: for not only is one object [the redress of wrong] secured in conjunction with another object [the king's inviolability] hitherto held irreconcilable, — but even with a view to the first object alone a much more effectual means is applied, because one which leads to no schism in the state, than could have been applied by the blank negation of the maxim; *i. e.* by lodging the responsibility exactly where the executive power [*ergo* the power of resisting this responsibility] was lodged. Here then is one example in illustration of my thesis — that the English constitution was in a great measure gradually evolved in the contest between the different parties in the reign of Charles I. Now, if this be so, it follows that for constitutional history no period is so important as that: and indeed, though it is true that the Revolution is the great era for the constitutional historian, because he there first finds the constitution fully developed as the ' bright consummate *flower*,' and what is equally important he there first finds the principles of our constitution *ratified* by a competent authority, — yet, to trace the *root* and growth of the constitution, the three reigns immediately preceding are still more properly the objects of his study. In proportion then as the reign

of Charles I. is important to the history of our constitution, in that proportion are those to be taxed with
the most dangerous of all possible falsifications of our
history, who have misrepresented either the facts or
the principles of those times.    Now I affirm that the
clergy of the Church of England have been in a perpetual conspiracy since the era of the restoration to
misrepresent both.    As an illustration of what I mean
I refer to the common edition of Hudibras by Dr.
Grey: for the proof I might refer to some thousands
of books.    Dr. Grey's is a disgusting case: for he
swallowed with the most anile credulity every story,
the most extravagant that the malice of those times
could invent against either the Presbyterians or the
Independents: and for this I suppose amongst other
deformities his notes were deservedly ridiculed by
Warburton.    But, amongst hundreds of illustrations
more respectable than Dr. Grey's I will refer the
reader to a work of our own days, the Ecclesiastical
Biography [in part a republication of Walton's Lives]
edited by the present master of Trinity College, Cambridge, who is held in the highest esteem wherever he
is known, and is I am persuaded perfectly conscientious
and as impartial as in such a case it is possible for a
high churchman to be.    Yet so it is that there is
scarcely one of the notes having any political reference
to the period of 1640 – 1660, which is not disfigured
by unjust prejudices: and the amount of the moral
which the learned .editor grounds upon the documents
before him — is this, that the young student is to
cherish the deepest abhorrence and contempt of all
who had any share on the parliamentary side in the
' confusions ' of the period from 1640 to 1660: that is

to say of men to whose immortal exertions it was owing that the very revolution of 1688, which Dr. W. will be the first to applaud, found us with any such stock of political principles or feelings as could make a beneficial revolution possible. Where, let me ask, would have been the willingness of some Tories to construe the flight of James II. into a virtual act of abdication, or to consider even the most formal act of abdication binding against the king, — had not the great struggle of Charles's days gradually substituted in the minds of all parties a rational veneration of the king's *office* for the old superstition in behalf of the king's *person*, which would have protected him from the effects of any acts however solemnly performed which affected injuriously either his own interests or the liberties of his people. Tempora mutantur : *nos et mutamur in illis.* Those whom we find in fierce opposition to the popular party about 1640 we find still in the same personal opposition fifty years after, but an opposition resting on far different principles : insensibly the principles of their antagonists had reached even them : and a courtier of 1689 was willing to concede more than a patriot of 1630 would have ventured to ask. Let me not be understood to mean that true patriotism is at all more shown in supporting the rights of the people than those of the king : as soon as both are defined and limited, the last are as indispensable to the integrity of the constitution — as the first : and popular freedom itself would suffer as much, though indirectly, from an invasion of Cæsar's rights — as by a more direct attack on itself. But in the 17th century the rights of the people were as yet *not* defined : throughout that century they were gradually defining

themselves — and, as happiness to all great practical
interests, defining themselves through a course of
fierce and bloody contests.   For the kingly rights
are almost inevitably carried too high in ages of imperfect civilization : and the well-known laws of Henry
the Seventh, by which he either broke or gradually
sapped the power of the aristocracy, had still more
extravagantly exalted them.   On this account it is just
to look upon democratic or popular politics as identical
in the 17th century with patriotic politics.   In later
periods, the democrat and the patriot have sometimes
been in direct opposition to each other : at that period
they were inevitably in conjunction.   All this, however, is in general overlooked by those who either
write English history or comment upon it.   Most
writers *of* or *upon* English history proceed either upon
servile principles, or upon no principles : and a good
*Spirit of English History*, that is, a history which
should abstract the tendencies and main results [as
to laws, manners, and constitution] from every age
of English history, is a work which I hardly hope
to see executed.   For it would require the concurrence of some philosophy, with a great deal of
impartiality.   How idly do we say, in speaking of the
events of our own time which affect our party feelings, — ' We stand too near to these events for an
impartial estimate : we must leave them to the judgment of posterity ! '   For it is a fact that of the many
books of memoirs written by persons who were not
merely contemporary with the great civil war, but
actors and even leaders in its principal scenes — there
is hardly one which does not exhibit a more impartial
picture of that great drama than the histories written at

this day. The historian of Popery does not display half so much zealotry and passionate prejudice in speaking of the many events which have affected the power and splendor of the Papal See for the last thirty years, and under his own eyes, as he does when speaking of a reformer who lived three centuries ago — of a translator of the Bible into a vernacular tongue who lived nearly five centuries ago — of an Anti-pope — of a Charlemagne or a Gregory the Great still further removed from himself. The recent events he looks upon as accidental and unessential: but in the great enemies, or great founders of the Romish temporal power, and in the history of their actions and their motives, he feels that the whole principle of the Romish cause and its pretensions are at stake. Pretty much under the same feeling have modern writers written with a rancorous party spirit of the political struggles in the 17th century: here they fancy that they can detect the *incunabula* of the revolutionary spirit: here some have been so sharpsighted as to read the features of pure jacobinism: and others[2] have gone so far as to assert that all the atrocities of the French revolution had their direct parallelisms in acts done or countenanced by the virtuous and august Senate of England in 1640! Strange distortion of the understanding which can thus find a brotherly resemblance between two great historical events, which of all that ever were put on record stand off from each other in most irreconcilable enmity: the one originating, as Mr. Coleridge has observed, in excess of principle; the other in the utter defect of all moral principle whatever; and the progress of each being answerable to its origin! Yet so it is. And not a memoir-writer

of that age is reprinted in this, but we have a preface
from some red-hot Anti-jacobin warning us with much
vapid common-place from the mischiefs and eventual
anarchy of too rash a spirit of reform as displayed in
the French revolution — *not* by the example of that
French revolution, but by that of our own in the age
of Charles I. The following passage from the Introduction to Sir William Waller's Vindication published
in 1793, may serve as a fair instance : ' He ' (Sir W.
Waller) ' was, indeed, at length sensible of the misery
which he had contributed to bring on his country ; '
(by the way, it is a suspicious circumstance — that Sir
William [3] first became sensible that his country was
miserable, when he became sensible that he himself
was not likely to be again employed ; and became
fully convinced of it, when his party lost their as-
cendancy :) ' he was convinced, by fatal experience,
that anarchy was a bad step towards a perfect government ; that the subversion of every establishment was
no safe foundation for a permanent and regular constitution : he found that pretences of reform were held
up by the designing to dazzle the eyes of the unwary,
&c. ; he found in short that reformation, by popular
insurrection, must end in the destruction and cannot
tend to the formation of a regular Government.' After
a good deal more of this well-meaning cant, the Intro
duction concludes with the following sentence : — the
writer is addressing the reformers of 1793, amongst
whom — ' both leaders and followers,' he says, ' may
together reflect — that, upon speculative and visionary
reformers,' (*i. e.* those of 1640) ' the severest punishment which God in his vengeance ever yet inflicted —
was to curse them with the complete gratification of

their own inordinate desires.' I quote this passage —
not as containing any thing singular, but for the very
reason that it is *not* singular: it expresses in fact the
universal opinion: notwithstanding which I am happy
to say that it is false. What 'complete gratification
of their own desires' was ever granted to the 'reformers' in question? On the contrary, it is well
known (and no book illustrates that particular fact so
well as Sir William Waller's) that as early as 1647
the army had too effectually subverted the just relations between itself and parliament — not to have
suggested fearful anticipations to all discerning patriots
of that unhappy issue which did in reality blight their
prospects. And, when I speak of an 'unhappy issue,'
I would be understood only of the immediate issue:
for the remote issue was — the revolution of 1688, as
I have already asserted. Neither is it true that even
the immediate issue was 'unhappy' to any extent
which can justify the ordinary language in which it is
described. Here again is a world of delusions. We
hear of 'anarchy,' of 'confusions,' of 'proscriptions,'
of 'bloody and ferocious tyranny.' All is romance;
there was no anarchy; no confusions; no proscriptions; no tyranny in the sense designed. The se-
questrations, forfeitures, and punishments of all sorts
which were inflicted by the conquering party on their
antagonists — went on by due course of law; and the
summary justice of courts martial was not resorted to
in England: except for the short term of the two
wars, and the brief intermediate campaign of 1648,
the country was in a very tranquil state. Nobody was
punished without an open trial; and all trials proceeded in the regular course, according to the ancient

forms, and in the regular courts of justice. And as to 'tyranny,' which is meant chiefly of the acts of Cromwell's government, it should be remembered that the Protectorate lasted not a quarter of the period in question (1640 – 1660); a fact which is constantly forgotten even by very eminent writers, who speak as though Cromwell had drawn his sword in January, 1649 — cut off the king's head — instantly mounted his throne — and continued to play the tyrant for the whole remaining period of his life (nearly ten years). Secondly, as to the *kind* of tyranny which Cromwell exercised, the misconception is ludicrous: continental writers have a notion, well justified by the language of English writers, that Cromwell was a ferocious savage who built his palace of human skulls and desolated his country. Meantime, he was simply a strong-minded — rough-built Englishman, with a character thoroughly English, and exceedingly good-natured. Gray valued himself upon his critical knowledge of English history: yet how thoughtlessly does he express the abstract of Cromwell's life in the line on the village Cromwell — 'Some Cromwell, guiltless of his country's blood!' How was Cromwell guilty of his country's blood? What blood did he cause to be shed? A great deal was shed no doubt in the wars (though less, by the way, than is imagined): but in those Cromwell was but a servant of the parliament: and no one will allege that he had any hand in causing a single war. After he attained the sovereign power, no more domestic wars arose: and as to a few persons who were executed for plots and conspiracies against his person, they were condemned upon evidence openly given and by due course of law. With respect to the general character of his government, it is evident that in the unsettled and revolutionary state of things which follows a civil war some critical cases will arise to demand an occasional ' vigor beyond the law ' — such' as the Roman government allowed of in the dictatorial power.   But in general, Cromwell's government was limited by law : and no reign in that century, prior to the revolution, furnishes fewer instances of attempts to tamper with the laws — to overrule them — to twist them to private interpretations — or to dispense with them.   As to his major-generals of counties, who figure in most histories of England as so many *Ali Pachas* that impaled a few prisoners every morning before breakfast — or rather as so many ogres that ate up good christian men, women and children alive, they were disagreeable people who were disliked much in the same way as our commissioners of the income-tax were disliked in the memory of us all ; and heartily they would have laughed at the romantic and bloody masquerade in which they are made to figure in the English histories.   What then was the ' tyranny ' of Cromwell's government, which is confessedly complained of even in those days ?   The word ' tyranny ' was then applied not so much to the mode in which his power was administered (except by the prejudiced) — as to its origin.   However mercifully a man may reign, — yet, if he have no right to reign at all, we may in one sense call him a tyrant; his power not being justly derived, and resting upon an unlawful (*i. e.* a military) basis.   As a usurper, and one who had diverted the current of a grand national movement to selfish and personal objects, Cromwell was and will be called a tyrant; but not in the more obvious sense of the word. Such are the misleading statements which disfigure the History of England in its most important chapter. They mislead by more than a simple error of fact: those, which I have noticed last, involve a moral anachronism; for they convey images of cruelty and barbarism such as could not co-exist with the national civilization at that time; and whosoever has not corrected this false picture by an acquaintance with the English literature of that age, must necessarily image to himself a state of society as rude and uncultured as that which prevailed during the wars of York and Lancaster — *i. e.* about two centuries earlier. But those, with which I introduced this article, are still worse; because they involve an erroneous view of constitutional history, and a most comprehensive act of ingratitude: the great men of the Long Parliament paid a heavy price for their efforts to purchase for their descendants a barrier to irresponsible power and security from the anarchy of undefined regal prerogative: in these efforts most of them made shipwreck of their own tranquillity and peace; that such sacrifices were made unavailingly (as it must have seemed to themselves), and that few of them lived to see the 'good old cause' finally triumphant, does not cancel their claims upon our gratitude — but rather strengthen them by the degree in which it aggravated the difficulty of bearing such sacrifices with patience. But whence come these falsifications of history? I believe, from two causes; first (as I have already said) from the erroneous tone impressed upon the national history by the irritated spirit of the clergy of the established church: to the religious zealotry of those times — the church was the object of especial attack ·

and its members were naturally exposed to heavy sufferings : hence their successors are indisposed to find
any good in a cause which could lead to such a result.
It is their manifest right to sympathize with their own
order in that day ; and in such a case it is almost tneir
duty to be incapable of an entire impartiality. Meantime they have carried this much too far : the literature
of England must always be in a considerable proportion lodged in their hands ; and the extensive
means thus placed at their disposal for injuriously
coloring that important part of history they have used
with no modesty or forbearance. There is not a page
of the national history even in its local subdivisions
which they have not stained with the atrabilious hue
of their wounded remembrances : hardly a town in
England, which stood a siege for the king or the parliament, but has some printed memorial of its constancy and its sufferings ; and in nine cases out of ten
the editor is a clergyman of the established church,
who has contrived to deepen ' the sorrow of the time '
by the harshness of his commentary. Surely it is
high time that the wounds of the 17th century should
close ; that history should take a more commanding
and philosophic station ; and that brotherly charity
should now lead us to a saner view of constitutional
politics ; or a saner view of politics to a more comprehensive charity. The other cause of this falsification
springs out of a selfishness which has less claim to
any indulgence — viz. the timidity with which the
English Whigs of former days and the party to whom
they [4] succeeded, constantly shrank from acknowledging any alliance with the great men of the Long Parliament under the nervous horror of being confounded

with the regicides of 1649. It was of such urgent importance to them, for any command over the public support, that they should acquit themselves of any sentiment of lurking toleration for regicide, with which their enemies never failed to load them, that no mode of abjuring it seemed sufficiently emphatic to them : hence it was that Addison, with a view to the interest of his party, thought fit when in Switzerland, to offer a puny insult to the memory of General Ludlow : hence it is that even in our own days, no writers have insulted Milton with so much bitterness and shameless irreverence as the Whigs ; though it is true that some few Whigs, more however in their literary than in their political character, have stepped forward in his vindication. At this moment I recollect a passage in the writings of a modern Whig bishop — in which, for the sake of creating a charge of falsehood against Milton, the author has grossly mis-translated a passage in the *Defensio pro Pop. Anglicano :* and, if that bishop were not dead, I would here take the liberty of rapping his knuckles — were it only for breaking Priscian's head. To return over to the clerical feud against the Long Parliament, — it was a passage in a very pleasing work of this day (*Ecclesiastical Bi-ography*) which suggested to me the whole of what I have now written. Its learned editor, who is incapable of uncandid feelings except in what concerns the in-terests of his order, has adopted the usual tone in regard to the men of 1640 throughout his otherwise valuable annotations : and somewhere or other (in the Life of Hammond, according to my remembrance) he has made a statement to this effect — That the custom prevalent among children in that age of asking their parents' blessing was probably first brought into disuse by the Puritans. Is it possible to imagine a perversity of prejudice more unreasonable? The unamiable side of the patriotic character in the seventeenth century was unquestionably its religious bigotry; which, however, had its ground in a real fervor of religious feeling and a real strength of religious principle somewhat exceeding the ordinary standard of the 19th century. But, however palliated, their bigotry is not to be denied; it was often offensive from its excess; and ludicrous in its direction. Many harmless customs, many ceremonies and rituals that had a high positive value, their frantic intolerance quarrelled with: and for my part I heartily join in the sentiment of Charles II. — applying it as he did, but a good deal more extensively, that their religion ' was not a religion for a gentleman ' indeed all sectarianism, but especially that which has a modern origin — arising and growing up within our own memories, unsupported by a grand traditional history of persecutions — conflicts — and martyrdoms, lurking moreover in blind alleys, holes, corners, and tabernacles, must appear spurious and mean in the eyes of him who has been bred up in the grand classic forms of the Church of England or the Church of Rome. But, because the bigotry of the Puritans was excessive and revolting, is *that* a reason for fastening upon them all the stray evils of omission or commission for which no distinct fathers can be found? The learned editor does not pretend that there is any positive evidence, or presumption even, for imputing to the Puritans a dislike to the custom in question: but, because he thinks it a good custom, his inference is that nobody could have abolished it but the Puritans. Now who does not see that, if this had been amongst the usages discountenanced by the Puritans, it would on that account have been the more pertinaciously maintained by their enemies in church and state? Or, even if this usage were of a nature to be prohibited by authority, as the public use of the liturgy — organs — surplices, &c., who does not see that with regard to *that* as well as to other Puritanical innovations there would have been a reflux of zeal at the restoration of the king which would have established them in more strength than ever? But it is evident to the unprejudiced that the usage in question gradually went out in submission to the altered spirit of the times. It was one feature of a general system of manners, fitted by its piety and simplicity for a pious and simple age, and which therefore even the 17th century had already outgrown. It is not to be inferred that filial affection and reverence have decayed amongst us, because they no longer express themselves in the same way. In an age of imperfect culture, all passions and emotions are in a more elementary state — 'speak a plainer language' — and express themselves *externally:* in such an age the frame and constitution of society is more picturesque; the modes of life rest more undisguisedly upon the basis of the absolute and original relation of things: the son is considered in his sonship, the father in his fatherhood: and the manners take an appropriate coloring. Up to the middle of the 17th century there were many families in which the children never presumed to sit down in their parents' presence. But with us, in an age of more complete intellectual culture, a thick disguise is spread over the naked foundations of human life; and the instincts of good taste banish from good company the expression of all the profounder emotions. A son therefore, who should kneel down in this age to ask his papa's blessing on leaving town for Brighton or Bath — would be felt by himself to be making a theatrical display of filial duty, such as would be painful to him in proportion as his feelings were sincere. All this would have been evident to the learned editor in any case but one which regarded the Puritans: they were at any rate to be molested: in default of any graver matter, a mere fanciful grievance is searched out. Still, however, nothing was effected; fanciful or real, the grievance must be connected with the Puritans: here lies the offence, there lies the Puritans: it would be very agreeable to find some means of connecting the one with the other: but how shall this be done? Why, in default of all other means, the learned editor *assumes* the connection. He leaves the reader with an impression that the Puritans are chargeable with a serious wound to the manners of the nation in a point affecting the most awful of the household charities: and he fails to perceive that for this whole charge his sole ground is — that it would be very agreeable to him if he had a ground. Such is the power of the *esprit de corps* to palliate and recommend as colorable the very weakest logic to a man of acknowledged learning and talent! — In conclusion I must again disclaim any want of veneration and entire affection for the Established Church: the very prejudices and injustice, with which I tax the English clergy, have a generous origin: but it is right to point the attention of historical students to their strength and the effect which they have had.

20

They have been indulged to excess; they have disfigured the grandest page in English history; they
have hid the true descent and tradition of our constitutional history; and, by impressing upon the literature
of the country a false conception of the patriotic party
in and out of Parliament, they have stood in the way
of a great work,—a work which, according to my
ideal of it, would be the most useful that could just
now be dedicated to the English public — viz. *a philosophic record of the revolutions of English History.*
The English Constitution, as proclaimed and ratified
in 1688 – 9, is in its kind, the noblest work of the
human mind working in conjunction with Time, and
what in such a case we may allowably call Providence. Of this *chef d'œuvre* of human wisdom it were
desirable that we should have a proportionable history: for such a history the great positive qualification
would be a philosophic mind: the great negative
qualification would be this [which to the established
clergy may now be recommended as a fit subject for
their magnanimity] ; viz. complete conquest over those
prejudices which have hitherto discolored the greatest
era of patriotic virtue by contemplating the great men
of that era under their least happy aspect — namely, in
relation to the Established Church.

Now that I am on the subject of English History, I
will notice one of the thousand mis-statements of
Hume's which becomes a memorable one from the
stress which he has laid upon it, and from the manner
and situation in which he has introduced it. Standing
in the current of a narrative, it would have merited a
silent correction in an unpretending note : but it occupies a much more assuming station; for it is intro-

duced in a philosophical essay; and being relied on for a particular purpose with the most unqualified confidence, and being alleged in opposition to the very highest authority [viz. the authority of an eminent person contemporary with the fact] it must be looked on as involving a peremptory defiance to all succeeding critics who might hesitate between the authority of Mr. Hume at the distance of a century from the facts and Sir William Temple speaking to them as a matter within his personal recollections. Sir William Temple had represented himself as urging in a conversation with Charles II., the hopelessness of any attempt on the part of an English king to make himself a despotic and absolute monarch, except indeed through the affections of his people.[5] This general thesis he had supported by a variety of arguments, and, amongst the rest, he had described himself as urging this — that even Cromwell had been unable to establish himself in unlimited power, though supported by a military force of *eighty thousand men.* Upon this Hume calls the reader's attention to the extreme improbability which there must beforehand appear to be in supposing that Sir W. Temple, — speaking of so recent a case, with so much official knowledge of that case at his command, uncontradicted moreover by the king whose side in the argument gave him an interest in contradicting Sir William's statement, and whose means of information were paramount to those of all others, — could under these circumstances be mistaken. Doubtless, the reader will reply to Mr. Hume, the improbability *is* extreme, and scarcely to be invalidated by any possible authority — which, at best, must terminate in leaving an equilibrium of opposing evidence. And yet, says Mr. Hume, Sir William was unquestionably wrong, and grossly wrong: Cromwel' never had an army at all approaching to the number of eighty thousand. Now here is a sufficient proof that Hume had never read Lord Clarendon's account of his own life: this book is not so common as his 'History of the Rebellion;' and Hume had either not met with it, or had neglected it. For, in the early part of this work, Lord Clarendon, speaking of the army which was assembled on Blackheath to welcome the return of Charles II., says that it amounted to fifty thousand men: and, when it is remembered that this army was exclusive of the troops in garrison — of the forces left by Monk in the North — and above all of the entire army in Ireland, — it cannot be doubted that the whole would amount to the number stated by Sir William Temple. Indeed Charles II. himself, in the year 1678 [*i. e.* about four years after this conversation] as Sir W. Temple elsewhere tells us, 'in six weeks' time raised an army of twenty thousand men, the completest — and in all appearance the bravest troops that could be any where seen, and might have raised many more; and it was confessed by all the Foreign Ministers that no king in Christendom could have made and completed such a levy as this appeared in such a time.' William III. again, about eleven years afterwards, raised twenty-three regiments with the same ease and in the same space of six weeks. It may be objected indeed to such cases, as in fact it *was* objected to the case of William III. by Howlett in his sensible Examination of Dr. Price's Essay on the Population of England, that, in an age when manufactures were so little extended, it could

never have been difficult to make such a levy of men —
provided there were funds for paying and equipping
them. But, considering the extraordinary funds which
were disposable for this purpose in Ireland, &c. during
the period of Cromwell's Protectorate, we may very
safely allow the combined authority of Sir William
Temple — of the king — and of that very prime
minister who disbanded Cromwell's army, to outweigh
the single authority of Hume at the distance of a century from the facts. Upon any question of fact, indeed,
Hume's authority 's none at all.

# NOTES.

———

THIS is remarked by her editor and descendant Julius Hutchinson, who adds some words to this effect — 'that *if* the patriots of that day were the inventors of the maxim [*The king can do no wrong*], we are much indebted to them.' The patriots certainly did not invent the maxim, for they found it already current: but they gave it its new and constitutional sense. I refer to the book, however, as I do to almost all books in these notes, from memory; writing most of them in situations where I have no access to books. By the way, Charles I., who used the maxim in the most odious sense, furnished the most colorable excuse for his own execution. He constantly maintained the irresponsibility of his ministers: but, if that were conceded, it would then follow that the king must be made responsible in his own person: — and that construction led of necessity to his trial and death.

## NOTE 2. Page 223.

Amongst these Mr. D'Israeli in one of the latter volumes of his 'Curiosities of Literature' has dedicated a chapter or so to a formal proof of this proposition. A reader who is familiar with the history of that age comes to the chapter with a previous indignation, knowing what sort of proof he has to expect. This indignation is not likely to be mitigated by what he will there find Because some one madman, fool, or scoundrel makes a monstrous proposal — which dies of itself unsupported, and is in violent contrast to all the acts and the temper of those times, —

[238]

this is to sully the character of the parliament and three-fourths of the people of England. If this proposal had grown out of the spirit of the age, that spirit would have produced many more proposals of the same character and acts corresponding to them. Yet upon this one infamous proposal, and two or three scandalous anecdotes from the libels of the day, does the whole *onus* of Mr. D'Israeli's parallel depend. *Tantamne rem tam negligenter?* — In the general character of an Englishman I have a right to complain that so heavy an attack upon the honor of England and her most virtuous patriots in her most virtuous age should be made with so much levity: a charge so solemn in its matter should have been prosecuted with a proportionate solemnity of manner. Mr. D'Israeli refers with just applause to the opinions of Mr. Coleridge: I wish that he would have allowed a little more weight to the striking passage in which that gentleman contrasts the French revolution with the English revolution of 1640 – 8. However, the general tone of honor and upright principle, which marks Mr. D'Israeli's work, encourages me and others to hope that he will cancel the chapter — and not persist in wounding the honor of a great people for the sake of a paral·lelism, which — even if it were true — is a thousand times too slight and feebly supported to satisfy the most accommodating reader.

### Note 3.   Page 224.

Sir William and his cousin Sir Hardress Waller, were both remarkable men. Sir Hardress had no conscience at all ; Sir William a very scrupulous one ; which, however, he was for ever tampering with — and generally succeeded in reducing into compliance with his immediate interest. He was, however, an accomplished gentleman : and as a man of talents worthy of the highest admiration.

### Note 4.   Page 229.

Until after the year 1688, I do not remember ever to have found the term Whig applied except to the religious characteristics of that party : whatever reference it might have to their political distinctions was only secondary and by implication.

### Note 5.   Page 235.

Sir William had quoted to Charles a saying from Gourville (a Frenchman whom the king esteemed, and whom Sir William himself considered the only foreigner he had ever known that understood England) to this effect : 'That a king of England, who will be the man of his people, is the greatest king in the world ; but, if he will be something more, by G— he is nothing at all.'

# A PERIPATETIC PHILOSOPHER.

HE was a man of very extraordinary genius. He has generally been treated by those who have spoken of him in print as a madman. But this is a mistake and must have been founded chiefly on the titles of his books. He was a man of fervid mind and of sub lime aspirations: but he was no madman; or, if he was, then I say that it is so far desirable to be a mad-man. In 1798 or 1799, when I must have been about thirteen years old, Walking Stewart was in Bath — where my family at that time resided. He frequented the pump-room, and I believe all public places — walking up and down, and dispersing his philosophic opinions to the right and the left, like a Grecian philos-opher. The first time I saw him was at a concert in the Upper Rooms; he was pointed out to me by one of my party as a very eccentric man who had walked over the habitable globe. I remember that Madame Mara was at that moment singing: and Walking Stewart, who was a true lover of music (as I after-wards came to know), was hanging upon her notes like a bee upon a jessamine flower. His countenance was striking, and expressed the union of benignity with philosophic habits of thought. In such health had his pedestrian exercises preserved him, connected

21                                                     [241]

with his abstemious mode of living, that though he must at that time have been considerably above forty, he did not look older than twenty-eight; at least the face which remained upon my recollection for some years was that of a young man. Nearly ten years afterwards I became acquainted with him. During the interval I had picked up one of his works in Bristol, — viz. his *Travels to discover the Source of Moral Motion*, the second volume of which is entitled *The Apocalypse of Nature*. I had been greatly impressed by the sound and original views which in the first volume he had taken of the national characters throughout Europe. In particular he was the first, and so far as I know the only writer who had noticed the profound error of ascribing a phlegmatic character to the English nation. ' English phlegm ' is the constant expression of authors when contrasting the English with the French. Now the truth is, that, beyond that of all other nations, it has a substratum of profound passion: and, if we are to recur to the old doctrine of temperaments, the English character must be classed not under the *phlegmatic* but under the *melancholic* temperament; and the French under the *sanguine*. The character of a nation may be judged of in this particular by examining its idiomatic language. The French, in whom the lower forms of passion are constantly bubbling up from the shallow and superficial character of their feelings, have appropriated all the phrases of passion to the service of trivial and ordinary life: and hence they have no language of passion for the service of poetry or of occasions really demanding it: for it has been already enfeebled by continual association with cases of an unimpassioned

order.  But a character of deeper passion has a perpetual standard in itself, by which as by an instinct it
tries all cases, and rejects the language of passion as
disproportionate and ludicrous where it is not fully
justified.  'Ah Heavens!' or 'Oh my God!' are
exclamations with us so exclusively reserved for cases
of profound interest, — that on hearing a woman even
(*i. e.* a person of the sex most easily excited) utter
such words, we look round expecting to see her child
in some situation of danger.  But, in France, 'Ciel!'
and 'Oh mon Dieu!' are uttered by every woman if a
mouse does but run across the floor.  The ignorant
and the thoughtless, however, will continue to class the
English character under the phlegmatic temperament,
whilst the philosopher will perceive that it is the exact
polar antithesis to a phlegmatic character.  In this
conclusion, though otherwise expressed and illustrated,
Walking Stewart's view of the English character will
be found to terminate : and his opinion is especially
valuable — first and chiefly, because he was a philosopher; secondly, because his acquaintance with man
civilized and uncivilized, under all national distinctions,
was absolutely unrivalled.  Meantime, this and others
of his opinions were expressed in language that if
literally construed would often appear insane or absurd.
The truth is, his long intercourse with foreign nations
had given something of a hybrid tincture to his diction;
in some of his works, for instance, he uses the French
word *hélas !* uniformly for the English *alas !* and
apparently with no consciousness of his mistake.  He
had also this singularity about him — that he was
everlastingly metaphysicizing against metaphysics.  To
me, who was buried in metaphysical reveries from my

earliest days, this was not likely to be an attraction, any more than the vicious structure of his diction was likely to please my scholarlike taste. All grounds of disgust, however, gave way before my sense of his powerful merits; and, as I have said, I sought his acquaintance. Coming up to London from Oxford about 1807 or 1808 I made inquiries about him; and found that he usually read the papers at a coffee-room in Piccadilly: understanding that he was poor, it struck me that he might not wish to receive visits at his lodgings, and therefore I sought him át the coffee-room. Here I took the liberty of introducing myself to him. He received me courteously, and invited me to his rooms — which at that time were in Sherrard-street, Golden-square — a street already memorable to me. I was much struck with the eloquence of his conversation; and afterwards I found that Mr. Wordsworth, himself the most eloquent of men in conversation, had been equally struck when he had met him at Paris between the years 1790 and 1792, during the early storms of the French revolution. In Sherrard-street I visited him repeatedly, and took notes of the conversations I had with him on various subjects. These I must have somewhere or other; and I wish I could introduce them here, as they would interest the reader. Occasionally in these conversations, as in his books, he introduced a few notices of his private history: in particular I remember his telling me that in the East Indies he had been a prisoner of Hyder's; that he had escaped with some difficulty; and that, in the service of one of the native princes as secretary or interpreter, he had accumulated a small fortune. This must have been too small, I fear, at that time to allow him even a philosopher's comforts: for some part of it, invested in the French funds, had been confiscated. I was grieved to see a man of so much ability, of gentlemanly manners, and refined habits, and with the infirmity of deafness, suffering under such obvious privations; and I once took the liberty, on a fit occasion presenting itself, of requesting that he would allow me to send him some books which he had been casually regretting that he did not possess; for I was at that time in the hey-day of my worldly prosperity. This offer, however, he declined with firmness and dignity, though not unkindly. And I now mention it, because I have seen him charged in print with a selfish regard to his own pecuniary interest. On the contrary, he appeared to me a very liberal and generous man; and I well remember that, whilst he refused to accept of any thing from me, he compelled me to receive as presents all the books which he published during my acquaintance with him: two of these, corrected with his own hand, viz. the *Lyre of Apollo* and the *Sophiometer*, I have lately found amongst other books left in London; and others he forwarded to me in Westmoreland. In 1809 I saw him often: in the spring of that year, I happened to be in London; and Mr. Wordsworth's tract on the Convention of Cintra being at that time in the printer's hands, I superintended the publication of it; and, at Mr. Wordsworth's request, I added a long note on Spanish affairs which is printed in the Appendix. The opinions I expressed in this note on the Spanish character at that time much calumniated, on the retreat to Corunna then fresh in the public mind, above all, the contempt I expressed for the superstition in respect to the French military prowess which was then universal and at its height, and which gave way in fact only to the campaigns of 1814 and 1815, fell in, as it happened, with Mr. Stewart's political creed in those points where at that time it met with most opposition. In 1812 it was, I think, that I saw him for the last time : and by the way, on the day of my parting with him, I had an amusing proof in my own experience of that sort of ubiquity ascribed to him by a witty writer in the London Magazine : I met him and shook hands with him under Somerset-house, telling him that I should leave town that evening for Westmoreland. Thence I went by the very shortest road (*i. e.* through Moor-street, Soho — for I am learned in many quarters of London) towards a point which necessarily led me through Tottenham-court-road : I stopped nowhere, and walked fast : yet so it was that in Tottenham-court-road I was not overtaken by (*that* was compre-prehensible), but overtook, Walking Stewart. Certainly, as the above writer alleges, there must have been three Walking Stewarts in London. He seemed no ways surprised at this himself, but explained to me that somewhere or other in the neighborhood of Tot-tenham-court-road there was a little theatre, at which there was dancing and occasionally good singing, be-tween which and a neighboring coffee-house he some-times divided his evenings. Singing, it seems, he could hear in spite of his deafness. In this street I took my final leave of him; it turned out such; and, anticipating at the time that it would be so, I looked after his white hat at the moment it was disappearing and exclaimed — 'Farewell, thou half-crazy and most eloquent man! I shall never see thy face again.' I did not intend, at that moment, to visit London again for some years: as it happened, I was there for a short time in 1814: and then I heard, to my great satisfaction, that Walking Stewart had recovered a considerable sum (about £14,000 I believe) from the East India Company; and from the abstract given in the London Magazine of the Memoir by his relation, I have since learned that he applied this money most wisely to the purchase of an annuity, and that he 'persisted in living' too long for the peace of an annuity office. So fare all companies' East and West, and all annuity offices, that stand opposed in interest to philosophers! In 1814, however, to my great regret, I did not see him; for I was then taking a great deal of opium, and never could contrive to issue to the light of day soon enough for a morning call upon a philosopher of such early hours; and in the evening I concluded that he would be generally abroad, from what he had formerly communicated to me of his own habits. It seems, however, that he afterwards held *conversaziones* at his own rooms; and did not stir out to theatres quite so much. From a brother of mine, who at one time occupied rooms in the same house with him, I learned that in other respects he did not deviate in his prosperity from the philosophic tenor of his former life. He abated nothing of his peripatetic exercises; and repaired duly in the morning, as he had done in former years, to St. James's Park, — where he sate in contemplative ease amongst the cows, inhaling their balmy breath and pursuing his philosophic reveries. He had also purchased an organ, or more than one, with which he solaced his solitude and beguiled himself of uneasy thoughts if he ever had any.

The works of Walking Stewart must be read with
some indulgence; the titles are generally too lofty and
pretending and somewhat extravagant; the composition is lax and unprecise, as I have before said; and
the doctrines are occasionally very bold, incautiously
stated, and too hardy and high-toned for the nervous
effeminacy of many modern moralists. But Walking
Stewart was a man who thought nobly of human
nature: he wrote therefore at times in the spirit and
with the indignation of an ancient prophet against the
oppressors and destroyers of the time. In particular I
remember that in one or more of the pamphlets which
I received from him at Grasmere he expressed himself
in such terms on the subject of Tyrannicide (distinguishing the cases in which it was and was not
lawful) as seemed to Mr. Wordsworth and myself
every way worthy of a philosopher; but, from the
way in which that subject was treated in the House of
Commons, where it was at that time occasionally introduced, it was plain that his doctrine was not fitted
for the luxurious and relaxed morals of the age. Like
all men who think nobly of human nature, Walking
Stewart thought of it hopefully. In some respects his
hopes were wisely grounded; in others they rested too
much upon certain metaphysical speculations which
are untenable, and which satisfied himself only because his researches in that track had been purely
self-originated and self-disciplined. He relied upon
his own native strength of mind; but in questions,
which the wisdom and philosophy of every age building successively upon each other have not been able
to settle, no mind, however strong, is entitled to build
wholly upon itself. In many things he shocked the

religious sense — especially as it exists in unphilosophic minds; he held a sort of rude and unscientific Spinos-. ism; and he expressed it coarsely and in the way most likely to give offence. And indeed there can be no stronger proof of the utter obscurity in which his works have slumbered than that they should all have escaped prosecution. He also allowed himself to look too lightly and indulgently on the afflicting spectacle of female prostitution as it exists in London and in all great cities. This was the only point on which I was disposed to quarrel with him; for I could not but view it as a greater reproach to human nature than the slave-trade or any sight of wretchedness that the sun looks down upon. I often told him so; and that I was at a loss to guess how a philosopher could allow himself to view it simply as part of the equipage of civil life, and as reasonably making part of the establishment and furniture of a great city as police-offices, lamp-lighting, or newspapers. Waiving however this one instance of something like compliance with the brutal spirit of the world, on all other subjects he was eminently unworldly, child-like, simple-minded, and upright. He would flatter no man: even when addressing nations, it is almost laughable to see how invariably he prefaces his counsels with such plain truths uttered in a manner so offensive as must have defeated his purpose if it had otherwise any chance of being accomplished. For instance, in addressing America, he begins thus: — 'People of America! since your separation from the mother-country your moral character has degenerated in the energy of thought and sense; produced by the absence of your association and intercourse with British officers and

merchants: you have no moral discernment to distinguish between the protective power of England and
the destructive power of France.' And his letter to
the Irish nation opens in this agreeable and conciliatory
manner : — 'People of Ireland! I address you as a
true philosopher of nature, foreseeing the perpetual
misery your irreflective character and total absence
of moral discernment are preparing for' &c. The
second sentence begins thus — 'You are sacrilegiously
arresting the arm of your parent kingdom fighting the
cause of man and nature, when the triumph of the
fiend of French police-terror would be your own
instant extirpation —.' And the letter closes thus : —
'I see but one awful alternative — that Ireland will be
a perpetual moral volcano, threatening the destruction
of the world, if the education and instruction of thought
and sense shall not be able to generate the faculty of
moral discernment among a very numerous class of
the population, who detest the civic calm as sailors the
natural calm — and make civic rights on which they
cannot reason a pretext for feuds which they delight
in.' As he spoke freely and boldly to others, so he
spoke loftily of himself: at p. 313, of 'The Harp of
Apollo,' on making a comparison of himself with
Socrates (in which he naturally gives the preference
to himself) he styles 'The Harp,' &c. 'this unparalleled work of human energy.' At p. 315, he
calls it 'this stupendous work;' and lower down on
the same page he says — 'I was turned out of school
at the age of fifteen for a dunce or blockhead, because
I would not stuff into my memory all the nonsense of
erudition and learning; and if future ages should discover the unparalleled energies of genius in this work,

it will prove my most important doctrine —· that the powers of the human mind must be developed in the education of thought and sense in the study of moral opinion, not arts and science.' Again, at p. 225 of his Sophiometer, he says : — ' The paramount thought that dwells in my mind incessantly is a question I put to myself — whether, in the event of my personal dissolution by death, I have communicated all the discoveries my unique mind possesses in the great master-science of man and nature.' In the next page he determines that he *has*, with the exception of one truth, — viz. ' the latent energy, physical and moral, of human nature as existing in the British people.' But here he was surely accusing himself without ground : for to my knowledge he has not failed in any one of his numerous works to insist upon this theme at least a billion of times. Another instance of his magnificent self-estimation is — that in the title pages of several of his works he announces himself as ' John Stewart, the only man of nature * that ever appeared in the world.'

By this time I am afraid the reader begins to suspect that he was crazy: and certainly, when I consider every thing, he must have been crazy when the wind was at NNE ; for who but Walking Stewart ever dated his books by a computation drawn — not from the creation, not from the flood, not from Nabonassar, or *ab urbe conditâ*, not from the Hegira — but from

---

* In Bath he was surnamed ' the Child of Nature ; ' — which arose from his contrasting on every occasion the existing man of our present experience with the ideal or Stewartian man that might be expected to emerge in some myriads of ages ; to which latter man he gave the name of the Child of Nature.

themselves, from their own day of publication, as constituting the one great era in the history of man by the side of which all other eras were frivolous and impertinent ?    Thus, in a work of his given to me in 1812 and probably published in that year, I find him incidentally recording of himself that he was at that time 'arrived at the age of sixty-three, with a firm state of health acquired by temperance, and a peace of mind almost independent of the vices of mankind — because my knowledge of life has enabled me to place my happiness beyond the reach or contact of other men's follies and passions, by avoiding all family connections, and all ambitious pursuits of profit, fame, or power.'    On reading this passage I was anxious to ascertain its date; but this, on turning to the title page, I found thus mysteriously expressed: 'In the 7000th year of Astronomical History, and the first day of Intellectual Life or Moral World, from the era of this work.'    Another slight indication of craziness appeared in a notion which obstinately haunted his mind that all the kings and rulers of the earth would confederate in every age against his works, and would hunt them out for extermination as keenly as Herod did the innocents in Bethlehem.    On this consideration, fearing that they might be intercepted by the long arms of these wicked princes before they could reach that remote Stewartian man or his precursor to whom they were mainly addressed, he recommended to all those who might be impressed with a sense of their importance to bury a copy or copies of each work properly secured from damp, &c. at a depth of seven or eight feet below the surface of the earth; and on their death-beds to communicate the knowledge of this fact to some con-

fidential friends, who in their turn were to send down
the tradition to some discreet persons of the next
generation; and thus, if the truth was not to be dispersed for many ages, yet the knowledge that here
and there the truth lay buried on this and that continent, in secret spots on Mount Caucasus — in the
sands of Biledulgerid — and in hiding-places amongst
the forests of America, and was to rise again in some
distant age and to vegetate and fructify for the universal benefit of man, — this knowledge at least was to
be whispered down from generation to generation;
and, in defiance of a myriad of kings crusading against
him, Walking Stewart was to stretch out the influence
of his writings through a long series of λαμπαδοφοροι to
that child of nature whom he saw dimly through a
vista of many centuries. If this were madness, it
seemed to me a somewhat sublime madness: and I
assured him of my co-operation against the kings,
promising that I would bury ' The Harp of Apollo ' in
my own orchard in Grasmere at the foot of Mount
Fairfield; that I would bury ' The Apocalypse of
Nature ' in one of the coves of Helvellyn, and several
other works in several other places best known to
myself. He accepted my offer with gratitude; but
he then made known to me that he relied on my
assistance for a still more important service — which
was this: in the lapse of that vast number of ages
which would probably intervene between the present
period and the period at which his works would have
reached their destination, he feared that the English
language might itself have mouldered away. ' No ! '
I said, ' *that* was not probable: considering its extensive diffusion, and that it was now transplanted into all

the continents of our planet, I would back the English language against any other on earth.' His own persuasion however was, that the Latin was destined to survive all other languages; it was to be the eternal as well as the universal language; and his desire was that I would translate his works, or some part of them, into that language.* This I promised; and I seriously designed at some leisure hour to translate into Latin a selection of passages which should embody an abstract of his philosophy. This would have been doing a service to all those who might wish to see a digest of his peculiar opinions cleared from the perplexities of his peculiar diction and brought into a narrow compass from the great number of volumes through which they are at present dispersed. However, like many another plan of mine, it went unexecuted.

On the whole, if Walking Stewart were at all crazy, he was so in a way which did not affect his natural genius and eloquence — but rather exalted them. The

---

* I was not aware until the moment of writing this passage that Walking Stewart had publicly made this request three years after making it to myself: opening the 'Harp of Apollo,' I have just now accidentally stumbled on the following passage, 'This stupendous work is destined, I fear, to meet a worse fate than the Aloe, which as soon as it blossoms loses its stalk. This first blossom of reason is threatened with the loss of both its stalk and its soil: for, if the revolutionary tyrant should triumph, he would destroy all the English books and energies of thought. I conjure my readers to translate this work into Latin, and to bury it in the ground, communicating on their death-beds only its place of concealment to men of nature.'

From the title page of this work, by the way, I learn that 'the 7000th year of Astronomical History' is taken from the Chinese tables, and coincides (as I had supposed) with the year 1812 of our computation.

old maxim, indeed, that 'Great wits to madness sure are near allied,' the maxim of Dryden and the popular maxim, I have heard disputed by Mr. Coleridge and Mr. Wordsworth, who maintain that mad people are the dullest and most wearisome of all people. As a body, I believe they are so. But I must dissent from the authority of Messrs. Coleridge and Wordsworth so far as to distinguish. Where madness is connected, as it often is, with some miserable derangement of the stomach, liver, &c. and attacks the principle of pleasurable life, which is manifestly seated in the central organs of the body (*i. e.* in the stomach and the apparatus connected with it), there it cannot but lead to perpetual suffering and distraction of thought; and there the patient will be often tedious and incoherent. People who have not suffered from any great disturbance in those organs are little aware how indispensable to the process of thinking are the momentary influxes of pleasurable feeling from the regular goings on of life in its primary function; in fact, until the pleasure is withdrawn or obscured, most people are not aware that they *have* any pleasure from the due action of the great central machinery of the system: proceeding in uninterrupted continuance, the pleasure as much escapes the consciousness as the act of respiration: a child, in the happiest state of its existence, does not *know* that it is happy. And generally whatsoever is the level state of the hourly feeling is never put down by the unthinking (*i. e.* by 99 out of 100) to the account of happiness: it is never put down with the positive sign, as equal to $+ x$; but simply as $= 0$. And men first become aware that it *was* a positive quantity, when they have lost it (*i. e.*

fallen into — $x$). Meantime the genial pleasure from the vital processes, though not represented to the consciousness, is *immanent* in every act — impulse — motion — word — and thought: and a philosopher sees that the idiots are in a state of pleasure, though they cannot see it themselves. Now I say that, where this principle of pleasure is not attached, madness is often little more than an enthusiasm highly exalted; the animal spirits are exuberant and in excess; and the madman becomes, if he be otherwise a man of ability and information, all the better as a companion. I have met with several such madmen; and I appeal to my brilliant friend, Professor W——, who is not a man to tolerate dulness in any quarter, and is himself the ideal of a delightful companion, whether he ever met a more amusing person than that madman who took a post-chaise with us from —— to Carlisle, long years ago, when he and I were hastening with the speed of fugitive felons to catch the Edinburgh mail. His fancy and his extravagance, and his furious attacks on Sir Isaac Newton, like Plato's suppers, refreshed us not only for that day but whenever they recurred to us; and we were both grieved when we heard some time afterwards from a Cambridge man that he had met our clever friend in a stage coach under the care of a brutal keeper. —— Such a madness, if any, was the madness of Walking Stewart: his health was perfect; his spirits as light and ebullient as the spirits of a bird in spring-time; and his mind unagitated by painful thoughts, and at peace with itself. Hence, if he was not an amusing companion, it was because the philosophic direction of his thoughts made him something more. Of anecdotes and matters of fact he was not communicative : of all that he had seen in the vast compass of his travels he never availed himself in conversation.  I do not remember at this moment that he ever once alluded to his own travels in his inter-course with me except for the purpose of weighing down by a statement grounded on his own great personal experience an opposite statement of many hasty and misjudging travellers which he thought injurious to human nature : the statement was this, that in all his countless rencontres with uncivilized tribes, he had never met with any so ferocious and brutal as to attack an unarmed and defenceless man who was able to make them understand that he threw himself upon their hospitality and forbearance.

On the whole, Walking Stewart was a sublime visionary : he had seen and suffered much amongst men ; yet not too much, or so as to dull the genial tone of his sympathy with the sufferings of others.  His mind was a mirror of the sentient universe. — The whole mighty vision that had fleeted before his eyes in this world, — the armies of Hyder-Ali and his son with oriental and barbaric pageantry, — the civic grandeur of England, the great deserts of Asia and America, — the vast capitals of Europe, — London with its eternal agitations, the ceaseless ebb and flow of its ' mighty heart,' — Paris shaken by the fierce torments of revolutionary convulsions, the silence of Lapland, and the solitary forests of Canada, with the swarming life of the torrid zone, together with innumerable recollections of individual joy and sorrow, that he had participated by sympathy — lay like a map beneath him, as if eternally co-present to his view ; so that, in the contemplation of the prodigious whole, he had no leisure

22

to separate the parts, or occupy his mind with details.
Hence came the monotony which the frivolous and the
desultory would have found in his conversation. I,
however, who am perhaps the person best qualified to
speak of him, must pronounce him to have been a man
of great genius; and, with reference to his conversation,
of great eloquence. That these were not better known
and acknowledged was owing to two disadvantages;
one grounded in his imperfect education, the other in
the peculiar structure of his mind. The first was this:
like the late Mr. Shelley he had a fine vague enthusiasm
and lofty aspirations in connection with human nature
generally and its hopes; and like him he strove to
give steadiness, a uniform direction, and an intelligible
purpose to these feelings, by fitting to them a scheme
of philosophical opinions. But unfortunately the philosophic system of both was so far from supporting their
own views and the cravings of their own enthusiasm,
that, as in some points it was baseless, incoherent, or
unintelligible, so in others it tended to moral results,
from which, if they had foreseen them, they would
have been themselves the first to shrink as contra-
dictory to the very purposes in which their system had
originated. Hence, in maintaining their own system
they both found themselves painfully entangled at
times with tenets pernicious and degrading to human
nature. These were the inevitable consequences of
the πρωτον ψευδος in their speculations; but were naturally charged upon them by those who looked carelessly
into their books as opinions which not only for the
sake of consistency they thought themselves bound to
endure, but to which they gave the full weight of their
sanction and patronage as to so many moving princi-

ples in their system. The other disadvantage under which Walking Stewart labored, was this : he was a man of genius, but not a man of talents ; at least his genius was out of all proportion to his talents, and wanted an organ as it were for manifesting itself; so that his most original thoughts were delivered in a crude state — imperfect, obscure, half developed, and not producible to a popular audience. He was aware of this himself ; and, though he claims everywhere the faculty of profound intuition into human nature, yet with equal candor he accuses himself of asinine stupidity, dulness, and want of talent. He was a disproportioned intellect, and so far a monster : and he must be added to the long list of original-minded men who have been looked down upon with pity and contempt by commonplace men of talent, whose powers of mind — though a thousand times inferior — were yet more manageable, and ran in channels more suited to common uses and common understandings.

# ON SUICIDE.

It is a remarkable proof of the inaccuracy with which most men read — that Donne's *Biathanatos* has been supposed to countenance Suicide; and those who reverence his name have thought themselves obliged to apologize for it by urging, that it was written before he entered the church. But Donne's purpose in this treatise was a pious one: many authors had charged the martyrs of the Christian church with Suicide — on the principle that if I put myself in the way of a mad bull, knowing that he will kill me — I am as much chargeable with an act of self-destruction as if I fling myself into a river. Several casuists had extended this principle even to the case of Jesus Christ: one instance of which, in a modern author, the reader may see noticed and condemned by Kant, in his *Religion innerhalb die gronzen der blossen Vernunft;* and another of much earlier date (as far back as the 13th century, I think), in a commoner book — Voltaire's notes on the little treatise of Beccaria, *Dei delitti e delle pene.* These statements tended to one of two results: either they unsanctified the characters of those who founded and nursed the Christian church; or they sanctified suicide. By way of meeting them, Donne wrote his book: and as the whole argument of his

[260]

opponents turned upon a false definition of suicide (not explicitly stated, but assumed), he endeavored to reconstitute the notion of what is essential to create an act of suicide. Simply to kill a man is not murder: *primâ facie*, therefore, there is some sort of presumption that simply for a man to kill himself—may not always be so: there is such a thing as simple homicide distinct from murder: there may, therefore, possibly be such a thing as self-homicide distinct from self-murder. There *may* be a ground for such a distinction, *ex analogiâ*. But, secondly, on examination, *is* there any ground for such a distinction? Donne affirms that there is; and, reviewing several eminent cases of spontaneous martyrdom, he endeavors to show that acts so motived and so circumstantiated will not come within the notion of suicide properly defined. Meantime, may not this tend to the encouragement of suicide in general, and without discrimination of its species? No: Donne's arguments have no prospective reference or application; they are purely retrospective. The circumstances necessary to create an act of mere self-homicide can rarely concur, except in a state of disordered society, and during the *cardinal* revolutions of human history: where, however, they *do* concur, there it will not be suicide. In fact, this is the natural and practical judgment of us all. We do not all agree on the particular cases which will justify self-destruction: but we all feel and involuntarily acknowledge (*implicitly* acknowledge in our admiration, though not explicitly in our words or in our principles), that there *are* such cases. There is no man, who in his heart would not reverence a woman that chose to die rather than to be dishonored: and,

if we do not say, tnat it is her duty to do so, *that* is
because the moralist must condescend to the weakness
and infirmities of human nature : mean and ignoble
natures must not be taxed up to the level of noble
ones.   Again, with regard to the other sex, corporal
punishment is its peculiar and *sexual* degradation ;
and if ever the distinction of Donne can be applied
safely to any case, it will be to the case of him who
chooses to die rather than to submit to that ignominy.
*At present*, however, there is but a dim and very confined sense, even amongst enlightened men (as we
may see by the debates of Parliament), of the injury
which is done to human nature by giving legal sanction to such brutalizing acts ; and therefore most men,
in seeking to escape it, would be merely shrinking
from a *personal* dishonor.   Corporal punishment is
usually argued with a single reference to the case of
him who suffers it ; and *so* argued, God knows that it
is worthy of all abhorrence : but the weightiest argument against it — is the foul indignity which is offered
to our common nature lodged in the person of him on
whom it is inflicted.   *His* nature is *our* nature : and,
supposing it possible that *he* were so far degraded as
to be unsusceptible of any influences but those which
address him through the brutal part of his nature, yet
for the sake of ourselves — No ! not merely for ourselves, or for the human race now existing, but for the
sake of human nature, which trancends all existing
participators of that nature — we should remember
that the evil of corporal punishment is not to be
measured by the poor transitory criminal, whose
memory and offence are soon to perish : these, in
the sum of things, are as nothing : the injury which

can be done him, and the injury which ne can do, have so momentary an existence that they may be safely neglected : but the abiding injury is to the most august interest which for the mind of man can have any existence, — viz. to his own nature : to raise and dignify which, I am persuaded, is the first — last — and holiest command * which the conscience imposes on the philosophic moralist. In countries, where the traveller has the pain of seeing human creatures performing the labors of brutes, † — surely the sorrow which the spectacle moves, if a wise sorrow, will not be chiefly directed to the poor degraded individual — too deeply degraded, probably, to be sensible of his own degrada-

* On which account, I am the more struck by the ignoble argument of those statesmen who have contended in the House of Commons that such and such classes of men in this nation are not accessible to any loftier influences. Supposing that there were any truth in this assertion, which is a libel not on this nation only, but on man in general, — surely it is the duty of lawgivers not to perpetuate by their institutions the evil which they find, but to presume and gradually to create a better spirit.

† Of which degradation, let it never be forgotten that France but thirty years ago presented as shocking cases as any country, even where slavery is tolerated. An eye-witness to the fact, who has since published it in print, told me, that in France, before the revolution, he had repeatedly seen a woman yoked with an ass to the plough ; and the brutal ploughman applying his whip indifferently to either. English people, to whom I have occasionally mentioned this as an exponent of the hollow refinement of manners in France, have uniformly exclaimed — ' *That* is more than I can believe ; ' and have taken it for granted that I had my information from some prejudiced Englishman. But who was my informer ? A Frenchman, reader, — M. Simond : and though now by adoption an American citizen, yet still French in his heart and in all his prejudices.

tion, but to the reflection that man's nature is thus exhibited in a state of miserable abasement; and, what is worst of all, abasement proceeding from man himself. Now, whenever this view of corporal punishment becomes general (as inevitably it will, under the influence of advancing civilization), I say, that Donne's principle will then become applicable to this case, and it will be the duty of a man to die rather than to suffer his own nature to be dishonored in that way. But so long as a man is not fully sensible of the dishonor, to him the dishonor, except as a personal one, does not wholly exist. In general, whenever a paramount interest of human nature is at stake, a suicide which maintains that interest is self-homicide: but, for a personal interest, it becomes self-murder. And into this principle Donne's may be resolved.

A doubt has been raised — whether brute animals ever commit suicide: to me it is obvious that they do not, and cannot. Some years ago, however, there was a case reported in all the newspapers of an old ram who committed suicide (as it was alleged) in the presence of many witnesses. Not having any pistols or razors, he ran for a short distance, in order to aid the impetus of his descent, and leaped over a precipice, at the foot of which he was dashed to pieces. His motive to the 'rash act,' as the papers called it, was supposed to be mere *tædium vitæ*. But, for my part, I doubted the accuracy of the report. Not long after a case occurred in Westmoreland which strengthened my doubts. A fine young blood horse, who could have no possible reason for making away with himself, unless it were the high price of oats at that time, was found one morning dead in his field. The case was certainly a suspicious one: for he was lying by the side of a stone-wall, the upper part of which wall his skull had fractured, and which had returned the compliment by fracturing his skull. It was argued, therefore, that in default of ponds, &c. he had deliberately hammered with his head against the wall; this, at first, seemed the only solution; and he was generally pronounced *felo de se*. However, a day or two brought the truth to light. The field lay upon the side of a hill: and, from a mountain which rose above it, a shepherd had witnessed the whole catastrophe, and gave evidence which vindicated the character of the horse. The day had been very windy; and the young creature being in high spirits, and, caring evidently as little for the corn question as for the bullion question, had raced about in all directions; and at length, descending too steep a part of the field, had been unable to check himself, and was projected by the impetus of his own descent like a battering ram against the wall.

Of human suicides, the most affecting I have ever seen recorded is one which I met with in a German book: the most calm and deliberate is the following, which is *said* to have occurred at Keswick, in Cumberland: but I must acknowledge, that I never had an opportunity, whilst staying at Keswick, of verifying the statement. A young man of studious turn, who is said to have resided near Penrith, was anxious to qualify himself for entering the church, or for any other mode of life which might secure to him a reasonable portion of literary leisure. His family, however,

23

thought that under the circumstances of his situation
he would have a better chance for success in life as a
tradesman; and they took the necessary steps for
placing him as an apprentice at some shopkeeper's in
Penrith. This he looked upon as an indignity, to
which he was determined in no case to submit. And
accordingly, when he had ascertained that all opposition to the choice of his friends was useless, he
walked over to the mountainous district of Keswick
(about sixteen miles distant) — looked about him in
order to select his ground — cooly walked up Lattrig
(a dependency of Skiddaw) — made a pillow of sods
— laid himself down with his face looking up to the
sky — and in that posture was found dead, with the
appearance of having died tranquilly.

# SUPERFICIAL KNOWLEDGE.

It is asserted that this is the age of Superficial Knowledge; and amongst the proofs of this assertion we find Encyclopædias and other popular abstracts of knowledge particularly insisted on. But in this notion and its alleged proofs there is equal error — wherever there is much diffusion of knowledge, there must be a good deal of superficiality: prodigious *extension* implies a due proportion of weak *intension;* a sea-like expansion of knowledge will cover large shallows as well as large depths. But in that quarter in which it is superficially cultivated the intellect of this age is properly opposed in any just comparison to an intellect without any culture at all : — leaving the deep soils out of the comparison, the shallow ones of the present day would in any preceding one have been barren wastes. Of this our modern encyclopædias are the best proof. For whom are they designed, and by whom used ?— By those who in a former age would have gone to the fountain heads ? No, but by those who in any age preceding the present would have drunk at no waters at all. Encyclopædias are the growth of the las; hundred years; not because those who were formerly students of higher learning have descended, but because those who were below encyclopædias have

ascended.  The greatness of the ascent is marked by
the style in which the more recent encyclopædias are
executed : at first they were mere abstracts of existing
books — well or ill executed : at present they contain
many *original* articles of great merit.  As in the
periodical literature of the age, so in the encyclopædias
it has become a matter of ambition with the publishers
to retain the most eminent writers in each several department.  And hence it is that our encyclopædias
now display one characteristic of this age — the very
opposite of superficiality (and which on other grounds
we are well assured of) — viz. its tendency in science,
no less than in other applications of industry, to extreme subdivision.  In all the employments which are
dependent in any degree upon the political economy
of nations, this tendency is too obvious to have been
overlooked.  Accordingly it has long been noticed for
congratulation in manufactures and the useful arts —
and for censure in the learned professions.  We have
now, it is alleged, no great and comprehensive lawyers
like Coke: and the study of medicine is subdividing
itself into a distinct ministry (as it were) not merely
upon the several organs of the body (oculists, aurists,
dentists, cheiropodists, &c.) but almost upon the several
diseases of the same organ : one man is distinguished
for the treatment of liver complaints of one class —
a second for those of another class; one man for
asthma — another for phthisis ; and so on.  As to the
law, the evil (if it be one) lies in the complex state of
society which of necessity makes the laws complex :
law itself is become unwieldy and beyond the grasp
of one man's term of life and possible range of expe
rience : and will never again come within them.

With respect to medicine, the case is no evil but a great benefit — so long as the subdividing principle does not descend too low to allow of a perpetual re-ascent into the generalizing principle (the τὸ commune) which secures the unity of the science. In ancient times all the evil of such a subdivision was no doubt realized in Egypt: for there a distinct body of professors took charge of each organ of the body, not (as we may be assured) from any progress of the science outgrowing the time and attention of the general professor, but simply from an ignorance of the organic structure of the human body and the reciprocal action of the whole upon each part and the parts upon the whole; an ignorance of the same kind which has led sailors seriously (and not merely, as may sometimes have happened, by way of joke) to reserve one ulcerated leg to their own management, whilst the other was given up to the management of the surgeon. With respect to law and medicine then, the difference between ourselves and our ancestors is not subjective but objective; not, *i. e.* in our faculties who study them, but in the things themselves which are the objects of study: not we (the students) are grown less, but they (the studies) are grown bigger; — and that our anecstors did not subdivide as much as we do — was something of their luck, but no part of their merit. Simply as subdividers therefore to the extent which now prevails, we are less superficial than any former age. In all parts of science the same principle of subdivision holds: here therefore, no less than in those parts of knowledge which are the subjects of distinct civil professions, we are of necessity more profound than our ancestors; but, for the same reason, less comprehen-

sive than they. Is it better to be a profound student,
or a comprehensive one? In some degree this must
depend upon the direction of the studies: but generally,
I think, it is better for the interests of knowledge that
the scholar should aim at profundity, and better for the
interests of the individual that he should aim at com
prehensiveness. A due balance and equilibrium of the
mind is but preserved · by a large and multiform
knowledge : but knowledge itself is but served by an
exclusive (or at least paramount) dedication of one
mind to one science. The first proposition is perhaps
unconditionally true : but the second with some limitations. There are such people as Leibnitzes on this
earth ; and their office seems not that of planets — to
revolve within the limits of one system, but that of
comets (according to the theory of some speculators)
— to connect different systems together. No doubt
there is much truth in this : a few Leibnitzes in every
age would be of much use : but neither are many men
fitted by nature for the part of Leibnitz ; nor would
the aspect of knowledge be better, if they were. We
should then have a state of Grecian life amongst us in
which every man individually would attain in a moderate
degree all the purposes of the sane understanding, —
but in which all the purposes of the sane understanding would be but moderately attained. What I mean
is this : — et all the objects of the understanding in
civil life o. in science be represented by the letters of
the alphabet; in Grecian life each man would separately go through all the letters in a tolerable way ;
whereas at present each letter is served by a distinct
body of men. Consequently the Grecian individual is
superior to the modern; but the Grecian whole is

ınferior: for the whole is made up of the individuals; and the Grecian individual repeats himself. Whereas in modern life the whole derives its superiority from the very circumstances which constitute the inferiority of the parts; for modern life is *cast* dramatically: and the difference is as between an army consisting of soldiers who should each individually be competent to go through the duties of a dragoon — of a hussar — of a sharp-shooter — of an artillery-man — of a pioneer, &e. and an army on its present composition, where the very inferiority of the soldier as an individual — his inferiority in compass and versatility of power and knowledge — is the very ground from which the army derives its superiority as a whole, viz. because it is the condition of the possibility of a total surrender of the individual to one exclusive pursuit. In science therefore, and (to speak more generally) in the whole evolution of the human faculties, no less than in Political Economy, the progress of society brings with it a necessity of sacrificing the ideal of what is excellent for the individual, to the ideal of what is excellent for the whole. We need therefore not trouble ourselves (except as a speculative question) with the comparison of the two states; because, as a practical question, it is precluded by the overruling tendencies of the age — which no man could counteract except in his own single case, *i. e.* by refusing to adapt himself as a part to the whole, and thus foregoing the advantages of either one state or the other. *

* The latter part of what is here said coincides, in a way which is rather remarkable, with a passage in an interesting work of Schiller's which I have since read, (*on the Æsthetic Education of Men*, in a series of letters: vid. letter the 6th.) ' With us in

order to obtain the representative *word* (as it were) of the total species, we must spell it out by the help of a series of individuals. So that on a survey of society as it actually exists, one might suppose that the faculties of the mind do really in actual experience show themselves in as separate a form, and in as much insulation, as psychology is forced to exhibit them in its analysis. And thus we see not only individuals, but whole classes of men, unfolding only one part of the germs which are laid in them by the hand of nature. In saying this I am fully aware of the advantages which the human species of modern ages has, when considered as a unity, over the best of antiquity : but the comparison should begin with the individuals : and then let me ask where is the modern individual that would have the presumption to step forward against the Athenian individual — man to man, and to contend for the prize of human excellence? The polypus nature of the Grecian republics, in which every individual enjoyed a separate life, and if it were necessary could become a whole, has now given place to an artificial watch-work, where many lifeless parts combine to form a mechanic whole. The state and the church, laws and manners, are now torn asunder : labor is divided from enjoyment, the means from the end, the exertion from the reward. Chained for ever to a little individual fraction of the whole, man himself is moulded into a fraction ; and, with the monotonous whirling of the wheel which he turns everlastingly in his ear, he never develops the harmony of his being ; and, instead of imaging the totality of human nature, becomes a bare abstract of his business or the science which he cultivates. The dead letter takes the place of the living understanding ; and a practised memory becomes a surer guide than genius and sensibility. Doubtless the power of genius, as we all know, will not fetter itself within the limits of its occupation ; but talents of mediocrity are all exhausted in the monotony of the employment allotted to them ; and that man must have no common head who brings with him the geniality of his powers unstripped of their freshness by the ungenial labors of life to the cultivation of the genial.' After insisting at some length on this wise, Schiller passes to the other side of the contemplation, and proceeds thus : — 'It suited my immediate purpose to point out the injuries of this condition of the species, without displaying

the compensations by which nature has balanced them. But I
will now readily acknowledge — that, little as this practical condition may suit the interests of the individual, yet the species
could in no other way have been progressive. Partial exercise
of the faculties (literally " *one-sidedness* in the exercise of the
faculties ") leads the individual undoubtedly into error, but the
species into truth. In no other way than by concentrating the
whole energy of our spirit, and by converging our whole being,
so to speak, into a single faculty, can we put wings as it were to
the individual faculty and carry it by this artificial flight far
beyond the limits within which nature has else doomed it to walk.
Just as certain as it is that all human beings could never, by
clubbing their visual powers together, have arrived at the power
of seeing what the telescope discovers to the astronomer ; just so
certain it is that the human intellect would never have arrived
at an analysis of the infinite or a *Critical Analysis of the Pure
Reason* (the principal work of Kant), unless individuals had
dismembered (as it were) and insulated this or that specific
faculty, and had thus armed their intellectual sight by the
keenest abstraction and by the submersion of the other powers
of their nature. Extraordinary men are formed then by ener-
getic and over-excited spasms as it were in the individual faculties ; though it is true that the equable exercise of all the faculties
in harmony with each other can alone make happy and perfect
men.' After this statement, from which it should seem that in
the progress of society nature has made it necessary for man to
sacrifice *his own* happiness to the attainment of *her* ends in the
development of his species, Schiller goes on to inquire whether
this evil result cannot be remedied ; and whether ' the totality
of our nature, which art has destroyed, might not be re-estab
lished by a higher art,' — but this, as leading to a discussion
beyond the limits of my own, I omit.

# ENGLISH DICTIONARIES.

IT has already, I believe, been said more than once in print that one condition of a good dictionary would be to exhibit the *history* of each word; that is, to record the exact succession of its meanings. But the philosophic reason for this has not been given; which reason, by the way, settles a question often agitated, viz. whether the true meaning of a word be best ascertained from its etymology, or from its present use and acceptation. Mr. Coleridge says, ' the best explanation of a word is often that which is suggested by its derivation' (I give the substance of his words from memory). Others allege that we have nothing to do with the primitive · meaning of the word; that the question is — what does it mean now? and they appeal, as the sole authority they acknowledge, to the received —

Usus, penes quem est jus et norma loquendi.

In what degree each party is right, may be judged from this consideration — that no word can ever deviate from its first meaning *per saltum :* each successive stage of meaning must always have been determined by that which preceded. ˙ And on this one law depends the whole philosophy of the case : for it thus appears

[274]

that the original and primitive sense of the word will contain virtually all which can ever afterwards arise: as in the *evolution*-theory of generation, the whole series of births is represented as involved in the first parent. Now, if the evolution of successive meanings has gone on rightly, *i. e.* by simply lapsing through a series of close affinities, there can be no reason for recurring to the primitive meaning of the word: but, if it can be shown that the evolution has been faulty, *i. e.* that the chain of true affinities has ever been broken through ignorance, then we have a right to reform the word, and to appeal from the usage ill-instructed to a usage better-instructed. Whether we ought to exercise this right, will depend on a consideration which I will afterwards notice. Meantime I will first give a few instances of faulty evolution.

1. *Implicit.* This word is now used in a most ignorant way; and from its misuse it has come to be a word wholly useless: for it is now never coupled, I think, with any other substantive than these two — faith and confidence: a poor domain indeed to have sunk to from its original wide range of territory. Moreover, when we say, *implicit faith*, or *implicit confidence*, we do not thereby indicate any specific *kind* of faith and confidence differing from other faith or other confidence: but it is a vague rhetorical word which expresses a great *degree* of faith and confidence; a faith that is unquestioning, a confidence that is unlimited; *i. e.* in fact, a faith that *is* a faith, a confidence that *is* a confidence. Such a use of the word ought to be abandoned to women: doubtless, when sitting in a bower in the month of May, it is pleasant to hear from a lovely mouth — 'I put implicit confi-

dence in your honor : ' but, though pretty and becoming to such a mouth, it is very unfitting to the mouth of a scholar : and I will be bold to affirm that no man, who had ever acquired a scholar's knowledge of the English language, has used the word in that lax and unmeaning way. The history of the word is this. — *Implicit* (from the Latin *implicitus*, involved in, folded up) was always used originally, and still is so by scholars, as the direct antithete of *explicit* (from the Latin *explicitus*, evolved, unfolded ) : and the use of both may be thus illustrated.

*Q.* 'Did Mr. A. ever say that he would marry Miss B. ? ' — *A.* 'No ; not explicitly (*i. e.* in so many words) ; but he did implicitly — by showing great displeasure if she received attentions from any other man ; by asking her repeatedly to select furniture for his house ; by consulting her on his own plans of life.'

*Q.* 'Did Epicurus maintain any doctrines such as are here ascribed to him ? ' — *A.* 'Perhaps not explicitly, either in words or by any other mode of direct sanction : on the contrary, I believe he denied them — and disclaimed them with vehemence : but he maintained them implicitly : for they are involved in other acknowledged doctrines of his, and may be deduced from them by the fairest and most irresistible logic.'

*Q.* 'Why did you complain of the man ? Had he expressed any contempt for your opinion ? ' — *A.* 'Yes, he had : not explicit contempt, I admit ; for he never opened his stupid mouth ; but implicitly he expressed the utmost that he could : for, when I had spoken two hours against the old newspaper, and in favor of the new one, he went instantly and put his name down as a subscriber to the old one.'

*Q.* 'Did Mr. —— approve of that gentleman's conduct and way of life?'—*A.* 'I don't know that I ever heard him speak about it: but he seemed to give it his implicit approbation by allowing both his sons to associate with him when the complaints ran highest against him.'

These instances may serve to illustrate the original use of the word; which use has been retained from the sixteenth century down to our own days by an uninterrupted chain of writers. In the eighteenth century this use was indeed nearly effaced; but still in the first half of that century it was retained by Saunderson the Cambridge professor of mathematics (see his Algebra, &c.), with three or four others, and in the latter half by a man to whom Saunderson had some resemblance in spring and elasticity of understanding, viz. by Edmund Burke. Since his day I know of no writers who have avoided the slang and unmeaning use of the word, excepting Messrs. Coleridge and Wordsworth; both of whom (but especially the last) have been remarkably attentive to the scholarlike * use of words, and to the history of their own language.

Thus much for the primitive use of the word *implicit*.

* Among the most shocking of the unscholarlike barbarisms, now prevalent, I must notice the use of the word '*nice*' in an objective instead of a subjective sense: '*nice*' does not and cannot express a quality of the object, but merely a quality of the subject: yet we hear daily of 'a very nice letter'—'a nice young lady,' &c., meaning a letter or a young lady that it is pleasant to contemplate: but 'a nice young lady'—means a fastidious young lady; and 'a nice letter' ought to mean a letter that is very delicate in its rating and in the choice of its company.

Now, with regard to the history of its transition into its present use, it is briefly this; and it will appear at once, that it has arisen through ignorance. When it was objected to a papist that his church exacted an assent to a great body of traditions and doctrines to which it was impossible that the great majority could be qualified, either as respected time — or knowledge — or culture of the understanding, to give any reason-able assent, — the answer was: ' Yes; but that sort of assent is not required of a poor uneducated man; all that he has to do — is to believe in the church: he is to have faith in *her* faith: by that act he adopts for his own whatsoever the church believes, though he may never have heard of it even : his faith is implicit, *i. e.* involved and wrapped up in the faith of the church, which faith he firmly believes to be the true faith upon the conviction he has that the church is preserved from all possibility of erring by the spirit of God.' *   Now, as this sort of believing by proxy or implicit belief (in which the belief was not *immediate* in the thing proposed to the belief, but in the authority of another person who believed in that thing and thus *mediately* in the thing itself) was constantly attacked by the learned assailants of popery, — it naturally happened that many unlearned readers of these pro-

---

* Thus Milton, who (in common with his contemporaries) always uses the word accurately, speaks of Ezekiel ' swallowing his implicit roll of knowledge ' — *i. e.* coming to the knowledge of many truths not separately and in detail, but by the act of arriving at some one master truth which involved all the rest. — So again, if any man or government were to suppress a book, that man or government might justly be reproached as the im-plicit destroyer of all the wisdom and virtue that might have been the remote products of that book.

testant polemics caught at a phrase which was so much bandied between the two parties: the spirit of the context sufficiently explained to them that it was used by protestants as a term of reproach, and indicated a faith that was an erroneous faith by being too easy — too submissive — and too passive: but the particular mode of this erroneousness they seldom came to understand, as learned writers naturally employed the term without explanation, presuming it to be known to those whom they addressed. Hence these ignorant readers caught at the last *result* of the phrase 'implicit faith' rightly, truly supposing it to imply a resigned and unquestioning faith; but they missed the whole immediate cause of meaning by which only the word 'implicit' could ever have been entitled to express that result.

I have allowed myself to say so much on this word 'implicit,' because the history of the mode by which its true meaning was lost applies almost to all other corrupted words — *mutatis mutandis*: and the amount of it may be collected into this formula, — that the *result* of the word is apprehended and retained, but the *schematismus* by which that result was ever reached is lost. This is the brief theory of all corruption of words. The word *schematismus* I have unwillingly used because no other expresses my meaning. So great and extensive a doctrine however lurks in this word, that I defer the explanation of it to a separate article. Meantime a passable sense of the word will occur to every body who reads Greek. I now go on to a few more instances of words that have forfeited their original meaning through the ignorance of those who used them.

'*Punctual.*' This word is now confined to the
meagre denoting of accuracy in respect to time —
fidelity to the precise moment of an appointment.
But originally it was just as often, and just as reasonably, applied to space as to time ; ' I cannot punctually
determine the origin of the Danube ; but I know in
general the district in which it rises, and that its
fountain is near that of the Rhine.' Not only, however,
was it applied to time and space, but it had a large
and very elegant figurative use.   Thus in the History
of the Royal Society by Sprat (an author who was
finical and nice in his use of words) — I remember a
sentence to this effect : ' the Society gave punctual
directions for the conducting of experiments ; ' *i. e.*
directions which descended to the minutiæ and lowest
details.   Again in the once popular romance of Paris-
mus Prince of Bohemia — ' She ' (I forget who) ' made
a punctual relation of the whole matter ; ' *i. e.* a relation which was perfectly circumstantial and true to
the minutest features of the case.

# DRYDEN'S HEXASTICH.

I⊤ is a remarkable fact, that the very finest epigram in the English language happens also to be the worst. *Epigram* I call it in the austere Greek sense; which thus far resembled our modern idea of an epigram, that something pointed and allied to wit was demanded in the management of the leading thought at its close, but otherwise nothing tending towards the comic or the ludicrous. The epigram I speak of is the well-known one of Dryden dedicated to the glorification of Milton. It is irreproachable as regards its severe brevity. Not one word is there that could be spared; nor could the wit of man have cast the movement of the thought into a better mould. There are three couplets. In the first couplet we are reminded of the fact that this earth had, in three different stages of its development, given birth to a trinity of transcendent poets; meaning narrative poets, or, even more narrowly, epic poets. The duty thrown upon the second couplet is to characterize these three poets, and to value them against each other, but in such terms as that, whilst nothing less than the very highest praise should be assigned to the two elder poets in this

trinity — the Greek and the Roman — nevertheless,
by some dexterous artifice, a higher praise than the
highest should suddenly unmask itself, and drop, as
it were, like a diadem from the clouds upon the brows
of their English competitor.   In the kind of expectation
raised, and in the extreme difficulty of adequately
meeting this expectation, there was pretty much the
same challenge offered to Dryden as was offered,
somewhere about the same time, to a British ambassador when dining with his political antagonists.   One
of these — the ambassador of France — had proposed
to drink his master, Louis XIV., under the character
of the sun, who dispensed life and light to the whole
political system.   To this there was no objection;
and immediately, by way of intercepting any further
draughts upon the rest of the solar system, the Dutch
ambassador rose, and proposed the health of their high
mightinesses the Seven United States, as the moon and
six * planets, who gave light in the absence of the sun.
The two foreign ambassadors, Monsieur and Mynheer,
secretly enjoyed the mortification of their English
brother, who seemed to be thus left in a state of
bankruptcy, 'no funds' being available for retaliation,
or so they fancied.   But suddenly our British repre
sentative toasted *his* master as Joshua, the son of Nun
that made the sun and moon stand still.   All had
seemed lost for England, when in an instant of time
both her antagonists were checkmated.   Dryden assumed something of the same position.   He gave
away the supreme jewels in his exchequer; apparently
nothing remained behind; all was exhausted.   To

---

* ' *Six planets* : ' — No more had then been discovered.

Homer he gave A; to Virgil he gave B; and, behold! after these were given away, there remained nothing at all that would not have been a secondary praise. But, in a moment of time, by giving A *and* B to Milton, at one sling of his victorious arm he raised him above Homer by the whole extent of B, and above Virgil by the whole extent of A. This felicitous eva- sion of the embarrassment is accomplished in the second couplet; and, finally, the third couplet winds up with graceful effect, by making a *resumé*, or recapi- tulation of the logic concerned in the distribution of prizes just announced. Nature, he says, had it not in her power to provide a third prize separate from the first and second; her resource was, to join the first and second in combination: 'To make a third, she joined the former two.'

Such is the abstract of this famous epigram; and, judged simply by the outline and tendency of the thought, it merits all the vast popularity which it has earned. But in the meantime, it is radically vicious as regards the filling in of this outline; for the par- ticular quality in which Homer is accredited with the pre-eminence, viz., *loftiness of thought*, happens to be a mere variety of expression for that quality, viz. *majesty*, in which the pre-eminence is awarded to Virgil. Homer excels Virgil in the very point in which lies Virgil's superiority to Homer; and that synthesis, by means of which a great triumph is reserved to Milton, becomes obviously impossible, when it is perceived that the supposed analytic elements of this synthesis are blank reiterations of each other

Exceedingly striking it is, that a thought should

have prospered for one hundred and seventy years, which, on the slightest steadiness of examination, turns out to be no thought at all, but mere blank vacuity. There is, however, this justification of the case, that the mould, the set of channels, into which the metal of the thought is meant to run, really *has* the felicity which it appears to have: the form is perfect; and it is merely in the *matter*, in the accidental filling up of the mould, that a fault has been committed. Had the Virgilian point of excellence been *loveliness* instead of *majesty*, or any word whatever suggesting the common antithesis of sublimity and beauty; or had it been power on the one side, matched against grace on the other, the true lurking tendency of the thought would have been developed, and the sub-conscious purpose of the epigram would have fulfilled itself to the letter.

*N. B.* — It is not meant that *loftiness of thought* and *majesty* are expressions so entirely interchangeable, as that no shades of difference could be suggested; it is enough that these 'shades' are not substantial enough, or broad enough, to support the weight of opposition which the epigram assigns to them. *Grace* and *elegance*, for instance, are far from being in all relations synonymous; but they are so to the full extent of any purposes concerned in this epigram. Nevertheless, it is probable enough that Dryden had moving in his thoughts a relation of the word *majesty*, which, if developed, would have done justice to his meaning. It was, perhaps, the decorum and sustained dignity of the *composition* — the workmanship apart from the native grandeur of the materials — the majestic style of the artistic treatment as distinguished from the original creative power — which Dryden, the translator of the Roman poet, familiar therefore with his weakness and with his strength, meant in this place to predicate as characteristically observable in Virgil.

# POPE'S RETORT UPON ADDISON.

THERE is nothing extraordinary, or that could merit a special notice, in a simple case of oversight, or in a blunder, though emanating from the greatest of poets.. But such a case challenges and forces our attention, when we know that the particular passage in which it occurs was wrought and burnished with excessive pains; or (which in this case is also known) when that particular passage is pushed into singular prominence as having obtained a singular success. In no part of his poetic mission did Pope so fascinate the gaze of his contemporaries as in his functions of satirist; which functions, in his latter years, absorbed all other functions. And one reason, I believe, why it was that the interest about Pope decayed so rapidly after his death (an accident somewhere noticed by Wordsworth), must be sought in the fact, that the most stinging of his personal allusions, by which he had given salt to his later writings, were continually losing their edge, and sometimes their intelligibility, as Pope's own contemporary generation was dying off. Pope alleges it as a palliation of his satiric malice, that it had been forced from him in the way of retaliation; forgetting that such a plea wilfully abjures the grandest justification of a satirist, viz., the deliberate assump-

[286]

tion of the character as something corresponding to
the prophet's mission amongst the Hebrews. It is no
longer the *facit indignatio versum*. Pope's satire,
where even it was most effective, was personal and
vindictive, and upon that argument alone could not be
philosophic. Foremost in the order of his fulminations
stood, and yet stands, the bloody castigation by which,
according to his own pretence, he warned and menaced
(but by which, in simple truth, he executed judgment
upon) his false friend, Addison.

To say that this drew vast rounds of applause upon
its author, and frightened its object into deep silence
for the rest of his life, like the *Quos ego* of angry
Neptune, sufficiently argues that the verses must have
ploughed as deeply as the Russian knout. Vitriol
could not scorch more fiercely. And yet the whole
passage rests upon a blunder; and the blunder is so
broad and palpable, that it implies instant forgetfulness
both in the writer and the reader. The idea which
furnishes the basis of the passage is this: that the
conduct ascribed to Addison is in its own nature so
despicable, as to extort laughter by its primary impulse; but that this laughter changes into weeping,
when we come to understand that the person concerned
in this delinquency is Addison. The change, the
transfiguration, in our mood of contemplating the
offence, is charged upon the discovery which we are
supposed to make as to the person of the offender;
that which by its baseness had been simply comic
when imputed to some corresponding author, passes
into a tragic *coup-de-théatre*, when it is suddenly traced
back to a man of original genius. The whole, therefore, of this effect is made to depend upon the sudden

scenical transition from a supposed petty criminal to
one of high distinction. And, meantime, no such stage
effect had been possible, since the knowledge that a
man of genius was the offender had been what we
started with from the beginning. 'Our laughter is
changed to tears,' says Pope, ' as soon as we discover
that the base act had a noble author.' And, behold!
the initial feature in the whole description of the case
is, that the libeller was one whom ' true genius fired : '

> ' Peace to all such !   But were there one whose mind
>    True genius fires,' &c.

Before the offence is described, the perpetrator is
already characterized as a man of genius: and, *in
spite of that knowledge*, we laugh.   But suddenly our
mood changes, and we weep, but why ? I beseech you.
Simply because we have ascertained the author to be
a man of genius.

> ' Who would not laugh, if such a man there be ?
>   Who would not weep, if Atticus were he ? '

The sole reason for weeping is something that we
knew already before we began to laugh.

It would not be right in logic, in fact, it would be a
mis-classification, if I should cite as at all belonging to
the same group several passages in Milton that come
very near to Irish bulls, by virtue of distorted language
One reason against such a classification would lie precisely in that fact — viz., that the assimilation to the
category of bulls lurks in the verbal expression, and
not (as in Pope's case) amongst the conditions. of the
thought.   And a second reason would lie in the strange
circumstance, that Milton had not fallen into this snare
of diction through any carelessness or oversight, but

with his eyes wide open, deliberately avowing his error as a special elegance; repeating it; and well aware of splendid Grecian authority for bis error, if anybody should be bold enough to call it an error. Every reader must be aware of the case —

> 'Adam the goodliest man of men since born
> His sons; the fairest of her daughters Eve' —

which makes Adam one of his own sons, Eve one of her own daughters. This, however, is authorized by Grecian usage in the severest writers. Neither can it be alleged that these might be bold poetic expressions, harmonizing with the Grecian idiom; for Poppo has illustrated this singular form of expression in a prose-writer, as philosophic and austere as Thucydides; a form which (as it offends against logic) must offend equally in all languages. Some beauty must have been described in the idiom, such as atoned for its solecism: for Milton recurs to the same idiom, and under the same entire freedom of choice, elsewhere; particularly in this instance, which has not been pointed out: 'And never,' says Satan to the abhorred phantoms of Sin and Death, when crossing his path,

> 'And never saw till now
> Sight more detestable than him and thee.'

Now, therefore, it seems, he *had* seen a sight more detestable than this very sight. He now looked upon something more hateful than X Y Z. What was it? It was X Y Z.

But the authority of Milton, backed by that of insolent Greece, would prove an overmatch for the logic of centuries. And I withdraw, therefore, from the rash attempt to quarrel with this sort of bull, in-

25

volving itself in the verbal expression. But the following, which lies rooted in the mere facts and incidents, is certainly the most extraordinary *practical* bull[1] that all literature can furnish. And a stranger thing, perhaps, than the oversight itself lies in this — that not any critic throughout Europe, two only excepted, but has failed to detect a blunder so memorable. All the rampant audacity of Bentley — ' slashing Bentley ' — all the jealous malignity of Dr. Johnson — who hated Milton without disguise as a republican, but secretly and under a mask *would* at any rate have hated him from jealousy of his scholarship — had not availed to sharpen these practised and these interested eyes into the detection of an oversight which argues a sudden Lethean forgetfulness on the part of Milton ; and in many generations of readers, however alive and awake with malice, a corresponding forgetfulness not less astonishing. Two readers only I have ever heard of that escaped this lethargic inattention ; one of which two is myself; and I ascribe my success partly to good luck, but partly to some merit on my own part in having cultivated a habit of systematically accurate reading. If I read at all, I make it a duty to read truly and faithfully. I profess allegiance for the time to the man whom I undertake to study ; and I am as loyal to all the engagements involved in such a contract, as if I had come under a *sacramentum militare.* So it was that, whilst yet a boy, I came to perceive, with a wonder not yet exhausted, that unaccountable blunder which Milton has committed in the main narrative on which the epic fable of the ' Paradise Lost ' turns as its hinges. And many a year afterwards I found that Paul Richter, whose vigilance nothing es-

caped, who carried with him through life ' the eye of
the hawk, and the fire therein,' had not failed to make
the same discovery. It is this: The archangel Satan
has designs upon man; he meditates his ruin; and it
is known that he does. Specially to counteract these
designs, and for no other purpose whatever, a choir
of angelic police is stationed at the gates of Paradise,
having (I repeat) one sole commission, viz., to keep
watch and ward over the threatened safety of the
newly created human pair. Even at the very first
this duty is neglected so thoroughly, that Satan gains
access without challenge or suspicion. That is awful:
for, ask yourself, reader, how a constable or an inspector of police would be received who had been
stationed at No. 6, on a secret information, and spent
the night in making love at No. 15. Through the
regular surveillance at the gates, Satan passes without
objection; and he is first of all detected by a purely
accidental collision during the rounds of the junior
angels. The result of this collision, and of the examination which follows, is what no reader can ever forget — so unspeakable is the grandeur of that scene
between the two hostile archangels, when the *Fiend*
(so named at the moment under the fine machinery
used by Milton for exalting or depressing the ideas of
his nature) finally takes his flight as an incarnation
of darkness.

' And fled<br>
Murmuring; and with him fled the shades of night.

The darkness flying with him, naturally we have the
feeling that he *is* the darkness, and that all darkness
has some essential relation to Satan.

But now, having thus witnessed his terrific expulsion,

naturally we ask what was the sequel. Four books, however, are interposed before we reach the answer to that question. This is the reason 'that we fail to remark the extraordinary oversight of Milton. Dislocated from its immediate plan in the succession of incidents, that sequel eludes our notice, which else and in its natural place would have shocked us beyond measure. The simple abstract of the whole story is, that Satan, being ejected, and sternly charged under Almighty menaces not to intrude upon the young Paradise of God, ' rides with darkness' for exactly one week, and, having digested his wrath rather than his fears on the octave of his solemn banishment, without demur, or doubt, or tremor, back he plunges into the very centre of Eden. On a Friday, suppose, he is expelled through the main entrance: on the Friday following he re-enters upon the forbidden premises through a clandestine entrance. The upshot is, that the heavenly police suffer, in the first place, the one sole enemy, who was or could be the object of their vigilance, to pass without inquest or suspicion; thus they *inaugurate* their task; secondly, by the merest accident (no thanks to their fidelity) they detect him, and with awful adjurations sentence him to perpetual banishment; but, thirdly, on his immediate return, in utter contempt of their sentence, they ignore him altogether, and apparently act upon Dogberry's direction, that, upon meeting a thief, the police may suspect him to be no true man; and, with such manner of men, the less they meddle or make, the more it will be for their honesty.

# NOTE.

### NOTE 1.  Page 290.

It is strange, or rather it is *not* strange, considering the
feebleness of that lady in such a field, that Miss Edgeworth
always fancied herself to have caught Milton in a bull, under
circumstances which, whilst leaving the shadow of a bull, effectually disown the substance. 'And in the lowest deep a lower
deep still opens to devour me.' This is the passage denounced
by Miss Edgeworth. 'If it was already the lowest deep,' said
the fair lady, ' how the deuce (no, perhaps it might be *I* that
said '*how the deuce* ') could it open into a lower deep? ' Yes,
how could it? In carpentry, it is clear to my mind that it could
*not.* But, in cases of deep imaginative feeling, no phenomenon
is more natural than precisely this never-ending growth of one
colossal grandeur chasing and surmounting another, or of abysses
that swallowed up abysses. Persecutions of this class oftentimes
are amongst the symptoms of fever, and amongst the inevitable
spontaneities of nature. Other people I have known who were
inclined to class amongst bulls Milton's all-famous expression
of '*darkness visible*,' whereas it is not even a bold or daring expression ; it describes a pure optical experience of very common
occurrence There are two separate darknesses or obscurities :
first, that obscurity *by* which you see dimly ; and secondly, that
obscurity *which* you see. The first is the atmosphere through
which vision is performed, and, therefore, part of the *subjective*
conditions essential to the act of seeing. The second is the *object*

[293]

of your sight.   In a glass-house at night illuminated by a sullen
fire in one corner, but else dark, you see the darkness massed in
the rear as a black object.   *That* is the ' visible darkness.'   And
on the other hand, the murky atmosphere between you and the
distant rear is not the object, but the medium, through or athwart
which you descry the black masses.   The first darkness is *subjective* darkness ;   that is, a darkness in your own eye, and
entangled with your very faculty of vision.   The second darkness
is perfectly different : it is *objective* darkness ; that is to say,
not any darkness which affects or modifies your faculty of seeing
either for better or worse ; but a darkness which is the *object*
of your vision ; a darkness which you see projected from yourself as a massy volume of blackness, and projected, possibly, to a
vast distance.

# MISCELLANEOUS ESSAYS.

# CONTENTS.

# MISCELLANEOUS ESSAYS.

## ON

## THE KNOCKING AT THE GATE

### IN MACBETH.

FROM my boyish days I had always felt a great perplexity on one point in Macbeth. It was this: the knocking at the gate, which succeeds to the murder of Duncan, produced to my feelings an effect for which I never could account. The effect was, that it reflected back upon the murder a peculiar awfulness and a depth of solemnity; yet, however obstinately I endeavored with my understanding to comprehend this, for many years I never could see *why* it should produce such an effect.

Here I pause for one moment to exhort the reader never to pay any attention to his understanding, when it stands in opposition to any other faculty of his mind. The mere understanding, however useful and indispensable, is the meanest faculty in the human mind, and the most to be distrusted; and yet the great majority

of people trust to nothing else; which may do for
ordinary life, but not for philosophical purposes. Of
this out of ten thousand instances that I might produce,
I will cite one. Ask of any person whatsoever, who is
not previously prepared for the demand by a knowledge
of perspective, to draw in the rudest way the commonest appearance which depends upon the laws of
that science; as, for instance, to represent the effect of
two walls standing at right angles to each other, or
the appearance of the houses on each side of a street,
as seen by a person looking down the street from one
extremity. Now, in all cases, unless the person has
happened to observe in pictures how it is that artists
produce these effects, he will be utterly unable to make
the smallest approximation to it. Yet why? For he
has actually seen the effect every day of his life. The
reason is — that he allows his understanding to overrule his eyes. His understanding, which includes no
intuitive knowledge of the laws of vision, can furnish
him with no reason why a line which is known and can
be proved to be a horizontal line, should not *appear* a
horizontal line; a line that made any angle with the
perpendicular, less than a right angle, would seem to
him to indicate that his houses were all tumbling down
together. Accordingly, he makes the line of his houses
a horizontal line, and fails, of course, to produce the
effect demanded. Here, then, is one instance out of
many, in which not only the understanding is allowed
to overrule the eyes, but where the understanding is
positively allowed to obliterate the eyes, as it were, for
not only does the man believe the evidence of his
understanding, in opposition to that of his eyes, but,
(what is monstrous!) the idiot is not aware that his

eyes ever gave such evidence. He does not know that he has seen (and therefore *quoad* his consciousness has *not* seen) that which he *has* seen every day of his life.

But to return from this digression, my understanding could furnish no reason why the knocking at the gate in Macbeth should produce any effect direct or reflected. In fact, my understanding said positively that it could *not* produce any effect. But I knew better; I felt that it did; and I waited and clung to the problem until further knowledge should enable me to solve it. At length, in 1812, Mr. Williams made his *début* on the stage of Ratcliffe Highway, and executed those unparalleled murders which have procured for him such a brilliant and undying reputation. On which murders, by the way, I must observe, that in one respect they have had an ill effect, by making the connoisseur in murder very fastidious in his taste, and dissatisfied by anything that has since been done in that line. All other murders look pale by the deep crimson of his; and, as an amateur once said to me in a querulous tone, 'There has been absolutely nothing *doing* since his time, or nothing that's worth speaking of.' But this is wrong; for it is unreasonable to expect all men to be great artists, and born with the genius of Mr. Williams. Now it will be remembered, that in the first of these murders, (that of the Marrs,) the same incident (of a knocking at the door, soon after the work of extermination was complete) did actually occur, which the genius of Shakspeare has invented; and all good judges, and the most eminent dilettanti, acknowledged the felicity of Shakspeare's suggestion, as soon as it was actually realized. Here, then, was a

fresh proof that I was right in relying on my own feeling, in opposition to my understanding; and I again set
myself to study the problem; at length I solved it to
my own satisfaction; and my solution is this.   Murder,
in ordinary cases, where the sympathy is wholly directed to the case of the murdered person, is an incident
of coarse and vulgar horror; and for this reason, that
it flings the interest exclusively upon the natural but
ignoble instinct by which we cleave to life; an instinct, which, as being indispensable to the primal
law of self-preservation, is the same in kind, (though
different in degree,) amongst all living creatures; this
instinct, therefore, because it annihilates all distinctions, and degrades the greatest of men to the level of
'the poor beetle that we tread on,' exhibits human nature in its most abject and humiliating attitude.   Such
an attitude would little suit the purposes of the poet.
What then must he do?   He must throw the interest
on the murderer.   Our sympathy must be with *him;*
(of course I mean a sympathy of comprehension, a
sympathy by which we enter into his feelings, and are
made to understand them, — not a sympathy[1] of pity
or approbation.)   In the murdered person, all strife
of thought, all flux and reflux of passion and of pur-

[1] It seems almost ludicrous to guard and explain my use of a
word, in a situation where it would naturally explain itself.
But it has become necessary to do so, in consequence of the
unscholarlike use of the word sympathy, at present so general,
by which, instead of taking it in its proper sense, as the act of
reproducing in our minds the feelings of another, whether for
hatred, indignation, love, pity, or approbation, it is made a
mere synonyme of the word *pity;* and hence, instead of saying
'sympathy *with* another,' many writers adopt the monstrous
barbarism of ' sympathy *for* another.'

pose, are crushed by one overwhelming panic; the fear of instant death smites him ' with its petrific mace.' But in the murderer, such a murderer as a poet will condescend to, there must be raging some great storm of passion, — jealousy, ambition, vengeance, hatred, — which will create a hell within him; and into this hell we are to look.

In Macbeth, for the sake of gratifying his own enormous and teeming faculty of creation, Shakspeare has introduced two murderers; and, as usual in his hands, they are remarkably discriminated: but, though in Macbeth the strife of mind is greater than in his wife, the tiger spirit not so awake, and his feelings caught chiefly by contagion from her, — yet, as both were finally involved in the guilt of murder, the murderous mind of necessity is finally to be presumed in both. This was to be expressed; and on its own account, as well as to make it a more proportionable antagonist to the unoffending nature of their victim, ' the gracious Duncan,' and adequately to expound ' the deep damnation of his taking off,' this was to be expressed with peculiar energy. We were to be made to feel that the human nature, *i. e.*, the divine nature of love and mercy, spread through the hearts of all creatures, and seldom utterly withdrawn from man, — was gone, vanished, extinct; and that the fiendish nature had taken its place. And, as this effect is marvellously accomplished in the *dialogues* and *soliloquies* themselves, so it is finally consummated by the expedient under consideration; and it is to this that I now solicit the reader's attention. If the reader has ever witnessed a wife, daughter, or sister, in a fainting fit, he may chance to have observed that the most affecting moment in

such a spectacle, is *that* in which a sigh and a stirring
announce the recommencement of suspended life.  Or,
if the reader has ever been present in a vast metropolis,
on the day when some great national idol was carried
in funeral pomp to his grave, and chancing to walk
near the course through which it passed, has felt powerfully, in the silence and desertion of the streets, and
in the stagnation of ordinary business, the deep interest
which at that moment was possessing the heart of man,
— if all at once he should hear the death-like stillness
broken up by the sound of wheels rattling away from
the scene, and making known that the transitory vision
was dissolved, he will be aware that at no moment was
his sense of the complete suspension and pause in
ordinary human concerns so full and affecting, as at
that moment when the suspension ceases, and the goings-
on of human life are suddenly resumed.  All action
in any direction is best expounded, measured, and made
apprehensible, by reaction.  Now apply this to the case
in Macbeth.  Here, as I have said, the retiring of the
human heart, and the entrance of the fiendish heart,
was to be expressed and made sensible.  Another
world has stept in; and the murderers are taken out
of the region of human things, human purposes, human
desires.  They are transfigured : Lady Macbeth is
' unsexed ; ' Macbeth has forgot that he was born of
woman ; both are conformed to the image of devils ;
and the world of devils is suddenly revealed.  But how
shall this be conveyed and made palpable ?  In order
that a new world may step in, this world must for a
time disappear.  The murderers, and the murder, must
be insulated — cut off by an immeasurable gulph from
the ordinary tide and succession of human affairs —

locked up and sequestered in some deep recess; we must be made sensible that the world of ordinary life is suddenly arrested — laid asleep — tranced — racked into a dread armistice; time must be annihilated; relation to things without abolished; and all must pass self-withdrawn into a deep syncòpe and suspension of earthly passion. Hence it is, that when the deed is done, when the work of darkness is perfect, then the world of darkness passes away like a pageantry in the clouds; the knocking at the gate is heard; and it makes known audibly that the reaction has commenced: the human has made its reflux upon the fiendish; the pulses of life are beginning to beat again; and the re-establishment of the goings-on of the world in which we live, first makes us profoundly sensible of the awful parenthesis that had suspended them.

O, mighty poet! Thy works are not as those of other men, simply and merely great works of art; but are also like the phenomena of nature, like the sun and the sea, the stars and the flowers, — like frost and snow, rain and dew, hail-storm and thunder, which are to be studied with entire submission of our own faculties, and in the perfect faith that in them there can be no too much or too little, nothing useless or inert, — but that, the further we press in our discoveries, the more we shall see proofs of design and self-supporting arrangement where the careless eye had seen nothing but accident!

# ON MURDER,

## CONSIDERED AS ONE OF THE FINE ARTS.

ADVERTISEMENT OF A MAN MORBIDLY VIRTUOUS.

MOST of us, who read books, have probably heard
of a Society for the Promotion of Vice, of the Hell-
Fire Club, founded in the last century by Sir Francis
D——, &c. At Brighton I think it was, that a Society was formed for the Suppression of Virtue. That
society was itself suppressed; but I am sorry to say
that another exists in London, of a character still more
atrocious. In tendency, it may be denominated a Society for the Encouragement of Murder; but, according to their own delicate ευφημισμός, it is styled, The
Society of Connoisseurs in Murder. They profess to
be curious in homicide; amateurs and dilettanti in the
various modes of bloodshed; and, in short, Murder-
Fanciers. Every fresh atrocity of that class which the
police annals of Europe bring up, they meet and criticize as they would a picture, statue, or other work of
art. But I need not trouble myself with any attempt
to describe the spirit of their proceedings, as the
reader will collect *that* much better from one of the
Monthly Lectures read before the society last year.
This has fallen into my hands accidentally, in spite of

2                                                    [17]

all the vigilance exercised to keep their transactions from the public eye. The publication of it will alarm them; and my purpose is, that it should. For I would much rather put them down quietly, by an appeal to public opinion, than by such an exposure of names as would follow an appeal to Bow Street; which last appeal, however, if this should fail, I must really resort to. For my intense virtue will not put up with such things in a Christian land. Even in a heathen land, the toleration of murder — viz., in the dreadful shows of the amphitheatre — was felt by a Christian writer to be the most crying reproach of the public morals. This writer was Lactantius; and with his words, as singularly applicable to the present occasion, I shall conclude : — 'Quid tam horribile,' says he, ' tam tetrum, quam hominis trucidatio ? Ideo severissimis legibus vita nostra munitur; ideo bella execrabilia sunt. Invenit tamen consuetudo quatenus homicidium sine bello ac sine legibus faciat : et hoc sibi voluptas quod scelus vindicavit. Quod si interesse homicidio sceleris conscientia est, — et eidem facinori spectator obstrictus est cui et admissor; ergo et in his gladiatorum cædibus non minus cruore profunditur qui spectat, quam ille qui facit : nec potest esse immunis à sanguine qui voluit effundi; aut videri non interfecisse, qui interfectori et favit et prœmium postulavit.' 'What is so dreadful,' says Lactantius, ' what so dismal and revolting, as the murder of a human creature ? Therefore it is, that life for us is protected by laws the most rigorous : therefore it is, that wars are objects of execration. And yet the traditional usage of Rome has devised a mode of authorizing murder apart from war, and in defiance of law ;

and the demands of taste (voluptas) are now become the same as those of abandoned guilt.' Let the Society of Gentlemen Amateurs consider this; and let me call their especial attention to the last sentence, which is so weighty, that I shall attempt to convey it in English: 'Now, if merely to be present at a murder fastens on a man the character of an accomplice; if barely to be a spectator involves us in one common guilt with the perpetrator, it follows, of necessity, that, in these murders of the amphitheatre, the hand which inflicts the fatal blow is not more deeply imbrued in blood than his who passively looks on; neither can *he* be clear of blood who has countenanced its shedding; nor that man seem other than a participator in murder, who gives his applause to the murderer, and calls for prizes on his behalf.' The '*præmia postulavit*' I have not yet heard charged upon the Gentlemen Amateurs of London, though undoubtedly their proceedings tend to that; but the '*interfectori favit*' is implied in the very title of this association, and expressed in every line of the lecture which follows. X. Y. Z.


## LECTURE.

GENTLEMEN,—I have had the honor to be appointed by your committee to the trying task of reading the Williams' Lecture on Murder, considered as one of the Fine Arts; a task which might be easy enough three or four centuries ago, when the art was little understood, and few great models had been exhibited; but in this age, when masterpieces of excellence have been executed by professional men, it must be evident, that in the style of criticism applied to them, the public will look for something of a corresponding improvement. Practice and theory must advance *pari passu*. People begin to see that something more goes to the composition of a fine murder than two blockheads to kill and be killed — a knife — a purse — and a dark lane. Design, gentlemen, grouping, light and shade, poetry, sentiment, are now deemed indispensable to attempts of this nature. Mr. Williams has exalted the ideal of murder to all of us; and to me, therefore, in particular, has deepened the arduousness of my task. Like Æschylus or Milton in poetry, like Michael Angelo in painting, he has carried his art to a point of colossal sublimity; and, as Mr. Wordsworth observes, has in a manner 'created the taste by which he is to be enjoyed.' To sketch the history of the art, and to examine its principles critically, now remains as a duty for the connoisseur, and for judges of quite another stamp from his Majesty's Judges of Assize.

Before I begin, let me say a word or two to certain prigs, who affect to speak of our society as if it were in some degree immoral in its tendency. Immoral! Jupiter protect me, gentlemen, what is it that people mean? I am for morality, and always shall be, and for virtue, and all that; and I do affirm, and always shall (let what will come of it), that murder is an improper line of conduct, highly improper; and I do not stick to assert, that any man who deals in murder, must have very incorrect ways of thinking, and truly inaccurate principles; and so far from aiding and abetting him by pointing out his victim's hiding-place, as a great moralist [1] of Germany declared it to be every good man's duty to do, I would subscribe one shilling and sixpence to have him apprehended, which is more by eighteenpence than the most eminent moralists have hitherto subscribed for that purpose. But what then? Everything in this world has two handles.. Murder, for instance, may be laid hold of by its moral handle (as it generally is in the pulpit, and at the Old Bailey); and *that*, I confess, is its weak side; or it may also be treated *æsthetically*, as the Germans call it — that is, in relation to good taste.

To illustrate this, I will urge the authority of three eminent persons; viz., S. T. Coleridge, Aristotle, and Mr. Howship the surgeon. To begin with S. T. C. One night, many years ago, I was drinking tea with him in Berners Street (which, by the way, for a short street, has been uncommonly fruitful in men of genius). Others were there besides myself; and, amidst some carnal considerations of tea and toast, we were all imbibing a dissertation on Plotinus from the attic lips of S. T. C. Suddenly a cry arose of, " *Fire — fire !* " upon which all of us, master and disciples, Plato and ὁι περὶ τον Πλάτωνα, rushed out, eager for the spectacle. The fire was in Oxford Street, at a pianoforte-maker's; and, as it promised to be a conflagration of merit, I was sorry that my engagements forced me away from Mr. Coleridge's party, before matters had come to a crisis. Some days after, meeting with my Platonic host, I reminded him of the case, and begged to know how that very promising exhibition had terminated. ' Oh, sir,' said he, ' it turned out so ill that we damned it unanimously.' Now, does any man suppose that Mr. Coleridge — who, for all he is too fat to be a person of active virtue, is undoubtedly a worthy

Christian — that this good S. T. C., I say, was an in-
cendiary, or capable of wishing any ill to the poor man
and his pianofortes (many of them, doubtless, with the
additional keys)?   On the contrary, I know him to be
that sort of man, that I durst stake my life upon it, he
would have worked an engine in a case of necessity,
although rather of the fattest for such fiery trials
of his virtue.   But how stood the case?   Virtue
was in no request.   On the arrival of the fire-engines,
morality had devolved wholly on the insurance office.
This being the case, he had a right to gratify his
taste.   He had left his tea.   Was he to have nothing
in return?

I contend that the most virtuous man, under the
premises stated, was entitled to make a luxury of the
fire, and to hiss it, as he would any other performance
that raised expectations in the public mind which afterwards it disappointed.   Again, to cite another great
authority, what says the Stagirite?   He (in the Fifth
Book, I think it is, of his Metaphysics) describes what
he calls κλεπτὴν τέλειον — i. e., a perfect thief; and as
to Mr. Howship, in a work of his on Indigestion, he
makes no scruple to talk with admiration of a certain
ulcer which he had seen, and which he styles ' a beautiful ulcer.'   Now, will any man pretend, that, ab-
stractedly considered, a thief could appear to Aristotle a perfect character, or that Mr. Howship could
be enamored of an ulcer?   Aristotle, it is well
known, was himself so very moral a character, that,
not content with writing his Nichomachéan Ethics, in
one volume octavo, he also wrote another system,
called Magna Moralia, or Big Ethics.   Now, it is impossible that a man who composes any ethics at all,

big or little, should admire a thief *per se;* and as to
Mr. Howship, it well known that he makes war upon
all ulcers, and, without suffering himself to be seduced
by their charms, endeavors to banish them from the
County of Middlesex. But the truth is, that, however objectionable *per se,* yet, relatively to others of
their class, both a thief and an ulcer may have infinite
degrees of merit. They are both imperfections, it is
true ; but, to be imperfect being their essence, the very
greatness of their imperfection becomes their perfection. *Spartam nactus es, hanc exorna.* A thief like
Autolycus, or the once famous George Barrington, and
a grim phagedænic ulcer, superbly defined, and running
regularly through all its natural stages, may no less
justly be regarded as ideals after *their* kind, than the
most faultless moss-rose amongst flowers, in its progress
from bud to ' bright consummate flower ; ' or, amongst
human flowers, the most magnificent young female,
apparelled in the pomp of womanhood. And thus not
only the ideal of an inkstand may be imagined (as Mr.
Coleridge illustrated in his celebrated correspondence
with Mr. Blackwood), in which, by the way, there is
not so much, because an inkstand is a laudable
sort of thing, and a valuable member of society ;
but even imperfection itself may have its ideal or perfect state.

Really, gentlemen, I beg pardon for so much philosophy at one time ; and now let me apply it. When
a murder is in the paulo-post-futurum tense — not
done, not even (according to modern purism) *being*
done, but only going to be done — and a rumor of it
comes to our ears, by all means let us treat it morally.
But suppose it over and done, and that you can say of

it, Τετέλεσαι, It is finished, or (in that adamantine mo-
lussus of Medea) εἴγασαι, Done it is : it is *fait accom-
pli ;* suppose the poor murdered man to be out of his
pain, and the rascal that did it off like a shot, nobody
knows whither; suppose, lastly, that we have done
our best, by putting out our legs, to trip up the fellow
in his flight, but all to no purpose — ' abiit, evasit,
excessit, erupit," &c.— why, then, I say, what's the use
of any more virtue ? Enough has been given to morality; now comes the turn of Taste and the Fine Arts.
A sad thing it was, no doubt, very sad; but *we* can't
mend it. Therefore let us make the best of a bad matter; and, as it is impossible to hammer anything out
of it for moral purposes, let us treat it æsthetically,
and see if it will turn to account in that way. Such
is the logic of a sensible man, and what follows? We
dry up our tears, and have the satisfaction, perhaps, to
discover that a transaction, which, morally considered,
was shocking, and without a leg to stand upon, when
tried by principles of Taste, turns out to be a very
meritorious performance. Thus all the world is pleased;
the old proverb is justified, that it is an ill wind which
blows nobody good; the amateur, from looking bilious
and sulky, by too close attention to virtue, begins to
pick up his crumbs; and general hilarity prevails.
Virtue has had her day; and henceforward, *Virtu,* so
nearly the same thing as to differ only by a single letter
— (which surely is not worth haggling or higgling
about) — *Virtu,* I repeat, and Connoisseurship, have
leave to provide for themselves. Upon this principle,
gentlemen I propose to guide your studies, from Cain to
Mr. Thurtell. Through this great gallery of murder,
therefore, together let us wander hand in hand, in de-

lighted admiration; while I endeavor to point your attention to the objects of profitable criticism.

The first murder is familiar to you all. As the inventor of murder, and the father of the art, Cain must have been a man of first-rate genius. All the Cains were men of genius. Tubal Cain invented tubes, I think, or some such thing. But, whatever might be the originality and genius of the artist, every art was then in its infancy, and the works must be criticized with a recollection of that fact. Even Tubal's work would probably be little approved at this day in Sheffield; and therefore of Cain (Cain senior, I mean) it is no disparagement to say, that his performance was but so-so. Milton, however, is supposed to have thought differently. By his way of relating the case, it should seem to have been rather a pet murder with him, for he retouches it with an apparent anxiety for its picturesque effect : —

> ' Whereat he inly raged; and, as they talk'd,
> Smote him into the midriff with a stone
> That beat out life: he fell; and, deadly pale,
> Groan'd out his soul *with gushing blood effused.*'
> *Par. Lost,* B. **xi.**

Upon this, Richardson the painter, who had an eye for effect, remarks as follows, in his ' Notes on Paradise Lost,' p. 497 : — ' It has been thought,' says he, ' that Cain beat (as the common saying is) the breath out of his brother's body with a great stone; Milton gives in to this, with the addition, however, of a large wound.' In this place it was a judicious addition; for the rudeness of the weapon, unless raised and enriched by a warm, sanguinary coloring, has too much

of the naked air of the savage school; as if the deed
were perpetrated by a Polypheme without science, pre-
meditation, or anything but a mutton bone. However, I am chiefly pleased with the improvement, as it
implies that Milton was an amateur. As to Shakspeare, there never was a better; witness his description of the murdered Duncan, Banquo, &c.; and,
above all, witness his incomparable miniature, in
' Henry VI.,' of the murdered Gloucester.[2]

The foundation of the art having been once laid, it
is pitiable to see how it slumbered without improvement for ages. In fact, I shall now be obliged to leap
over all murders, sacred and profane, as utterly unworthy of notice, until long after the Christian era.
Greece, even in the age of Pericles, produced no murder, or at least none is recorded, of the slightest merit;
and Rome had too little originality of genius in any of
the arts to succeed where her model failed her.[3]  In
fact, the Latin language sinks under the very idea of
murder. ' The man was murdered;' — how will this
sound in Latin? *Interfectus est, interemptus est* —
which simply expresses a homicide; and hence the
Christian Latinity of the middle ages was obliged to
introduce a new word, such as the feebleness of classic
conceptions never ascended to. *Murdratus est*, says
the sublimer dialect of the Gothic ages. Meantime, the
Jewish school of murder kept alive whatever was yet
known in the art, and gradually transferred it to the
Western World. Indeed, the Jewish school was always respectable, even in its medieval stages, as the
case of Hugh of Lincoln shows, which was honored
with the approbation of Chaucer, on occasion of another
performance from the same school, which he puts into
the mouth of the Lady Abbess.

Recurring, however, for one moment, to classical antiquity, I cannot but think that Catiline, Clodius, and some of that coterie, would have made first-rate artists ; and it is on all accounts to be regretted, that the priggism of Cicero robbed his country of the only chance she had for distinction in this line. As the *subject* of a murder, no person could have answered better than himself. Oh Gemini ! how he would have howled with panic, if he had heard Cethegus under his bed. It would have been truly diverting to have listened to him ; and satisfied I am, gentlemen, that he would have preferred the *utile* of creeping into a closet, or even into a *cloaca*, to the *honestum* of facing the bold artist.

To come now to the dark ages — (by which we that speak with precision mean, *par excellence*, the tenth century as a meridian line, and the two centuries immediately before and after, full midnight being from A. D. 888 to A. D. 1111) — these ages ought naturally to be favorable to the art of murder, as they were to church architecture, to stained glass, &c. ; and, accordingly, about the latter end of this period, there arose a great character in our art, I mean the Old Man of the Mountains. He was a shining light, indeed, and I need not tell you, that the very word 'assassin' is deduced from him. So keen an amateur was he, that on one occasion, when his own life was attempted by a favorite assassin, he was so much pleased with the talent shown, that, notwithstanding the failure of the artist, he created him a duke upon the spot, with remainder to the female line, and settled a pension on him for three lives. Assassination is a branch of the art which demands a separate notice ; and it is possible

that I may devote an entire lecture to it.   Meantime,
I shall only observe how odd it is, that this branch of
the art has flourished by intermitting fits.   It never
rains, but it pours.   Our own age can boast of some
fine specimens, such, for instance, as Bellingham's
affair with the prime minister Percival, the Duc de
Berri's case at the Parisian Opera House, the Maré-
chal Bessieres' case at Avignon ; and about two and a
half centuries ago, there was a most brilliant constellation of murders in this class.   I need hardly say, that
I allude especially to those seven splendid works —
the assassinations of William I., of Orange ; of the
three French Henries, viz., — Henri, Duke of Guise,
that had a fancy for the throne of France; of Henry III.,
last prince in the line of Valois, who then occupied
that throne ; and finally of Henri IV., his brother-in-
law, who succeeded to that throne as first prince in the
line of Bourbon ; not eighteen years later came the
5th on that roll, viz., that of our Duke of Buckingham,
(which you will find excellently described in the letters
published by Sir Henry Ellis, of the British Museum),
6thly, of Gustavus Adolphus, and 7thly, of Wallen-
stein.   What a glorious Pleiad of murders !   And it
increases one's admiration — that this bright constellation of artistic displays, comprehending 3 Majesties, 3
Serene Highnesses, and 1 Excellency, all lay within so
narrow a field of time as between A. D. 1588 and 1635.
The King of Sweden's assassination, by the by, is
doubted by many writers, Harte amongst others ; but
they are wrong.   He was murdered ; and I consider
his murder unique in its excellence ; for he was murdered at noon-day, and on the field of battle — a feature of original conception, which occurs in no other

work of art that I remember. To conceive the idea of a secret murder on private account, as enclosed within a little parenthesis on a vast stage of public battle-carnage, is like Hamlet's subtle device of a tragedy within a tragedy. Indeed, all of these assassinations may be studied with profit by the advanced connois-seur. They are all of them *exemplaria* model murders, pattern murders, of which one may say, —

‘ Nocturnâ versate manu, versate diurna; ’

especially *nocturnâ*.

In these assassinations of princes and statesmen, there is nothing to excite our wonder; important changes often depend on their deaths; and, from the eminence on which they stand, they are peculiarly ex-posed to the aim of every artist who happens to be possessed by the craving for scenical effect. But there is another class of assassinations, which has prevailed from an early period of the seventeenth century, that really *does* surprise me: I mean the assassination of philosophers. For, gentlemen, it is a fact, that every philosopher of eminence for the two last centuries has either been murdered, or, at the least, been very near it; insomuch, that if a man calls himself a philosopher, and never had his life attempted, rest assured there is nothing in him; and against Locke's philosophy in particular, I think it an unanswerable objection (if we needed any), that, although he carried his throat about with him in this world for seventy-two years, no man ever condescended to cut it. As these cases of philos-ophers are not much known, and are generally good and well composed in their circumstances, I shall here read an excursus on that subject, chiefly by way of showing my own learning.

The first great philosopher of the seventeenth century (if we except Bacon and Galileo) was Des Cartes; and if ever one could say of a man that he was all *but* murdered — murdered within an inch — one must say it of him. The case was this, as reported by Baillet in his 'Vie De M. Des Cartes,' tom. I. p. 102 – 3. In the year 1621, when Des Cartes might be about twenty-six years old, he was touring about as usual (for he was as restless as a hyena); and, coming to the Elbe, either at Gluckstadt or at Hamburg, he took shipping for East Friezland. What he could want in East Friezland no man has ever discovered; and perhaps he took this into consideration himself; for, on reaching Embden, he resolved to sail instantly for *West* Friezland; and being very impatient of delay, he hired a bark, with a few mariners to navigate it. No sooner had he got out to sea, than he made a pleasing discovery, viz., that he had shut himself up in a den of murderers. His crew, says M. Baillet, he soon found out to be 'des scélérats' — not *amateurs*, gentlemen, as we are, but professional men — the height of whose ambition at that moment was to cut his individual throat. But the story is too pleasing to be abridged; I shall give it, therefore, accurately, from the French of his biographer: " M. Des Cartes had no company but that of his servant, with whom he was conversing in French. The sailors, who took him for a foreign merchant, rather than a cavalier, concluded that he must have money about him. Accordingly, they came to a resolution by no means advantageous to his purse. There is this difference, however, between sea-robbers and the robbers in forests, that the latter may, without hazard, spare the lives of their victims; whereas the others cannot put a passenger on shore in such a case without running the risk of being apprehended. The crew of M. Des Cartes arranged their measures with a view to evade any danger of that sort. They observed that he was a stranger from a distance, without acquaintance in the country, and that nobody would take any trouble to inquire about him, in case he should never come to hand (*quand il viendroit à manquer*).' Think, gentlemen, of these Friezland dogs discussing a philosopher as if he were a puncheon of rum consigned to some ship-broker. 'His temper, they remarked, was very mild and patient; and, judging from the gentleness of his deportment, and the courtesy with which he treated themselves, that he could be nothing more than some green young man, without station or root in the world, they concluded that they should have all the easier task in disposing of his life. They made no scruple to discuss the whole matter in his presence, as not supposing that he understood any other language than that in which he conversed with his servant; and the amount of their deliberation was — to murder him, then to throw him into the sea, and to divide his spoils.'

Excuse my laughing, gentlemen; but the fact is, I always *do* laugh when I think of this case — two things about it seem so droll. One is, the horrid panic or 'funk' (as the men of Eton call it) in which Des Cartes must have found himself, upon hearing this regular drama sketched for his own death — funeral — succession and administration to his effects. But another thing which seems to me still more funny about this affair is, that if these Friezland hounds had

been 'game,' we should have no Cartesian philosophy; and how we could have done without *that*, considering the world of books it has produced, I leave
to any respectable trunk-maker to declare.

However, to go on: spite of his enormous funk,
Des Cartes showed fight, and by that means awed
these Anti-Cartesian rascals. 'Finding,' says M.
Baillet, 'that the matter was no joke, M. Des Cartes
leaped upon his feet in a trice, assumed a stern countenance that these cravens had never looked for, and,
addressing them in their own language, threatened to
run them through on the spot if they dared to give
him any insult.' Certainly, gentlemen, this would
have been an honor far above the merits of such inconsiderable rascals — to be spitted like larks upon a
Cartesian sword; and therefore I am glad M. Des
Cartes did not rob the gallows by executing his threat,
especially as he could not possibly have brought his
vessel to port, after he had murdered his crew; so
that he must have continued to cruise for ever in the
Zuyder Zee, and would probably have been mistaken
by sailors for the *Flying Dutchman*, homeward bound.
'The spirit which M. Des Cartes manifested,' says
his biographer, 'had the effect of magic on these
wretches. The suddenness of their consternation
struck their minds with a confusion which blinded
them to their advantage, and they conveyed him to his
destination as peaceably as he could desire.'

Possibly, gentlemen, you may fancy that, on the
model of Cæsar's address to his poor ferryman — '*Cæ-
sarem vehis et fortunas ejus*' — M. Des Cartes needed
only to have said, 'Dogs, you cannot cut my throat,
for you carry Des Cartes and his philosophy,' and

might safely have defied them to do their worst. A German emperor had the same notion, when, being cautioned to keep out of the way of a cannonading, he replied, 'Tut! man. Did you ever hear of a cannon-ball that killed an emperor?'[4] As to an emperor I cannot say, but a less thing has sufficed to smash a philosopher; and the next great philosopher of Europe undoubtedly *was* murdered. This was Spinosa.

I know very well the common opinion about him is, that he died in his bed. Perhaps he did, but he was murdered for all that; and this I shall prove by a book published at Brussels in the year 1731, entitled 'La Vie de Spinosa, par M. Jean Colerns,' with many additions, from a MS. life, by one of his friends. Spinosa died on the 21st February, 1677, being then little more than forty-four years old. This, of itself, looks suspicious; and M. Jean admits, that a certain expression in the MS. life of him would warrant the conclusion, 'que sa mort n'a pas été-à-fait naturelle.' Living in a damp country, and a sailor's country, like Holland, he may be thought to have indulged a good deal in grog, especially in punch,[5] which was then newly discovered. Undoubtedly he might have done so; but the fact is, that he did not. M. Jean calls him ' extrêmement sobre en son boire et en son manger.' And though some wild stories were afloat about his using the juice of mandragora (p. 140) and opium (p. 144), yet neither of these articles is found in his druggist's bill. Living, therefore, with such sobriety, how was it possible that he should die a natural death at forty-four? Hear his biographer's account : — 'Sunday morning, the 21st of February, before it was church time, Spinosa came down stairs, and conversed

with the master and mistress of the house. At this
time, therefore, perhaps ten o'clock on Sunday morning, you see that Spinosa was alive, and pretty well.
But it seems ' he had summoned from Amsterdam a
certain physician, whom,' says the biographer, ' I shall
not otherwise point out to notice than by these two
letters, L. M.'  This L. M. had directed the people of
the house to purchase ' an ancient cock,' and to have
him boiled forthwith, in order that Spinosa might take
some broth about noon ; which in fact he did ; and ate
some of the *old cock* with a good appetite, after the
landlord and his wife had returned from church.

' In the afternoon, L. M. staid alone with Spinosa,
the people of the house having returned to church ; on
coming out from which, they learned, with much surprise, that Spinosa had died about three o'clock, in the
presence of L. M., who took his departure for Amsterdam that same evening, by the night-boat, without
paying the least attention to the deceased,' and probably without paying very much attention to the payment of his own little account.  ' No doubt he was
the readier to dispense with these duties, as he had
possessed himself of a ducatoon, and a small quantity
of silver, together with a silver-hafted knife, and had
absconded with his pillage.'  Here you see, gentlemen, the murder is plain, and the manner of it.  It
was L. M. who murdered Spinosa for his money.  Poor
Spinosa was an invalid, meagre and weak: as no blood
was observed, L. M. no doubt threw him down, and
smothered him with pillows — the poor man being
already half suffocated by his infernal dinner.  After
masticating that ' ancient cock,' which I take to mean
a cock of the preceding century, in what condition

could the poor invalid find nimself for a stand-up fight
with L. M.? But who was L. M.? It surely never
could be Lindley Murray, for I saw him at York in
1825; and, besides, I do not think he would do such
a thing — at least, not to a brother grammarian: for you
know, gentlemen, that Spinosa wrote a very respectable
Hebrew grammar.

Hobbes — but why, or on what principle, I never
could understand — was not murdered. This was a
capital oversight of the professional men of the seventeenth century; because in every light he was a fine
subject for murder, except, indeed, that he was lean
and skinny; for I can prove that he had money, and
(what is very funny) he had no right to make the least
resistance; since, according to himself, irresistible
power creates the very highest species of right, sc
that it is rebellion of the blackest dye to refuse to be
murdered, when a competent force appears to murder
you. However, gentlemen, though he was not murdered, I am happy to assure you that (by his own account) he was three times very near being murdered,
which is consolatory. The first time was in the spring
of 1640, when he pretends to have circulated a little
MS. on the king's behalf against the Parliament; he
never could produce this MS., by the by; but he says,
that, ' Had not His Majesty dissolved the Parliament '
(in May), ' it had brought him into danger of his life.'
Dissolving the Parliament, however, was of no use;
for in November of the same year the Long Parliament
assembled, and Hobbes, a second time fearing he should
be murdered, ran away to France. This looks like the
madness of John Dennis, who thought that Louis XIV.
would never make peace with Queen Anne, unless he

(Dennis, to wit) were given up to French vengeance;
and actually ran away from the sea-coast under that
belief.   In France, Hobbes managed to take care of his
throat pretty well for ten years; but at the end of that
time, by way of paying court to Cromwell, he published his 'Leviathan.'   The old coward now began
to 'funk' horribly for the third time; he fancied the
swords of the cavaliers were constantly at his throat,
recollecting how they had served the Parliament ambassadors at the Hague and Madrid.   'Tum,' says
he, in his dog-Latin life of himself,

> 'Tum venit in mentem mihi Dorislaus et Ascham ;
> Tanquam proscripto terror ubique aderat.'

And accordingly he ran home to England.   Now, certainly, it is very true that a man deserved a cudgelling
for writing 'Leviathan;' and two or three cudgel-
lings for writing a pentameter ending so villanously as
'terror ubique aderat!'   But no man ever thought
him worthy of anything beyond cudgelling.   And, in
fact, the whole story is a bounce of his own.   For, in
a most abusive letter which he wrote 'to a learned
person' (meaning Wallis the mathematician), he gives
quite another account of the matter, and says (p. 8),
he ran home 'because he would not trust his safety
with the French clergy;' insinuating that he was likely
to be murdered for his religion, which would have been
a high joke indeed — Tom's being brought to the stake
for religion.

Bounce or not bounce, however, certain it is that
Hobbes, to the end of his life, feared that somebody
would murder him.   This is proved by the story I am
going to tell you: it is not from a manuscript, but (as
Mr. Coleridge says) it is as good as manuscript; for it

comes from a book now entirely forgotten, viz., 'The
Creed of Mr. Hobbes Examined : in a Conference between him and a Student in Divinity' (published
about ten years before Hobbes's death). The book is
anonymous, but it was written by Tennison, the same
who, about thirty years after, succeeded Tillotson as
Archbishop of Canterbury. The introductory anecdote
is as follows : — ' A certain divine' (no doubt Tennison himself) ' took an annual tour of one month to
different parts of the island." In one of these excursions (1670), he visited the Peak in Derbyshire, partly
in consequence of Hobbes's description of it. Being
in that neighborhood, he could not but pay a visit to
Buxton ; and at the very moment of his arrival, he was
fortunate enough to find a party of gentlemen dis-
mounting at the inn-door, amongst whom was a long
thin fellow, who turned out to be no less a person than
Mr. Hobbes, who probably had ridden over from Chatsworth.[6]   Meeting so great a lion, a tourist, in search
of the picturesque, could do no less than present himself in the character of bore. And luckily for this
scheme, two of Mr. Hobbes's companions were suddenly
summoned away by express ; so that, for the rest of his
stay at Buxton, he had Leviathan entirely to himself,
and had the honor of bowsing with him in the evening.   Hobbes, it seems, at first showed a good deal of
stiffness, for he was shy of divines ; but this wore off,
and he became very sociable and funny, and they
agreed to go into the bath together. How Tennison
could venture to gambol in the same water with Leviathan, I cannot explain ; but so it was : they frolicked
about like two dolphins, though Hobbes must have
been as old as the hills ; and 'in those intervals

wherein they abstained from swimming and plunging themselves ' (*i. e.*, diving), ' they discoursed of many things relating to the Baths of the Ancients, and the Origine of Springs. When they had in this manner passed away an hour, they stepped out of the bath; and, having dried and cloathed themselves, they sate down in expectation of such a supper as the place afforded; designing to refresh themselves like the *Deipnosophistæ*, and rather to reason than to drink profoundly. But in this innocent intention they were interrupted by the disturbance arising from a little quarrel, in which some of the ruder people in the house were for a short time engaged. At this Mr. Hobbes seemed much concerned, though he was at some distance from the persons.' And why was he concerned, gentlemen? No doubt, you fancy, from some benign and disinterested love of peace worthy of an old man and a philosopher. But listen — ' For a while he was not composed, but related it once or twice as to himself, with a low and careful, *i. e.* anxious, tone, how Sextus Roscius was murthered after supper by the Balneæ Palatinæ. Of such general extent is that remark of Cicero, in relation to Epicurus the Atheist, of whom he observed, that he of all men dreaded most those things which he contemned — Death and the Gods.' Merely because it was supper time, and in the neighborhood of a bath, Mr. Hobbes must have the fate of Sextus Roscius. He must be mur*th*ered, because Sextus Roscius was mur*th*ered. What logic was there in this, unless to a man who was always dreaming of murder? Here was Leviathan, no longer afraid of the daggers of English cavaliers or French clergy, but ' frightened from his propriety ' by a row in an ale-house between some honest clodhoppers of Derbyshire, whom his own gaunt scarecrow of a person, that belonged to quite another century, would have frightened out of their wits.

Malebranche, it will give you pleasure to hear, was murdered. The man who murdered him is well known: it was Bishop Berkeley. The story is familiar, though hitherto not put in a proper light. Berkeley, when a young man, went to Paris, and called on Père Malebranche. He found him in his cell cooking. Cooks have ever been a *genus irritabile*; authors still more so. Malebranche was both. A dispute arose; the old father, warm already, became warmer; culinary and metaphysical irritations united to derange his liver: he took to his bed and died. Such is the common version of the story. 'So the whole ear of Denmark is abused.' The fact is, that the matter was hushed up, out of consideration for Berkeley, who (as Pope justly observes) had 'every virtue under heaven:' else it was well known that Berkeley, feeling himself nettled by the waspishness of the old Frenchman, squared at him; a *turn-up* was the consequence; Malebranche was floored in the first round; the conceit was wholly taken out of him; and he would perhaps have given in; but Berkeley's blood was now up, and he insisted on the old Frenchman's retracting his doctrine of Occasional Causes. The vanity of the man was too great for this; and he fell a sacrifice to the impetuosity of Irish youth, combined with his own absurd obstinacy.

Leibnitz, being every way superior to Malebranche, one might, *a fortiori*, have counted on *his* being murdered; which, however, was not the case. I believe

he was nettled at this neglect, and felt himself insulted
by the security in which he passed his days. In no
other way can I explain his conduct at the latter end
of his life, when he chose to grow very avaricious,
and to hoard up large sums of gold, which he kept in
his own house. This was at Vienna, where he died;
and letters are still in existence, describing the immeasurable anxiety which he entertained for his throat.
Still his ambition, for being *attempted* at least, was so
great, that he would not forego the danger. A late
English pedagogue, of Birmingham manufacture — viz.,
Dr. Parr — took a more selfish course under the same
circumstance. He had amassed a considerable quantity of gold and silver plate, which was for some time
deposited in his bedroom at his parsonage house, Hatton. But growing every day more afraid of being
murdered, which he knew that he could not stand
(and to which, indeed, he never had the slightest pretensions), he transferred the whole to the Hatton
blacksmith; conceiving, no doubt, that the murder of
a blacksmith would fall more lightly on the *salus
reipublicæ*, than that of a pedagogue. But I have
heard this greatly disputed; and it seems now generally agreed, that one good horseshoe is worth about
two and a quarter Spital sermons.[7]

As Leibnitz, though not murdered, may be said to
have died, partly of the fear that he should be murdered, and partly of vexation that he was not, Kant,
on the other hand — who manifested no ambition in
that way — had a narrower escape from a murderer
than any man we read of, except Des Cartes. So absurdly does fortune throw about her favors! The
case is told, I think, in an anonymous life of this very

great man.  For health's sake, Kant imposed upon himself, at one time, a walk of six miles every day along a high-road.  This fact becoming known to a man who had his private reasons for committing murder, at the third milestone from Königsberg, he waited for his 'intended,' who came up to time as duly as a mail-coach.

But for an accident, Kant was a dead man.  This accident lay in the scrupulous, or what Mrs. Quickly would have called the *peevish*, morality of the murderer.  An old professor, he fancied, might be laden with sins.  Not so a young child.  On this consideration, he turned away from Kant at the critical moment, and soon after murdered a child of five years old.  Such is the German account of the matter; but my opinion is, that the murderer was an amateur, who felt how little would be gained to the cause of good taste by murdering an old, arid, and adust metaphysician; there was no room for display, as the man could not possibly look more like a mummy when dead, than he had done alive.

Thus, gentlemen, I have traced the connection between philosophy and our art, until insensibly I find that I have wandered into our own era.  This I shall not take any pains to characterize apart from that which preceded it, for, in fact, they have no distinct character.  The seventeenth and eighteenth centuries, together with so much of the nineteenth as we have yet seen, jointly compose the Augustan age of murder.  The finest work of the seventeenth century is, unquestionably, the murder of Sir Edmondbury Godfrey, which has my entire approbation.  In the grand fea-

ture of *mystery*, which in some shape or other ought
to color every judicious attempt at murder, it is excellent; for the mystery is not yet dispersed. The
attempt to fasten the murder upon the Papists, which
would injure it as much as some well-known Correg-
gios have been injured by the professional picture-
cleaners, or would even ruin it by translating it into
the spurious class of mere political or partisan murders,
thoroughly wanting in the murderous *animus*, I exhort
the society to discountenance. In fact, this notion is
altogether baseless, and arose in pure Protestant
fanaticism. Sir Edmondbury had not distinguished
himself amongst the London magistrates by any sever-
ity against the Papists, or in favoring the attempts of
zealots to enforce the penal laws against individuals.
He had not armed against himself the animosities of
any religious sect whatever. And as to the droppings
of wax lights upon the dress of the corpse when first
discovered in a ditch, from which it was inferred at
the time that the priests attached to the Popish
Queen's Chapel had been concerned in the murder,
either these were mere fraudulent artifices devised by
those who wished to fix the suspicion upon the Papists, or else the whole allegation — wax-droppings,
and the suggested cause of the droppings — might be
a bounce or fib of Bishop Burnet; who, as the Duchess
of Portsmouth used to say, was the one great master
of fibbing and romancing in the seventeenth century.
At the same time, it must be observed that the quantity of murder was not great in Sir Edmondbury's
century, at least amongst our own artists; which, perhaps, is attributable to the want of enlightened patronage. *Sint Mæcenates, non deerunt, Flacce, Marones.*

Consulting Grant's 'Observations on the Bills of Mortality' (4th edition, Oxford, 1665), I find, that, out of 229,250, who died in London during one period of twenty years in the seventeenth century, not more than eighty-six were murdered; that is, about four three-tenths per annum. A small number this, gentlemen, to found an academy upon; and certainly, where the quantity is so small, we have a right to expect that the quality should be first-rate. Perhaps it was; yet still I am of opinion that the best artist in this century was not equal to the best in that which followed. For instance, however praiseworthy the case of Sir Edmondbury Godfrey may be (and nobody can be more sensible of its merits than I am), still, I cannot consent to place it on a level with that of Mrs. Ruscombe of Bristol, either as to originality of design, or boldness and breadth of style. This good lady's murder took place early in the reign of George III. — a reign which was notoriously favorable to the arts generally. She lived in College Green, with a single maid-servant, neither of them having any pretension to the notice of history but what they derived from the great artist whose workmanship I am recording. One fine morning, when all Bristol was alive and in motion, some suspicion arising, the neighbors forced an entrance into the house, and found Mrs. Ruscombe murdered in her bedroom, and the servant murdered on the stairs. This was at noon; and, not more than two hours before, both mistress and servant had been seen alive. To the best of my remembrance, this was in 1764; upwards of sixty years, therefore, have now elapsed, and yet the artist is still undiscovered. The suspicions of posterity have settled upon two pretend-

ers — a baker and a chimney-sweeper. But posterity
is wrong; no unpractised artist could have conceived
so bold an idea as that of a noonday murder in the
heart of a great city. It was no obscure baker, gentlemen, or anonymous chimney-sweeper, be assured, that
executed this work. I know who it was. (*Here there
was a general buzz, which at length broke out into
open applause; upon which the lecturer blushed, and
went on with much earnestness.*) For Heaven's sake,
gentlemen, do not mistake me; it was not I that did
it. I have not the vanity to think myself equal to any
such achievement; be assured that you greatly over-
rate my poor talents; Mrs. Ruscombe's affair was far
beyond my slender abilities. But I came to know
who the artist was, from a celebrated surgeon who
assisted at his dissection. This gentleman had a private museum in the way of his profession, one corner
of which was occupied by a cast from a man of remarkably fine proportions.

'That,' said the surgeon, 'is a cast from the celebrated Lancashire highwayman, who concealed his profession for some time from his neighbors, by drawing
woollen stockings over his horse's legs, and in that
way muffling the clatter which he must else have made
in riding up a flagged alley that led to his stable. At
the time of his execution for highway robbery, I was
studying under Cruickshank: and the man's figure
was so uncommonly fine, that no money or exertion
was spared to get into possession of him with the least
possible delay. By the connivance of the under-
sheriff, he was cut down within the legal time, and
instantly put into a chaise-and-four; so that, when he
reached Cruickshank's, he was positively not dead.

Mr. ——, a young student at that time, had the honor
of giving him the *coup de grace*, and finishing the sentence of the law.' This remarkable anecdote, which
seemed to imply that all the gentlemen in the dissect-
ing-room were amateurs of our class, struck me a good
deal ; and I was repeating it one day to a Lancashire
lady, who thereupon informed me, that she had herself
lived in the neighborhood of that highwayman, and
well remembered two circumstances, which combined,
in the opinion of all his neighbors, to fix upon him the
credit of Mrs. Ruscombe's affair. One was, the fact
of his absence for a whole fortnight at the period of
that murder ; the other, that, within a very little time
after, the neighborhood of this highwayman was deluged with dollars. Now, Mrs. Ruscombe was known
to have hoarded about two thousand of that coin. Be
the artist, however, who he might, the affair remains a
durable monument of his genius ; for such was the impression of awe, and the sense of power left behind, by
the strength of conception manifested in this murder,
that no tenant (as I was told in 1810) had been found
up to that time for Mrs. Ruscombe's house.

But, whilst I thus eulogize the Ruscombian case, let
me not be supposed to overlook the many other specimens of extraordinary merit spread over the face of this
century. Such cases, indeed, as that of Miss Bland, or
of Captain Donnellan, and Sir Theophilus Boughton,
shall never have any countenance from me. Fie on
these dealers in poison, say I : can they not keep to
the old honest way of cutting throats, without introducing such abominable innovations from Italy ? I
consider all these poisoning cases, compared with the
legitimate style, as no better than waxwork by the

side of sculpture, or a lithographic print by the side of
a fine Volpato. But, dismissing these, there remain
many excellent works of art in a pure style, such as
nobody need be ashamed to own ; and this every candid connoisseur will admit. *Candid*, observe, I say ;
for great allowances must be made in these cases ; no
artist can ever be sure of carrying through his own fine
preconception. Awkward disturbances will arise ;
people will not submit to have their throats cut
quietly ; they will run, they will kick, they will bite ;
and whilst the portrait painter often has to complain
of too much torpor in his subject, the artist in our line
is generally embarrassed by too much animation. ˙At
the same time, however disagreeable to the artist, this
tendency in murder to excite and irritate the subject is
certainly one of its advantages to the world in general,
which we ought not to overlook, since it favors the
development of latent talent. Jeremy Taylor notices
with admiration the extraordinary leaps which people
will take under the influence of fear. There was a
striking instance of this in the recent case of the
M'Keans : the boy cleared a height, such as he will
never clear again to his dying day. Talents also of
the most brilliant description for thumping, and, indeed, for all the gymnastic exercises, have sometimes
been developed by the panic which accompanies our
artists ; talents else buried and hid under a bushel, to
the possessors as much as to their friends. I remember an interesting illustration of this fact, in a case
which I learned in Germany.

Riding one day in the neighborhood of Munich, I
overtook a distinguished amateur of our society, whose
name, for obvious reasons, I shall conceal. This gen-

tleman informed me that, finding himself wearied with the frigid pleasures (such he esteemed them) of mere amateurship, he had quitted England for the Continent — meaning to practise a little professionally. For this purpose he resorted to Germany, conceiving the police in that part of Europe to be more heavy and drowsy than elsewhere. His *debut* as a practitioner took place at Mannheim; and, knowing me to be a brother amateur, he freely communicated the whole of his maiden adventure. 'Opposite to my lodging,' said he, 'lived a baker; he was somewhat of a miser, and lived quite alone. Whether it were his great expanse of chalky face, or what else, I know not, but the fact was, I "fancied" him, and resolved to commence business upon his throat, which, by the way, he always carried bare — a fashion which is very irritating to my desires. Precisely at eight o'clock in the evening, I observed that he regularly shut up his windows. One night I watched him when thus engaged — bolted in after him — locked the door — and, addressing him with great suavity, acquainted him with the nature of my errand; at the same time advising him to make no resistance, which would be mutually unpleasant. So saying, I drew out my tools; and was proceeding to operate But at this spectacle the baker, who seemed to have been struck by catalepsy at my first announcement, awoke into tremendous agitation. 'I will *not* be murdered!' he shrieked aloud; 'what for will I' (meaning *shall* I) 'lose my precious throat?' 'What for?' said I; 'if for no other reason, for this — that you put alum into your bread. But no matter, alum or no alum' (for I was resolved to forestall any argument on that point), 'know that I am a virtuoso in the **art of**

murder — am desirous of improving myself in its
details — and am enamored of your vast surface of
throat, to which I am determined to be a customer.'
' Is it so?' said he, ' but I'll find you a customer in
another line;' and so saying, he threw himself into a
boxing attitude. The very idea of his boxing struck
me as ludicrous. It is true, a London baker had distinguished himself in the ring, and became known to
fame under the title of the Master of the Rolls; but
he was young and unspoiled; whereas, this man was
a monstrous feather-bed in person, fifty years old, and
totally out of condition. Spite of all this, however,
and contending against me, who am a master in the
art, he made so desperate a defence, that many times I
feared he might turn the tables upon me; and that I,
an amateur, might be murdered by a rascally baker.
What a situation! Minds of sensibility will sympathize with my anxiety. How severe it was, you may
understand by this, that for the first thirteen rounds
the baker positively had the advantage. Round the
14th, I received a blow on the right eye, which closed
it up; in the end, I believe, this was my salvation;
for the anger it roused in me was so great, that, in the
next, and every one of the three following rounds, I
floored the baker.

' Round 19th. The baker came up piping, and
manifestly the worse for wear. His geometrical ex-
ploits in the four last rounds had done him no good.
However, he showed some skill in stopping a message which I was sending to his cadaverous mug; in
delivering which, my foot slipped, and I went down.

' Round 20th. Surveying the baker, I became
ashamed of having been so much bothered by a shape-

less mass of dough ; and I went in fiercely, and administered some severe punishment. A rally took place — both went down — baker undermost — ten to three on amateur.

'Round 21st. The baker jumped up with surprising agility ; indeed, he managed his pins capitally, and fought wonderfully, considering that he was drenched in perspiration ; but the shine was now taken out of him, and his game was the mere effect of panic. It was now clear that he could not last much longer. In the course of this round we tried the weaving system, in which I had greatly the advantage, and hit him repeatedly on the conk. My reason for this was, that his conk was covered with carbuncles ; and I thought I should vex him by taking such liberties with his conk, which in fact I did.

'The three next rounds, the master of the rolls staggered about like a cow on the ice. Seeing how matters stood, in round 24th I whispered something into his ear, which sent him down like a shot. It was nothing more than my private opinion of the value of his throat at an annuity office. This little confidential whisper affected him greatly ; the very perspiration was frozen on his face, and for the next two rounds I had it all my own way. And when I called *time* for the 27th round, he lay like a log on the floor.'

After which, said I to the amateur, ' It may be presumed that you accomplished your purpose.' ' You are right,' said he mildly, ' I did ; and a great satisfaction, you know, it was to my mind, for by this means I killed two birds with one stone ; ' meaning that he had both thumped the baker and murdered him. Now, for the life of me, I could not see *that* ; for, on

5

the contrary, to my mind it appeared that he had
taken two stones to kill one bird, having been obliged
to take the conceit out of him first with his fist, and then
with his tools. But no matter for his logic. The
moral of his story was good, for it showed what an
astonishing stimulus to latent talent is contained in
any reasonable prospect of being murdered. A pursy,
.unwieldy, half cataleptic baker of Mannheim had
absolutely fought seven-and-twenty rounds with an
accomplished English boxer, merely upon this inspiration ; so great was natural genius exalted and sublimed
by the genial presence of his murderer.

Really, gentlemen, when one hears of such things
as these, it becomes a duty, perhaps, a little to soften
that extreme asperity with which most men speak of
murder. To hear people talk, you would suppose
that all the disadvantages and inconveniences were on
the side of being murdered, and that there were none
at all in *not* being murdered. But considerate men
think otherwise. ' Certainly,' says Jeremy Taylor,
' it is a less temporal evil to fall by the rudeness of a
sword than the violence of a fever : and the axe ' (to
which he might have added the ship-carpenter's mallet
and the crowbar), ' a much less affliction than a stran-
gury.' Very true ; the bishop talks like a wise man
and an amateur, as I am sure he was ; and another
great philosopher, Marcus Aurelius, was equally above
the vulgar prejudices on this subject. He declares
it to be one of ' the noblest functions of reason to
know whether it is time to walk out of the world or
not.' (Book iii., Collers' Translation.) No sort of
knowledge being rarer than this, surely *that* man must
be a most philanthropic character, who undertakes to

instruct people in this branch of knowledge gratis, and at no little hazard to himself. All this, however, I throw out only in the way of speculation to future moralists; declaring in the meantime my own private conviction, that very few men commit murder upon philanthropic or patriotic principles, and repeating what I have already said once at least — that, as to the majority of murderers, they are very incorrect characters.

With respect to the Williams' murders, the sublimest and most entire in their excellence that ever were committed, I shall not allow myself to speak incidentally. Nothing less than an entire lecture, or even an entire course of lectures, would suffice to expound their merits. But one curious fact connected with his case I shall mention, because it seems to imply that the blaze of his genius absolutely dazzled the eye of criminal justice. You all remember, I doubt not, that the instruments with which he executed his first great work (the murder of the Marrs) were a ship-carpenter's mallet and a knife. Now, the mallet belonged to an old Swede, one John Peterson, and bore his initials. This instrument Williams left behind him in Marr's house, and it fell into the hands of the magistrates. But, gentlemen, it is a fact that the publication of this circumstance of the initials led immediately to the apprehension of Williams, and, if made earlier, would have prevented his second great work (the murder of the Williamsons), which took place precisely twelve days after. Yet the magistrates kept back this fact from the public for the entire twelve days, and until that second work was accomplished. That finished, they published it, apparently feeling that Williams had now done enough for his fame, and that his glory was at length placed beyond the reach of accident.

As to Mr. Thurtell's case, I know not what to say Naturally, I have every disposition to think highly of my predecessor in the chair of this society; and I acknowledge that his lectures were unexceptionable. But, speaking ingenuously, I do really think that his principal performance, as an artist, has been much overrated. I admit, that at first, I was myself carried away by the general enthusiasm. On the morning when the murder was made known in London, there was the fullest meeting of amateurs that I have ever known since the days of Williams; old bedridden connoisseurs, who had got into a peevish way of sneering and complaining ' that there was nothing doing,' now hobbled down to our club-room: such hilarity, such benign expression of general satisfaction, I have rarely witnessed. On every side you saw people shaking hands, congratulating each other, and forming dinner parties for the evening; and nothing was to be heard but triumphant challenges of — ' Well! will *this* do?' ' Is *this* the right thing?' 'Are you satisfied at last?' But in the middle of the row, I remember, we all grew silent, on hearing the old cynical amateur L. S—— stumping along with his wooden leg; he entered the room with his usual scowl; and, as he advanced, he continued to growl and stutter the whole way — 'Mere plagiarism — base plagiarism from hints that I threw out! Besides, his style is as harsh as Albert Durer, and as coarse as Fuseli.' Many thought that this was mere jealousy, and general waspishness; but I confess that, when the first glow of enthusiasm had subsided, I have found most judicious critics to agree that there was something *falsetto* in the style of Thurtell. The fact is, he was a member of our society, which naturally gave a friendly bias to our judgments; and his person was universally familiar to the 'fancy,' which gave him, with the whole London public, a temporary popularity, that his pretensions are not capable of supporting; for *opinionum commenta delet dies, naturæ judicia confirmat.* There was, however, an unfinished design of Thurtell's for the murder of a man with a pair of dumb-bells, which I admired greatly; it was a mere outline, that he never filled in; but to my mind it seemed every way superior to his chief work. I remember that there was great regret expressed by some amateurs that this sketch should have been left in an unfinished state: but there I cannot agree with them; for the fragments and first bold outlines of original artists have often a felicity about them which is apt to vanish in the management of the details.

The case of the M'Keans I consider far beyond the vaunted performance of Thurtell — indeed, above all praise; and bearing that relation, in fact, to the immortal works of Williams, which the 'Æneid' bears to the 'Iliad.'

But it is now time that I should say a few words about the principles of murder, not with a view to regulate your practice, but your judgment: as to old women, and the mob of newspaper readers, they are pleased with anything, provided it is bloody enough. But the mind of sensibility requires something more. *First*, then, let us speak of the kind of person who is adapted to the purpose of the murderer; *secondly*, of the place where; *thirdly*, of the time when, and other little circumstances.

As to the person, I suppose that it is evident that he ought to be a good man; because, if he were not, he might himself, by possibility, be contemplating murder at the very time; and such 'diamond-cut-diamond' tussles, though pleasant enough where nothing better is stirring, are really not what a critic can allow himself to call murders. I could mention some people (I name no names) who have been murdered by other people in a dark lane; and so far all seemed correct enough; but, on looking farther into the matter, the public have become aware that the murdered party was himself, at the moment, planning to rob his murderer, at the least, and possibly to murder him, if he had been strong enough. Whenever that is the case, or may be thought to be the case, farewell to all the genuine effects of the art. For the final purpose of murder, considered as a fine art, is precisely the same as that of tragedy, in Aristotle's account of it; viz., ' to cleanse the heart by means of pity and terror.' Now, terror there may be, but how can there be any pity for one tiger destroyed by another tiger?

It is also evident that the person selected ought not to be a public character. For instance, no judicious artist would have attempted to murder Abraham Newland.[8] For the case was this: everybody read so much about Abraham Newland, and so few people ever saw him, that to the general belief he was a mere abstract idea. And I remember, that once, when I happened to mention that I had dined at a coffee-house in company with Abraham Newland, everybody looked scornfully at me, as though I had pretended to

lave played at billiards with Prester John, or to have
nad an affair of honor with the Pope. And, by the
way, the Pope would be a very improper person to
murder: for he has such a virtual ubiquity as the
father of Christendom, and, like the cuckoo, is so
often heard but never seen, that I suspect most people
regard *him* also as an abstract idea. Where, indeed,
a public man is in the habit of giving dinners, ' with
every delicacy of the season,' the case is very different: every person is satisfied that *he* is no abstract
idea; and, therefore, there can be no impropriety in
murdering him, only that his murder will fall into the
class of assassinations, which I have not yet treated.

*Thirdly.* The subject chosen ought to be in good
health: for it is absolutely barbarous to murder a sick
person, who is usually quite unable to bear it. On
this principle, no tailor ought to be chosen who is
above twenty-five, for after that age he is sure to be
dyspeptic. Or at least, if a man will hunt in that
warren, he will of course think it his duty, on the old
established equation, to murder some multiple of 9 —
say 18, 27, or 36. And here, in this benign attention
to the comfort of sick people, you will observe the
usual effect of a fine art to soften and refine the feelings. The world in general, gentlemen, are very
bloody-minded; and all they want in a murder is a
copious effusion of blood; gaudy display in this point
is enough for *them.* But the enlightened connoisseur
is more refined in his taste; and from our art, as from
all the other liberal arts when thoroughly mastered,
the result is, to humanize the heart; so true is it, that

' Ingenuas didicisse fideliter artes,
Emollit mores, nec sinit esse feros.'

A philosophic friend, well known for his philan‑
thropy and general benignity, suggests that the subject
chosen ought also to have a family of young chil‑
dren wholly dependent upon his exertions, by way of
deepening the pathos. And, undoubtedly, this is a
judicious caution. Yet I would not insist too keenly
on such a condition. Severe good taste unquestiona‑
bly suggests it; but still, where the man was other‑
wise unobjectionable in point of morals and health, I
would not look with too curious a jealousy to a re‑
striction which might have the effect of narrowing the
artist's sphere.

So much for the person. As to the time, the place,
and the tools, I have many things to say, which at
present I have no room for. The good sense of the
practitioner has usually directed him to night and
privacy. Yet there have not been wanting cases
where this rule was departed from with excellent
effect. In respect to time, Mrs. Ruscombe's case is a
beautiful exception, which I have already noticed; and
in respect both to time and place, there is a fine ex‑
ception in the annals of Edinburgh (year 1805), familiar
to every child in Edinburgh, but which has unac‑
countably been defrauded of its due portion of fame
amongst English amateurs. The case I mean is that
of a porter to one of the banks, who was murdered,
whilst carrying a bag of money, in broad daylight, on
turning out of the High Street, one of the most public
streets in Europe; and the murderer is to this hour
undiscovered.

> ' Sed fugit interea, fugit irreparabile tempus,
> Singula dum capti circumvectamur amore.'

And now, gentlemen, in conclusion, let me again

solemnly disclaim all pretensions on my own part to the character of a professional man. I never attempted any murder in my life, except in the year 1801, upon the body of a tom-cat; and *that* turned out differently from my intention. My purpose, I own, was downright murder. 'Semper ego auditor tantum?' said I, 'nunquamne reponam?' And I went down stairs in search of Tom at one o'clock on a dark night, with the 'animus,' and no doubt with the fiendish looks, of a murderer. But when I found him, he was in the act of plundering the pantry of bread and other things. Now this gave a new turn to the affair; for the time being one of general scarcity, when even Christians were reduced to the use of potato-bread, rice-bread, and all sorts of things, it was downright treason in a tom-cat to be wasting good wheaten-bread in the way he was doing. It instantly became a patriotic duty to put him to death; and, as I raised aloft and shook the glittering steel, I fancied myself rising, like Brutus, effulgent from a crowd of patriots, and, as I stabbed him, I

'Call'd aloud on Tully's name,
And bade the father of his country hail!'

Since then, what wandering thoughts I may have had of attempting the life of an ancient ewe, of a superannuated hen, and such 'small deer,' are locked up in the secrets of my own breast; but, for the higher departments of the art, I confess myself to be utterly unfit. My ambition does not rise so high. No, gentlemen, in the words of Horace,

'Fungar vice cotis, acutum
Reddere quæ ferrum valet, exsors ipsa secandi.'

# SUPPLEMENTARY PAPER ON MURDER,

## CONSIDERED AS ONE OF THE FINE ARTS.

A GOOD many years ago, the reader may remember that I came forward in the character of a *dilettante* in murder. Perhaps *dilettante* is too strong a word. *Connoisseur* is better suited to the scruples and infirmity of public taste. I suppose there is no harm in *that*, at least. A man is not bound to put his eyes, ears, and understanding into his breeches-pocket when he meets with a murder. If he is not in a downright comatose state, I suppose he must see that one murder is better or worse than another, in point of good taste. Murders have their little differences and shades of merit, as well as statues, pictures, oratorios, cameos, intaglios, or what not. You may be angry with the man for talking too much, or too publicly (as to the too much, that I deny — a man can never cultivate his taste too highly); but you must allow him to think, at any rate. Well, would you believe it? all my neighbors came to hear of that little æsthetic essay which I had published; and, unfortunately, hearing at the very same time of a club that I was connected with, and a dinner at which I presided — both tending to the same little object as the essay, viz., the diffusion of a just taste among Her [9] Majesty's subjects, they got up the most barbarous calumnies against me. In particular, they said that I, or that the club (which comes to the

[58]

same thing), had offered bounties on well-conducted homicides — with a scale of drawbacks, in case of any one defect or flaw, according to a table issued to private friends. Now, let me tell the whole truth about the dinner and the club, and it will be seen how malicious the world is. But first, confidentially, allow me to say what my real principles are upon the matter in question.

As to murder, I never committed one in my life. It's a well-known thing amongst all my friends. I can get a paper to certify as much, signed by lots of people. Indeed, if you come to that, I doubt whether many people could produce as strong a certificate. Mine would be as big as a breakfast tablecloth. There is indeed one member of the club, who pretends to say he caught me once making too free with his throat on a club night, after everybody else had retired. But, observe, he shuffles in his story according to his state of civilation. When not far gone, he contents himself with saying that he caught me ogling his throat; and that I was melancholy for some weeks after, and that my voice sounded in a way expressing, to the nice ear of a connoisseur, *the sense of opportunities lost;* but the club all know that he is a disappointed man himself, and that he speaks querulously at times about the fatal neglect of a man's coming abroad without his tools. Besides, all this is an affair between two amateurs, and everybody makes allowances for little asperities and fibs in such a case. 'But,' say you, 'if no murderer, you may have encouraged, or even have bespoken a murder.' No, upon my honor — no. And that was the very point I wished to argue for your satisfaction. The truth is, I am a very particular man in everything relating to murder; and perhaps I carry my delicacy too far. The Stagirite most justly, and possibly with a view to my case, placed virtue in the τὸ μέσον, or middle point between two extremes. A golden mean is certainly what every man should aim at. But it is easier talking than doing; and, my infirmity being notoriously too much milkiness of heart, I find it difficult to maintain that steady equatorial line between the two poles of too much murder on the one hand, and too little on the other. I am too soft — and people get excused through me — nay, go through life without an attempt made upon them, that ought *not* to be excused. I believe, if I had the management of things, there would hardly be a murder from year's end to year's end. In fact, I'm for peace, and quietness, and fawningness, and what may be styled *knocking-under-ness*. A man came to me as a candidate for the place of my servant, just then vacant. He had the reputation of having dabbled a little in our art; some said, not without merit. What startled me, however, was, that he supposed this art to be part of his regular duties in my service, and talked of having it considered in his wages. Now, that was a thing I would not allow; so I said at once, ' Richard (or James, as the case might be), you misunderstand my character. If a man will and must practise this difficult (and allow me to add, dangerous) branch of art — if he has an over-ruling genius for it, why, in that case, all I say is, that he might as well pursue his studies whilst living in my service as in another's. And also, I may observe, that it can do no harm either to himself or to the subject on whom he operates, that he should be guided by men of more taste than himself. Genius may do

much, but long study of the art must always entitle a
man to offer advice. So far I will go — general principles I will suggest. But as to any particular case,
once for all I will have nothing to do with it. Never
tell me of any special work of art you are meditating
— I set my face against it *in toto*. For, if once a man
indulges himself in murder, very soon he comes to
think little of robbing; and from robbing he comes
next to drinking and Sabbath-breaking, and from that
to incivility and procrastination. Once begin upon
this downward path, you never know where you are
to stop. Many a man has dated his ruin from some
murder or other that perhaps he thought little of at
the time. *Principiis obsta* — that's my rule.' Such
was my speech, and I have always acted up to it; so,
if that is not being virtuous, I should be glad to know
what is. But now about the dinner and the club.
The club was not particularly of my creation; it arose
pretty much as other similar associations, for the propagation of truth and the communication of new ideas;
rather from the necessities of things, than upon any
one man's suggestion. As to the dinner, if any man
more than another could be held responsible for that,
it was a member known amongst us by the name of
*Toad-in-the-hole*. He was so called from his gloomy,
misanthropical disposition, which led him into constant
disparagements of all modern murders as vicious abor-
tions, belonging to no authentic school of art. The
finest performances of our own age he snarled at cyn-
ically; and at length this querulous humor grew upon
him so much, and he became so notorious as a *laudator
temporis acti*, that few people cared to seek his society.
This made him still more fierce and truculent. He

went about muttering and growling; wherever you
met him, he was soliloquizing, and saying, 'despicable
pretender — without grouping — without two ideas
upon handling — without' — and there you lost him.
At length existence seemed to be painful to him; he
rarely spoke, he seemed conversing with phantoms in
the air; his housekeeper informed us that his reading
was nearly confined to 'God's Revenge upon Murder,'
by Reynolds, and a more ancient book of the same
title, noticed by Sir Walter Scott in his 'Fortunes of
Nigel.' Sometimes, perhaps, he might read in the
'Newgate Calendar' down to the year 1788, but he
never looked into a book more recent. In fact, he
had a theory with regard to the French Revolution, as
having been the great cause of degeneration in murder. 'Very soon, sir,' he used to say, 'men will have
lost the art of killing poultry: the very rudiments of
the art will have perished!' In the year 1811, he
retired from general society. Toad-in-the-hole was
no more seen in any public resort. We missed him
from his wonted haunts — 'nor up the lawn, nor at
the wood was he.' By the side of the main conduit
his listless length at noontide he would stretch, and
pore upon the filth that muddled by. 'Even dogs,'
this pensive moralist would say, 'are not what they
were, sir — not what they should be. I remember in
my grandfather's time that some dogs had an idea of
murder. I have known a mastiff, sir, that lay in am-
bush for a rival, yes, sir, and finally murdered him,
with pleasing circumstances of good taste. I also was
on intimate terms of acquaintance with a tom-cat that
was an assassin. But now' —— and then, the subject growing too painful, he dashed his hand to his

forehead, and went off abruptly in a homeward direction towards his favorite conduit, where he was seen by an amateur in such a state, that he thought it dangerous to address him. Soon after Toad shut himself entirely up; it was understood that he had resigned himself to melancholy; and at length the prevailing notion was, that Toad-in-the-hole had hanged himself.

The world was wrong *there*, as it had been on some other questions. Toad-in-the-hole might be sleeping, but dead he was not; and of that we soon had ocular proof. One morning in 1812, an amateur surprised us with the news that he had seen Toad-in-the-hole brushing with hasty steps the dews away, to meet the postman by the conduit side. Even that was something: how much more, to hear that he had shaved his beard — had laid aside his sad-colored clothes, and was adorned like a bridegroom of ancient days. What could be the meaning of all this? Was Toad-in-the-hole mad? or how? Soon after the secret was explained — in more than a figurative sense 'the murder was out.' For in came the London morning papers, by which it appeared that but three days before a murder, the most superb of the century by many degrees, had occurred in the heart of London. I need hardly say, that this was the great exterminating *chef-d'œuvre* of Williams at Mr. Marr's, No. 29 Ratcliffe Highway. That was the *début* of the artist; at least for anything the public knew. What occurred at Mr. Williamson's twelve nights afterwards — the second work turned out from the same chisel — some people pronounced even superior. But Toad-in-the-hole always 'reclaimed,' he was even angry, at such comparisons. 'This vulgar *gout de comparaison*, as La Bruyère calls it,' he would often remark, ' will be our ruin ; each work has its own separate characteristics — each in and for itself is incomparable. One perhaps might suggest the ' Iliad ' — the other the ' Odyssey : ' but what do you get by such comparisons ? Neither ever was, or will be surpassed ; and when you've talked for hours, you must still come back to that.' Vain, however, as all criticism might be, he often said that volumes might be written on each case for itself; and he even proposed to publish in quarto on the subject.

Meantime, how had Toad-in-the-hole happened to hear of this great work of art so early in the morning? He had received an account by express, despatched by a correspondent in London, who watched the progress of art on *Toad's* behalf, with a general commission to send off a special express, at whatever cost, in the event of any estimable works appearing. The express arrived in the night-time ; Toad-in-the-hole was then gone to bed; he had been muttering and grumbling for hours, but of course he was called up. On reading the account, he threw his arms round the express, declared him his brother and his preserver, and expressed his regret at not having it in his power to knight him. We, amateurs, having heard that he was abroad, and therefore had *not* hanged himself, made sure of soon seeing him amongst us. Accordingly he soon arrived ; seized every man's hand as he passed him — wrung it almost frantically, and kept ejaculating, ' Why, now, here's something like a murder ! — this is the real thing — this is genuine — this is what you can approve, can recommend to a friend : this — says every man, on reflection — this is the thing that ought to be ! Such works are enough to make us all young.'. And in fact the general opinion is, that Toad-in-the-hole would have died but for this regeneration of art, which he called a second age of Leo the Tenth; and it was our duty, he said, solemnly to commemorate it. At present, and *en attendant*, he proposed that the club should meet and dine together. A dinner, therefore, was given by the club; to which all amateurs were invited from a distance of one hundred miles.

Of this dinner, there are ample short-hand notes amongst the archives of the club. But they are not 'extended,' to speak diplomatically; and the reporter, who only could give the whole report *in extenso*, is missing — I believe murdered. Meantime, in years long after that day, and on an occasion perhaps equally interesting, viz., the turning up of Thugs and Thuggism, another dinner was given. Of this I myself kept notes, for fear of another accident to the short-hand reporter. And I here subjoin them. Toad-in-the-hole, I must mention, was present at this dinner. In fact, it was one of its sentimental incidents. Being as old as the valleys at the dinner of 1812, naturally he was as old as the hills at the Thug dinner of 1838. He had taken to wearing his beard again; why, or with what view, it passes my persimmon to tell you. But so it was. And his appearance was most benign and venerable. Nothing could equal the angelic radiance of his smile, as he inquired after the unfortunate reporter (whom, as a piece of private scandal, I should tell you that he was himself supposed to have murdered, in a rapture of creative art): the answer was, with roars of laughter, from the under-sheriff of our county — '*Non est inventus.*' Toad-in-the-hole laughed outrageously at this: in fact, we all thought he was

6

choking ; and, at the earnest request of the company, a
musical composer furnished a most beautiful glee upon
the occasion, which was sung five times after dinner,
with universal applause and inextinguishable laughter,
the words being these (and the chorus so contrived, as
most beautifully to mimic the peculiar laughter of
Toad-in-the-hole) : —

' Et interrogatum est à Toad-in-the-hole — Ubi est ille reporter ?
Et responsum est cum cachinno — *Non est inventus.*'

*Chorus.*

' Delnde iteratum est ab omnibus, cum cachinnatione undulante
trepidante — *Non est inventus.*'

Toad-in-the-hole, I ought to mention, about nine
years before, when an express from Edinburgh brought
him the earliest intelligence of the Burke-and-Hare
revolution in the art, went mad upon the spot ; and, instead of a pension to the express for even one life, or a
knighthood, endeavored to Burke him ; in consequence
of which he was put into a strait-waistcoat. And that
was the reason we had no dinner then. But now all
of us were alive and kicking, strait-wasitcoaters and
others ; in fact, not one absentee was reported upon
the entire roll. There were also many foreign amateurs present.

Dinner being over, and the cloth drawn, there was
a general call made for the new glee of *Non est inventus ;* but, as this would have interfered with the requisite gravity of the company during the earlier toasts,
I overruled the call. After the national toasts had
been given, the first official toast of the day was, *The
Old Man of the Mountains* — drunk in solemn silence.

Toad-in-the-hole returned thanks in a neat speech.

He likened nimself to the Old Man of the Mountains, in a few brief allusions, that made the company
yell with laughter ; and he concluded with giving the
health of

*Mr. Von Hammer,* with many thanks to him for his
learned History of the Old Man and his subjects the
assassins.

Upon this I rose and said, that doubtless most of the
company were aware of the distinguished place assigned by orientalists to the very learned Turkish
scholar, Von Hammer the Austrian ; that he had made
the profoundest researches into our art, as connected
with those early and eminent artists, the Syrian assassins in the period of the Crusaders ; that his work had
been for several years deposited, as a rare treasure of
art, in the library of the club. Even the author's
name, gentlemen, pointed him out as the historian of
our art — Von Hammer ——

' Yes, yes,' interrupted Toad-in-the-hole, ' Von
Hammer — he's the man for a *malleus hæreticorum.*
You all know what consideration Williams bestowed
on the hammer, or the ship-carpenter's mallet, which
is the same thing. Gentlemen, I give you another
great hammer — Charles the Hammer, the Marteau, or,
in old French, the Martel — he hammered the Saracens
till they were all as dead as door-nails.'

' *Charles the Hammer,* with all the honors.'

But the explosion of Toad-in-the-hole, together
with the uproarious cheers for the grandpapa of Charlemagne, had now made the company unmanageable.
The orchestra was again challenged with shouts the
stormiest for the new glee. I foresaw a tempestuous
evening ; and I ordered myself to be strengthened with

three waiters on each side ; the vice-president with as many. Symptoms of unruly enthusiasm were beginning to show out; and I own that I myself was considerably excited, as the orchestra opened with its storm of music, and the impassioned glee began — 'Et interrogatum est à Toad-in-the-hole — Ubi est ille Reporter ?' And the frenzy of the passion became absolutely convulsing, as the full chorus fell in — 'Et iteratum est ab omnibus — *Non est inventus.*'

The next toast was — *The Jewish Sicarii.*

Upon which I made the following explanation to the company : — 'Gentlemen, I am sure it will interest you all to hear that the assassins, ancient as they were, had a race of predecessors in the very same country. All over Syria, but particularly in Palestine, during the early years of the Emperor Nero, there was a band of murderers, who prosecuted their studies in a very novel manner. They did not practise in the night-time, or in lonely places ; but, justly considering that great crowds are in themselves a sort of darkness by means of the dense pressure, and the impossibility of finding out who it was that gave the blow, they mingled with mobs everywhere; particularly at the great paschal feast in Jerusalem; where they actually had the audacity, as Josephus assures us, to press into the temple — and whom should they choose for operating upon but Jonathan himself, the Pontifex Maximus ? They murdered him, gentlemen, as beautifully as if they had had him alone on a moonless night in a dark lane. And when it was asked, who was the murderer, and where he was ———'

'Why then, it was answered,' interrupted Toad-in-the-hole, " *Non est inventus.*"' And then, in spite of all I could do or say, the orchestra opened, and the whole company began — ' Et interrogatum est à Toad-in-the-hole — Ubi est ille Sicarius ? Et responsum est ab omnibus — *Non est inventus.*'

When the tempestuous chorus had subsided, I began again : — ' Gentlemen, you will find a very circumstantial account of the Sicarii in at least three different parts of Josephus ; once in Book XX., sec. v. c. 8, of his " Antiquities ; " once in Book I. of his " Wars : " but in sec. x. of the chapter first cited you will find a particular description of their tooling. This is what he says : — " They tooled with small scimitars not much different from the Persian *acinacæ*, but more curved, and for all the world most like the Roman semi-lunar *sicæ*." It is perfectly magnificent, gentlemen, to hear the sequel of their history. Perhaps the only case on record where a regular army of murderers was assembled, a *justus exercitus*, was in the case of these *Sicarii*. They mustered in such strength in the wilderness, that Festus himself was obliged to march against them with the Roman legionary force. A pitched battle ensued ; and this army of amateurs was all cut to pieces in the desert. Heavens, gentlemen, what a sublime picture ! The Roman legions — the wilderness — Jerusalem in the distance — an army of murderers in the foreground ! '

The next toast was — ' To the further improvement of Tooling, and thanks to the committee for their services.'

Mr. L., on behalf of the Committee who had reported on that subject, returned thanks. He made an interesting extract from the report, by which it appeared how very much stress had been laid formerly on the mode of tooling by the fathers, both Greek and Latin. In confirmation of this pleasing fact, he made a very striking statement in reference to the earliest work of antediluvian art. Father Mersenne, that learned French Roman Catholic, in page one thousand four hundred and thirty-one [10] of his operose Commentary on Genesis, mentions, on the authority of several rabbis, that the quarrel of Cain with Abel was about a young woman ; that, according to the various accounts, Cain had tooled with his teeth (Abelem fuisse *morsibus* dilaceratum à Cain) ; according to many others, with the jaw-bone of an ass, which is the tooling adopted by most painters. But it is pleasing to the mind of sensibility to know that, as science expanded, sounder views were adopted. One author contends for a pitchfork, St. Chrysostom for a sword, Irenæus for a scythe, and Prudentius, the Christian poet of the fourth century, for a hedging-bill. This last writer delivers his opinion thus : —

' Frater, probatæ sanctitatis æmulus,
  Germana curvo colla frangit sarculo : '

*i. e.,* his brother, jealous of his attested sanctity, fractures his fraternal throat with a curved hedging-bill. ' All which is respectfully submitted by your committee, not so much as decisive of the question (for it is not), but in order to impress upon the youthful mind the importance which has ever been attached to the quality of the tooling by such men as Chrysostom and Irenæus.'

' Irenæus be hanged !' said Toad-in-the-hole, who now rose impatientiy to give the next toast : — ' Our Irish friends ; wishing them a speedy revolution in

their mode of tooling, as well as in everything else connected with the art!'

'Gentlemen, I'll tell you the plain truth. Every
day of the year we take up a paper, we read the opening of a murder. We say, this is good, this is charm-
ing, this is excellent! But, behold you! scarcely have
we read a little farther, before the word Tipperary or
Ballina-something betrays the Irish manufacture. Instantly we loathe it; we call to the waiter; we say,
" waiter, take away this paper; send it. out of the
house; it is absolutely a scandal in the nostrils of all
just taste." I appeal to every man, whether, on finding a murder (otherwise perhaps promising enough) to
be Irish, he does not feel himself as much insulted as
when, Madeira being ordered, he finds it to be Cape;
or when, taking up what he takes to be a mushroom,
it turns out what children call a toad-stool. Tithes,
politics, something wrong in principle, vitiate every
Irish murder. Gentlemen, this must be reformed, or
Ireland will not be a land to live in; at least, if we do
live there, we must import all our murders, that's
clear.' Toad-in-the-hole sat down, growling with
suppressed wrath; and the uproarious ' Hear, hear!'
clamorously expressed the general concurrence.

The next toast was — ' The sublime epoch of Burkism and Harism!'

This was drunk with enthusiasm; and one of the
members, who spoke to the question, made a very
curious communication to the company: — 'Gentlemen, we fancy Burkism to be a pure invention of our
own times: and in fact no Pancirollus has ever enu-
merated this branch of art when writing *de rebus
deperditis*. Still, I have ascertained that the essential

principle of this variety in the art *was* known to the
ancients; although, like the art of painting upon glass,
of making the myrrhine cups, &c., it was lost in the
dark ages for want of encouragement.    In the famous
collection of Greek epigrams made by Planudes, is one
upon a very fascinating case of Burkism : it is a per-
feet little gem of art.    The epigram itself I cannot lay
my hand upon at this moment; but the following is
an abstract of it by Salmasius, as I find it in his notes
on Vopiscus :  " Est et elegans epigramma Lucilii, ubi
medicus et pollinctor de compacto sic egerunt, ut
medicus ægros omnes curæ suæ commissos occideret :
this was the basis of the contract, you see, that on the
one part the doctor, for himself and his assigns, doth
undertake and contract duly and truly to murder all
the patients committed to his charge : but why?
There lies the beauty of the case — Et ut pollinctori
amico suo traderet pollingendos."    The *pollinctor*,
you are aware, was a person whose business it was to
dress and prepare dead bodies for burial.    The orginal
ground of the transaction appears to have been sentimental :  " He was my friend," says the murderous
doctor ;  " he was dear to me," in speaking of the pollinctor.    But the law, gentlemen, is stern and harsh :
the law will not hear of these tender motives : to sustain a contract of this nature in law, it is essential that
a " consideration " should be given.    Now what *was*
the consideration ?    For thus far all is on the side of
the pollinctor : he will be well paid for his services ;
but, meantime, the generous, the noble-minded doctor gets nothing.    What *was* the equivalent, again I
ask, which the law would insist on the doctor's taking,
in order to establish that " consideration," without

which the contract had no force? You shall hear:
" Et ut pollinctor vicissim τελαμῶνάς quos furabatar de
pollinctione mortuorum medico mitteret donis ad alli-
ganda vulnera eorum quos curabat;" *i. e.*, and that
reciprocally the pollinctor should transmit to the physician, as free gifts for the binding-up of wounds in
those whom he treated medically, the belts or trusses
(τελαμῶνας) which he had succeeded in purloining in
the course of his functions about the corpses.

'Now, the case is clear: the whole went on a principle of reciprocity which would have kept up the
trade for ever. The doctor was also a surgeon: he
could not murder *all* his patients: some of the patients must be retained intact. For these he wanted
linen bandages. But, unhappily, the Romans wore
woollen, on which account it was that they bathed so
often. Meantime, there *was* linen to be had in Rome;
but it was monstrously dear; and the τελαμῶνας, or
linen swathing bandages, in which superstition obliged
them to bind up corpses, would answer capitally for
the surgeon. The doctor, therefore, contracts to furnish his friend with a constant succession of corpses,
provided, and be it understood always, that his said
friend, in return, should supply him with one-half of
the articles he would receive from the friends of the
parties murdered or to be murdered. The doctor
invariably recommended his invaluable friend the
pollinctor (whom let us call the undertaker); the
undertaker, with equal regard to the sacred rights of
friendship, uniformly recommended the doctor. Like
Pylades and Orestes, they were models of a perfect
friendship: in their lives they were lovely: and on
the gallows, it is to be hoped, they were not divided.

'Gentlemen, it makes me laugh horribly, when I think of those two friends drawing and re-drawing on each other: "Pollinctor in account with Doctor, debtor by sixteen corpses: creditor by forty-five bandages, two of which damaged." Their names unfortunately are lost; but I conceive they must have been Quintus Burkius and Publius Harins. By the way, gentlemen, has anybody heard lately of Hare? I understand he is comfortably settled in Ireland, considerably to the west, and does a little business now and then; but, as he observes with a sigh, only as a retailer — nothing like the fine thriving wholesale concern so carelessly blown up at Edinburgh. "You see what comes of neglecting business" — is the chief moral, the ἐπιμύθιον, as Æsop would say, which Hare draws from his past experience.'

At length came the toast of the day — *Thugdom in all its branches.*

The speeches *attempted* at this crisis of the dinner were past all counting. But the applause was so furious, the music so stormy, and the crashing of glasses so incessant, from the general resolution never again to drink an inferior toast from the same glass, that I am unequal to the task of reporting. Besides which, Toad-in-the-hole now became ungovernable. He kept firing pistols in every direction; sent his servant for a blunderbuss, and talked of loading with ball-cartridge. We conceived that his former madness had returned at the mention of Burke and Hare; or that, being again weary of life, he had resolved to go off in a general massacre. This we could not think of allowing; it became indispensable, therefore, to kick him out; which we did with universal consent, the whole company lending their toes *uno pede*, as I may say, though pitying his gray hairs and his angelic smile. During the operation, the orchestra poured in their old chorus. The universal company sang, and (what surprised us most of all) Toad-in-the-hole joined us furiously in singing —

'Et interrogatum est ab omnibus — Ubi est ille Toad-in-the-hole ?

Et responsum est ab omnibus — *Non est inventus* '

# NOTES.

## NOTE 1. Page 20.

Kant — who carried his demands of unconditional veracity to so extravagant a length as to affirm, that, if a man were to see an innocent person escape from a murderer, it would be his duty, on being questioned by the murderer, to tell the truth, and to point out the retreat of the innocent person, under any certainty of causing murder. Lest this doctrine should be supposed to have escaped him in any heat of dispute, on being taxed with it by a celebrated French writer, he solemnly re-affirmed it, with his reasons.

## NOTE 2. Page 26.

The passage occurs in the *second* part (act 3) of 'Henry VI.,' and is doubly remarkable — first, for its critical fidelity to nature, were the description meant only for *poetic* effect ; but, secondly, for the *judicial* value impressed upon it when offered (as here it *is* offered) in silent corroboration legally of a dreadful whisper all at once arising, that foul play had been dealing with a great prince, clothed with an official state character. It is the Duke of Gloucester, faithful guardian and loving uncle of the simple and imbecile king, who has been found dead in his bed. How shall this event be interpreted ? Had he died under some natural visitation of Providence, or by violence from his enemies ? The two court factions read the circumstantial indications of the case into opposite constructions. The affectionate and afflicted young king, whose position almost pledges him to neutrality, cannot, nevertheless, disguise his overwhelming suspicions of hellish conspiracy in the background. Upon this, a leader of the queen's faction endeavors to break the force of this royal frankness, countersigned and echoed most impressively by

Lord Warwick. 'What *instance*,' he asks — meaning by *instance* not example or illustration, as thoughtless commentators have constantly supposed, but in the common scholastic sense — what *instantia*, what pressure of argument, what urgent plea, can Lord Warwick put forward in support of his ' dreadful oath ' — an oath, namely, that, as surely as he hopes for the life eternal, so surely

> ' I do believe that violent hands were laid
> Upon the life of this thrice-faméd duke.'

Ostensibly the challenge is to Warwick, but substantially it is meant for the king. And the reply of Warwick, the argument on which he builds, lies in a solemn array of all the changes worked in the duke's features by death, as irreconcilable with any other hypothesis than that this death had been a violent one. What argument have I that Gloucester died under the hands of murderers ? Why, the following roll-call of awful changes, affecting head, face, nostrils, eyes, hands, &c., which do not belong indifferently to *any* mode of death, but exclusively to a death by violence : —

> ' But see, his face is black and full of blood;
> His eyeballs farther out than when he lived,
> Staring full ghastly, like a strangled man;
> His hair uprear'd, his nostrils stretch'd with struggling;
> His hands abroad display'd, as one that grasp'd
> And tugg'd for life, and was by strength subdued.
> Look on the sheets : — his hair, you see, is sticking;
> His well-proportion'd beard made rough and rugged,
> Like to the summer's corn by tempest lodged.
> It cannot be but he was murder'd here;
> The least of all these signs were probable.'

As the logic of the case, let us not for a moment forget, that, to be of any value, the signs and indications pleaded must be sternly *diagnostic*. The discrimination sought for is between death that is natural, and death that is violent. All indications, therefore, that belong equally and indifferently to either, are equivocal, useless, and alien from the very purpose of the signs here registered by Shakspeare.

## NOTE 3.  Page 26.

At the time of writing this, I held the common opinion upon that subject.  Mere inconsideration it was that led to so erroneous a judgment.  Since then, on closer reflection, I have seen ample reason to retract it : satisfied I now am, that the Romans, in every art which allowed to them any parity of advantages, had merits as racy, native, and characteristic, as the best of the Greeks.  Elsewhere I shall plead this cause circumstantially, with the hope of converting the reader.  In the meantime, I was anxious to lodge my protest against this ancient error; an error which commenced in the time-serving sycophancy of Virgil, the court-poet.  With the base purpose of gratifying Augustus in his vindictive spite against Cicero, and by way of introducing, therefore, the little clause *orabunt Causas melius* as applying to all Athenian against all Roman orators, Virgil did not scruple to sacrifice by wholesale the just pretensions of his compatriots collectively.

## NOTE 4.  Page 33.

This same argument has been employed at least once too often.  Some centuries back a dauphin of France, when admonished of his risk from small-pox, made the same demand as the emperor — ' Had any gentleman heard of a dauphin killed by small-pox ? '  No ; not any gentleman *had* heard of such a case.  And yet, for all that, this dauphin died of that same small-pox.

## NOTE 5.  Page 33.

' June 1, 1675. — Drinke part of three boules of punch (a liquor very strainge to me),' says the Rev. Mr. Henry Teonge, in his Diary published by C. Knight.  In a note on this passage, a reference is made to Fryer's Travels to the East Indies, 1672, who speaks of ' that enervating liquor called *paunch* (which is Hindostanee for five), from five ingredients.'  Made thus, it seems the medical men called it diapente; if with four only, diatessaron.  No doubt, it was this evangelical name that recommended it to the Rev. Mr. Teonge.

### Note 6.   Page 37.

Chatsworth was then, as now, the superb seat of the Caven-dishes in their highest branch — in those days Earl, at present Duke, of Devonshire.   It is to the honor of this family that, through two generations, they gave an asylum to Hobbes.   It is noticeable that Hobbes was born in the year of the Spanish Ar-mada, *i. e.*, in 1588 : such, at least, is my belief.   And, there-fore, at this meeting with Tennison in 1670, he must have been about 82 years old.

### Note 7.   Page 40.

' *Spital Sermons :* ' — Dr. Parr's chief public appearances as an author, after his original appearance in the famous Latin preface to Bellendĕnus (don't say Bellendĕnus), occurred in cer-tain Sermons at periodic intervals, delivered on behalf of some hospital (I really forget what) which retained for its official de-signation the old word *Spital ;* and thus it happened that the Sermons themselves were generally known by the title of *Spital* Sermons.

### Note 8.   Page 54.

Abraham Newland is now utterly forgotten.   But when this was written, his name had not ceased to ring in British ears, as the most familiar and most significant that perhaps has ever ex-isted.   It was the name which appeared on the face of all Bank of England notes, great or small; and had been, for more than a quarter of a century (especially through the whole career of the French Revolution), a short-hand expression for paper money in its safest form.

### Note 9.   Page 58.

*Her* Majesty : — In the lecture, having occasion to refer to the reigning sovereign, I said ' *His* Majesty ; ' for at that time William IV. was on the throne : but between the lecture and this supplement had occurred the accession of our present Queen.

### Note 10.   Page 70.

' Page one thousand four hundred and thirty-one:' — *literally,* good reader, and no joke at all.

# JOAN OF ARC.[1]

IN REFERENCE TO M. MICHELET'S HISTORY OF
FRANCE.

WHAT is to be thought of *her*? What is to be
thought of the poor shepherd girl from the hills and
forests of Lorraine, that — like the Hebrew shepherd
boy from the hills and forests of Judæa — rose suddenly out of the quiet, out of the safety, out of the religious inspiration, rooted in deep pastoral solitudes, to
a station in the van of armies, and to the more perilous
station at the right hand of kings? The Hebrew boy
inaugurated his patriotic mission by an *act*, by a victorious *act*, such as no man could deny. But so did the
girl of Lorraine, if we read her story as it was read by
those who saw her nearest. Adverse armies bore witness to the boy as no pretender; but so they did to
the gentle girl. Judged by the voices of all who saw
them *from a station of good-will*, both were found true
and loyal to any promises involved in their first acts.
Enemies it was that made the difference between their
subsequent fortunes. The boy rose to a splendor and
a noonday prosperity, both personal and public, that
rang through the records of his people, and became a
by-word amongst his posterity for a thousand years,
until the sceptre was departing from Judah. The poor,
forsaken girl, on the contrary, drank not herself ·from
that cup of rest which she had secured for France.
She never sang together with the songs that rose in her

native Domrémy, as echoes to the departing steps of
invaders. She mingled not in the festal dances at
Vaucouleurs which celebrated in rapture the redemp-
tion of France. No! for her voice was then silent:
no! for her feet were dust. Pure, innocent, noble-
hearted girl! whom, from earliest youth, ever I believed in as full of truth and self-sacrifice, this was
amongst the strongest pledges for *thy* truth, that never
once — no, not for a moment of weakness — didst thou
revel in the vision of coronets and honor from man.
Coronets for thee! O no! Honors, if they come when
all is over, are for those that share thy blood.[2]  Daughter of Domrémy, when the gratitude of thy king shall
awaken, thou wilt be sleeping the sleep of the dead.
Call her, King of France, but she will not hear thee!
Cite her by thy apparitors to come and receive a robe
of honor, but she will be found *en contumace*.  When
the thunders of universal France, as even yet may happen, shall proclaim the grandeur of the poor shepherd
girl that gave up all for her country, thy ear, young
shepherd girl, will have been deaf for five centuries.
To suffer and to do, that was thy portion in this life;
that was thy destiny; and not for a moment was it
hidden from thyself. Life, thou saidst, is short: and
the sleep which is in the grave is long! Let me use
that life, so transitory, for the glory of those heavenly
dreams destined to comfort the sleep which is so long.
This pure creature — pure from every suspicion of
even a visionary self-interest, even as she was pure in
senses more obvious — never once did this holy child,
as regarded herself, relax from her belief in the darkness that was travelling to meet her. She might not
prefigure the very manner of her death; she saw not

in vision, perhaps, the aerial altitude of the fiery scaffold, the spectators without end on every road pouring into Rouen as to a coronation, the surging smoke, the volleying flames, the hostile faces all around, the pitying eye that lurked but here and there, until nature and imperishable truth broke loose from artificial restraints; — these might not be apparent through the mists of the hurrying future. But the vioice that called her to death, *that* she heard for ever.

Great was the throne of France even in those days, and great was he that sat upon it : but well Joanna knew that not the throne, nor he that sat upon it, was for *her ;* but, on the contrary, that she was for *them ;* not she by them, but they by her, should rise from the dust. Gorgeous were the lilies of France, and for centuries had the privilege to spread their beauty over land and sea, until, in another century, the wrath of God and man combined to wither them; but well Joanna knew, early at Domrémy she had read that bitter truth, that the lilies of France would decorate no garland for *her.* Flower nor bud, bell nor blossom, would ever bloom for *her.*

.    .    .    .    .    .    .    .    .

But stay. What reason is there for taking up this subject of Joanna precisely in the spring of 1847? Might it not have been left till the spring of 1947; or, perhaps, left till called for ? Yes, but it *is* called for ; and clamorously. You are aware, reader, that amongst the many original thinkers whom modern France has produced, one of the reputed leaders is M. Michelet. All these writers are of a revolutionary cast; not in a political sense merely, but in all senses ; mad, oftentimes, as March hares ; crazy with the laughing gas of

recovered liberty; drunk with the wine-cup of their
mighty revolution, snorting, whinnying, throwing up
their heels, like wild horses in the boundless Pampas,
and running races of defiance with snipes, or with the
winds, or with their own shadows, if they can find
nothing else to challenge. Some time or other I, that
have leisure to read, may introduce *you*, that have not,
to two or three dozen of these writers; of whom I can
assure you beforehand, that they are often profound,
and at intervals are even as impassioned as if they
were come of our best English blood. But now, con-
fining our attention to M. Michelet, we in England —
who know him best by his worst book, the book
against priests, &c. — know him disadvantageously.
That book is a rhapsody of incoherence. But his
' History of France ' is quite another thing. A
man, in whatsoever craft he sails, cannot stretch
away out of sight when he is linked to the windings
of the shore by towing ropes of history. Facts, and
the consequences of facts, draw the writer back to the
falconer's lure from the giddiest heights of speculation.
Here, therefore — in his ' France ' — if not always free
from flightiness, if now and then off like a rocket for
an airy wheel in the clouds, M. Michelet, with natural
politeness, never forgets that he has left a large audience waiting for him on earth, and gazing upwards in
anxiety for his return : return, therefore, he does.
But history, though clear of certain temptations in one
direction, has separate dangers of its own. It is impossible so to write a history of France, or of England
— works becoming every hour more indispensable to
the inevitably-political man of this day — without perilous openings for error. If I, for instance, on the part

of England, should happen to turn my labors in that channel, and (on the model of Lord Percy going to Chevy Chase)

'A vow to God should make
My pleasure in the Michelet woods
Three summer days to take,'

probably, from simple delirium, I might hunt M. Michelet into *delirium tremens*. Two strong angels stand by the side of history, whether French history or English, as heraldic supporters : the angel of research on the left hand, that must read millions of dusty parchments, and of pages blotted with lies; the angel of meditation on the right hand, that must cleanse these lying records with fire, even as of old the draperies of *asbestos* were cleansed, and must quicken them into regenerated life. Willingly I acknowledge that no man will ever avoid innumerable errors of detail; with so vast a compass of ground to traverse, this is impossible; but such errors (though I have a bushel on hand, at M. Michelet's service) are not the game I chase; it is the bitter and unfair spirit in which M. Michelet writes against England. Even *that*, after all, is but my secondary object; the real one is Joanna the Pucelle d'Orleans for herself.

I am not going to write the History of *La Pucelle* : to do this, or even circumstantially to report the history of her persecution and bitter death, of her struggle with false witnesses and with ensnaring judges, it would be necessary to have before us *all* the documents, and therefore the collection only [3] now forthcoming in Paris. But *my* purpose is narrower. There have been great thinkers, disdaining the careless judgments of contemporaries, who have thrown themselves

boldly on the judgment of a far posterity, that should
have had time to review, to ponder, to compare. There
have been great actors on the stage of tragic humanity
that might with the same depth of confidence, have
appealed from the levity of compatriot friends — too
heartless for the sublime interest of their story, and
too impatient for the labor of sifting its perplexities —
to the magnanimity and justice of enemies. To this
class belongs the Maid of Arc. The ancient Romans
were too faithful to the ideal of grandeur in themselves
not to relent, after a generation or two, before the
grandeur of Hannibal. Mithridates — a more doubtful person — yet merely for the magic perseverance of
his indomitable malice, won from the same Romans the
only real honor that ever he received on earth. And
we English have ever shown the same homage to stub-
born enmity. To work unflinchingly for the ruin of
England ; to say through life, by word and by deed,
*Delenda est Anglia Victrix !* that one purpose of malice, faithfully pursued, has quartered some people upon
our national funds of homage as by a perpetual annuity. Better than an inheritance of service rendered
to England herself, has sometimes proved the most
insane hatred to England. Hyder Ali, even his son
Tippoo, though so far inferior, and Napoleon, have all
benefited by this disposition amongst ourselves to exaggerate the merit of diabolic enmity. Not one of
these men was ever capable, in a solitary instance, of
praising an enemy [what do you say to *that*, reader?],
and yet in *their* behalf, we consent to forget, not their
crimes only, but (which is worse) their hideous bigotry
and anti-magnanimous egotism, for nationality it was
not. .Suffrein, and some half dozen of other French

nautical heroes, because rightly they did us all the mischief they could (which was really great), are names justly reverenced in England. On the same principle, La Pucelle d'Orleans, the victorious enemy of·England, has been destined to receive her deepest commemoration from the magnanimous justice of Englishmen.

Joanna, as we in England should call her, but, according to her own statement, Jeanne (or, as M. Michelet asserts, Jean [4]) D'Arc, was born at Domrémy, a village on the marches of Lorraine and Champagne, and dependent upon the town of Vaucouleurs. I have called her a Lorrainer, not simply because the word is prettier, but because Champagne too odiously reminds us English of what are for *us* imaginary wines, which, undoubtedly, *La Pucelle* tasted as rarely as we English ; we English, because the Champagne of London is chiefly grown in Devonshire ; *La Pucelle*, because the Champagne of Champagne never, by any chance, flowed into the fountain of Domrémy, from which only she drank. M. Michelet will have her to be a *Champenoise*, and for no better reason than that she ' took after her father,' who happened to be a *Champenois*.

These disputes, however, turn on refinements too nice. Domrémy stood upon the frontiers, and, like other frontiers, produced a *mixed* race representing the *cis* and the *trans*. A river (it is true) formed the boundary-line at this point — the river Meuse ; and *that*, in old days, might have divided the populations ; but in these days it did not : there were bridges, there were ferries, and weddings crossed from the right bank to the left. Here lay two great roads, not so much for travellers that were few, as for armies that were

too many by half.   These two roads, one of which
was the great high road between France and Germany,
*decussated* at this very point; which is a learned way
of saying, that they formed a St. Andrew's cross, or
letter X.   I hope the compositor will choose a good
large X, in which case the point of intersection, the
*locus* of conflux and intersection for these four diverg-
ing arms, will finish the reader's geographical education, by showing him to a hair's-breadth where it was
that Domrémy stood.   Those roads, so grandly situated, as great trunk arteries between two mighty
realms,[5] and haunted for ever by wars, or rumors of
wars, decussated (for anything I know to the contrary)
absolutely under Joanna's bedroom window; one rolling away to the right, past Monsieur D'Arc's old barn,
and the other unaccountably preferring to sweep round
that odious man's pigsty to the left.

On whichever side of the border chance had thrown
Joanna, the same love to France would have been nur-
tured.   For it is a strange fact, noticed by M. Michelet
and others, that the Dukes of Bar and Lorraine had
for generations pursued the policy of eternal warfare
with France on their own account, yet also of eternal
amity and league with France, in case anybody else
presumed to attack her.   Let peace settle upon France,
and before long you might rely upon seeing the little
vixen Lorraine, flying at the throat of France.   Let
France be assailed by a formidable enemy, and instantly you saw a Duke of Lorraine insisting on having his own throat cut in support of France; which
favor accordingly was cheerfully granted to him in
three great successive battles — twice by the English,
viz., at Crécy and Agincourt, once by the Sultan at
Nicopolis.

This sympathy with France during great eclipses, in those that during ordinary seasons were always teasing her with brawls and guerilla inroads, strengthened the natural piety to France of those that were confessedly the children of her own house. The outposts of France, as one may call the great frontier provinces, were of all localities the most devoted to the Fleurs de Lys. To witness, at any great crisis, the generous devotion to these lilies of the little fiery cousin that in gentler weather was for ever tilting at the breast of France, could not but fan the zeal of France's legitimate daughters: whilst to occupy a post of honor on the frontiers against an old hereditary enemy of France, would naturally stimulate this zeal by a sentiment of martial pride, by a sense of danger always threatening, and of hatred always smouldering. That great four-headed road was a perpetual memento to patriotic ardor. To say, this way lies the road to Paris, and that other way to Aix-la-Chapelle — this to Prague, that to Vienna — nourished the warfare of the heart by daily ministrations of sense. The eye that watched for the gleams of lance or helmet from the hostile frontier, the ear that listened for the groaning of wheels, made the high road itself, with its relations to centres so remote, into a manual of patriotic duty.

The situation, therefore, *locally*, of Joanna was full of profound suggestions to a heart that listened for the stealthy steps of change and fear that too surely were in motion. But, if the place were grand, the time, the burden of the time, was far more so. The air overhead in its upper chambers was *hurtling* with the obscure sound; was dark with sullen fermenting of storms that had been gathering for a hundred and thirty years. The battle of Agincourt in Joanna's childhood had re-opened the wounds of France. Crécy and Poictiers, those withering overthrows for the chivalry of France, had, before Agincourt occurred, been tranquillized by more than half a century; but this resurrection of their trumpet wails made the whole series of battles and endless skirmishes take their stations as parts in one drama. The graves that had closed sixty years ago, seemed to fly open in sympathy with a sorrow that echoed their own. The monarchy of France labored in extremity, rocked and reeled like a ship fighting with the darkness of monsoons. The madness of the poor king (Charles VI.) falling in at such a crisis, like the case of women laboring in childbirth during the storming of a city, trebled the awfulness of the time. Even the wild story of the incident which had immediately occasioned the explosion of this madness — the case of a man unknown, gloomy, and perhaps maniacal himself, coming out of a forest at noonday, laying his hand upon the bridle of the king's horse, checking him for a moment to say, 'Oh, king, thou art betrayed,' and then vanishing, no man knew whither, as he had appeared for no man knew what — fell in with the universal prostration of mind that laid France on her knees, as before the slow unweaving of some ancient prophetic doom. The famines, the extraordinary diseases, the insurrections of the peasantry up and down Europe — these were chords struck from the same mysterious harp; but these were transitory chords. There have been others of deeper and more ominous sound. The termination of the Crusades, the destruction of the Templars, the Papal interdicts, the tragedies caused or suffered by the house of Anjou, and by the emperor — these were full of a more permanent significance. But, since then, the colossal figure of feudalism was seen standing, as it were, on tiptoe, at Crécy, for flight from earth: that was a revolution unparalleled; yet *that* was a trifle, by comparison with the more fearful revolutions that were mining below the church. By her own internal schisms, by the abominable spectacle of a double pope — so that no man, except through political bias, could even guess which was Heaven's vicegerent, and which the creature of hell — the church was rehearsing, as in still earlier forms she had already rehearsed, those vast rents in her foundations which no man should ever heal.

These were the loftiest peaks of the cloudland in the skies, that to the scientific gazer first caught the colors of the *new* morning in advance. But the whole vast range alike of sweeping glooms overhead, dwelt upon all meditative minds, even upon those that could not distinguish the tendencies nor decipher the forms. It was, therefore, not her own age alone, as affected by its immediate calamities, that lay with such weight upon Joanna's mind; but her own age, as one section in a vast mysterious drama, unweaving through a century back, and drawing nearer continually to some dreadful crisis. Cataracts and rapids were heard roaring ahead; and signs were seen far back, by help of old men's memories, which answered secretly to signs now coming forward on the eye, even as locks answer to keys. It was not wonderful that in such a haunted solitude, with such a haunted heart, Joanna should see angelic visions, and hear angelic voices. These voices whispered to her for ever the duty, self-

imposed, of delivering France. Five years she listened
to these monitory voices with internal struggles. At
length she could resist no longer. Doubt gave way;
and she left her home for ever in order to present herself at the dauphin's court.

The education of this poor girl was mean according
to the present standard: was ineffably grand, according to a purer philosophic standard: and only not good
for our age, because for us it would be unattainable.
She read nothing, for she could not read; but she had
heard others read parts of the Roman martyrology.
She wept in sympathy with the sad *Misereres* of the
Romish church; she rose to heaven with the glad triumphant *Te Deums* of Rome : she drew her comfort and
her vital strength from the rites of the same church.
But, next after these spiritual advantages, she owed most
to the advantages of her situation. The fountain of Domrémy was on the brink of a boundless forest; and it was
haunted to that degree by fairies, that the parish priest
(*curé*) was obliged to read mass there once a-year, in
order to keep them in any decent bounds. Fairies are,
important, even in a statistical view: certain weeds
mark poverty in 'the soil, fairies mark its solitude. As
surely as the wolf retires before cities, does the fairy
sequester herself from the haunts of the licensed vict-
ualler. A village is too much for her nervous delicacy :
at most, she can tolerate a distant view of a hamlet.
We may judge, therefore, by the uneasiness and extra
trouble which they gave to the parson, in what
strength the fairies mustered at Domrémy; and, by a
satisfactory consequence, how thinly sown with men
and women must have been that region even in its
inhabited spots. But the forests of Domrémy — those

were the glories of the land: for in them abode mysterious power and ancient secrets that towered into tragic strength. 'Abbeys there were, and abbey windows,' — 'like Moorish temples of the Hindoos,' that exercised even princely power both in Lorraine and in the German Diets. These had their sweet bells that pierced the forests for many a league at matins or vespers, and each its own dreamy legend. Few enough, and scattered enough, were these abbeys, so as in no degree to disturb the deep solitude of the region; yet many enough to spread a network or awning of Christian sanctity over what else might have seemed a heathen wilderness. This sort of religious talisman being secured, a man the most afraid of ghosts (like myself, suppose, or the reader) becomes armed into courage to wander for days in their sylvan recesses. The mountains of the Vosges, on the eastern frontier of France, have never attracted much notice from Europe, except in 1813—14 for a few brief months, when they fell within Napoleon's line of defence against the Allies. But they are interesting for this, amongst other features, that they do not, like some loftier ranges, repel woods: the forests and the hills are on sociable terms. *Live and let live*, is their motto. For this reason, in part, these tracts in Lorraine were a favorite hunting-ground with the Carlovingian princes. About six hundred years before Joanna's childhood, Charlemagne was known to have hunted there. That, of itself, was a grand incident in the traditions of a forest or a chase. In these vast forests, also, were to be found (if anywhere to be found) those mysterious fawns that tempted solitary hunters into visionary and perilous pursuits. Here

was seen (if anywhere seen) that ancient stag **who**
was already nine hundred years old, but possibly **a**
hundred or two more, when met by Charlemagne ; and
the thing was put beyond doubt by the inscription
upon his golden collar. I believe Charlemagne knight-
ed the stag ; and, if ever he is met again by a king, **he**
ought to be made an earl — or, being upon the marches
of France, a marquis. Observe, I don't absolutely
vouch for all these things : my own opinion varies.
On a fine breezy forenoon I am audaciously sceptical ;
but, as twilight sets in, my credulity grows steadily,
till it becomes equal to anything that could be desired.
And I have heard candid sportsmen declare that, outside of these very forests, they laughed loudly at all
the dim tales connected with their haunted solitudes ;
but, on reaching a spot notoriously eighteen miles
deep within them, they agreed with Sir Roger de Cov-
erley, that a good deal might be said on both sides.

Such traditions, or any others that (like the stag)
connect distant generations with each other, are, for
that cause, sublime ; and the sense of the shadowy,
connected with such appearances that reveal themselves
or not according to circumstances, leaves a coloring of
sanctity over ancient forests, even in those minds that
utterly reject the legend as a fact.

But, apart from all distinct stories of that order, in
any solitary frontier between two great empires, as
here, for instance, or in the desert between Syria and
the Euphrates, there is an inevitable tendency in
minds of any deep sensibility, to people the solitudes
with phantom images of powers that were of old so
vast. Joanna, therefore, in her quiet occupation of a
shepherdess, would be led continually to brood over

the political condition of her country, by the traditions of the past no less than by the mementoes of the local present.

M. Michelet, indeed, says that La Pucelle was *not* a shepherdess. I beg his pardon: she *was*. What he rests upon, I guess pretty well: it is the evidence of a woman called Haumette, the most confidential friend of Joanna. Now, she is a good witness, and a good girl, and I like her; for she makes a natural and affectionate report of Joanna's ordinary life. But still, however good she may be as a witness, Joanna is better; and she, when speaking to the dauphin, calls herself in the Latin report *Bergereta*. Even Haumette confesses, that Joanna tended sheep in her girlhood. And I believe, that if Miss Haumette were taking coffee alone with me this very evening (February 12, 1847) — in which there would be no subject for scandal for or maiden blushes, because I am an intense philosopher, and Miss H. would be hard upon four hundred and fifty years old — she would admit the following comment upon her evidence to be right. A Frenchman, about forty years ago, M. Simond, in his 'Travels,' mentions incidently the following hideous scene as one steadily observed and watched by himself in chivalrous France, not very long before the French Revolution: — A peasant was ploughing; the team that drew his plough was a donkey and a woman. Both were regularly harnessed: both pulled alike. This is bad enough; but the Frenchman adds, that, in distributing his lashes, the peasant was obviously desirous of being impartial; or, if either of the yoke-fellows had a right to complain, certainly it was not the donkey. Now, in any country where such degradation of fe-

males could be tolerated by the state of manners, a
woman of delicacy would shrink from acknowledging,
either for herself or her friend, that she had ever been
addicted to any mode of labor not strictly domestic;
because, if once owning herself a prædial servant, she
would be sensible that this confession extended by probability in the hearer's thoughts to the having incurred
indignities of this horrible kind.  Haumette clearly
thinks it more dignified for Joanna to have been darning the stockings of her horny-hoofed father, Monsieur
D'Arc, than keeping sheep, lest she. might then be
suspected of having ever done something worse.  But,
luckily, there was no danger of *that:* Joanna never
was in service; and my opinion is, that her father
should have mended his own stockings, since probably
he was the party to make holes in them, as many a
better man than D'Arc does; meaning by *that* not myself, because, though probably a better man than D'Arc,
I protest against doing anything of the kind.  If I
lived even with Friday in Juan Fernandez, either Friday must do all the darning, or else it must go un-
done.  The better men that I meant were the sailors
'n the British navy, every man of whom mends his
own stockings.  Who else is to do it?  Do you suppose, reader, that the junior lords of the admiralty are
under articles to darn for the navy?

The reason, meantime, for my systematic hatred of
D'Arc is this.  There was a story current in France
before the Revolution, framed to ridicule the pauper
aristocracy, who happened to have long pedigrees and
short rent rolls, viz., that a head of such a house, dating
from the Crusades, was overheard saying to his son, a
Chevalier of St. Louis, ' *Chevalier, as-tu donné au*

*cochon à manger !* ' Now, it is clearly made out by the surviving evidence, that D'Arc would much have preferred continuing to say, ' *Ma fille as-tu donné au cochon à manger ?* ' to saying, *Pucelle d'Orleans, as-tu sauvé los fleurs-de-lys ?* ' There is an old English copy of verses which argues thus : —

> ' If the man that turnips cries,
> Cry not when his father dies —
> Then 'tis plain the man had rather —
> Have a turnip than his father.'

I cannot say that the logic in these verses was ever *entirely* to my satisfaction. I do not see my way through it as clearly as could be wished. But I see my way most clearly through D'Arc ; and the result is — that he would greatly have preferred not merely a turnip to his father, but saving a pound or so of bacon to saving the Oriflamme of France.

It is probable (as M. Michelet suggests) that the title of Virgin, or *Pucelle*, had in itself, and apart from the miraculous stories about her, a secret power over the rude soldiery and partisan chiefs of that period ; for, in such a person, they saw a representative manifestation of the Virgin Mary, who in a course of centuries, had grown steadily upon the popular heart.

As to Joanna's supernatural detection of the dauphin (Charles VII.) amongst three hundred lords and knights, I am surprised at the credulity which could ever lend itself to that theatrical juggle. Who admires more than myself the sublime enthusiasm, the rapturous faith in herself, of this pure creature ? But I am far from admiring stage artifices, which not *La Pucelle*, but the court, must have arranged ; nor can

surrender myself to the conjurer's *legerdemain*, such
as may be seen every day for a shilling. Southey's
' Joan of Arc ' was published in 1796. Twenty years
after, talking with Southey, I was surprised to find
him still owning a secret bias in favor of Joan, founded
on her detection of the dauphin. The story, for the
benefit of the reader new to the case, was this : — *La
Pucelle* was first made known to the dauphin, and presented to his court, at Chinon : and here came her
first trial. By way of testing her supernatural pretensions, she was to find out the royal personage
amongst the whole ark of clean and unclean creatures.
Failing in this *coup d'essai*, she would not simply disappoint many a beating heart in the glittering crowd
that on different motives yearned for her success, but
she would ruin herself — and, as the oracle within had
told her, would, by ruining herself, ruin France. Our
own sovereign lady Victoria rehearses annually a trial
not so severe in degree, but the same in kind. She
' pricks ' for sheriffs. Joanna pricked for a king. But
observe the difference : our own lady pricks for two
men out of three ; Joanna for one man out of three
hundred. Happy Lady of the islands and the orient !
— she *can* go astray in her choice only by one half ;
to the extent of one half she *must* have the satisfaction
of being right. And yet, even with these tight limits
to the misery of a boundless discretion, permit me,
liege Lady, with all loyalty, to submit — that now and
then you prick with your pin the wrong man. But
the poor child from Domrémy, shrinking under the
gaze of a dazzling court — not *because* dazzling (for in
visions she had seen those that were more so), but
because some of them wore a scoffing smile on their

features — how should *she* throw her line into so deep a river to angle for a king, where many a gay creature was sporting that masqueraded as kings in dress? Nay, even more than any true king would have done: for, in Southey's version of the story, the dauphin says, by way of trying the virgin's magnetic sympathy with royalty,

> 'On the throne,
> I the while mingling with the menial throng,
> Some courtier shall be seated.'

This usurper is even crowned : 'the jewelled crown shines on a menial's head.' But, really, that is '*un peu fort;*' and the mob of spectators might raise a scruple whether our friend the jackdaw upon the throne, and the dauphin himself, were not grazing the shins of treason. For the dauphin could not lend more than belonged to him. According to the popular notion, he had no crown for himself; consequently none to lend, on any pretence whatever, until the consecrated Maid should take him to Rheims. This was the *popular* notion in France. But, certainly, it was the dauphin's interest to support the popular notion, as he meant to use the services of Joanna. For, if he were king already, what was it that she could do for him beyond Orleans? That is to say, what more than a mere *military* service could she render him? And, above all, if he were king without a coronation, and without the oil from the sacred ampulla, what advantage was yet open to him by celerity above his competitor the English boy? Now was to be a race for a coronation: he that should win *that* race, carried the superstition of France along with him : he that should first be drawn from the ovens of Rheims, was under that superstition baked into a king.

La Pucelle, before she could be allowed to practise as a warrior, was put through her manual and platoon exercise, as a pupil in divinity, at the bar of six eminent men in wigs. According to Southey (v. 393, Book III., in the original edition of his ' Joan of Arc '), she ' appalled the doctors.' It's not easy to do *that :* but they had some reason to feel bothered, as that surgeon would assuredly feel bothered, who, upon proceeding to dissect a subject, should find the subject retaliating as a dissector upon himself, especially if Joanna ever made the speech to them which occupies v. 354–391, B. III. It is a double impossibility : 1st, because a piracy from Tindal's ' Christianity as old as the Creation ' — a piracy *à parte ante,* and by three centuries ; 2dly, it is quite contrary to the evidence on Joanna's trial. Southey's ' Joan,' of A. D. 1796 (Cottle, Bristol), tells the doctors, amongst other secrets, that she never in her life attended — 1st, Mass ; nor 2d, the Sacramental table ; nor 3d, Confession. In the meantime, all this deistical confession of Joanna's, besides being suicidal for the interest of her cause, is opposed to the depositions upon *both* trials. The very best witness called from first to last, deposes that Joanna attended these rites of her church even too often ; was taxed with doing so ; and, by blushing, owned the charge as a fact, though certainly not as a fault. Joanna was a girl of natural piety, that saw God in forests, and hills, and fountains ; but did not the less seek him in chapels and consecrated oratories.

This peasant girl was self-educated through her own natural meditativeness. If the reader turns to that

divine passage in ' Paradise Regained,' which Milton
has put into the mouth of our Saviour when first entering the wilderness, and musing upon the tendency
of those great impulses growing within himself—

> ' Oh, what a multitude of thoughts at once
> Awaken'd in me swarm, while I consider
> What from within I feel myself, and hear
> What from without comes often to my ears,
> Ill sorting with my present state compared!
> When I was yet a child, no childish play
> To me was pleasing; all my mind was set
> Serious to learn and know, and thence to do
> What might be public good; myself I thought
> Born to that end ' —

he will have some notion of the vast reveries which
brooded over the heart of Joanna in early girlhood,
when the wings were budding that should carry her
from Orleans to Rheims; when the golden chariot was
dimly revealing itself, that should carry her from the
kingdom of *France Delivered* to the eternal kingdom.

It is not requisite, for the honor of Joanna, nor is
there, in this place, room to pursue her brief career of
*action*. That, though wonderful, forms the earthly
part of her story : the spiritual part is the saintly passion of her imprisonment, trial, and execution. It is
unfortunate, therefore, for Southey's ' Joan of Arc '
(which, however, should always be regarded as a
*juvenile* effort), that, precisely when her real glory
begins, the poem ends. But this limitation of the
interest grew, no doubt, from the constraint inseparably
attached to the law of epic unity. Joanna's history
bisects into two opposite hemispheres, and both coul-
not have been presented to the eye in one poem, un
.ess by sacrificing all unity of theme, or else by involv-

ing the earlier half, as a narrative episode, in the latter; which, however, might have been done, for it might have been communicated to a fellow-prisoner, or a confessor, by Joanna herself. It is sufficient, as concerns *this* section of Joanna's life, to say that she fulfilled, to the height of her promises, the restoration of the prostrate throne. France had become a province of England; and for the ruin of both, if such a yoke could be maintained. Dreadful pecuniary exhaustion caused the English energy to droop; and that critical opening *La Pucelle* used with a corresponding felicity of audacity and suddenness (that were in themselves portentous) for introducing the wedge of French native resources, for rekindling the national pride, and for planting the dauphin once more upon his feet. When Joanna appeared, he had been on the point of giving up the struggle with the English, distressed as they were, and of flying to the south of France. She taught him to blush for such abject counsels. She liberated Orleans, that great city, so decisive by its fate for the issue of the war, and then beleagured by the English with an elaborate application of engineering skill unprecedented in Europe. Entering the city after sunset, on the 29th of April, she sang mass on Sunday, May 8, for the entire disappearance of the besieging force. On the 29th of June, she fought and gained over the English the decisive battle of Patay; on the 9th of July, she took Troyes by a coup-de-main from a mixed garrison of English and Burgundians; on the 15th of that month, she carried the dauphin into Rheims; on Sunday the 17th, she crowned him; and there she rested from her labor of triumph. All that was to be *done,* she had now accomplished: what remained was — to *suffer*.

All this forward movement was her own: excepting one man, the whole council was against her. Her enemies were all that drew power from earth. Her supporters were her own strong enthusiasm, and the headlong contagion by which she carried this sublime frenzy into the hearts of women, of soldiers, and of all who lived by labor. Henceforwards she was thwarted; and the worst error that she committed was, to· lend the sanction of her presence to counsels which she had ceased to approve. But she had now accomplished the capital objects which her own visions had dictated. These involved all the rest. Errors were now less important; and doubtless it had now become more difficult for herself to pronounce authentically what *were* errors. The noble girl had achieved, as by a rapture of motion, the capital end of clearing out a free space around her sovereign, giving him the power to move his arms with effect; and, secondly, the inappreciable end of winning for that sovereign what seemed to all France the heavenly ratification of his rights, by crowning him with the ancient solemnities. She had made it impossible for the English now to step before her. They were caught in an irretrievable blunder, owing partly to discord amongst the uncles of Henry VI., partly to a want of funds, but partly to the very impossibility which they believed to press with tenfold force upon any French attempt to forestall theirs. They laughed at such a thought; and whilst they laughed, she *did* it. Henceforth the single redress for the English of this capital oversight, but which never *could* have redressed it effectually, was, to vitiate

and taint the coronation of Charles VII. as the work
of a witch. That policy, and not malice (as M.
Michelet is so happy to believe), was the moving
principle in the subsequent prosecution of Joanna.
Unless they unhinged the force of the first coronation
in the popular mind, by associating it with power given
from hell, they felt that the sceptre of the invader
was broken.

But she, the child that, at nineteen, had wrought
wonders so great for France, was she not elated? Did
she not lose, as men so often *have* lost, all sobriety of
mind when standing upon the pinnacle of success so
giddy? Let her enemies declare. During the progress of her movement, and in the centre of ferocious
struggles, she had manifested the temper of her feelings, by the pity which she had everywhere expressed
for the suffering enemy. She forwarded to the English
leaders a touching invitation to unite with the French,
as brothers, in a common crusade against infidels, thus
opening the road for a soldierly retreat. She interposed to protect the captive or the wounded—she
mourned over the excesses of her countrymen—she
threw herself off her horse to kneel by the dying
English soldier, and to comfort him with such ministrations, physical or spiritual, as his situation allowed.
' Nolebat,' says the evidence, ' uti ense suo, aut quem-
quam interficere.' She sheltered the English, that
invoked her aid, in her own quarters. She wept as
she beheld, stretched on the field of battle, so many
brave enemies that had died without confession. And,
as regarded herself, her elation expressed itself thus:
—On the day when she had finished her work, she
wept; for she knew that, when her *triumphal* task was

done, her end must be approaching. Her aspirations pointed only to a place, which seemed to her more than usually full of natural piety, as one in which it would give her pleasure to die. And she uttered, between smiles and tears, as a wish that inexpressibly fascinated her heart, and yet was half-fantastic, a broken prayer, that God would return her to the solitudes from which he had drawn her, and suffer her to become a shepherdess once more. It was a natural prayer, because nature has laid a necessity upon every human heart to seek for rest, and to shrink from torment. Yet, again, it was a half-fantastic prayer, because, from childhood upwards, visions that she had no power to mistrust, and the voices which sounded in her ear for ever, had long since persuaded her mind, that for *her* no such prayer could be granted. Too well she felt that her mission must be worked out to the end, and that the end was now at hand. All went wrong from this time. She herself had created the *funds* out of which the French restoration should grow; but she was not suffered to witness their development, or their prosperous application. More than one military plan was entered upon which she did not approve. But she still continued to expose her person as before. Severe wounds had not taught her caution. And at length, in a sortie from Compeigne (whether through treacherous collusion on the part of her own friends is doubtful to this day), she was made prisoner by the Burgundians, and finally surrendered to the English.

Now came her trial. This trial, moving of course under English influence, was conducted in chief by the Bishop of Beauvais. He was a Frenchman, sold to

English interests, and hoping, by favor of the English leaders, to reach the highest preferment. *Bishop
that art, Archbishop that shalt be, Cardinal that mayest
be,* were the words that sounded continually in his ear ;
and doubtless, a whisper of visions still higher, of a
triple crown, and feet upon the necks of kings, sometimes stole into his heart.   M. Michelet is anxious to
keep us in mind that this bishop was but an agent of
the English.   True.   But it does not better the case
for his countryman — that, being an accomplice in the
crime, making himself the leader in the persecution
against the helpless girl, he was willing to be all this
in the spirit, and with the conscious vileness of a cat's-
paw.   Never from the foundations of the earth was
there such a trial as this, if it were laid open in all its
beauty of defence, and all its hellishness of attack.   Oh,
child of France ! shepherdess, peasant girl ! trodden
under foot by all around thee, how I honor thy flashing intellect, quick as God's lightning, and true as
God's lightning to its mark, that ran before France
and laggard Europe by many a century, confounding
the malice of the ensnarer, and making dumb the
oracles of falsehood !   Is it not scandalous, is it
not humiliating to civilization, that, even at this
day, France exhibits the horrid spectacle of judges
examining the prisoner against himself; seducing
him, by fraud, into treacherous conclusions against
his own head ; using the terrors of their power for
extorting confessions from the frailty of hope ; nay
(which is worse), using the blandishments of conde-
scension and snaky kindness for thawing into compli-
ances of gratitude those whom they had failed to
freeze into terror ?   Wicked judges ! Barbarian juris-

prudence! that, sitting in your own conceit on the summits of social wisdom, have yet failed to learn the first principles of criminal justice; sit ye humbly and with docility at the feet of this girl from Domrémy, that tore your webs of cruelty into shreds and dust. 'Would you examine me as a witness against myself?' was the question by which many times she defied their arts. Continually she showed that their interrogations were irrelevant to any business before the court, or that entered into the ridiculous charges against her. General questions were proposed to her on points of casuistical divinity; two-edged questions, which not one of themselves could have answered without, on the one side, landing himself in heresy (as then inter-preted), or, on the other, in some presumptuous expression of self-esteem. Next came a wretched Dominican, that pressed her with an objeetion, which, if applied to the Bible would tax every one of its miracles with unsoundness. The monk had the excuse of never having read the Bible. M. Michelet has no such excuse; and it makes one blush for him, as a philosopher, to find him describing such an argument as 'weighty,' whereas it is but a varied expression of rude Mahometan metaphysics. Her answer to this, if there were room to place the whole in a clear light, was as shattering as it was rapid. Another thought to entrap her by asking what language the angelic visitors of her solitude had talked; as though heavenly counsels could want polyglot interpreters for every word, or that God needed language at all in whisper-ing thoughts to a human heart. Then came a worse devil, who asked her whether the archangel Michael had appeared naked. Not comprehending the vile insinua-

tion, Joanna, whose poverty suggested to her simplicity
that it might be the *costliness* of suitable robes which
caused the demur, asked them if they fancied God,
who clothed the flowers of the valleys, unable to find
raiment for his servants.   The answer of Joanna
moves a smile of tenderness, but the disappointment
of her judges makes one laugh exultingly.   Others
succeeded by troops, who upbraided her with leaving
her father; as if that greater Father, whom she believed
herself to have been serving, did not retain the power
of dispensing with his own rules, or had not said,
that, for a less cause than martyrdom, man and woman
ˉhould leave both father and mother.

On Easter Sunday, when the trial had been long
proceeding, the poor girl fell so ill as to cause a belief
that she had been poisoned.   It was not poison.   Nobody had any interest in hastening a death so certain.
M. Michelet, whose sympathies with all feelings are so
quick, that one would gladly see them always as justly
directed, reads the case most truly.   Joanna had a
twofold malady.   She was visited by a paroxysm of
the complaint called *home-sickness;* the cruel nature
of her imprisonment, and its length, could not but
point her solitary thoughts, in darkness and in chains
(for chained she was), to Domrémy,   And the season,
which was the most heavenly period of the spring,
added stings to this yearning.   That was one of her
maladies — *nostalgia,* as medicine calls it; the other
was weariness and exhaustion from daily combats with
malice.   She saw that everybody hated her, and
thirsted for her blood; nay, many kind-hearted creatures that would have pitied her profoundly, as regarded all political charges, had their natural feelings

warped by the belief that she had dealings with fiendish powers. She knew she was to die; that was *not*
the misery: the misery was, that this consummation
could not be reached without so much intermediate
strife, as if she were contending for some chance
(where chance was none) of happiness, or were dreaming for a moment of escaping the inevitable. Why,
then, *did* she contend? Knowing that she would reap
nothing from answering her persecutors, why did she
not retire by silence from the superfluous contest? It
was because her quick and eager loyalty to truth would
not suffer her to see it darkened by frauds, which *she*
could expose, but others, even of candid listeners,
perhaps could not; it was through that imperishable
grandeur of soul, which taught her to submit meekly
and without a struggle to her punishment, but taught
her *not* to submit — no, not for a moment — to calumny as to facts, or to misconstruction as to motives.
Besides, there were secretaries all around the court
taking down her words. That was meant for no good
to *her*. But the end does not always correspond to
the meaning. And Joanna might say to herself — these
words that will be used against me to-morrow and the
next day, perhaps in some nobler generation may rise
again for my justification. Yes, Joanna, they *are* rising
even now in Paris, and for more than justification.

Woman, sister — there are some things which you
do not execute as well as your brother, man; no, nor
ever will. Pardon me, if I doubt whether you will
ever produce a great poet from your choirs, or a Mozart, or a Phidias, or a Michael Angelo, or a great
philosopher, or a great scholar. By which last is
meant — not one who depends simply on an infinite

memory, but also on an infinite and electrical power
of combination; bringing together from the four winds,
like the angel of the resurrection, what else were dust
from dead men's bones, into the unity of breathing
life. If you *can* create yourselves into any of these
great creators, why have you not?

Yet, sister woman, though I cannot consent to find
a Mozart or a Michael Angelo in your sex, cheerfully,
and with the love that burns in depths of admiration,
I acknowledge that you can do one thing as well as
the best of us men — a greater thing than even Milton
is known to have done, or Michael Angelo — you can
die grandly, and as goddesses would die, were goddesses mortal. If any distant worlds (which *may* be
the case) are so far ahead of us Tellurians in optical
resources, as to see distinctly through their telescopes
all that we do on earth, what is the grandest sight to
which we ever treat them? St. Peter's at Rome, do
you fancy, on Easter Sunday, or Luxor, or perhaps the
Himalayas? Oh, no! my friend: suggest something
better; these are baubles to *them;* they see in other
worlds, in their own, far better toys of the same kind.
These, take my word for it, are nothing. Do you give
it up? The finest thing, then, we have to show them,
is a scaffold on the morning of execution. I assure
you there is a strong muster in those far telescopic
worlds, on any such morning, of those who happen to
find themselves occupying the right hemisphere for a
peep at *us*. How, then, if it be announced in some
such telescopic world by those who make a livelihood
of catching glimpses at our newspapers, whose lan
guage they have long since deciphered, that the poor
victim in the morning's sacrifice is a woman? How,

if it be published in that distant world, that the sufferer wears upon her head, in the eyes of many, the garlands of martyrdom? How, if it should be some Marie Antoinette, the widowed queen, coming forward on the scaffold, and presenting to the morning air her head turned gray by sorrow, daughter of Cæsars kneeling down humbly to kiss the guillotine, as one that worships death? How, if it were the noble Charlotte Corday, that in the bloom of youth, that with the loveliest of persons, that with homage waiting upon her smiles wherever she turned her face to scatter them — homage that followed those smiles as surely as the carols of birds, after showers in spring, follow the re-appearing sun and the racing of sunbeams over the hills — yet thought all these things cheaper than the dust upon her sandals, in comparison of deliverance from hell for her dear suffering France! Ah! these were spectacles indeed for those sympathizing people in distant worlds; and some, perhaps would suffer a sort of martyrdom themselves, because they could not testify their wrath, could not bear witness to the strength of love and to the fury of hatred that burned within them at such scenes; could not gather into golden urns some of that glorious dust which rested in the catacombs of earth.

On the Wednesday after Trinity Sunday in 1431, being then about nineteen years of age, the Maid of Arc underwent her martyrdom. She was conducted before mid-day, guarded by eight hundred spearmen, to a platform of prodigious height, constructed of wooden billets supported by occasional walls of lath and plaster, and traversed by hollow spaces in every direction for the creation of air-currents. The pile 'struck terror,' says M. Michelet, 'by its height;' and, as usual, the English purpose in this is viewed as one of pure malignity. But there are two ways of explaining all that. It is probable that the purpose was merciful. On the circumstances of the execution I shall not linger. Yet, to mark the almost fatal felicity of M. Michelet in finding out whatever may injure the English name, at a moment when every reader will be interested in Joanna's personal appearance, it is really edifying to notice the ingenuity by which he draws into light from a dark corner a very unjust account of it, and neglects, though lying upon the high road, a very pleasing one. Both are from English pens. Grafton, a chronicler but little read, being a stiff-necked John Bull, thought fit to say, that no wonder Joanna should be a virgin, since her 'foule face' was a satisfactory solution of that particular merit. Holinshead, on the other hand, a chronicler somewhat later, every way more important, and at one time universally read, has given a very pleasing testimony to the interesting character of Joanna's person and engaging manners. Neither of these men lived till the following century, so that personally this evidence is none at all. Grafton sullenly and carelessly believed as he wished to believe; Holinshead took pains to inquire, and reports undoubtedly the general impression of France. But I cite the case as illustrating M. Michelet's candor.[6]

The circumstantial incidents of the execution, unless with more space than I can now command, I should be unwilling to relate. I should fear to injure, by imperfect report, a martyrdom which to myself appears so unspeakably grand. Yet for a purpose, pointing not at Joanna, but at M. Michelet — viz., to convince him that an Englishman is capable of thinking more highly of *La Pucelle* than even her admiring countryman, I shall, in parting, allude to one or two traits in Joanna's demeanor on the scaffold, and to one or two in that of the bystanders, which authorize me in questioning an opinion of his upon this martyr's firmness. The reader ought to be reminded that Joanna D'Arc was subjected to an unusually unfair trial of opinion. Any of the elder Christian martyrs had not much to fear of *personal* rancor. The martyr was chiefly regarded as the enemy of Cæsar; at times, also, where any knowledge of the Christian faith and morals existed, with the enmity that arises spontaneously in the worldly against the spiritual. But the martyr, though disloyal, was not supposed to be, therefore, anti-national; and still less was *individually* hateful. What was hated (if anything) belonged to his class, not to himself separately. Now, Joanna, if hated at all, was hated personally, and in Rouen on national grounds. Hence there would be a certainty of calumny arising against *her*, such as would not affect martyrs in general. That being the case, it would follow of necessity that some people would impute to her a willingness to recant. No innocence could escape *that*. Now, had she really testified this willingness on the scaffold, it would have argued nothing at all but the weakness of a genial nature shrinking from the instant approach of torment. And those will often pity that weakness most, who, in their own persons, would yield to it least. Meantime, there never was a calumny uttered that drew less support from the recorded circumstances. It rests upon no *positive* testimony, and it has a weight of contra-

10

dicting testimony to stem. And yet, strange **to**
say, M. Michelet, who at times seems to admire the
Maid of Arc as much as I do, is the one sole writer
amongst her *friends* who lends some countenance to
this odious slander. His words are, that, if she did
not utter this word *recant* with her lips, she uttered it
in her heart. ' Whether she *said* the word is uncertain; but I affirm that she *thought* it.'

Now, I affirm that she did not ; not in any sense of·
the word ' *thought* ' applicable to the case. Here is
France calumniating *La Pucelle :* here is England defending her. M. Michelet can only mean that, on *à
priori* principles, every woman must be liable to such
a weakness : that Joanna was a woman ; *ergo*, that she
was liable to such a weakness. That is, he only supposes her· to have uttered the word by an argument
which presumes it impossible for anybody to have done
otherwise. I, on the contrary, throw the *onus* of the
argument not on presumable tendencies of nature, but
on the known facts of that morning's execution, as recorded by multitudes. What else, I demand, than
mere weight of metal, absolute nobility of deportment,
broke the vast line of battle then arrayed against her ?
What else but her meek, saintly demeanor won from
the enemies, that till now had believed her a witch,
tears of rapturous admiration ? ' Ten thousand men,'
says M. Michelet himself, ' ten thousand men wept ; '
and of these ten thousand the majority were political
enemies knitted together by cords of superstition.
What else was it but her constancy, united with her
angelic gentleness, that drove the fanatic English soldier — who had sworn to throw a faggot on her‿ scaffold, as *his* tribute of abhorrence, that *did* so, that ful-

filled his vow — suddenly to turn away a penitent for life, saying everywhere that he had seen a dove rising upon wings to heaven from the ashes where she had stood ? What else drove the executioner to kneel at every shrine for pardon to *his* share in the tragedy! And if all this were insufficient, then I cite the closing act of her life, as valid on her behalf, were all other testimonies against her. The executioner had been directed to apply his torch from below. He did so. The fiery smoke rose upwards in billowing volumes. A Dominican monk was then standing almost at her side. Wrapped up in his sublime office, he saw not the danger, but still persisted in his prayers. Even then, when the last enemy was racing up the fiery stairs to seize her, even at that moment did this noblest of girls think only for *him*, the one friend that would not forsake her, and not for herself; bidding him with her last breath to care for his own preservation, but to leave *her* to God. That girl, whose latest breath ascended in this sublime expression of self-oblivion, did not utter the word *recant* either with her lips or in her heart. No ; she did not, though one should rise from the dead to swear it.

. . . . . . . . . . .

Bishop of Beauvais ! thy victim died in fire upon a scaffold — thou upon a down bed. But for the departing minutes of life, both are oftentimes alike. At the farewèll crisis, when the gates of death are opening, and flesh is resting from its struggles, oftentimes the tortured and torturer have the same truce from carnal torment ; both sink together into sleep ; together both, sometimes, kindle into dreams. When the mortal mists were gathering fast upon you two, bishop and shepherd girl — when the pavilions of life

were closing up their shadowy curtains about you —
let us try, through the gigantic glooms, to decipher the
flying features of your separate visions.

The shepherd girl that had delivered France — she,
from her dungeon, she, from her baiting at the stake,
she, from her duel with fire, as she entered her last
dream — saw Domrémy, saw the fountain of Domrémy,
saw the pomp of forests in which her childhood had
wandered. That Easter festival, which man had denied to her languishing heart — that resurrection of
spring-time, which the darkness of dungeons had intercepted from *her*, hungering after the glorious liberty
of forests — were by God given back into her hands,
as jewels that had been stolen from her by robbers.
With those, perhaps (for the minutes of dreams can
stretch into ages), was given back to her by God the
bliss of childhood. By special privilege, for *her* might
be created, in this farewell dream, a second childhood,
innocent as the first; but not, like *that*, sad with the
gloom of a fearful mission in the rear. The mission
had now been fulfilled. The storm was weathered, the
skirts even of that mighty storm were drawing off.
The blood that she was to reckon for had been exacted; the tears that she was to shed in secret had
been paid to the last. The hatred to herself in all
eyes had been faced steadily, had been suffered, had
been survived. And in her last fight upon the scaffold
she had triumphed gloriously; victoriously she had
tasted the stings of death. For all, except this comfort from her farewell dream, she had died — died,
amidst the tears of ten thousand enemies — died,
amidst the drums and trumpets of armies — died,
amidst peals redoubling upon peals, volleys upon volleys, from the saluting clarions of martyrs.

Bishop of Beauvais! because • the guilt-burdened man is in dreams haunted and waylaid by the most frightful of his crimes, and because upon that fluctuating mirror — rising (like the mocking mirrors of *mirage* in Arabian deserts) from the fens of death — most of all are reflected the sweet countenances which the man has laid in ruins ; therefore I know, bishop, that you also, entering your final dream, saw Domrémy. That fountain, of which the witnesses spoke so much, showed itself to your eyes in pure morning dews : but neither dews, nor the holy dawn, could cleanse away the bright spots of innocent blood upon its surface. By the fountain, bishop, you saw a woman seated, that hid her face. But as *you* draw near, the woman raises her wasted features. Would Domrémy know them again for the features of her child ? ˙Ah, but *you* know them, bishop, well! Oh, mercy! what a groan was *that* which the servants, waiting outside the bishop's dream at his bedside, heard from his laboring heart, as at this moment he turned away from the fountain and the woman, seeking rest in the forests afar off. Yet not *so* to escape the woman, whom once again he must behold before he dies. In the forests to which he prays for pity, will he find a respite ? What a tumult, what a gathering of feet is there! In glades, where only wild deer should run, armies and nations are assembling ; towering in the fluctuating crowd are phantoms that belong to departed hours. There is the great English Prince, Regent of France. There is my Lord of Winchester, the princely cardinal, that died and made no sign. There is the Bishop of Beauvais, clinging to the shelter of thickets. What building is that which hands so rapid are raising ? Is it a martyr's scaffold ? Will

they burn the child.of Domrémy a second time? **No:**
it is a tribunal that rises to the clouds ; and two nations
stand around it, waiting for a trial.   Shall my Lord
of Beauvais sit again upon the judgment-seat, and
again number the hours for the innocent?  Ah! no:
he is the prisoner at the bar.   Already all is waiting :
the mighty audience is gathered, the Court is hurrying
to their seats, the witnesses are arrayed, the trumpets
are sounding, the judge is taking his place.   Oh! but
this is sudden.   My lord, have you no counsel?  'Counsel I have none : in heaven above, or on earth beneath, counsellor there is none now that would take a
brief from *me :* all are silent.'   Is it, indeed, come to
this ?   Alas the time is short, the tumult is wondrous,
the crowd stretches away into infinity, but yet I will
search in it for somebody to take your brief: I know
of somebody that will be your counsel.  .Who is this
that cometh from Domrémy?   Who is she in bloody
coronation robes from Rheims?  Who is she that
cometh with blackened flesh from walking the fur-
naces of Rouen?   This is she, the shepherd girl, counsellor that had none for herself, whom I choose, bishop,
for yours.   She it is, I engage, that shall take my
lord's brief.   She it is, bishop, that would plead for
you : yes, bishop, SHE — when heaven and earth are
silent.

# NOTES.

### Note 1.   Page 81.

'*Arc :*'— Modern France, that should know a great deal better than myself, insists that the name is not D'Arc — *i. e.*, of Arc — but *Darc*.   Now it happens sometimes, that if a person, whose position guarantees his access to the best information, will content himself with gloomy dogmatism, striking the table with his fist, and saying in a terrific voice, 'It *is* so; and there's an end of it,' one bows deferentially, and submits.   But if, unhappily for himself, won by this docility, he relents too amiably into reasons and arguments, probably one raises an insurrection against him that may never be crushed; for in the fields of logic one can skirmish, perhaps, as well as he.   Had he confined himself to dogmatism, he would have entrenched his position in darkness, and have hidden his own vulnerable points.   But, coming down to base reasons, he lets in light, and one sees where to plant the blows.   Now, the worshipful reason of modern France for disturbing the old received spelling, is — that Jean Hordal, a descendant of *La Pucelle's* brother, spelled the name *Darc*, in 1612.   But what of that?   It is notorious that what small matter of spelling Providence had thought fit to disburse amongst man in the seventeenth century, was all monopolized by printers; now, M. Hordal was *not* a printer.

### Note 2.   Page 82.

'*Those that share thy blood :*' — a collateral relative of Joanne's was subsequently ennobled by the title of *Du Lys*.

### Note 3.   Page 85.

'Only *now* forthcoming :' — In 1847 *began* the publication (from official records) of Joanna's trial.   It was interrupted, I fear, by the convulsions of 1848; and whether even yet finished, I do not know.

## NOTE 4.   Page 87.

' *Jean:* ' — M. Michelet asserts, that there was a mystical meaning at that era in calling a child *Jean;* it implied a secret commendation of a child, if not a dedication, to St. John the evangelist, the beloved disciple, the apostle of love and mysterious visions. But, really, as the name was so exceedingly common, few people will detect a mystery in calling a *boy* by the name of Jack, though it *does* seem mysterious to call a girl Jack. It may be less so in France, where a beautiful practice has always pre-vailed of giving to a boy his mother's name — preceded and strengthened by a male name, as *Charles Anne, Victor Vic toire.* In cases where a mother's memory has been unusually dear to a son, this vocal memento of her, locked into the circle of his own name, gives to it the tenderness of a testamentary relique, or a funeral ring. I presume, therefore, that *La Pucelle* must have borne the baptismal names of Jeanne Jean; the latter with no reference, perhaps, to so sublime a person as St. John, but simply to some relative.

## NOTE 5.   Page 88.

And reminding one of that inscription, so justly admired by Paul Richter, which a Russian Czarina placed on a guide-post near Moscow — *This is the road that leads to Constantinople.*

## NOTE 6.   Page 112.

Amongst the many ebullitions of M. Michelet's fury against us poor English, are four which will be likely to amuse the reader ; and they are the more conspicuous in collision with the justice which he sometimes does us, and the very indignant admiration which, under some aspects, he grants to us.

1. Our English literature he admires with some gnashing of teeth. He pronounces it ' fine and sombre,' but, I lament to add, ' sceptical, Judaic, Satanic — in a word, Anti-Christian.' That Lord Byron should figure as a member of this diabolical corpora-tion, will not surprise men. It *will* surprise them to hear that Milton is one of its Satanic leaders. Many are the generous and eloquent Frenchmen, besides Chateaubriand, who have, in the course of the last thirty years, nobly suspended their own burn-

ing nationality, in order to render a more rapturous homage at the feet of Milton; and some of them have raised Milton almost to a level with angelic natures. Not one of them has thought of looking for him *below* the earth. As to Shakspeare, M. Michelet detects in him a most extraordinary mare's nest. It is this: he does 'not recollect to have seen the name of God' in any part of his works. On reading such words, it is natural to rub one's eyes, and suspect that all one has ever seen in this world may have been a pure ocular delusion. In particular, I begin myself to suspect, that the word '*la gloire*' never occurs in any Parisian journal. 'The great English nation,' says M. Michelet, 'has one immense profound vice,' to wit, 'pride.' Why, really that may be true; but we have a neighbor not absolutely clear of an 'immense profound vice,' as like ours in color and shape as cherry to cherry. In short, M. Michelet thinks us, by fits and starts, admirable, only that we are detestable; and he would adore some of our authors, were it not that so intensely he could have wished to kick them.

2. M. Michelet thinks to lodge an arrow in our sides by a very odd remark upon Thomas a Kempis: which is, that a man of any conceivable European blood — a Finlander, suppose, or a Zantiote — might have written Tom; only not an Englishman. Whether an Englishman could have forged Tom, must remain a matter of doubt, unless the thing had been tried long ago. That problem was intercepted for ever by Tom's perverseness in choosing to manufacture himself. Yet, since nobody is better aware than M. Michelet that this very point of Kempis *having* manufactured Kempis is furiously and hopelessly litigated, three or four nations claiming to have forged his work for him, the shocking old doubt will raise its snaky head once more — whether this forger, who rests in so much darkness, might not, after all, be of English blood. Tom, it may be feared, is known to modern English literature chiefly by an irreverent mention of his name in a line of Peter Pindar's (Dr. Wolcot) fifty years back, where he is described as

'Kempis Tom,
Who clearly shows the way to Kingdom Come.'

Few in these days can have read him, unless in the Methodist version of John Wesley. Amongst those few, however, happens

**11**

to be myself; which arose from the accident of having, when a
boy of eleven, received a copy of the ' De Imitatione Christi,' as
a bequest from a relation, who died very young; from which
cause, and from the external prettiness of the book, being a
Glasgow reprint, by the celebrated Foulis, and gayly bound, I
was induced to look into it; and finally read it many times over,
partly out of some sympathy which, even in those days, I had
with its simplicity and devotional fervor; but much more from
the savage delight I found in laughing at Tom's Latinity. *That,*
I freely grant to M. Michelet, is inimitable. Yet, after all, it is
not certain whether the original *was* Latin. But, however *that*
may have been, if it is possible that M. Michelet * can be accurate in saying that there are no less than *sixty* French versions
(not editions, observe, but separate versions) existing of the ' De ·
Imitatione,' how prodigious must have been the adaptation of the
book to the religious heart of the fifteenth century ! Excepting
the Bible, but excepting *that* only, in Protestant lands, no book
known to man has had the same distinction. It is the most
marvellous bibliographical fact on record.

3. Our English girls, it seems, are as faulty in one way as we
English males in another. None of us men could have written
the *Opera Omnia* of Mr. à Kempis; neither could any of our
girls have assumed male attire like *La Pucelle*. But why?
Because, says Michelet, English girls and German think so much

---

* ' *If M. Michelet can be accurate :* '— However, on consideration, this statement does not depend on Michelet. The bibli-
ographer Barbier has absolutely *specified* sixty in a separate
dissertation, *soixante traductions,* amongst those even that have
not escaped the search. The Italian translations are said to be
thirty. As to mere *editions*, not counting the early MSS. for
half a century before printing was introduced, those in Latin
amount to two thousand, and those in French to one thousand.
Meantime, it is very clear to me that this astonishing popularity,
so entirely unparalleled in literature, could not have existed except in Roman Catholic times, nor subsequently have lingered in
any Protestant land. It was the denial of Scripture fountains to
thirsty lands which made this slender rill of Scripture truth so
passionately welcome.

of an indecorum. Well, that is a good fault, generally speaking. But M. Michelet ought to have remembered a fact in the martyrologies which justifies both parties — the French heroine for doing, and the general choir of English girls for *not* doing. A female saint, specially renowned in France, had, for a reason as weighty as Joanna's — viz., expressly to shield her modesty amongst men — worn a male military harness. That reason and that example authorized *La Pucelle ;* but our English girls, as a body, have seldom any such reason, and certainly no such saintly example, to plead. This excuses *them.* Yet, still, if it is indispensable to the national character that our young women should now and then trespass over the frontier of decorum, it then becomes a patriotic duty in me to assure M. Michelet that we have such ardent females amongst us, and in a long series ; some detected in naval hospitals, when too sick to remember their disguise; some on fields of battle; multitudes never detected at all; some only suspected; and others discharged without noise by war offices and other absurd people. In our navy, both royal and commercial, and generally from deep remembrances of slighted love, women have sometimes served in disguise for many years, taking contentedly their daily allowance of burgoo, biscuit, or cannon-balls — anything, in short, digestible or indigestible, that it might please Providence to send. One thing, at least, is to their credit : never any of these poor masks, with their deep silent remembrances, have been detected through murmuring, or what is nautically understood by ' skulking.' So, for once, M. Michelet has an *erratum* to enter upon the fly-leaf of his book in presentation copies.

4. But the last of these ebullitions is the most lively. We English, at Orleans, and after Orleans (which is not quite so extraordinary, if all were told), fled before the Maid of Arc. Yes, says M. Michelet, you *did :* deny it, if you can. Deny it, *mon cher ?* I don't mean to deny it. Running away, in many cases, is a thing so excellent, that no philosopher would, at times, condescend to adopt any other step. All of us nations in Europe, without one exception, have shown our philosophy in that way at times. Even people, ' *qui ne se rendent pas,*' have deigned both to run and to shout, ' *Sauve qui peut!* ' at odd times of sunset ; though, for my part, I have no pleasure in recalling unpleasant

remembrances to brave men ; and yet, really, being so philosophic, they ought *not* to be unpleasant.    But the amusing feature in M. Michelet's reproach is the way in which he *improves*
and varies against us the charge of running, as if he were singing
a catch.    Listen to him.    They '*showed their backs*,' did these
English.    (Hip, hip, hurrah! three times three !)    '*Behind
good walls, they let themselves be taken*.'    (Hip, hip ! nine times
nine !)    They '*ran as fast as their legs could carry them*.'
(Hurrah ! twenty-seven times twenty-seven !)    They '*ran before
a girl;*' they did.    (Hurrah ! eighty-one times eighty-one !)
This reminds one of criminal indictments on the old model in
English courts, where (for fear the prisoner should escape) the
crown lawyer varied the charge perhaps through forty counts.
The law laid its guns so as to rake the accused at every possible
angle.    Whilst the indictment was reading, he seemed a monster
of crime in his own eyes; and yet, after all, the poor fellow had
but committed one offence, and not always *that*.    N. B. — Not
having the French original at hand, I make my quotations from
a friend's copy of Mr. Walter Kelly's translation, which seems
to me faithful, spirited, and idiomatically English — liable, in
fact, only to the single reproach of occasional provincialisms.

# THE ENGLISH MAIL-COACH.

## SECTION THE FIRST. — THE GLORY OF MOTION.

SOME twenty or more years before I matriculated at Oxford, Mr. Palmer, at that time M. P. for Bath, had accomplished two things, very hard to do on our little planet, the Earth, however cheap they may be held by eccentric people in comets — he had invented mail-coaches, and he had married the daughter [1] of a duke. He was, therefore, just twice as great a man as Galileo, who did certainly invent (or which is the same thing, [2] discover) the satellites of Jupiter, those very next things extant to mail-coaches in the two capital pretensions of speed and keeping time, but, on the other hand, who did not marry the daughter of a duke.

These mail-coaches, as organzied by Mr. Palmer, are entitled to a circumstantial notice from myself, having had so large a share in developing the anarchies of my subsequent dreams; an agency which they accomplished, 1st, through velocity, at that time unprecedented — for they first revealed the glory of motion; 2dly, through grand effects for the eye between lamp-light and the darkness upon solitary roads; 3dly, through animal beauty and power so often displayed in the class of horses selected for this mail service; 4thly, through the conscious presence of a central intellect, that, in the midst of vast distances [3] — of storms, of darkness, of danger — overruled all

obstacles into one steady co-operation to a national
result.   For my own feeling, this post-office service
spoke as by some mighty orchestra, where a thousand
instruments, all disregarding each other, and so far in
danger of discord, yet all obedient as slaves to the
supreme *baton* of some great leader, terminate in a
perfection of harmony like that of heart, brain, and
lungs, in a healthy animal organization.   But, finally,
that particular element in this whole combination
which most impressed myself, and through which it is
that to this hour Mr. Palmer's mail-coach system ty-
rannizes over my dreams by terror and terrific beauty,
lay in the awful *political* mission which at that time it
fulfilled.   The mail-coach it was that distributed over
the face of the land, like the opening of apocalyptic
vials, the heart-shaking news of Trafalgar, of Salamanca, of Vittoria, of Waterloo.   These were the
harvests that, in the grandeur of their reaping, redeemed the tears and blood in which they had been
sown.   Neither was the meanest peasant so much
below the grandeur and the sorrow of the times as to
confound battles such as these, which were gradually
moulding the destinies of Christendom, with the vulgar conflicts of ordinary warfare, so often no more
than gladiatorial trials of national prowess.   The
victories of England in this stupendous contest rose
of themselves as natural *Te Deums* to heaven; and it
was felt by the thoughtful that such victories, at such
a crisis of general prostration, were not more beneficial to ourselves than finally to France, our enemy,
and to the nations of all western or central Europe,
through whose pusillanimity it was that the French
domination had prospered.

The mail-coach, as the national organ for publishing these mighty events thus diffusively influential, became itself a spiritualized and glorified object to an impassioned heart; and naturally, in the Oxford of that day, *all* hearts were impassioned, as being all (or nearly all) in *early* manhood. In most universities there is one single college; in Oxford there were five-and-twenty, all of which were peopled by young men, the *élite* of their own generation; not boys, but men; none under eighteen. In some of these many colleges, the custom permitted the student to keep what are called 'short terms;' that is, the four terms of Michaelmas, Lent, Easter, and Act, were kept by a residence, in the aggregate of ninety-one days, or thirteen weeks. Under this interrupted residence, it was possible that a student might have a reason for going down to his home four times in the year. This made eight journeys to and fro. But, as the homes lay dispersed through all the shires of the island, and most of us disdained all coaches except his majesty's mail, no city out of London could pretend to so extensive a connection with Mr. Palmer's establishment as Oxford. Three mails, at the least, I remember as passing every day through Oxford, and benefiting by my personal patronage — viz., the Worcester, the Gloucester, and the Holyhead mail. Naturally, therefore, it became a point of some interest with us, whose journeys revolved every six weeks on an average, to look a little into the executive details of the system. With some of these Mr. Palmer had no concern; they rested upon bye-laws enacted by posting-houses for their own benefit, and upon other bye-laws, equally stern, enacted by the inside passengers for the illustration of their own

haughty exclusiveness.   These last were of a nature to
rouse our scorn, from which the transition was not
very long to systematic mutiny.   Up to this time, say
1804, or 1805 (the year of Trafalgar), it had been the
fixed assumption of the four inside people (as an old
tradition of all public carriages derived from the reign
of Charles II.), that they, the illustrious quaternion,
constituted a porcelain variety of the human race,
whose dignity would have been compromised by exchanging one word of civility with the three miserable
delf-ware outsides.   Even to have kicked an outsider,
might have been held to attaint the foot concerned in
that operation ;  so that, perhaps, it would have required an act of parliament to restore its purity of
blood.   What words, then, could express the horror,
and the sense of treason, in that case, which *had* happened, where all three outsides (the trinity of Pariahs)
made a vain attempt to sit down at the same breakfast-
table or dinner-table with the consecrated four ?   I
myself witnessed such an attempt; and on that occasion a benevolent old gentleman endeavored to soothe
his three holy associates, by suggesting that, if the
outsides were indicted for this criminal attempt at the
next assizes, the court would regard it as a case of
lunacy, or *delirium tremens*, rather than of treason.
England owes much of her grandeur to the depth of
the aristocratic element in her social composition, when
pulling against her strong democracy.   I am not the
man to laugh at it.   But sometimes, undoubtedly, it
expressed itself in comic shapes.   The course taken
with the infatuated outsiders, in the particular attempt
which I have noticed, was, that the waiter, beckoning
them away from the privileged *salle-à-manger*, sang

out, 'This way, my good men,' and then enticed these good men away to the kitchen. But that plan had not always answered. Sometimes, though rarely, cases occurred where the intruders, being stronger than usual, or more vicious than usual, resolutely refused to budge, and so far carried their point, as to have a separate table arranged for themselves in a corner of the general room. Yet, if an Indian screen could be found ample enough to plant them out from the very eyes of the high table, or *dais*, it then became possible to assume as a fiction of law — that the three delf fellows, after all, were not present. They could be ignored by the porcelain men, under the maxim, that objects not appearing, and not existing, are governed by the same logical construction.[4]

Such being, at that time, the usages of mail-coaches, what was to be done by us of young Oxford? We, the most aristocratic of people, who were addicted to the practice of looking down superciliously even upon the insides themselves as often very questionable characters — were we, by voluntarily going outside, to court indignities? If our dress and bearing sheltered us, generally, from the suspicion of being ' raff' (the name at that period for ' snobs '[5]), we really *were* such constructively, by the place we assumed. If we did not submit to the deep shadow of eclipse, we entered at least the skirts of its penumbra. And the analogy of theatres was valid against us, where no man can complain of the annoyances incident to the pit or gallery, having his instant remedy in paying the higher price of the boxes. But the soundness of this analogy we disputed. In the case of the theatre, it cannot be pretended that the inferior situations have any separate attractions, unless the pit may be supposed to have an advantage for the purposes of the critic or the dramatic reporter. But the critic or reporter is a rarity. For most people, the sole benefit is in the price. Now, on the contrary, the outside of the mail had its own incommunicable advantages. These we could not forego. The higher price we would willingly have paid, but not the price connected with the condition of riding inside; which condition we pronounced insufferable. The air, the freedom of prospect, the proximity to the horses, the elevation of seat — these were what we required; but, above all, the certain anticipation of purchasing occasional opportunities of driving.

Such was the difficulty which pressed us; and under the coercion of this difficulty, we instituted a searching inquiry into the true quality and valuation of the different apartments about the mail. We conducted this inquiry on metaphysical principles; and it was ascertained satisfactorily, that the roof of the coach, which by some weak men had been called the attics, and by some the garrets, was in reality the drawing-room; in which drawing-room the box was the chief ottoman or sofa; whilst it appeared that the *inside*, which had been traditionally regarded as the only room tenantable by gentlemen, was, in fact, the coal-cellar in disguise.

Great wits jump. The very same idea had not long before struck the celestial intellect of China. Amongst the presents carried out by our first embassy to that country was a state-coach. It had been specially selected as a personal gift by George III.; but the exact mode of using it was an immense mystery to Pekin. The ambassador, indeed (Lord Macartney), had made some imperfect explanations upon this point; but, as his excellency communicated these in a diplomatic whisper, at the very moment of his departure, the celestial intellect was very feebly illuminated, and it became necessary to call a cabinet council on the grand state question, 'Where was the emperor to sit?' The hammer-cloth happened to be unusually gorgeous; and partly on that consideration, but partly also because the box offered the most elevated seat, was nearest to the moon, and undeniably went foremost, it was resolved by acclamation that the box was the imperial throne, and for the scoundrel who drove, he might sit where he could find a perch. The horses, therefore, being harnessed, solemnly his imperial majesty ascended his new English throne under a flourish of trumpets, having the first lord of the treasury on his right hand, and the chief jester on his left. Pekin gloried in the spectacle; and in the whole flowery people, constructively present by representation, there was but one discontented person, and *that* was the coachman. This mutinous individual audaciously shouted, 'Where am *I* to sit?' But the privy council, incensed by his disloyalty, unanimously opened the door, and kicked him into the inside. He had all the inside places to himself; but such is the rapacity of ambition, that he was still dissatisfied. 'I say,' he cried out in an extempore petition, addressed to the emperor through the window — 'I say, how am I to catch hold of the reins?' — 'Anyhow,' was the imperial answer; ' don't trouble *me*, man, in my glory. How catch the reins? Why, through the windows, through the keyholes — *any*how.' Finally this contumacious coachman lengthened the check-strings into a sort of jury-reins, communicating with the horses; with these he drove as steadily as Pekin had any right to expect. The emperor returned after the briefest of circuits; he descended in great pomp from his throne, with the severest resolution never to remount it. A public thanksgiving was ordered for his majesty's happy escape from the disease of broken neck; and the state-coach was dedicated thenceforward as a votive offering to the god Fo, Fo — whom the learned more accurately called Fi, Fi.

A revolution of this same Chinese character did young Oxford of that era effect in the constitution of mail-coach society. It was a perfect French revolution; and we had good reason to say, *ça ira*. In fact, it soon became *too* popular. The 'public,' a well-known character, particularly disagreeable, though slightly respectable, and notorious for affecting the chief seats in synagogues — had at first loudly opposed this revolution; but when the opposition showed itself to be ineffectual, our disagreeable friend went into it with headlong zeal. At first it was a sort of race between us; and, as the public is usually from thirty to fifty years old, naturally we of young Oxford, that averaged about twenty, had the advantage. Then the public took to bribing, giving fees to horse-keepers, &c., who hired out their persons as warming-pans on the box-seat. *That*, you know, was shocking to all moral sensibilities. Come to bribery, said we, and there is an end to all morality, Aristotle's, Zeno's, Cicero's, or anybody's. And, besides, of what use was it? For *we* bribed also. And as our bribes to those of the public were as five shillings to sixpence, here again young Oxford had the advantage. But the contest was ruinous to the principles of the stables connected with the mails. This whole corporation was constantly bribed, rebribed, and often sur-rebribed; a mail-coach yard was like the hustings in a contested election; and a horse-keeper, hostler, or helper, was held by the philosophical at that time to be the most corrupt character in the nation.

There was an impression upon the public mind, natural enough from the continually augmenting velocity of the mail, but quite erroneous, that an outside seat on this class of carriages was a post of danger. On the contrary, I maintained that, if a man had become nervous from some gipsy prediction in his childhood, allocating to a particular moon now approaching some unknown danger, and he should inquire earnestly, 'Whither can I fly for shelter? Is a prison the safest retreat? or a lunatic hospital? or the British Museum?' I should have replied, 'Oh, no; I'll tell you what to do. Take lodgings for the next forty days on the box of his majesty's mail. Nobody can touch you there. If it is by bills at ninety days after date that you are made unhappy — if noters and protesters are the sort of wretches whose astrological shadows darken the house of life — then note you what I vehemently protest — viz., that no matter though the sheriff and under-sheriff in every county should be running after you with his *posse*, touch a hair of your head he cannot whilst you keep house, and have your legal domicile on the box of the mail. It is felony to stop the mail; even the sheriff cannot do that. And an *extra* touch of the whip to the leaders (no great matter if it grazes the sheriff) at any time guarantees your safety.' In fact, a bedroom in a quiet house

seems a safe enough retreat, yet it is liable to its own
notorious nuisances — to robbers by night, to rats, to
fire.  But the mail laughs at these terrors.  To robbers,
the answer is packed up and ready for delivery in the
barrel of the guard's blunderbuss.  Rats again! — there
*are* none about mail-coaches, any more than snakes in
Von Troil's Iceland; [6] except, indeed, now and then a
parliamentary rat, who always hides his shame in what
I have shown to be the ' coal-cellar.'   And as to fire,
I never knew but one in a mail-coach, which was in
the Exeter mail, and caused by an obstinate sailor
bound to Devonport.  Jack, making light of the law
and the lawgiver that had set their faces against his
offence, insisted on taking up a forbidden seat [7] in the
rear of the roof, from which he could exchange his
own yarns with those of the guard.  No greater offence was then known to mail-coaches; it was treason,
it was *læsa majestas*, it was by tendency arson; and
the ashes of Jack's pipe, falling amongst the straw of
the hinder boot containing the mail-bags, raised a
flame which (aided by the wind of our motion) threatened a revolution in the republic of letters.  Yet even
this left the sanctity of the box unviolated.  In dignified repose, the coachman and myself sat on, resting
with benign composure upon our knowledge that the
fire would have to burn its way through four inside
passengers before it could reach ourselves.  I remarked to the coachman, with a quotation from Virgil's
' Æneid ' really too hackneyed —

> ' Jam proximus ardet
> Ucalegon.'

But, recollecting that the Virgilian part of the coachman's education might have been neglected, I inter-

preted so far as to say, that perhaps at that moment the flames were catching hold of our worthy brother and inside passenger, Ucalegon. The coachman made no answer, which is my own way when a stranger addresses me either in Syriac or in Coptic, but by his faint sceptical smile he seemed to insinuate that he knew better; for that Ucalegon, as it happened, was not in the way-bill, and therefore could not have been booked.

No dignity is perfect which does not at some point ally itself with the mysterious. The connection of the mail with the state and the executive government — a connection obvious, but yet not strictly defined — gave to the whole mail establishment an official grandeur which did us service on the roads, and invested us with seasonable terrors. Not the less impressive were those terrors, because their legal limits were imperfectly ascertained. Look at those turnpike gates; with what deferential hurry, with what an obedient start, they fly open at our approach! Look at that long line of carts and carters ahead, audaciously usurping the very crest of the road. Ah! traitors, they do not hear us as yet; but, as soon as the dreadful blast of our horn reaches them with proclamation of our approach, see with what frenzy of trepidation they fly to their horses' heads, and deprecate our wrath by the precipitation of their crane-neck quarterings. Treason they feel to be their crime; each individual carter feels himself under the ban of confiscation and attainder; his blood is attainted through six generations; and nothing is wanting but the headsman and his axe, the block and the saw-dust, to close up the vista of his horrors. What! shall it be within

benefit of clergy to delay the king's message on the
high road? — to interrupt the great respirations, ebb
and flood, *systole* and *diastole*, of the national intercourse? — to endanger the safety of tidings, running
day and night between all nations and languages?
Or can it be fancied, amongst the weakest of men,
that the bodies of the criminals will be given up to
their widows for Christian burial? Now the doubts
which were raised as to our powers did more to wrap
them in terror, by wrapping them in uncertainty, than
could have been effected by the sharpest definitions of
the law from the Quarter Sessions. We, on our parts
(we, the collective mail, I mean), did our utmost to
exalt the idea of our privileges by the insolence with
which we wielded them. Whether this insolence
rested upon law that gave it a sanction, or upon conscious power that haughtily dispensed with that sanction, equally it spoke from a potential station; and
the agent, in each particular insolence of the moment,
was viewed reverentially, as one having authority.

Sometimes after breakfast his majesty's mail would
become frisky; and in its difficult wheelings amongst
the intricacies of early markets, it would upset an
apple-cart, a cart loaded with eggs, &c. Huge was
the affliction and dismay, awful was the smash. I, as
far as possible, endeavored in such a case to represent
the conscience and moral sensibilities of the mail;
and, when wildernesses of eggs were lying poached
under our horses' hoofs, then would I stretch forth
my hands in sorrow saying (in words too celebrated at
that time, from the false echoes[8] of Marengo), 'Ah!
wherefore have we not time to weep over you?' which
was evidently impossible, since, in fact, we had not

time to laugh over them. Tied to post-office allowance, in some cases of fifty minutes for eleven miles,
could the royal mail pretend to undertake the offices
of sympathy and condolence? Could it be expected
to provide tears for the accidents of the road? If
even it seemed to trample on humanity, it did so, I
felt, in discharge of its own more peremptory duties.

Upholding the morality of the mail, *à fortiori* I
upheld its rights; as a matter of duty, I stretched to
the uttermost its privilege of imperial precedency, and
astonished weak minds by the feudal powers which I
hinted to be lurking constructively in the charters of
this proud establishment. Once I remember being on
the box of the Holyhead mail, between Shrewsbury
and Oswestry, when a tawdry thing from Birmingham,
some 'Tallyho' or 'Highflyer,' all flaunting with
green and gold, came up alongside of us. What a
contrast to our royal simplicity of form and color in
this plebeian wretch! The single ornament on our
dark ground of chocolate color was the mighty
shield of the imperial arms, but emblazoned in proportions as modest as a signet-ring bears to a seal of
office. Even this was displayed only on a single
panel, whispering, rather than proclaiming, our relations to the mighty state; whilst the beast from Birmingham, our green-and-gold friend from false, fleet-
ing, perjured Brummagem, had as much writing and
painting on its sprawling flanks as would have puzzled
a decipherer from the tombs of Luxor. For some
time this Birmingham machine ran along by our side
— a piece of familiarity that already of itself seemed
to me sufficiently jacobinical. But all at once a movement of the horses announced a desperate intention of

12

leaving us behind. 'Do you see *that*?' I said to the coachman. — 'I see,' was his short answer. He was wide awake, yet he waited longer than seemed prudent ; for the horses of our audacious opponent had a disagreeable air of freshness and power. But his motive was loyal ; his wish was, that the Birmingham conceit should be full-blown before he froze it. When *that* seemed right, he unloosed, or, to speak by a stronger word, he *sprang*, his known resources : he slipped our royal horses like cheetahs, or hunting-leopards, after the affrighted game. How they could retain such a reserve of fiery power after the work they had accomplished, seemed hard to explain. But on our side, besides the physical superiority, was a tower of moral strength, namely, the king's name, ' which they upon the adverse faction wanted.' Passing them without an effort, as it seemed, we threw them into the rear with so lengthening an interval between us, as proved in itself the bitterest mockery of their presumption ; whilst our guard blew back a shattering blast of triumph, that was really too painfully full of derision.

I mention this little incident for its connection with what followed. A Welsh rustic, sitting behind me, asked if I had not felt my heart burn within me during the progress of the race? I said, with philosophic calmness, *No ;* because we were not racing with a mail, so that no glory could be gained. In fact, it was sufficiently mortifying that such a Birmingham thing should dare to challenge us. The Welshman replied, that he didn't see *that ;* for that a cat might look at a king, and a Brummagem coach might lawfully race the Holyhead mail. ' *Race* us, if you like,' I replied, ' though even *that* has an air of sedition, but not *beat* us. This would have been treason; and for its own sake I am glad that the "Tallyho" was disappointed.' So dissatisfied did the Welshman seem with this opinion, that at last I was obliged to tell him a very fine story from one of our elder dramatists — viz., that once, in some far oriental kingdom, when the sultan of all the land, with his princes, ladies, and chief omrahs, were flying their falcons, a hawk suddenly flew at a majestic eagle ; and in defiance of the eagle's natural advantages, in contempt also of the eagle's traditional royalty, and before the whole assembled field of astonished spectators from Agra, and Lahore, killed the eagle on the spot. Amazement seized the sultan at the unequal contest, and burning admiration for its unparalleled result. He commanded that the hawk should be brought before him; he caressed the bird with enthusiasm; and he ordered that, for the commemoration of his matchless courage, a diadem of gold and rubies should be solemnly placed on the hawk's head; but then that, immediately after this solemn coronation, the bird should be led off to execution, as the most valiant indeed of traitors, but not the less a traitor, as having dared to rise rebelliously against his liege lord and anointed sovereign, the eagle. ' Now,' said I to the Welshman, ' to you and me, as men of refined sensibilities, how painful it would have been that this poor Brummagem brute, the "Tallyho," in the impossible case of a victory over us, should have been crowned with Birmingham tinsel, with paste diamonds, and Roman pearls, and then led off to instant execution.' The Welshman doubted if that could be warranted by law. And when I hinted

at the 6th of Edward Longshanks, chap. 18, for regu‑
lating the precedency of coaches, as being probably
the statute relied on for the capital punishment of
such offences, he replied drily, that if the attempt to
pass a mail really were treasonable, it was a pity that
the 'Tallyho' appeared to have so imperfect an ac-
· quaintance with law.

The modern modes of travelling cannot compare
with the old mail-coach system in grandeur and
power.    They boast of more velocity, not, however,
as a consciousness, but as a fact of our lifeless knowledge, resting upon *alien* evidence; as, for instance,
because somebody *says* that we have gone fifty miles
in the hour, though we are far from feeling it as a personal experience, or upon the evidence of a result, as
that actually we find ourselves in York four hours
after leaving London.    Apart from such an assertion,
or such a result, I myself am little aware of the pace.
But, seated on the old mail-coach, we needed no evidence out of ourselves to indicate the velocity.    On
this system the word was, *Non magna loquimur*, as
upon railways, but *vivimus*.    Yes, 'magna *vivimus;*'
we do not make verbal ostentation of our grandeurs,
we realize our grandeurs in act, and in the very experience of life.    The vital experience of the glad
animal sensibilities made doubts impossible on the
question of our speed; we heard our speed, we saw it,
we felt it as a thrilling; and this speed was not the
product of blind insensate agencies, that had no sympathy to give, but was incarnated in the fiery eyeballs
of the noblest amongst brutes, in his dilated nostril,
spasmodic muscles, and thunder-beating hoofs.    The
sensibility of the horse, uttering itself in the maniac

fight of his eye, might be the last vibration of such a movement; the glory of Salamanca might be the first. But the intervening links that connected them, that spread the earthquake of battle into the eyeball of the horse, were the heart of man and its electric thrillings — kindling in the rapture of the fiery strife, and then propagating its own tumults by contagious shouts and gestures to the heart of his servant the horse.

But now, on the new system of travelling, iron tubes and boilers have disconnected man's heart from the ministers of his locomotion. Nile nor Trafalgar has power to raise an extra bubble in a steam-kettle. The galvanic cycle is broken up for ever; man's imperial nature no longer sends itself forward through the electric sensibility of the horse; the inter-agencies are gone in the mode of communication between the horse and his master, out of which grew so many aspects of sublimity under accidents of mists that hid, or sudden blazes that revealed, of mobs that agitated, or midnight solitudes that awed. Tidings, fitted to convulse all nations, must henceforwards travel by culinary process; and the trumpet that once announced from afar the laurelled mail, heart-shaking, when heard screaming on the wind, and proclaiming itself through the darkness to every village or solitary house on its route, has now given way for ever to the pot-wallopings of the boiler.

Thus have perished multiform openings for public expressions of interest, scenical yet natural, in great national tidings; for revelations of faces and groups that could not offer themselves amongst the fluctuating mobs of a railway station. The gatherings of gazers about a laurelled mail had one centre, and acknowl-

edged one sole interest. But the crowds attending **at**
a railway station have as little unity as running **water,**
and own as many centres as there are separate **car-**
riages in the train.

How else, for example, than as a constant watcher
for the dawn, and for the London mail that in summer
months entered about daybreak amongst the lawny
thickets of Marlborough forest, couldst thou, sweet
Fanny of the Bath road, have become the glorified
inmate of my dreams? Yet Fanny, as the loveliest
young woman for face and person that perhaps in my
whole life I have beheld, merited the station which
even now, from a distance of forty years, she holds in
my dreams; yes, though by links of natural association
she brings along with her a troop of dreadful creatures,
fabulous and not fabulous, that are more abominable
to the heart, than Fanny and the dawn are delightful.

Miss Fanny of the Bath road, strictly speaking,
lived at a mile's distance from the road; but came so
continually to meet the mail, that I on my frequent
transits rarely missed her, and naturally connected her
image with the great thoroughfare where only I had
ever seen her. Why she came so punctually, I do not
exactly know; but I believe with some burden of
commissions to be executed in Bath, which had gathered to her own residence as a central rendezvous for
converging them. The mail-coachman who drove the
Bath mail, and wore the royal livery,[9] happened to be
Fanny's grandfather. A good man he was, that loved
his beautiful granddaughter; and, loving her wisely,
was vigilant over her deportment in any case where
young Oxford might happen to be concerned. Did my
vanity then suggest that I myself, individually, could fall

within the line of his terrors? Certainly not, as regarded any physical pretensions that I could plead; for Fanny (as a chance passenger from her own neighborhood once told me) counted in her train a hundred and ninety-nine professed admirers, if not open aspirants to her favor; and probably not one of the whole brigade but excelled myself in personal advantages. Ulysses even, with the unfair advantage of his accursed bow, could hardly have undertaken that amount of suitors. So the danger might have seemed slight — only that woman is universally aristocratic; it is amongst her nobilities of heart that she *is* so. Now, the aristocratic distinctions in my favor might easily with Miss Fanny have compensated my physical deficiencies. Did I then make love to Fanny? Why, yes; about as much love as one *could* make whilst the mail was changing horses — a process which, ten years later, did not occupy above eighty seconds; but *then* — viz., about Waterloo — it occupied five times eighty. Now, four hundred seconds offer a field quite ample enough for whispering into a young woman's ear a great deal of truth, and (by way of parenthesis) some trifle of falsehood. Grandpapa did right, therefore, to watch me. And yet, as happens too often to the grandpapas of earth, in a contest with the admirers of granddaughters, how vainly would he have watched me had I meditated any evil whispers to Fanny! She, it is my belief, would have protected herself against any man's evil suggestions. But he, as the result showed, could not have intercepted the opportunities for such suggestions. Yet, why not? Was he not active? Was he not blooming? Blooming he was as Fanny herself.

‘ Say, all our praises why should lords ——’
Stop, that’s not the line.

‘ Say, all our roses why should girls engross ? ’

The coachman showed rosy blossoms on his face
deeper even than his granddaughter’s — *his* being
drawn from the ale cask, Fanny’s from the fountains
of the dawn.   But, in spite of his blooming face, some
infirmities he had; and one particularly in which he
too much resembled a crocodile.   This lay in a monstrous inaptitude for turning round.   The crocodile, I
presume, owes that inaptitude to the absurd *length* of
his back; but in our grandpapa it arose rather from
the absurd *breadth* of his back, combined, possibly,
with some growing stiffness in his legs.   Now, upon
this crocodile infirmity of his I planted a human advantage for tendering my homage to Miss Fanny.   In
defiance of all his honorable vigilance, no sooner had
he presented to us his mighty Jovian back (what a
field for displaying to mankind his royal scarlet!’),
whilst inspecting professionally the buckles, the straps,
and the silvery turrets [10] of his harness, than I raised
Miss Fanny’s hand to my lips, and, by the mixed tenderness and respectfulness of my manner, caused her
easily to understand how happy it would make me to
rank upon her list as No. 10 or 12, in which case a
few casualties amongst her lovers (and observe, they
*hanged* liberally in those days might have promoted
me speedily to the top of the tree ; as, on the other
hand, with how much loyalty of submission I acqui-
esced by anticipation in her award, supposing that she
should plant me in the very rearward of her favor, as
No. 199 + 1.   Most truly I loved this beautiful and
ingenuous girl; and had it not been for the Bath

mail, timing all courtships by post-office allowance, heaven only knows what might have come of it. People talk of being over head and ears in love; now, the mail was the cause that I sank only over ears in love, which, you know, still left a trifle of brain to overlook the whole conduct of the affair.

Ah, reader! when I look back upon those days, it seems to me that all things change — all things perish ' Perish the roses and the palms of kings : ' perish even the crowns and trophies of Waterloo : thunder and lightning are not the thunder and lightning which I remember. Roses are degenerating. The Fannies of our island — though this I say with reluctance — are not visibly improving ; and the Bath road is notoriously superannuated. Crocodiles, you will say, are stationary. Mr. Waterton tells me that the crocodile does *not* change ; that a cayman, in fact, or an alligator, is just as good for riding upon as he was in the time of the Pharaohs. *That* may be ; but the reason is, that the crocodile does not live fast — he is a slow coach. I believe it is generally understood among naturalists, that the crocodile is a blockhead. It is my own impression that the Pharaohs were also blockheads. Now, as the Pharaohs and the crocodile domineered over Egyptian society, this accounts for a singular mistake that prevailed through innumerable generations on the Nile. The crocodile made the ridiculous blunder of supposing man to be meant chiefly for his own eating. Man, taking a different view of the subject, naturally met that mistake by another : he viewed the crocodile as a thing sometimes to worship, but always to run away from. And this continued until Mr. Waterton[11] changed the relations between the animals.

13

The mode of escaping from the reptile he showed **to** be, not by running away, but by leaping on its back, booted and spurred.    The two animals had misunderstood each other.    The use of the crocodile has now been cleared up — viz., to be ridden; and the final cause of man is, that he may improve the health of the crocodile by riding him a fox-hunting before breakfast. And it **is** pretty certain that any crocodile, who has been regularly hunted through the season, and is master of the weight he carries, will take a six-barred gate now as well as ever he would have done in the infancy of the pyramids.

If, therefore, the crocodile does *not* change, all things else undeniably *do :* even the shadow of the pyramids grows less.    And often the restoration in vision of Fanny and the Bath road, makes me too pathetically sensible of that truth.    Out of the darkness, if I happen to call back the image of Fanny, up rises suddenly from a gulf of forty years a rose in June; or, if I think for an instant of the rose in June, up rises the heavenly face of Fanny.    One after the other, like the antiphonies in the choral service, rise Fanny and the rose in June, then back again the rose in June and Fanny. Then come both together, as in a chorus — roses and Fannies, Fannies and roses, without end, thick as blossoms in paradise.    Then comes a venerable crocodile, in a royal livery of scarlet and gold, with sixteen capes; and the crocodile is driving four-in-hand from the box of the Bath mail.    And suddenly we upon the mail are pulled up by a mighty-dial, sculptured with the hours, that mingle with the heavens and the heavenly host.    Then all at once we are arrived at Marlborough forest, amongst the lovely households [12] of the roe-deer; the deer and their fawns retire into the dewy thickets; the thickets are rich with roses ; once again the roses call up the sweet countenance of Fanny ; and she, being the granddaughter of a crocodile, awakens a dreadful host of semi-legendary animals—griffins, dragons, basilisks, sphinxes — till at length the whole vision of fighting images crowds into one towering armorial shield, a vast emblazonry of human charities and human loveliness that have perished, but quartered heraldically with unutterable and demoniac natures, whilst over all rises, as a surmounting crest, one fair female hand, with the forefinger pointing, in sweet, sorrowful admonition, upwards to heaven, where is sculptured the eternal writing which proclaims the frailty of earth and her children.

### GOING DOWN WITH VICTORY.

But the grandest chapter of our experience, within the whole mail-coach service, was on those occasions when we went down from London with the news of victory. A period of about ten years stretched from Trafalgar to Waterloo; the second and third years of which period (1806 and 1807) were comparatively sterile ; but the other nine (from 1805 to 1815 inclusively) furnished a long succession of victories; the least of which, in such a contest of Titans, had an inappreciable value of position — partly for its absolute interference with the plans of our enemy, but still more from its keeping alive through central Europe the sense of a deep-seated vulnerability in France. Even to tease the coasts of our enemy, to mortify them by continual blockades, to insult them by capturing if it were but a baubling schooner under the eyes of their

arrogant armies, repeated from time to time a sullen
proclamation of power lodged in one quarter to which
the hopes of Christendom turned in secret.   How much
more loudly must this proclamation have spoken in the
audacity[13] of having bearded the *élite* of their troops,
and having beaten them in pitched battles ! Five years
of life it was worth paying down for the privilege of an
outside place on a mail-coach, when carrying down the
first tidings of any such event.  And it is to be noted
that, from our insular situation, and the multitude of
our frigates disposable for the rapid transmission of
intelligence, rarely did any unauthorized rumor steal
away a prelibation from the first aroma of the regular
despatches.   The government news was generally the
earliest news.

From eight P. M., to fifteen or twenty minutes later,
imagine the mails assembled on parade in Lombard
Street, where, at that time,[14] and not in St. Martin's-
le-Grand, was seated the General Post-office.   In what
exact strength we mustered I do not remember; but,
from the length of each separate *attelage*, we filled the
street, though a long one, and though we were drawn
up in double file.   On *any* night the spectacle was
beautiful.   The absolute perfection of all the appoint-
ments about the carriages and the harness, their
strength, their brilliant cleanliness, their beautiful
simplicity — but, more than all, the royal magnificence
of the horses — were what might first have fixed the
attention.   Every carriage, on every morning in the
year, was taken down to an official inspector for examination — wheels, axles, linchpins, poles, glasses, lamps,
were all critically probed and tested.   Every part of
every carriage had been cleaned, every horse had been

groomed, with as much rigor as if they belonged to a
private gentleman; and that part of the spectacle
offered itself always. But the night before us is a
night of victory; and, behold! to the ordinary display,
what a heart-shaking addition! — horses, men, carriages, all are dressed in laurels and flowers, oak-leaves
and ribbons. The guards, as being officially his Majesty's servants, and of the coachmen such as are within
the privilege of the post-office, wear the royal liveries
cf course; and as it is summer (for all the *land* victories were naturally won in summer), they wear, on this
fine evening, these liveries exposed to view, without
any covering of upper coats. Such a costume, and the
elaborate arrangement of the laurels in their hats, dilate
their hearts, by giving to them openly a personal connection with the great news, in which already they
have the general interest of patriotism. That great
national sentiment surmounts and quells all sense of
ordinary distinctions. Those passengers who happen
to be gentlemen are now hardly to be distinguished as
such except by dress; for the usual reserve of their
manner in speaking to the attendants has on this night
melted away. One heart, one pride, one glory, connects every man by the transcendent bond of his
national blood. The spectators, who are numerous
beyond precedent, express their sympathy with these
fervent feelings by continual hurrahs. Every moment
are shouted aloud by the post-office servants, and summoned to draw up, the great ancestral names of cities
known to history through a thousand years — Lincoln,
Winchester, Portsmouth, Gloucester, Oxford, Bristol,
Manchester, York, Newcastle, Edinburgh, Glasgow,
Perth, Stirling, Aberdeen — expressing the grandeur

of the empire by the antiquity of its towns, and the grandeur of the mail establishment by the diffusive radiation of its separate missions.   Every moment you hear thunder of lids locked down upon the mail-bags. That sound to each individual mail is the signal for drawing off, which process is the finest part of the entire spectacle.   Then come the horses into play. Horses! can these be horses that bound off with the action and gestures of leopards?   What stir! — what sea-like ferment! — what a thundering of wheels! — what a trampling of hoofs! — what a sounding of trumpets! — what farewell cheers — what redoubling peals of brotherly congratulation, connecting the name of the particular mail — ' Liverpool for ever! ' — with the name of the particular victory — ' Badajoz for ever!' or 'Salamanca for ever!'   The half-slumbering consciousness that, all night long and all the next day — perhaps for even a longer period — many of these mails, like fire racing along a train of gunpowder, will be kindling at every instant new successions of burning joy, has an obscure effect of multiplying the victory itself, by multiplying to the imagination into infinity the stages of its progressive diffusion.   A fiery arrow seems to be let loose, which from that moment is destined to travel, without intermission, westwards for three hundred [15] miles — northwards for six hundred; and the sympathy of our Lombard Street friends at parting is exalted a hundredfold by a sort of visionary sympathy with the yet slumbering sympathies which in so vast a succession we are going to awake.

Liberated from the embarrassments of the city, and issuing into the broad uncrowded avenues of the northern suburbs, we soon begin to enter upon our natural pace of ten miles an hour. In the broad light of the summer evening, the sun, perhaps, only just at the point of setting, we are seen from every story of every house. Heads of every age crowd to the windows — young and old understand the language of our victorious symbols — and rolling volleys of sympathizing cheers ran along us, behind us, and before us. The beggar, rearing himself against the wall, forgets his lameness — real or assumed — thinks not of his whining trade, but stands erect, with bold exulting smiles, as we pass him. The victory has healed him, and says, Be thou whole! Women and children, from garrets alike and cellars, through infinite London, look down or look up with loving eyes upon our gay ribbons and our martial laurels; sometimes kiss their hands; sometimes hang out, as signals of affection, pocket-handkerchiefs, aprons, dusters, anything that, by catching the summer breezes, will express an aerial jubilation. On the London side of Barnet, to which we draw near within a few minutes after nine, observe that private carriage which is approaching us. The weather being so warm, the glasses are all down; and one may read, as on the stage of a theatre, everything that goes on within. It contains three ladies — one likely to be ' mamma,' and two of seventeen or eighteen, who are probably her daughters. What lovely animation, what beautiful unpremeditated pantomime, explaining to us every syllable that passes, in these ingenuous girls! By the sudden start and raising of the hands, on first discovering our laurelled equipage! — by the sudden movement and appeal to the elder lady from both of them — and by the heightened color on their animated countenances, we can almost hear them saying, 'See, see! Look at their laurels! Oh, mamma! there has been a great battle in Spain, and it has been a great victory.' In a moment we are on the point of passing them. We passengers — I on the box, and the two on the roof behind me — raise our hats to the ladies; the coachman makes his professional salute with the whip; the guard even, though punctilious on the matter of his dignity as an officer under the crown, touches his hat. The ladies move to us, in return, with a winning graciousness of gesture; all smile on each side in a way that nobody could misunderstand, and that nothing short of a grand national sympathy could so instantaneously prompt. Will these ladies say that we are nothing to *them*? Oh, no; they will not say *that*. They cannot deny — they do not deny — that for this night they are our sisters; gentle or simple, scholar or illiterate servant, for twelve hours to come, we on the outside have the honor to be their brothers. Those poor women, again, who stop to gaze upon us with delight at the entrance of Barnet, and seem, by their air of weariness, to be returning from labor — do you mean to say that they are washerwomen and . charwomen? Oh, my poor friend, you are quite mistaken. I assure you they stand in a far higher rank; for this one night they feel themselves by birthright to be daughters of England, and answer to no humbler title.

Every joy, however, even rapturous joy — such is the sad law of earth — may carry with it grief, or fear of grief, to some. Three miles beyond Barnet, we see approaching us another private carriage, nearly repeating the circumstances of the former case. Here, also, the glasses are all down — here, also, is an elderly lady seated; but the two daughters are missing; for the single young person sitting by the lady's side, seems to be an attendant — so I judge from her dress, and her air of respectful reserve. The lady is in mourning; and her countenance expresses sorrow. At first she does not look up; so that I believe she is not aware of our approach, until she hears the measured beating of our horses' hoofs. Then she raises her eyes to settle them painfully on our triumphal equipage. Our decorations explain the case to her at once; but she beholds them with apparent anxiety, or even with terror. Some time before this, I, finding it difficult to hit a flying mark, when embarrassed by the coachman's person and reins intervening, had given to the guard a ' Courier' evening paper, containing the gazette, for the next carriage that might pass. Accordingly he tossed it in, so folded that the huge capitals expressing some such legend as — GLORIOUS VICTORY, might catch the eye at once. To see the paper, however, at all, interpreted as it was by our ensigns of triumph, explained everything; and, if the guard were right in thinking the lady to have received it with a gesture of horror it could not be doubtful that she had suffered some deep personal affliction in connection with this Spanish war.

Here, now, was the case of one who, having formerly suffered, might, erroneously perhaps, be distressing herself with anticipations of another similar suffering. That same night, and hardly three hours later, occurred the reverse case. A poor woman, who too probably would find herself, in a day or two, to have suffered the heaviest afflictions by the battle, blindly allowed herself to express an exultation so unmeasured in the news and its details, as gave to her the appearance which amongst Celtic Highlanders is called *fey*. This was at some little town where we changed horses an hour or two after midnight. Some fair or wake had kept the people up out of their beds, and had occasioned a partial illumination of the stalls and booths, presenting an unusual but very impressive effect. We saw many lights moving about as we drew near; and perhaps the most striking scene on the whole route was our reception at this place. The flashing of torches and the beautiful radiance of blue lights (technically, Bengal lights) upon the heads of our horses; the fine effect of such a showery and ghostly illumination falling upon our flowers and glittering laurels; [16] whilst all around ourselves, thàt formed a centre of light, the darkness gathered on the rear and flanks in massy blackness; these optical splendors, together with the prodigious enthusiasm of the people, composed a picture at once scenical and affecting, theatrical and holy. As we staid for three or four minutes, I alighted; and immediately from a dismantled stall in the street, where no doubt she had been presiding through the earlier part of the night, advanced eagerly a middle-aged woman. The sight of my newspaper it was that had drawn her attention upon myself. The victory which we were carrying down to the provinces on *this* occasion, was the imperfect one of Talavera — imperfect for its results, such was the virtual treachery of the Spanish general, Cuesta, but not imperfect in its ever-memorable heroism   I told her the main outline of the battle.

The agitation of her enthusiasm had been so conspicuous when listening, and when first applying for information, that I could not but ask her if she had not some relative in the Peninsular army. Oh, yes; her only son was there. In what regiment? He was a trooper in the 23d Dragoons. My heart sank within me as she made that answer. This sublime regiment, which an Englishman should never mention without raising his hat to their memory, had made the most memorable and effective charge recorded in military annals. They leaped their horses — *over* a trench where they could, *into* it, and with the result of death or mutilation when they could *not*. What proportion cleared the trench is nowhere stated. Those who *did*, closed up and went down upon the enemy with such divinity of fervor (I use the word *divinity* by design : the inspiration of God must have prompted this movement to those whom even then he was calling to his presence), that two results followed. As regarded the enemy, this 23d Dragoons, not, I believe, originally three hundred and fifty strong, paralyzed a French column, six thousand strong, then ascended the hill, and fixed the gaze of the whole French army. As regarded themselves, the 23d were supposed at first to have been barely not annihilated ; but eventually, I believe, about one in four survived. And this, then, was the regiment — a regiment already for some hours glorified and hallowed to the ear of all London. as lying stretched, by a large majority, upon one bloody aceldama — in which the young trooper served whose mother was now talking in a spirit of such joyous enthusiasm. Did I tell her the truth? Had I the heart to break up her dreams? No. To-morrow, said I to myself — to-morrow, or the next day, will publish the worst. For one night more, wherefore should she not sleep in peace? After to-morrow, the chances are too many that peace will forsake her pillow. This brief respite, then, let her owe to *my* gift and *my* forbearance. But, if I told her not of the bloody price that had been paid, not, therefore, was I silent on the contributions from her son's regiment to that day's service and glory. I showed her not the funeral banners under which the noble regiment was sleeping. I lifted not the overshadowing laurels from the bloody trench in which horse and rider lay mangled together. But I told her how these dear children of England, officers and privates, had leaped their horses over all obstacles as gayly as hunters to the morning's chase. I told her how they rode their horses into the mists of death (saying to myself, but not saying to *her*), and laid down their young lives for thee, O mother England! as willingly — poured out their noble blood as cheerfully — as ever, after a long day's sport, when infants, they had rested their wearied heads upon their mother's knees, or had sunk to sleep in her arms. Strange it is, yet true, that she seemed to have no fears for her son's safety, even after this knowledge that the 23d Dragoons had been memorably engaged ; but so much was she enraptured by the knowledge that *his* regiment, and therefore that *he*, had rendered conspicuous service in the dreadful conflict — a service which had actually made them, within the last twelve hcurs, the foremost topic of conversation in London — so absolutely was fear swallowed up in joy — that, in the mere simplicity of her fervent nature, the poor woman threw her arms round my neck, as she thought of her son, and gave to *me* the kiss which secretly was meant for *him*.

# THE ENGLISH MAIL-COACH.

## SECTION THE SECOND. — THE VISION OF SUDDEN DEATH.

WHAT is to be taken as the predominant opinion of man, reflective and philosophic, upon SUDDEN DEATH? It is remarkable that, in different conditions of society, sudden death has been variously regarded as the consummation of an earthly career most fervently to be desired, or, again, as that consummation which is with most horror to be deprecated. Cæsar the Dictator, at his last dinner party (*cœna*), on the very evening before his assassination, when the minutes of his earthly career were numbered, being asked what death, in *his* judgment, might be pronounced the most eligible, replied, 'That which should be most sudden.' On the other hand, the divine Litany of our English Church, when breathing forth supplications, as if in some representative character for the whole human race prostrate before God, places such a death in the very van of horrors : — 'From lightning and tempest; from plague, pestilence, and famine; from battle and murder, and from SUDDEN DEATH — *Good Lord, deliver us.*' Sudden death is here made to crown the climax in a grand ascent of calamities; it is ranked among the last of curses; and yet, by the noblest of

[157]

Romans, it was ranked as the first of blessings.   In
that difference, most readers will see little more than
the essential difference between Christianity and Paganism.   But this, on consideration, I doubt.   The
Christian Church may be right in its estimate of sudden death; and it is a natural feeling, though after all
t may also be an infirm one, to wish for a quiet dismissal from life ·— as that which *seems* most reconcil-
able with meditation, with penitential retrospects, and
with the humilities of farewell prayer.   There does
not, however, occur to me any direct scriptural warrant for this earnest petition of the English Litany,
unless under a special construction of the word ‘ sudden.’   It seems a petition — indulged rather and conceded to human infirmity, than exacted from human
piety.   It is not so much a doctrine built upon the
eternities of the Christian system, as a plausible opinion built upon special varieties of physical temperament.   Let that, however, be as it may, two remarks
suggest themselves as prudent restraints upon a doctrine, which else *may* wander, and *has* wandered, into
an uncharitable superstition.   The first is this : that
many people are likely to exaggerate the horror of a
sudden death, from the disposition to lay a false stress
upon words or acts, simply because by an accident
they have become *final* words or acts.   If a man dies,
for instance, by some sudden death when he happens
to be intoxicated, such a death is falsely regarded with
peculiar horror ; as though the intoxication were suddenly exalted into a blasphemy.   But *that* is unphilosophic.   The man was, or he was not, *habitually* a
drunkard.   If not, if his intoxication were a solitary
accident, there can be no reason for allowing special

emphasis to this act, simply because through misfortune it became his final act. Nor, on the other hand, if it were no accident, but one of his *habitual* transgressions, will it be the more habitual or the more a transgression, because some sudden calamity surprising him, has caused this habitual transgression to be also a final one. Could the man have had any reason even dimly to foresee his own sudden death, there would have been a new feature in his act of intemperance — feature of presumption and irreverence, as in one that, having known himself drawing near to the presence of God, should have suited his demeanor to an expectation so awful. But this is no part of the case supposed. And the only new element in the man's act is not any element of special immorality, but simply of special misfortune.

The other remark has reference to the meaning of the word *sudden*. Very possibly Cæsar and the Christian Church do not differ in the way supposed; that is, do not differ by any difference of doctrine as between Pagan and Christian views of the moral temper appropriate to death, but perhaps they are contemplating different cases. Both contemplate a violent death, a βιαθανατος — death that is βιαιος, or, in other words, death that is brought about, not by internal and spontaneous change, but by active force, having its origin from without. In this meaning the two authorities agree. Thus far they are in harmony. But the difference is, that the Roman by the word ' sudden ' means *unlingering;* whereas the Christian Litany by ' sudden death ' means a death *without warning*, consequently without any available summons to religious preparation. The poor mutineer, who kneels down to gather into his heart the bullets from twelve firelocks of his pitying comrades, dies by a most sudden death in Cæsar's sense; one shock, one mighty spasm, one (possibly *not* one) groan, and all is over. But in the sense of the Litany, the mutineer's death is far from sudden; his offence originally, his imprisonment, his trial, the interval between his sentence and its execution, having all furnished him with separate warnings of his fate — having all summoned him to meet it with solemn preparation.

Here at once, in this sharp verbal distinction, we comprehend the faithful earnestness with which a holy Christian Church pleads on behalf of her poor departing children, that God would vouchsafe to them the last great privilege and distinction possible on a death-bed — viz., the opportunity of untroubled preparation for facing this mighty trial. Sudden death, as a mere variety in the modes of dying, where death in some shape is inevitable, proposes a question of choice which, equally in the Roman and the Christian sense, will be variously answered according to each man's variety of temperament. Meantime, one aspect of sudden death there is, one modification, upon which no doubt can arise, that of all martyrdoms it is the most agitating — viz., where it surprises a man under circumstances which offer (or which seem to offer) some hurrying, flying, inappreciably minute chance of evading it. Sudden as the danger which it affronts, must be any effort by which such an evasion can be accomplished. Even *that*, even the sickening necessity for hurrying in extremity where all hurry seems destined to be vain, even that anguish is liable to a hideous exasperation in one particular case — viz., where the appeal is made not exclusively to the instinct of self-preservation, but to the conscience, on behalf of some other life besides your own, accidentally thrown upon *your* protection. To fail, to collapse in a service merely your own, might seem comparatively venial; though, in fact, it is far from venial. But to fail in a case where Providence has suddenly thrown into your hands the final interests of another — a fellow-creature shuddering between the gates of life and death; this, to a man of apprehensive conscience, would mingle the misery of an atrocious criminality with the misery of a bloody calamity. You are called upon, by the case supposed, possibly to die; but to die at the very moment when, by any even partial failure, or effeminate collapse of your energies, you will be self-denounced as a murderer. You had but the twinkling of an eye for your effort, and that effort might have been unavailing; but to have risen to the level of such an effort, would have rescued you, though not from dying, yet from dying as a traitor to your final and farewell duty.

The situation here contemplated exposes a dreadful ulcer, lurking far down in the depths of human nature. It is not that men generally are summoned to face such awful trials. But potentially, and in shadowy outline, such a trial is moving subterraneously in perhaps all men's natures. Upon the secret mirror of our dreams such a trial is darkly projected, perhaps, to every one of us. That dream, so familiar to childhood, of meeting a lion, and, through languishing prostration in hope and the energies of hope, that constant sequel of lying down before the lion, publishes the secret frailty of human nature — reveals its

deep-seated falsehood to itself — records its abysmal
treachery.  Perhaps not one of us escapes that dream;
perhaps, as· by some sorrowful doom of man, that
dream repeats for every one of us, through every
generation, the original temptation in Eden.  Every
one of us, in this dream, has a bait offered to the
infirm places of his own individual will; once again
a snare is presented for tempting him into captivity to
a luxury of ruin; once again, as in aboriginal Paradise, the man falls by his own choice; again, by
infinite iteration, the ancient Earth groans to Heaven,
through her secret caves, over the weakness of her
child: ‘Nature, from her seat, sighing through all her
works,’ again ‘ gives signs of wo that all is lost; ’ and
again the counter sigh is repeated to the sorrowing
heavens for the endless rebellion against God.  It is
not without probability that in the world of dreams
every one of us ratifies for himself the original transgression.  In dreams, perhaps under some secret
conflict of the midnight sleeper, lighted up to the
consciousness at the time, but darkened to the memory as soon as all is finished, each several child of our
mysterious race completes for himself the treason of
the aboriginal fall.

.    .    .    .    .    .    .    .    .    .    .

The incident, so memorable in itself by its features
of horror, and so scenical by its grouping for the eye,
which furnished the text for this reverie upon *Sudden
Death*, occurred to myself in the dead of night, as a
solitary spectator, when seated on the box of the
Manchester and Glasgow mail, in· the second or third
summer after Waterloo.  I find it necessary to relate
the circumstances, because they are such as could not

have occurred unless under a singular combination of accidents. In those days, the oblique and lateral communications with many rural post-offices were so arranged, either through necessity or through defect of system, as to make it requisite for the main north-western mail (*i. e.*, the *down* mail), on reaching Manchester, to halt for a number of hours; how many, I do not remember; six or seven, I think; but the result was, that, in the ordinary course, the mail recommenced its journey northwards about midnight. Wearied with the long detention at a gloomy hotel, I walked out about eleven o'clock at night for the sake of fresh air; meaning to fall in with the mail and resume my seat at the post-office. The night, however, being yet dark, as the moon had scarcely risen, and the streets being at that hour empty, so as to offer no opportunities for asking the road, I lost my way; and did not reach the post-offiee until it was considerably past midnight; but, to my great relief (as it was important for me to be in Westmoreland by the morning), I saw in the huge saucer eyes of the mail, blazing through the gloom, an evideuce that my chance was not yct lost. Past the time it was, but, by some rare accident, the mail was not even yet ready to start. I ascended to my seat on the box, where my cloak was still lying as it had lain at the Bridgewater Arms. I had left it there in imitation of a nautical discoverer, who leaves a bit of bunting on the shore of his discovery, by way of warning off the ground the whole human race, and notifying to the Christian and the heathen worlds, with his best compliments, that he has hoisted his pocket-handker-chief once and for ever upon that virgin soil; thence-

forward claiming the *jus dominii* to the top of **the**
atmosphere above it, and also the right of driving
shafts to the centre of the earth below it; so that all
people found after this warning, either aloft in upper
chambers of the atmosphere, or groping in subterrane-
ous shafts, or squatting audaciously on the surface of
the soil, will be treated as trespassers — kicked, that is
to say, or decapitated, as circumstances may suggest, by
their very faithful servant, the owner of the said pocket-
handkerchief.    In the present case, it is probable that
my cloak might not have been respected, and the *jus
gentium* might have been cruelly violated in my person
— for, in the dark, people commit deeds of darkness,
gas being a great ally of morality — but it so happened that, on this night, there was no other outside
passenger; and thus the crime, which else was but too
probable, missed fire for want of a criminal.

Having mounted the box, I took a small quantity of
laudanum, having already travelled two hundred and
fifty miles — viz., from a point seventy miles beyond
London.    In the taking of laudanum there was nothing
extraordinary.    But by accident it drew upon me the
special attention of my assessor on the box, the coachman.    And in *that* also there was nothing extraordinary.    But by accident, and with great delight, it
drew my own attention to the fact that this coachman
was a monster in point of bulk, and that he had but
one eye.    In fact, he had been foretold by Virgil as

‘Monstrum horrendum, informe, ingens cui lumen ademptum.’

He answered to the conditions in every one of the
items:— 1, a monster he was; 2, dreadful; 3, shape-
less; 4, huge; 5, who had lost an eye.    But why

should *that* delight me? Had he been one of the Calendars in the 'Arabian Nights,' and had paid down his eye as the price of his criminal curiosity, what right had *I* to exult in his misfortune? I did *not* exult: I delighted in no man's punishment, though it were even merited. But these personal distinctions (Nos. 1, 2, 3, 4, 5) identified in an instant an old friend of mine, whom I had known in the south for some years as the most masterly of mail-coachmen. He was the man in all Europe that could (if *any* could) have driven six-in-hand full gallop over *Al Sirat* — that dreadful bridge of Mahomet, with no side battlements, and of *extra* room not enough for a razor's edge — leading right across the bottomless gulf. Under this eminent man, whom in Greek I cognominated Cyclops *diphrélates* (Cyclops the charioteer), I, and others known to me, studied the diphrelatic art. Excuse, reader, a word too elegant to be pedantic. As a pupil, though I paid extra fees, it is to be lamented that I did not stand high in his esteem. It showed his dogged honesty (though, observe, not his discernment), that he could not see my merits. Let us excuse his absurdity in this particular, by remembering his want of an eye. Doubtless *that* made him blind to my merits. In the art of conversation, however, he admitted that I had the whip-hand of him. On this present occasion, great joy was at our meeting. But what was Cyclops doing here? Had the medical men recommended northern air, or how? I collected, from such explanations as he volunteered, that he had an interest at stake in some suit-at-law now pending at Lancaster; so that probably he had got himself transferred to this station, for the purpose of connecting with his professional pursuits an instant readiness for the calls of his lawsuit.

. Meantime, what are we stopping for? Surely we have now waited long enough. Oh, this procrastinating mail, and this procrastinating post-office! Can't they take a lesson upon that subject from *me*? Some people have called *me* procrastinating. Yet you are witness, reader, that I was kept here waiting for the post-offiee. Will the post-office lay its hand on its heart, in its moments of sobriety, and assert that ever it waited for me? What are they about? The guard tells me that there is a large extra accumulation of foreign mails this night, owing to irregularities caused by war, by wind, by weather, in the .packet service, which as yet does not benefit at all by steam. For an *extra* hour, it seems, the post-offiee has been engaged in threshing out the pure wheaten correspondence of Glasgow, and winnowing it from the chaff of all baser intermediate towns. But at last all is finished. Sound your horn, guard. Manchester, good-by; we've lost an hour by your criminal conduct at the post-offiee: which, however, though I do not mean to part with a serviceable ground of complaint, and one which really *is* such for the horses, to me secretly is an advantage, since it compels us to look sharply for this lost hour amongst the next eight or nine, and to recover it (if we can) at the rate of one mile extra per hour. . Off we are at last, and at eleven miles per hour: and for the moment I detect no changes in the energy or in the skill of Cyclops.

· From Manchester to Kendal, which virtually (though not in law) is the capital of Westmoreland, there were at this time seven stages of eleven miles each. The first five of these, counting from Manchester, terminate in Lancaster, which is therefore fifty-five miles north of Manchester, and the same distance exactly from Liverpool. The first three stages terminate in Preston (called, by way of distinction from other towns of that name, *proud* Preston), at which place it is that the separate roads from Liverpool and from Manchester to the north become confluent.[17] Within these first three stages lay the foundation, the progress, and termination of our night's adventure. During the first stage, I found out that Cyclops was mortal: he was liable to the shocking affection of sleep — a thing which previously I had never suspected. If a man indulges in the vicious habit of sleeping, all the skill in aurigation of Apollo himself, with the horses of Aurora to execute his notions, avail him nothing. ' Oh, Cyclops!' I exclaimed, 'thou art mortal. My friend, thou snorest.' Through the first eleven miles, however, this infirmity — which I grieve to say that he shared with the whole Pagan Pantheon — betrayed itself only by brief snatches. On waking up, he made an apology for himself, which, instead of mending matters, laid open a gloomy vista of coming disasters. The summer assizes, he reminded me, were now going on at Lancaster: in consequence of which, for three nights and three days, he had not lain down in a bed. During the day, he was waiting for his own summons as a witness on the trial in which he was interested: or else, lest he should be missing at the critical moment, was drinking with the other witnesses, under the pastoral surveillance of the attorneys. During the night, or that part of it which at sea would form the middle watch, he was driving. This explanation certainly accounted for his drowsiness, but in a way which made it much more alarming; since now, after several days resistance to this infirmity, at length he was steadily giving way. Throughout the second stage he grew more and more drowsy. In the second mile of the third stage, he surrendered himself finally and without a struggle to his perilous temptation. All his past resistance had but deepened the weight of this final oppression. Seven atmospheres of sleep rested upon him; and to consummate the case, our worthy guard, after singing 'Love amongst the Roses' for perhaps thirty times, without invitation, and without applause, had in revenge moodily resigned himself to slumber — not so deep, doubtless, as the coachman's, but deep enough for mischief. And thus at last, about ten miles from Preston, it came about that I found myself left in charge of his Majesty's London and Glasgow mail, then running at the least twelve miles an hour.

What made this negligence less criminal than else it must have been thought, was the condition of the roads at night during the assizes. At that time, all the law business of populous Liverpool, and also of populous Manchester, with its vast cincture of populous rural districts, was called up by ancient usage to the tribunal of Lilliputian Lancaster. To break up this old traditional usage required, 1, a conflict with powerful established interests; 2, a large system of new arrangements; and 3, a new parliamentary statute. But as yet this change was merely in contemplation. As things were at present, twice in the year [18] so vast a body of business rolled northwards, from the southern quarter of the county, that for a fortnight at least it occupied the severe exertions of two judges in its despatch. The consequence of this was, that every horse available for such a service, along the whole line of road, was exhausted in carrying down the multitudes of people who were parties to the different suits. By sunset, therefore, it usually happened that, through utter exhaustion amongst men and horses, the roads sank into profound silence. Except the exhaustion in the vast adjacent county of York from a contested election, no such silence succeeding to no such fiery uproar was ever witnessed in England.

On this occasion, the usual silence and solitude prevailed along the road. Not a hoof nor a wheel was to be heard. And to strengthen this false luxurious confidence in the noiseless roads, it happened also that the night was one of peculiar solemnity and peace. For my own part, though slightly alive to the possibilities of peril, I had so far yielded to the influence of the mighty calm as to sink into a profound reverie. The month was August, in the middle of which lay my own birth-day — a festival to every thoughtful man suggesting solemn and often sigh-born [19] thoughts. The county was my own native county — upon which, in its southern section, more than upon any equal area known to man past or present, had descended the original curse of labor in its heaviest form, not mastering the bodies only of men as of slaves, or criminals in mines, but working through the fiery will. Upon no equal space of earth was, or ever had been, the same energy of human power put forth daily. At this particular season also of the assizes, that dreadful hurricane of flight and pursuit, as it might have seemed to a stranger, which swept to and from Lancaster all day long, hunting the county up and down, and regularly

15

subsiding back into silence about sunset, could not **fail** (when united with this permanent distinction of Lancashire as the very metropolis and citidal of labor) to point the thoughts pathetically upon that counter vision of rest, of saintly repose from strife and sorrow, towards which, as to their secret haven, the profounder aspirations of man's heart are in solitude continually travelling. Obliquely upon our left we were nearing the sea, which also must, under the present circumstances, be repeating the general state of halcyon repose. The sea, the atmosphere, the light, bore each an orchestral part in this universal lull. Moonlight, and the first timid tremblings of the dawn, were by this time blending; and the blendings were brought into a still more exquisite state of unity by a slight silvery mist, motionless and dreamy, that covered the woods and fields, but with a veil of equable transpareney. Except the feet of our own horses, which, running on a sandy margin of the road, made but little disturbance, there was no sound abroad. In the clouds, and on the earth, prevailed the same majestic peace; and in spite of all that the villain of a schoolmaster has done for the ruin of our sublimer thoughts, which are the thoughts of our infancy, we still believe in no such nonsense as a limited atmosphere. Whatever we may swear with our false feigning lips, in our faithful hearts we still believe, and must for ever believe, in fields of air traversing the total gulf between earth and the central heavens. Still in the confidence of children that tread without fear *every* chamber in their father's house, and to whom no door is closed, we, in that Sabbatic vision which sometimes is revealed **for an** hour upon nights like this, ascend with **easy** steps from the sorrow-stricken fields of earth, upwards to the sandals of God.

Suddenly, from thoughts like these, I was awakened to a sullen sound, as of some motion on the distant road. It stole upon the air for a moment; I listened in awe; but then it died away. Once roused, however, I could not but observe with alarm the quickened motion of our horses. Ten years' experience had made my eye learned in the valuing of motion; and I saw that we were now running thirteen miles an hour. I pretend to no presence of mind. On the contrary, my fear is, that I am miserably and shamefully deficient in that quality as regards action. The palsy of doubt and distraction hangs like some guilty weight of dark unfathomed remembrances upon my energies, when the signal is flying for *action*. But, on the other hand, this accursed gift I have, as regards *thought*, that in the first step towards the possibility of a misfortune, I see its total evolution; in the radix of the series I see too certainly and too instantly its entire expansion; in the first syllable of the dreadful sentence, I read already the last. It was not that I feared for ourselves. *Us*, our bulk and impetus charmed against peril in any collision. And I had ridden through too many hundreds of perils that were frightful to approach, that were matter of laughter to look back upon, the first face of which was horror — the parting face a jest, for any anxiety to rest upon *our* interests. The mail was not built, I felt assured, nor bespoke, that could betray *me* who trusted to its protection. But any carriage that we could meet would be frail and light in comparison of ourselves. And I remark this ominous accident of our situation. We

were on the wrong side of the road.   But then, it may
be said, the other party, if other there was, might also
be on the wrong side; and two wrongs might make a
right.   *That* was not likely.   The same motive which
had drawn *us* to the right-hand side of the road —
viz., the luxury of the soft beaten sand, as contrasted
with the paved centre — would prove attractive to
others.   The two adverse carriages would therefore, to
a certainty, be travelling on the same side; and from
this side, as not being ours in law, the crossing over to
the other would, of course, be looked for from *us*.[20]
Our lamps, still lighted, would give the impression of
vigilance on our part.   And every creature that met
us, would rely upon *us* for quartering.[21]   All this, and
if the separate links of the anticipation had been a
thousand times more, I saw, not discursively, or by
effort, or by succession, but by one flash of horrid
simultaneous intuition.

Under this steady though rapid anticipation of the
evil which *might* be gathering ahead, ah ! what a sullen mystery of fear, what a sigh of wo, was that which
stole upon the air, as again the far-off sound of a wheel
was heard ?   A whisper it was — a whisper from,
perhaps, four miles off — secretly announcing a ruin
that, being foreseen, was not the less inevitable ; that,
being known, was not, therefore, healed.   What could
be done — who was it that could do it — to check the
storm-flight of these maniacal horses ?   Could I not
seize the reins from the grasp of the slumbering coachman ?   You, reader, think that it would have been in
*your* power to do so.   And I quarrel not with your
estimate of yourself.   But, from the way in which the
coachman's hand was viced between his upper and

ᴧower thigh, this was impossible. Easy, was it? See, then, that bronze equestrian statue. The cruel rider has kept the bit in his horse's mouth for two centuries. Unbridle him, for a minute, if you please, and wash his mouth with water. Easy, was it? Unhorse me, then, that imperial rider; knock me those marble feet from those marble stirrups of Charlemagne.

The sounds ahead strengthened, and were now too clearly the sounds of wheels. Who and what could it be? Was it industry in a taxed cart? Was it youthful gayety in a gig? Was it sorrow that loitered, or joy that raced? For as yet the snatches of sound were too intermitting, from distance, to decipher the character of the motion. Whoever were the travellers, something must be done to warn them. Upon the other party rests the active responsibility, but upon *us* — and, wo is me! that *us* was reduced to my frail opium-shattered self — rests the responsibility of warning. Yet how should this be accomplished? Might I not sound the guard's horn? Already, on the first thought, I was making my way over the roof to the guard's seat. But this, from the accident which I have mentioned, of the foreign mails' being piled upon the roof, was a difficult and even dangerous attempt to one cramped by nearly three hundred miles of outside travelling. And, fortunately, before I had lost much time in the attempt, our frantic horses swept round an angle of the road, which opened upon us that final stage where the collision must be accomplished, and the catastrophe sealed. All was apparently finished. The court was sitting; the case was heard; the judge had finished; and the only verdict was yet in arrear.

Before us lay an avenue, straight as an arrow, six hundred yards, perhaps, in length; and the umbrageous trees, which rose in a regular line from either side, meeting high overhead, gave to it the character of a cathedral aisle. These trees lent a deeper solemnity to the early light; but there was still light enough to perceive, at the further end of this Gothic aisle, a frail reedy gig, in which were seated a young man, and by his side a young lady. Ah, young sir! what are you about? If it is requisite that you should whisper your communications to this young lady — though really I see nobody, at an hour and on a road so solitary, likely to overhear you — is it therefore requisite that you should carry your lips forward to hers? The little carriage is creeping on at one mile an hour; and the parties within it being thus tenderly engaged, are naturally bending down their heads. Between them and eternity, to all human calculation, there is but a minute and a-half. Oh heavens! what is it that I shall do? Speaking or acting, what help can I offer? Strange it is, and to a mere auditor of the tale might seem laughable, that I should need a suggestion from the 'Iliad' to prompt the sole resource that remained. Yet so it was. Suddenly I remembered the shout of Achilles, and its effect. But could I pretend to shout like the son of Peleus, aided by Pallas? No: but then I needed not the shout that should alarm all Asia militant; such a shout would suffice as might carry terror into the hearts of two thoughtless young people, and one gig horse. I shouted — and the young man heard me not. A second time I shouted — and now he heard me, for now he raised his head.

Here, then, all had been done that, by me, *could* be

done: more on *my* part was not possible. Mine had been the first step; the second was for the young man; the third was for God. If, said I, this stranger is a brave man, and if, indeed, he loves the young girl at his side — or, loving her not, if he feels the obligation, pressing upon every man worthy to be called a man, of doing his utmost for a woman confided to his protection — he will, at least, make some effort to save her. If *that* fails, he will not perish the more, or by a death more cruel, for having made it; and he will die as a brave man should, with his face to the danger, and with his arm about the woman that he sought in vain to save. But, if he makes no effort, shrinking, without a struggle, from his duty, he himself will not the less certainly perish for this baseness of poltroonery. He will die no less: and why not? Wherefore should we grieve that there is one craven less in the world? No; *let* him perish, without a pitying thought of ours wasted upon him; and, in that case, all our grief will be reserved for the fate of the helpless girl who now, upon the least shadow of failure in *him*, must, by the fiercest of translations — must, without time for a prayer — must, within seventy seconds, stand before the judgment-seat of God.

But craven he was not: sudden had been the call upon him, and sudden was his answer to the call. He saw, he heard, he comprehended, the ruin that was coming down: already its gloomy shadow darkened above him; and already he was measuring his strength to deal with it. Ah! what a vulgar thing does courage seem, when we see nations buying it and selling it for a shilling a-day: ah! what a sublime thing does courage seem, when some fearful summons on the great deeps of life carries a man, as if running before a hurricane, up to the giddy crest of some tumultuous crisis, from which lie two courses, and a voice says to him audibly, ' One way lies hope ; take the other, and mourn for ever ! ' How grand a triumph, if, even then, amidst the raving of all around him, and the frenzy of the danger, the man is able to confront his situation — is able to retire for a moment into solitude with God, and to seek his counsel from *him !*

For seven seconds, it might be, of his seventy, the stranger settled his countenance steadfastly upon us, as if to search and value every element in the conflict before him.   For five seconds more of his seventy he sat immovably, like one that mused on some great purpose.   For five more, perhaps, he sat with eyes upraised, like one that prayed in sorrow, under some extremity of doubt, for light that should guide him to the better choice.   Then suddenly he rose ;   stood upright ;   and by a powerful strain upon the reins, raising his horse's fore-feet from the ground, he slewed him round on the pivot of his hind-legs, so as to plant the little equipage in a position nearly at right angles to ours.   Thus far his condition was not improved, except as a first step had been taken to-wards the possibility of a second.   If no more were done, nothing was done ; for the little carriage still occupied the very centre of our path, though in an altered direction.   Yet even now it may not be too late : fifteen of the seventy seconds may still be unex-hansted ; and one almighty bound may avail to clear the ground.   Hurry, then, hurry ! for the flying mo-ments — *they* hurry !   Oh, hurry, hurry, my brave

young man! for the cruel hoofs of our horses — *they*
also hurry! Fast are the flying moments, faster are the
hoofs of our horses. But fear not for *him*, if human
energy can suffice; faithful was he that drove to his
terrific duty; faithful was the horse to *his* command.
One blow, one impulse given with voice and hand,
by the stranger, one rush from the horse, one bound
as if in the act of rising to a fence, landed the docile
creature's fore-feet upon the crown or arching centre
of the road. The larger half of the little equipage
had then cleared our overtowering shadow: *that* was
evident even to my own agitated sight. But it mat-
tered little that one wreck should float off in safety,
if upon the wreck that perished were embarked the
human freightage. The rear part of the carriage —
was *that* certainly beyond the line of absolute ruin?
What power could answer the question? Glance of
eye, thought of man, wing of angel, which of these
had speed enough to sweep between the question and
the answer, and divide the one from the other?
Light does not tread upon the steps of light more
indivisibly, than did our all-conquering arrival upon
the escaping efforts of the gig. *That* must the young
man have felt too plainly. His back was now turned
to us; not by sight could he any longer communicate
with the peril; but by the dreadful rattle of our
harness, too truly had his ear been instructed — that
all was finished as regarded any further effort of *his*.
Already in resignation he had rested from his struggle;
and perhaps in his heart he was whispering, ' Father,
which art in heaven, do thou finish above what I on
earth have attempted.' Faster than ever mill-race we
ran past them in our inexorable flight. Oh, raving of

hurricanes that must have sounded in their young ears at the moment of our transit! Even in that moment the thunder of collision spoke aloud. Either with the swingle-bar, or with the haunch of our near leader, we had struck the off-wheel of the little gig, which stood rather obliquely, and not quite so far advanced, as to be accurately parallel with the near-wheel. The blow, from the fury of our passage, resounded terrifically. I rose in horror, to gaze upon the ruins we might have caused. From my elevated station I looked down, and looked back upon the scene, which in a moment told its own tale, and wrote all its records on my heart for ever.

Here was the map of the passion that now had finished. The horse was planted immovably, with his fore-feet upon the paved crest of the central road. He of the whole party might be supposed untouched by the passion of death. The little cany carriage — partly, perhaps, from the violent torsion of the wheels in its recent movement, partly from the thundering blow we had given to it — as if it sympathized with human horror, was all alive with tremblings and shiverings. The young man trembled not, nor shivered. He sat like a rock. But *his* was the steadiness of agitation frozen into rest by horror. As yet he dared not to look round; for he knew that, if anything remained to do, by him it could no longer be done. And as yet he knew not for certain if their safety were accomplished. But the lady ——

But the lady ——! Oh, heavens! will that spectacle ever depart from my dreams, as she rose and sank upon her seat, sank and rose, threw up her arms wildly to heaven, clutched at some visionary object in the air, fainting, praying, raving, despairing? Figure to yourself, reader, the elements of the case; suffer me to recall before your mind the circumstances of that unparalleled situation. From the silence and deep peace of this saintly summer night — from the pathetic blending of this sweet moonlight, dawnlight, dreamlight — from the manly tenderness of this flattering, whispering, murmuring love — suddenly as from the woods and fields — suddenly as from the chambers of the air opening in revelation — suddenly as from the ground yawning at her feet, leaped upon her, with the flashing of cataracts, Death the crownéd phantom, with all the equipage of his terrors, and the tiger roar of his voice.

The moments were numbered; the strife was finished; the vision was closed. In the twinkling of an eye, our flying horses had carried us to the termination of the umbrageous aisle; at right angles we wheeled into our former direction; the turn of the road carried the scene out of my eyes in an instant, and swept it into my dreams for ever.

# THE ENGLISH MAIL-COACH.

## SECTION THE THIRD. — DREAM-FUGUE.

### FOUNDED ON THE PRECEDING THEME OF SUDDEN DEATH

'Whence the sound
Of instruments, that made melodious chime,
Was heard, of harp and organ ; and who moved
Their stops and chords, was seen ; his volant touch
Instinct through all proportions, low and high,
Fled and pursued transverse the resonant fugue.'
*Par. Lost*, B xi.

*Tumultuosissimamente.*

PASSION of sudden death ! that once in youth I read
and interpreted by the shadows of thy averted signs ! [29]
— rapture of panic taking the shape (which amongst
tombs in churches I have seen) of woman bursting
her sepulchral bonds — of woman's Ionic form bending from the ruins of her grave with arching foot, with
eyes upraised, with clasped adoring hands — waiting,
watching, trembling, praying for the trumpet's call to
rise from dust for ever ! Ah, vision too fearful of
shuddering humanity on the brink of almighty abysses !
— vision that didst start back, that didst reel away,
like a shrivelling scroll from before the wrath of fire
racing on the wings of the wind ! Epilepsy so brief
of horror, wherefore is it that thou canst not die ?
Passing so suddenly into darkness, wherefore is it that
still thou sheddest thy sad funeral blights upon the
gorgeous mosaics of dreams ? Fragment of music too

[180]

passionate, heard once, and heard no more, what aileth thee, that thy deep rolling chords come up at intervals through all the worlds of sleep, and after forty years, have lost no element of horror?

## I.

Lo, it is summer — almighty summer! The ever-lasting gates of life and summer are thrown open wide; and on the ocean, tranquil and verdant as a savannah, the unknown lady from the dreadful vision and I myself are floating — she upon a fiery pinnace, and I upon an English three-decker. Both of us are wooing gales of festal happiness within the domain of our common country, within that ancient watery park, within that pathless chase of ocean, where England takes her pleasure as a huntress through winter and summer, from the rising to the setting sun. Ah, what a wilderness of floral beauty was hidden, or was suddenly revealed, upon the tropic islands through which the pinnace moved! And upon her deck what a bevy of human flowers — young women how lovely, young men how noble, that were dancing together, and slowly drifting towards *us* amidst music and incense, amidst blossoms from forests and gorgeous corymbi from vintages, amidst natural carolling and the echoes of sweet girlish laughter. Slowly the pinnace nears us, gaily she hails us, and silently she disappears beneath the shadow of our mighty bows. But then, as at some signal from heaven, the music, and the carols, and the sweet echoing of girlish laughter — all are hushed. What evil has smitten the pinnace, meeting or overtaking her? Did ruin to our friends couch within our own dreadful shadow? Was our shadow the shadow of death? I looked over the bow for an answer, and, behold! the pinnace was dismantled; the revel and the revellers were found no more; the glory of the vintage was dust; and the forests with their beauty were left without a witness upon the seas. 'But where,' and I turned to our crew — 'where are the lovely women that danced beneath the awning of flowers and clustering corymbi! Whither have fled the noble young men that danced with *them*?' Answer there was none. But suddenly the man at the masthead, whose countenance darkened with alarm, cried out, 'Sail on the weather beam! Down she comes upon us: in seventy seconds she also will founder.'

## II.

I looked to the weather side, and the summer had departed. The sea was rocking, and shaken with gathering wrath. Upon its surface sat mighty mists, which grouped themselves into arches and long cathedral aisles. Down one of these, with the fiery pace of a quarrel from a cross-bow, ran a frigate right athwart our course. 'Are they mad?' some voice exclaimed from our deck. 'Do they woo their ruin?' But in a moment, she was close upon us, some impulse of a heady current or local vortex gave a wheeling bias to her course, and off she forged without a shock. As she ran past us, high aloft amongst the shrouds stood the lady of the pinnace. The deeps opened ahead in malice to receive her, towering surges of foam ran after her, the billows were fierce to catch her. But far away she was borne into desert spaces of the sea: whilst still by sight I followed her as she ran before the howling gale, chased by angry sea-birds and by maddening billows; still I saw her, as at the moment when she ran past us, standing amongst the shrouds, with her white draperies streaming before the wind. There she stood, with hair dishevelled, one hand clutched amongst the tackling — rising, sinking, fluttering, trembling, praying — there for leagues I saw her as she stood, raising at intervals one hand to heaven, amidst the fiery crests of the pursuing waves and the raving of the storm; until at last, upon a sound from afar of malicious laughter and mockery, all was hidden for ever in driving showers; and afterwards, but when I know not, nor how.

### III.

Sweet funeral bells from some incalculable distance, wailing over the dead that die before the dawn, awakened me as I slept in a boat moored to some familiar shore. The morning twilight even then was breaking; and, by the dusky revelations which it spread, I saw a girl, adorned with a garland of white roses about her head for some great festival, running along the solitary strand in extremity of haste. Her running was the running of panic; and often she looked back as to some dreadful enemy in the rear. But when I leaped ashore, and followed on her steps to warn her of a peril in front, alas! from me she fled as from another peril, and vainly I shouted to her of quicksands that lay ahead. Faster and faster she ran; round a promontory of rocks she wheeled out of sight; in an instant I also wheeled round it, but only to see the treacherous sands gathering above her head. Already her person was buried; only the fair young head and the diadem

of white roses around it were still visible to the pitying heavens: and, last of all, was visible one white
marble arm.  I saw by the early twilight this fair
young head, as it was sinking down to darkness — saw
this marble arm, as it rose above her head and her
treacherous grave, tossing, faltering, rising, clutching
as at some false deceiving hand stretched out from the
clouds — saw this marble arm uttering her dying hope,
and then uttering her dying despair.  The head, the
diadem, the arm — these all had sunk; at last over
these also the cruel quicksand had closed; and no
memorial of the fair young girl remained on earth,
except my own solitary tears, and the funeral bells
from the desert seas, that, rising again more softly,
sang a requiem over the grave of the buried child, and
over her blighted dawn.

I sat, and wept in secret the tears that men have
ever given to the memory of those that died before
the dawn, and by the treachery of earth, our mother.
But suddenly the tears and funeral bells were hushed
by a shout as of many nations, and by a roar as from
some great king's artillery, advancing rapidly along
the valleys, and heard afar by echoes from the mountains.  'Hush!' I said, as I bent my ear earthwards
to listen — 'nush! — this either is the very anarchy
of strife, or else' — and then I listened more profoundly, and whispered as I raised my head — 'or
else, oh heavens! it is *victory* that is final, victory that
swallows up all strife.'

## IV.

Immediately, in trance, I was carried over land and
sea to some distant kingdom, and placed upon a tri-

umphal car, amongst companions crowned with laurel. The darkness of gathering midnight, brooding over all the land, hid from us the mighty crowds that were weaving restlessly about ourselves as a centre: we heard them, but saw them not. Tidings had arrived, within an hour, of a grandeur that measured itself against centuries; too full of pathos they were, too full of joy, to utter themselves by other language than by tears, by restless anthems, and *Te Deums* reverberated from the choirs and orchestras of earth. These tidings we that sat upon the laurelled car had it for our privilege to publish amongst all nations. And already, by signs audible through the darkness, by snortings and tramplings, our angry horses, that knew no fear of fleshy weariness, upbraided us with delay. Wherefore *was* it that we delayed? We waited for a secret word that should bear witness to the hope of nations, as now accomplished for ever. At midnight the secret word arrived; which word was — Waterloo and Recovered Christendom! The dreadful word shone by its own light; before us it went; high above our leaders' heads it rode, and spread a golden light over the paths which we traversed. Every city, at the presence of the secret word, threw open its gates. The rivers were conscious as we crossed. All the forests, as we ran along their margins, shivered in homage to the secret word. And the darkness comprehended it.

Two hours after midnight we approached a mighty Minster. Its gates, which rose to the clouds, were closed. But when the dreadful word, that rode before us, reached them with its golden light, silently they moved back upon their hinges; and at a flying gallop our equipage entered the grand aisle of the cathedral.

16

Headlong was our pace; and at every altar, in the little chapels and oratories to the right hand and left of our course, the lamps, dying or sickening, kindled anew in sympathy with the secret word that was flying past. Forty leagues we might have run in the cathedral, and as yet no strength of morning light had reached us, when before us we saw the aerial galleries of organ and choir. Every pinnacle of the fretwork, every station of advantage amongst the traceries, was crested by white-robed choristers, that sang deliverance; that wept no more tears, as once their fathers had wept; but at intervals that sang together to the generations, saying,

'Chant the deliverer's praise in every tongue,'
and receiving answers from afar,
'Such as once in heaven and earth were sung.'
And of their chanting was no end; of our headlong pace was neither pause nor slackening.

Thus, as we ran like torrents — thus, as we swept with bridal rapture over the Campo Santo [23] of the cathedral graves — suddenly we became aware of a vast necropolis rising upon the far-off horizon — a city of sepulchres, built within the saintly cathedral for the warrior dead that rested from their feuds on earth. Of purple granite was the necropolis; yet, in the first minute, it lay like a purple stain upon the horizon, so mighty was the distance. In the second minute it trembled through many changes, growing into terraces and towers of wondrous altitude, so mighty was the pace. In the third minute already, with our dreadful gallop, we were entering its suburbs. Vast sarcophagi rose on every side, having towers and turrets that, upon the limits of the central aisle, strode forward

with haughty intrusion, that ran back with mighty
shadows into answering recesses.   Every scarcophagus
showed many bas-reliefs — bas-reliefs of battles and
of battle-fields; battles from forgotten ages — battles
from yesterday — battle-fields that, long since, nature
had healed and reconciled to herself with the sweet
oblivion of flowers — battle-fields that were yet angry
and crimson with carnage.   Where the terraces ran,
there did *we* run; where the towers curved, there did
*we* curve.   With the flight of swallows our horses
swept round every angle.   Like rivers in flood, wheeling round headlands — like hurricanes that ride into
the secrets of forests — faster than ever light unwove
the mazes of darkness, our flying equipage carried
earthly passions, kindled warrior instincts, amongst
the dust that lay around us — dust oftentimes of our
noble fathers that had slept in God from Créci to Trafalgar.   And now had we reached the last sarcophagus,
now were we abreast of the last bas-relief, already had
we recovered the arrow-like flight of the illimitable
central aisle, when coming up this aisle to meet us we
beheld afar off a female child, that rode in a carriage
as frail as flowers.   The mists, which went before her,
hid the fawns that drew her, but could not hide the
shells and tropic flowers with which she played — but
could not hide the lovely smiles by which she uttered
her trust in the mighty cathedral, and in the cherubim
that looked down upon her from the mighty shafts of
its pillars.   Face to face she was meeting us; face to
face she rode, as if danger there were none.   'Oh,
baby!' I exclaimed, 'shalt thou be the ransom for
Waterloo?   Must we, that carry tidings of great joy
to every people, be messengers of ruin to thee!'   In

horror I rose at the thought; but then also, in horror
at the thought, rose one that was sculptured on a bas-
relief — a Dying Trumpeter. Solemnly from the field
of battle he rose to his feet; and, unslinging his stony
trumpet, carried it, in his dying anguish, to his stony
lips — sounding once, and yet once again; proclamation that, in *thy* ears, oh baby! spoke from the battlements of death. Immediately deep shadows fell
between us, and aboriginal silence. The choir had
ceased to sing. The hoofs of our horses, the dreadful
rattle of our harness, the groaning of our wheels,
alarmed the graves no more. By horror the bas-relief
had been unlocked into life. By horror we, that were
so full of life, we men and our horses, with their fiery
fore-legs rising in mid air to their everlasting gallop,
were frozen to a bas-relief. Then a third time the
trumpet sounded; the seals were taken off all pulses;
life, and the frenzy of life, tore into their channels
again; again the choir burst forth in sunny grandeur,
as from the muffling of storms and darkness; again
the thunderings of our horses carried temptation into ·
the graves. One cry burst from our lips, as the clouds,
drawing off from the aisle, showed it empty before us
— 'Whither has the infant fled? — is the young child
caught up to God?' Lo! afar off, in a vast recess,
rose three mighty windows to the clouds; and on a
level with their summits, at height insuperable to man,
rose an altar of purest alabaster. On its eastern face
was trembling a crimson glory. A glory was it from
the reddening dawn that now streamed *through* the
windows? Was it from the crimson robes of the
martyrs painted *on* the windows? Was it from the
bloody bas-reliefs of earth? There, suddenly, within

that crimson radiance, rose the apparition of a woman's head, and then of a woman's figure. The child it was — grown up to woman's height. Clinging to the horns of the altar, voiceless she stood — sinking, rising, raving, despairing; and behind the volume of incense, that, night and day, streamed upwards from the altar, dimly was seen the fiery font, and the shadow of that dreadful being who should have baptized her with the baptism of death. But by her side was kneeling her better angel, that hid his face with wings; that wept and pleaded for *her*; that prayed when *she* could *not*; that fought with Heaven by tears for *her* deliverance; which also, as he raised his immortal countenance from his wings, I saw, by the glory in his eye, that from Heaven he had won at last.

## V.

Then was completed the passion of the mighty fugue. The golden tubes of the organ, which as yet had but muttered at intervals — gleaming amongst clouds and surges of incense — threw up, as from fountains unfathomable, columns of heart-shattering music. Choir and anti-choir were filling fast with unknown voices. Thou also, Dying Trumpeter! — with thy love that was victorious, and thy anguish that was finishing — didst enter the tumult; trumpet and echo — farewell love, and farewell anguish — rang through the dreadful *sanctus*. Oh, darkness of the grave! that from the crimson altar and from the fiery font wert visited and searched by the effulgence in the angel's eye — were these indeed thy children? Pomps of life, that, from the burials of centuries, rose again to the voice of perfect joy, did ye indeed mingle with

the festivals of Death? Lo! as I looked back for
seventy leagues through the mighty cathedral, I saw
the quick and the dead that sang together to God,
together that sang to the generations of man. All
the hosts of jubilation, like armies that ride in pursuit, moved with one step. Us, that, with laurelled
heads, were passing from the cathedral, they overtook,
and, as with a garment, they wrapped us round with
thunders greater than our own. As brothers we moved
together; to the dawn that advanced — to the stars
that fled; rendering thanks to God in the highest —
that, having hid his face through one generation behind thick clouds of War, once again was ascending —
from the Campo Santo of Waterloo was ascending —
in the visions of Peace; rendering thanks for thee,
young girl! whom, having overshadowed with his in-
effable passion of death, suddenly did God relent;
suffered thy angel to turn aside his arm; and even in
thee, sister unknown! shown to me for a moment only
to be hidden for ever, found an occasion to glorify his
goodness. A thousand times, amongst the phantoms
of sleep, have I seen thee entering the gates of the
golden dawn — with the secret word riding before
thee — with the armies of the grave behind thee:
seen thee sinking, rising, raving, despairing; a thousand times in the worlds of sleep have seen thee followed by God's angel through storms; through desert
seas; through the darkness of quicksands; through
dreams, and the dreadful revelations that are in dreams
— only that at the last, with one sling of his victorious
arm, he might snatch thee back from ruin, and might
emblazon in thy deliverance the endless resurrections
of his love!

# NOTES.

### Note 1.   Page 125.

Lady Madeline Gordon.

### Note 2.   Page 125.

' *The same thing :* '— Thus, in the calendar of the Church Fes_tivals, the discovery of the true cross (by Helen, the mother of Constantine) is recorded (and one might think — with the ex_press consciousness of sarcasm) as the *Invention* of the Cross.

### Note 3.   Page 125.

' *Vast distances :* ' — One case was familiar to mail-coach trav_ellers, where two mails in opposite directions, north and south, starting at the same minute from points six hundred miles apart, met almost constantly at a particular bridge which bisected the total distance.

### Note 4.   Page 129.

*De non apparentibus, &c.*

### Note 5.   Page 129.

' *Snobs,*' and its antithesis, ' *nobs,*' arose among the internal factions of shoemakers perhaps ten years later.   Possibly enough, the terms may have existed much earlier; but they were then first made known, picturesquely and effectively, by a trial at some assizes which happened to fix the public attention.

### Note 6.   Page 134.

' *Von Troil's Iceland :* ' — The allusion to a well-known chap_ter in Von Troil's work, entitled, ' Concerning the Snakes of

Iceland.' The entire chapter consists of these six words — '*There are no snakes in Iceland.*'

### NOTE 7.    Page 134.

'*Forbidden seat:*' — The very sternest code of rules was enforced upon the mails by the Post-office. Throughout England, only three outsides were allowed, of whom one was to sit on the box, and the other two immediately behind the box; none, under any pretext, to come near the guard; an indispensable caution; since else, under the guise of passenger, a robber might by any one of a thousand advantages — which sometimes are created, but always are favored, by the animation of frank, social intercourse — have disarmed the guard. Beyond the Scottish border, the regulation was so far relaxed as to allow of *four* outsides, but not relaxed at all as to the mode of placing them. · One, as before, was seated on the box, and the other three on the front of the roof, with a determinate and ample separation from the little insulated chair of the guard. This relaxation was conceded by way of compensating to Scotland her disadvantages in point of population. England, by the superior density of her population, might always count upon a large fund of profits in the fractional trips of chance passengers riding for short distances of two or three stages. In Scotland, this chance counted for much less. And therefore, to make good the deficiency, Scotland was allowed a compensatory profit upon one *extra* passenger.

### NOTE 8.    Page 136.

'*False echoes:*' — Yes, false! for the words ascribed to Napoleon, as breathed to the memory of Desaix, never were uttered at all. They stand in the same category of theatrical fictions as the cry of the foundering line-of-battle ship Vengeur, as the vaunt of General Cambronne at Waterloo, '*La Garde meurt, mais ne se rend pas,*' or as the repartees of Talleyrand.

### NOTE 9.    Page 142.

'*Wore the royal livery:*' — The general impression was, that the royal livery belonged of right to the mail-coachmen as their professional dress. But that was an error. To the guard it *did* belong, I believe, and was obviously essential as an official warrant, and as a means of instant identification for his person, in the discharge of his important public duties. But the coachman, and especially if his place in the series did not connect him immediately with London and the General Post-office, obtained the scarlet coat only as an honorary distinction after long (or, if not long, trying and special) service.

### Note 10. Page 144.

' *Turrets* : ' — As one who loves and venerates Chaucer for his unrivalled merits of tenderness, of picturesque characterization, and of narrative skill, I noticed with great pleasure that the word *torrettes* is used by him to designate the little devices through which the reins are made to pass. This same word, in the same exact sense, I heard uniformly used by many scores of illustrious mail-coachmen, to whose confidential friendship I had the honor of being admitted in my younger days.

### Note 11. Page 145.

' *Mr. Waterton* : ' — Had the reader lived through the last generation, he would not need to be told that some thirty or thirty-five years back, Mr. Waterton, a distinguished country gentleman of ancient family in Northumberland, publicly mounted and rode in top-boots a savage old crocodile, that was restive and very impertinent, but all to no purpose. The crocodile jibbed and tried to kick, but vainly. He was no more able to throw the squire, than Sinbad was to throw the old scoundrel who used his back without paying for it, until he discovered a mode (slightly immoral, perhaps, though some think not) of murdering the old fraudulent jockey, and so circuitously of unhorsing him.

### Note 12. Page 146.

' *Households* : ' — Roe-deer do not congregate in herds like the fallow or the red deer, but by separate families, parents and children; which feature of approximation to the sanctity of human hearths, added to their comparatively miniature and graceful proportions, conciliate to them an interest of peculiar tenderness, supposing even that this beautiful creature is less characteristically impressed with the grandeurs of savage and forest life.

17

### NOTE 13.    Page 148.

'*Audacity :*'—Such the French accounted it; and it has struck me that Soult would not have been so popular in London. at the period of her present Majesty's coronation, or in Manchester, on occasion of his visit to that town, if they had been aware of the insolence with which he spoke of us in notes written at intervals from the field of Waterloo.  As though it had been mere felony in our army to look a French one in the face, he said in more notes than one, dated from two to four P. M., on the field of Waterloo, ' Here are the English — we have them; they are caught *en flagrant delit.*'  Yet no man should have known us better; no man had drunk deeper from the cup of humiliation than Soult had in 1809, when ejected by us with headlong violence from Oporto, and pursued through a long line of wrecks to the frontier of Spain; subsequently at Albuera, in the bloodiest of recorded battles, to say nothing of Toulouse, he should have learned our pretensions.

### NOTE 14.    Page 148.

'*At that time :* '—I speak of the era previous to Waterloo.

### NOTE 15.    Page 150.

' *Three hundred :*' — Of necessity, this scale of measurement, to an American, if he happens to be a thoughtless man, must sound ludicrous.   Accordingly, I remember a case in which an American writer indulges himself in the luxury of a little fibbing, by ascribing to an Englishman a pompous account of the Thames, constructed entirely upon American ideas of grandeur, and concluding in something like these terms : — ' And, sir, arriving at London, this mighty father of rivers attains a breadth of at least two furlongs, having, in its winding course, traversed the astonishing distance of one hundred and seventy miles.'   And this the candid American thinks it fair to contrast with the scale of the Mississippi.   Now, it is hardly worth while to answer a pure fiction gravely, else one might say that no Englishman out of Bedlam ever thought of looking in an island for the rivers of a continent; nor, consequently could have thought of looking for the peculiar grandeur of the Thames in the length of its course or in the extent of soil which it drains; yet, if he *had* been so absurd, the American might have recollected that a river, not to be compared with the Thames even as to volume of water — viz , the Tiber — has contrived to make itself heard of in this world for twenty-five centuries to an extent not reached as yet by any river, however corpulent, of his own land. The glory of the Thames is measured by the destiny of the population to which it ministers, by the commerce which it supports, by the grandeur of the empire in which, though far from the largest, it is the most influential stream. Upon some such scale, and not by a transfer of Columbian standards, is the course of our English mails to be valued. The American may fancy the effect of his own valuations to our English ears, by supposing the case of a Siberian glorifying his country in these terms : — ' These wretches, sir, in France and England, cannot march half a mile in any direction without finding a house where food can be had and lodging; whereas, such is the noble desolation of our magnificent country, that in many a direction for a thousand miles, I will engage that a dog shall not find shelter from a snow-storm, nor a wren find an apology for breakfast.'

### Note 16.    Page 154.

' *Glittering laurels :* '— I must observe, that the color of *green* suffers almost a spiritual change and exaltation under the effect of Bengal lights.

### Note 17.    Page 167.

' *Confluent:* '— Suppose a capital Y (the Pythagorean letter) : Lancaster is at the foot of this letter; Liverpool at the top of the *right* branch; Manchester at the top of the *left;* proud Preston at the centre, where the two branches unite. It is thirty-three miles along either of the two branches; it is twenty-two miles along the stem — viz., from Preston in the middle, to Lancaster at the root. There's a lesson in geography for the reader.

### Note 18.    Page 168.

' *Twice in the year :* ' — There were at that time only two assizes even in the most populous counties — viz., the Lent Assizes, and the Summer Assizes.

### Note 19. Page 169.

' *Sigh-born :* ' — 1 owe the suggestion of this word to an obscure remembrance of a beautiful phrase in ' Giraldus Cambrensis ' — viz., *suspiriosæ cogitationes.*

### Note 20. Page 172.

It is true that, according to the law of the case as established by legal precedents, all carriages were required to give way before Royal equipages, and therefore before the mail as one of them. But this only increased the danger, as being a regulation very imperfectly made known, very unequally enforced, and therefore often embarrassing the movements on both sides.

### Note 21. Page 172.

' *Quartering :* ' — This is the technical word, and, I presume, derived from the French *cartayer*, to evade a rut or any obstacle.

### Note 22. Page 180.

' *Averted signs :* ' —I read the course and changes of the lady's agony in the succession of her involuntary gestures ; but it must be remembered that I read all this from the rear, never once catching the lady's full face, and even her profile imperfectly.

### Note 23. Page 186.

' *Campo Santo :* ' — It is probable that most of my readers will be acquainted with the history of the Campo Santo (or cemetery) at Pisa, composed of earth brought from Jerusalem for a bed of sanctity, as the highest prize which the noble piety of crusaders could ask or imagine. To readers who are unacquainted with England, or who (being English) are yet unacquainted with the cathedral cities of England, it may be right to mention that the graves within-side the cathedrals often form a flat pavement over which carriages and horses *might* run ; and perhaps a boyish remembrance of one particular cathedral, across which I had seen passengers walk and burdens carried, as about two centuries back they were through the middle of St. Paul's in London, may have assisted my dream.

# DINNER, REAL, AND REPUTED.

GREAT misconceptions have always prevailed about the Roman *dinner*. Dinner [*cœna*] was the only meal which the Romans as a nation took. It was no accident, but arose out of their whole social economy. This I shall endeavor to show, by running through the history of a Roman day. *Ridentem dicere verum quid vetat?* And the course of this review will expose one or two important truths in ancient political economy, which have been too much overlooked.

With the lark it was that the Roman rose. Not that the earliest lark rises so early in Latium as the earliest lark in England ; that, is, during summer : but then, on the other hand, neither does it ever rise so late. The Roman citizen was stirring with the dawn — which, allowing for the shorter longest-day and longer shortest-day of Rome, you may call about four in summer — about seven in winter. Why did he do this? Because he went to bed at a very early hour. But why did he do that? By backing in this way, we shall surely back into the very well of truth : always, where it is possible, let us have the *pourquoi* of the *pourquoi*. The Roman went to bed early for two remarkable reasons. 1st, Because in Rome, built for a martial destiny, every habit of life had reference to

the usages of war.   Every citizen, if he were not a
mere proletarian animal kept at the public cost, with a
view to his *proles* or offspring, held himself a soldier-
elect : the more noble he was, the more was his lia-
bility to military service ; in short, all Rome, and at
all times, was consciously ' in procinct.' [1]   Now it was
a principle of ancient warfare, that every hour of daylight had a triple worth, as valued against hours of
darkness.   That was one reason — a reason suggested
by the understanding.   But there was a second reason,
far more remarkable ; and this was a reason suggested
by a blind necessity.   It is an important fact, that this
planet on which we live, this little industrious earth of
ours, has developed her wealth by slow stages of increase.   She was far from being the rich little globe in
Cæsar's days that she is at present.   The earth in our
days is incalculably richer, as a whole, than in the
time of Charlemagne ; and at that time she was richer,
by many a million of acres, than in the era of Augustus.   In that Augustan era we descry a clear belt of
cultivation, averaging perhaps six hundred miles in
depth, running in a ring-fence about the Mediterranean.   This belt, *and no more*, was in decent cultivation.   Beyond that belt, there was only a wild Indian
cultivation ; generally not so much.   At present, what
a difference !   We have that very belt, but much richer, all things considered, *æquatis æquandis*, than in the
Roman era and much beside.   The reader must not
look to single cases, as that of Egypt or other parts of
Africa, but take the whole collectively.   On that
scheme of valuation, we have the old Roman belt, the
circum Mediterranean girdle not much tarnished, and
we have all the rest of Europe to boot.   Such being

the case, the earth, being (as a whole) in that Pagan
era so incomparably poorer, could not in the Pagan
era support the expense of maintaining great empires
in cold latitudes.   Her purse would not reach that
cost.   Wherever she undertook in those early ages to
rear man in great abundance, it must be where nature
would consent to work in partnership with herself;
where *warmth* was to be had for nothing ; where
*clothes* were not so entirely indispensable, but that a
ragged fellow might still keep himself warm ; where
slight *shelter* might serve ; and where the *soil*, if not
absolutely richer in reversionary wealth, was more
easily cultured.   Nature, in those days of infancy,
must come forward liberally, and take a number of
shares in every new joint-stock concern before it could
move.   Man, therefore, went to bed early in those
ages, simply because his worthy mother earth could not
afford him candles.   She, good old lady (or good
young lady, for geologists know not [2] whether she is
in that stage of her progress which corresponds to
gray hairs, or to infancy, or to 'a *certain* age ') — she,
good lady, would certainly have shuddered to hear any
of her nations asking for candles.   ' Candles, indeed !'
she would have said, ' who ever heard of such a thing ?
and with so much excellent daylight running to waste,
as I have provided *gratis !*   What will the wretches
want next ? '

The daylight, furnished *gratis*, was certainly ' undeniable ' in its quality, and quite sufficient for all purposes that were honest.   Seneca, even in his own
luxurious period, called those men ' *lucifugæ*,' and by
other ugly names, who lived chiefly by candle-light.
None but rich and luxurious men, nay, even amongst

these, none but idlers, *did* live or *could* live by candle-
light.   An immense majority of men in Rome never
lighted a candle, unless sometimes in the early dawn.
And this custom of Rome was the custom also of all
nations that lived round the great lake of the Mediterranean.   In Athens, Egypt, Palestine, Asia Minor,
everywhere, the ancients went to bed, like good boys,
from seven to nine o'clock.[3]  The Turks and other
people, who have succeeded to the stations and the
habits of the ancients, do so at this day.

The Roman, therefore, who saw no joke in sitting
round a table in the dark, went off to bed as the darkness began.   Everybody did so.   Old Numa Pom-
pilius himself was obliged to trundle off in the dusk.
Tarquinius might be a very superb fellow ; but I doubt
whether he ever saw a farthing rushlight.   And,
though it may be thought that plots and conspiracies
would flourish in such a city of darkness, it is to be
considered, that the conspirators themselves had no more
candles than honest men : both parties were in the dark.

Being up, then, and stirring not long after the lark,
what mischief did the Roman go about first ?   Now-a-
days, he would have taken a pipe or a cigar.   But,
alas for the ignorance of the poor heathen creatures !
they had neither the one nor the other.   In this point,
I must tax our mother earth with being really *too*
stingy.   In the case of the candles, I approve of her
parsimony.   Much mischief is brewed by candle-
light.   But it was coming it too strong to allow no
tobacco.   Many a wild fellow in Rome, your Gracchi,
Syllas, Catilines, would not have played ' h— and
Tommy ' in the way they did, if they could have
soothed their angry stomachs with a cigar : a pipe

has intercepted many an evil scheme. But the thing is past helping now. At Rome, you must do as 'they does' at Rome. So, after shaving (supposing the age of the *Barbati* to be past), what is the first business that our Roman will undertake? Forty to one he is a poor man, born to look upwards to his fellow-men — and not to look down upon anybody but slaves. He goes, therefore, to the palace of some grandee, some top-sawyer of the senatorian order. This great man, for all his greatness, has turned out even sooner than himself. For he also has had no candles and no cigars; and he well knows, that before the sun looks into his portals, all his halls will be overflowing and buzzing with the matin susurrus of courtiers — the 'mane salutantes.' 4 It is as much as his popularity is worth to absent himself, or to keep people waiting. But surely, the reader may think, this poor man he might keep waiting. No, he might not; for, though poor, being a citizen, the man is a gentleman. That was the consequence of keeping slaves. Wherever there is a class of slaves, he that enjoys the *jus suffragii* (no matter how poor) is a gentleman. The true Latin word for a gentleman is *ingenuus* — a freeman and the son of a freeman.

Yet even here there were distinctions. Under the emperors, the courtiers were divided into two classes: with respect to the superior class, it was said of the sovereign — that he *saw* them ('*videbat*'); with respect to the other — that he *was seen* ('*videbatur*'). Even Plutarch mentions it as a common boast in his times, ἡμας ειδεν ὁ βασιλευς — *Cæsar is in the habit of seeing me;* or, as a common plea for evading a suit, ἑτερȣς ὁρα μαλλον — *I am sorry to say he is more inclined to look upon others.* And this usage derived itself (mark that well !) from the *republican* era. The aulic spirit was propagated by the empire, but from a republican root.

Having paid his court, you will suppose that our friend comes home to breakfast. Not at all : no such discovery as ' breakfast' had then been made : breakfast was not invented for many centuries after that. I have always admired, and always shall admire, as the very best of all human stories, Charles Lamb's account of *roast-pork*, and its traditional origin in China. Ching Ping, it seems, had suffered his father's house to be burned down : the outhouses were burned along with the house : and in one of these the pigs, by accident, were roasted to a turn. Memorable were the results for all future China and future civilization. Ping, who (like all China beside) had hitherto eaten his pig raw, now for the first time tasted it in a state of torrefaction. Of course he made his peace with his father by a part (tradition says a leg) of the new dish. The father was so astounded with the discovery, that he burned his house down once a-year for the sake of coming at an annual banquet of a roast pig. A curious prying sort of a fellow, one Chang Pang, got to know of this. He also burned down a house with a pig in it, and had his eyes opened. The secret was ill kept — the discovery spread — many great conversions were made — houses were blazing in every part of the Celestial Empire. The insurance offices took the matter up. One Chong Pong, detected in the very act of shutting up a pig in his drawing-room, and then firing a train, was indicted on a charge of arson. The chief justice of Pekin, on that occasion, requested an officer of the court to hand him up a piece of the roast pig, the *corpus delicti*: pure curiosity it was, liberal curiosity, that led him to taste; but within two days after, it was observed, says Lamb, that his lordship's town-house was on fire. In short, all China apostatized to the new faith; and it was not until some centuries had passed, that a man of prodigious genius arose, viz., Chung Pung, who, established the second era in the history of roast pig by showing that it could be had without burning down a house.

No such genius had yet arisen in Rome. Breakfast was not suspected. No prophecy, no type of breakfast, had been' published. In fact, it took as much time and research to arrive at that great discovery as at the Copernican system. True it is, reader, that you have heard of such a word as *jentaculum;* and your dictionary translates that old heathen word by the Christian word *breakfast.* But dictionaries are dull deceivers. Between *jentaculum* and *breakfast* the differences are as wide as between a horse-chestnut and a chestnut horse; differences in the *time when*, in the *place where*, in the *manner how*, but pre-eminently in the *thing which.*

Galen is a good authority upon such a subject, since, if (like other Pagans) he ate no breakfast himself, in some sense he may be called the cause of breakfast to other men, by treating of those things which could safely be taken upon an empty stomach. As to the time, he (like many other authors) says, περι τριτην, η (το μακροτερον) περι τεταρτην· about the third, or at farthest about the fourth hour: and so exact is he, that he assumes the day to lie exactly between six and six o'clock, and to be divided into thirteen equal portions. So the time will be a few minntes before nine, or a

204 DINNER, REAL, AND REPUTED.

few minutes before ten, in the forenoon. That seems
fair enough. But it is not time in respect to its location
that we are concerned with, so much as time in respect
to its duration. Now, heaps of authorities take it
for granted, that you are not to sit down — you are to
stand; and, as to the place, that any place will do —
'any corner of the forum,' says Galen, 'any corner
that you fancy:' which is like referring a man for his
*salle à manger* to Westminster Hall or Fleet Street.
Augustus, in a letter still surviving, tells us that he
*jentabat*, or took his *jentaculum*, in his carriage; sometimes in a wheel carriage (*in essedo*), sometimes in a
litter or palanquin (*in lecticâ*). This careless and dis-
orderly way as to time and place, and other circumstances of haste, sufficiently indicate the quality of the
meal you are to expect. Already you are 'sagacious
of your quarry from so far.' Not that we would presume, excellent reader, to liken you to Death, or to
insinuate that you are a 'grim feature.' But would
it not make a saint 'grim' to hear of such preparations for the morning meal? And then to hear of
such consummations as *panis siccus*, dry bread; or (if
the learned reader thinks it will taste better in Greek),
αϱτος ξηϱος! And what may this word *dry* happen
to mean? 'Does it mean *stale?*' says Salmasius.
'Shall we suppose,' says he, in querulous words,
'*molli et recenti opponi*,' that it is placed in antithesis
to soft and new bread, what English sailors call '*soft
tommy?*' and from that antithesis conclude it to be,
'*durum et non recens coctum, eoque sicciorem?*' Hard
and stale, and in that proportion more arid? Not
quite so bad as that, we hope. Or again — '*siccum
pro biscocto, ut hodie vocamus, sumemus?*' [5] By *hodie*

Salmasius means, amongst his countrymen of France, where *biscoctus* is verbatim reproduced in the word *bis* (twice), *cuit* (baked) ; whence our own *biscuit*. Biscuit might do very well, could we be sure that it was cabin biscuit ; but Salmasius argues that — in this case he takes it to mean ' *buccellatum, qui est panis nauticus ;* ' that is, the ship company's biscuit, broken with a sledge-hammer. In Greek, for the benefit again of the learned reader, it is termed δίπυρος, indicating that it has passed twice under the action of fire.

'Well,' you say, 'no matter if it had passed through the fires of Moloch ; only let us have this biscuit, such as it is.' In good faith, then, fasting reader, you are not likely to see much more than you *have* seen. It is a very Barmecide feast, we do assure you — this same ' jentaculum ; ' at which abstinence and patience are much more exercised than the teeth : faith and hope are the chief graces cultivated, together with that species of the *magnificum* which is founded on the *ignotum*. Even this biscuit was allowed in the most limited quantities ; for which reason it is that the Greeks called this apology for a meal by the name of βυκκισμος, a word formed (as many words were in the Post-Augustan ages) from a Latin word — viz., *buccea*, a mouthful ; not literally such, but so much as a polished man could allow himself to put into his mouth at once. 'We took a mouthful,' says Sir William Waller, the parliamentary general — ' took a mouthful ; paid our reckoning ; mounted ; and were off.' But there Sir William means, by his plausible ' mouthful,' something very much beyond either nine or nineteen ordinary quantities of that denomination, whereas the Roman ' jentaculum ' was literally such ;

and, accordingly, one of the varieties under which the ancient vocabularies express this model of evanescent quantities is *gustatio*, a mere tasting; and again, it is called by another variety *gustus*, a mere taste [whence comes the old French word *gouster* for a refection or luncheon, and then (by the usual suppression of the *s*) *gouter*]. Speaking of his uncle, Pliny the Younger says: 'Post solem plerumque lavabatur: deinde gustabat; dormiebat minimum; mox, quasi alio die, studebat in cœnæ tempus.' 'After taking the air, generally speaking, he bathed; after that he broke his fast on a morsel of biscuit, and took a very slight *siesta :* which done, as if awaking to a new day, he set in regularly to his studies, and pursued them to dinner-time.' *Gustabat* here meant that nondescript meal which arose at Rome when *jentaculum* and *prandium* were fused into one, and that only a *taste* or mouthful of biscuit, as we shall show farther on.

Possibly, however, most excellent reader, like some epicurean traveller, who, in crossing the Alps, finds himself weather-bound at St. Bernard's on Ash-Wednesday, you surmise a remedy: you descry some opening from 'the loopholes of retreat,' through which a few delicacies might be insinuated to spread verdure on this arid wilderness of biscuit. Casuistry can do much. A dead hand at casuistry has often proved more than a match for Lent with all his quarantines. But sorry I am to say that, in this case, no relief is hinted at in any ancient author. A grape or two (not a bunch of grapes), a raisin or two, a date, an olive — these are the whole amount of relief[6] which the chancery of the Roman kitchen granted in such cases. All things here hang together, and prove each other

—the time, the place, the mode, the thing. Well might man eat standing, or eat in public, such a trifle as this. Go home, indeed, to such a breakfast? You would as soon think of ordering a cloth to be laid in order to eat a peach, or of asking a friend to join you in an orange. No man in his senses makes ' two bites of a cherry.' So let us pass on to the other stages of the day. Only, in taking leave of this morning's stage, throw your eyes back with me, Christian reader, upon this truly heathen meal, fit for idolatrous dogs like your Greeks and your Romans; survey, through the vista of ages, that thrice-accursed biscuit, with half a fig, perhaps, by way of garnish, and a huge hammer by its side, to secure the certainty of mastica-tion, by previous comminution. Then turn your eyes to a Christian breakfast — hot rolls, eggs, coffee, beef; but down, down, rebellious visions; we need say no more! You, reader, like myself, will breathe a male-diction on the Classical era, and thank your stars for making you a Romanticist. Every morning I thank mine for keeping me back from the Augustan age, and reserving me to a period in which breakfast had been already invented. In the words of Ovid, I say : —

' Prisca juvent alios : ego me nunc denique natum
Gratulor. Hæc ætas moribus apta meis.'

Our friend, the Roman cit, has therefore thus far, in his progress through life, obtained no breakfast, if he ever contemplated an idea so frantic. But it occurs to you, my faithful reader, that perhaps he will not always be thus unhappy. I could bring wagon-loads of sentiments, Greek as well as Roman, which prove, more clearly than the most eminent pikestaff, that, as

the wheel of fortune revolves, simply out of the fact
that it has carried a man downwards, it must subsequently carry him upwards, no matter what dislike
that wheel, or any of its spokes, may bear to that
man : ' non si male nunc sit, et olim sic erit : ' and
that if a man, through the madness of his nation,
misses coffee and hot rolls at nine, he may easily run
into a leg of mutton at twelve.   True it is he may do
so : truth is commendable ; and I will not deny that a
man may sometimes, by losing a breakfast, gain a
dinner. , Such things have been in various ages, and
will be again, but not at Rome.   There were reasons
against it.   We have heard of men who consider life
under the idea of a wilderness — dry as a ' remainder
biscuit after a voyage :' and who consider a day under
the idea of a little life.   Life is the macrocosm, or
world at large ; day is the microcosm, or world in miniature.   Consequently, if life is a wilderness, then day,
as a little life, is a little wilderness.   And this wilderness can be safely traversed only by having relays of
fountains, or stages for refreshment.   Such stages,
they conceive, are found in the several meals which
Providence has stationed at due intervals through the
day, whenever the perverseness of man does not break
the chain, or derange the order of succession.

   These are the anchors by which man rides in that
billowy ocean between morning and night.   The first
anchor, viz., breakfast, having given way in Rome, the
more need there is that he should pull up by the
second ; and that is often reputed to be dinner.   And
as your dictionary, good reader, translated *breakfast* by
that vain word *jentaculum*, so doubtless it will translate
*dinner* by that still vainer word *prandium*.   Sincerely

I hope that your own dinner on this day, and through all time coming, may have a better root in fact and substance than this most visionary of all baseless things — the Roman *prandium*, of which I shall presently show you that the most approved translation is *moonshine*.

Reader, I am anything but jesting here. In the very spirit of serious truth, I assure you that the delusion about 'jentaculum' is even exceeded by this other delusion about 'prandium.' Salmasius himself, for whom a natural prejudice of place and time partially obscured the truth, admits, however, that *prandium* was a meal which the ancients rarely took ; his very words are — '*raro prandebant veteres.*' Now, judge for yourself of the good sense which is shown in translating by the word *dinner*, which must of necessity mean the chief meal, a Roman word which represents a fancy meal, a meal of caprice, a meal which few people took.    At this moment, what is the single point of agreement between the noon meal of the English laborer and the evening meal of the English gentleman ? What is the single circumstance common to both, which causes us to denominate them by the common name of *dinner?*    It is, that in both we recognize the *principal* meal of the day, the meal upon which is thrown the *onus* of the day's support.    In everything else they are as wide asunder as the poles ; but they agree in this one point of their function.    Is it credible now, that, to represent such a meal amongst ourselves, we select a Roman word so notoriously expressing a mere shadow, a pure apology, that very few people ever tasted it — nobody sat down to it — not many washed their hands after it, and gradually the very name of it

18

became interchangeable with another name, implying
the slightest possible act of tentative tasting or sipping? ' *Post lavationem sine mensâ prandium,*' says
Seneca, ' *post quod non sunt lavandæ manus ;* ' that is,
' after bathing, I take a *prandium* without sitting down
to table, and such a *prandium* as brings after itself no
need of washing the hands.' No ; moonshine as little
soils the hands as it oppresses the stomach.

Reader ! I, as well as Pliny, had an uncle, an East
Indian uncle ; doubtless you have such an uncle ;
everybody has an Indian uncle. Generally such a
person is ' rather yellow, rather yellow ' (to quote
Canning *versus* Lord Durham), that is the chief fault
with his physics ; but, as to his morals, he is universally a man of princely aspirations and habits. He is
not always so orientally rich as he is reputed ; but he
is always orientally munificent. Call upon him at any
hour from two to five, he insists on your taking *tiffin :*
and such a tiffin ! The English corresponding term is
luncheon ; but how meagre a shadow is the European
meal to its glowing Asiatic cousin ! Still, gloriously as
tiffin shines, does anybody imagine that it is a vicarious
dinner, or ever meant to be the substitute and *locum
tenens* of dinner ? Wait till eight, and you will have
your eyes opened on that subject. So of the Roman
*prandium :* had it been as luxurious as it was simple,
still it was always viewed as something meant only to
stay the stomach, as a prologue to something beyond.
The *prandium* was far enough from giving the feeblest
idea even of the English luncheon ; yet it stood in the
same relation to the Roman day. Now to Englishmen that meal scarcely exists ; and were it not for
women, whose delicacy of organization does not allow

them to fast so long as men, would probably be abolished.    It is singular in this, as in other points, how nearly England and ancient Rome approximate.    We all know how hard it is to tempt a man generally into spoiling his appetite, by eating before dinner.    The same dislike of violating what they called the integrity of the appetite (*integram famem*), existed at Rome. *Integer* means what is *intact*, unviolated by touch. Cicero, when protesting against spoiling his appetite for dinner, by tasting anything beforehand, says, *integram famem ad cœnam afferam;* I intend bringing to dinner an appetite untampered with.    Nay, so much stress did the Romans lay on maintaining this primitive state of the appetite undisturbed, that any prelusions with either *jentaculum* or *prandium* were said, by a very strong phrase indeed, *polluere famem*, to pollute the sanctity of the appetite.    The appetite was regarded as a holy vestal flame, soaring upwards towards dinner throughout the day : if undebauched, it tended to its natural consummation in *cœna :* expiring like a phœnix, to rise again out of its own ashes.    On this theory, to which language had accommodated itself, the two prelusive meals of nine or ten o'clock A. M., and of one P. M., so far from being ratified by the public sense, and adopted into the economy of the day, were regarded gloomily as gross irregularities, enormities, debauchers of the natural instinct ; and, in so far as they thwarted that instinct, lessened it, or depraved it, were almost uniformly held to be full of pollution ; and, finally, to *profane* a sacred motion of nature.    Such was the language.

But we guess what is passing in the reader's mind. He thinks that all this proves the *prandium* to have

been a meal of little account ; and in very many cases
absolutely unknown.   But still he thinks all this
might happen to the English dinner — *that* also might
be neglected ; supper might be generally preferred ;
and, nevertheless, dinner would be as truly entitled to
the name of dinner as before.   Many a student
neglects his dinner ; enthusiasm in any pursuit must
often have extinguished appetite for all of us.   Many
a time and oft did this happen to Sir Isaac Newton.
Evidence is on record, that such a deponent at eight
o'clock A. M. found Sir Isaac with one stocking on, one
off ; at two, said deponent called him to dinner.
Being interrogated whether Sir Isaac had pulled on
the *minus* stocking, or gartered the *plus* stocking, witness replied that he had not.   Being asked if Sir
Isaac came to dinner, replied that he did not.   Being
again asked, 'At sunset, did you look in on Sir
Isaac?' witness replied, 'I did.'   'And now, upon
your conscience, sir, by the virtue of your oath, in what
state were the stockings?'   *Ans.* — '*In statu quo ante
bellum.*'   It seems Sir Isaac had fought through that
whole battle of a long day, so trying a campaign to
many people — he had traversed that whole sandy
Zaarah, without calling, or needing to call, at one of
those fountains, stages, or *mansiones*,[7] by which (according to our former explanation) Providence has re-
lieved the continuity of arid soil, which else disfigures
that long dreary level.   This happens to all ; but was
dinner not dinner, and did supper become dinner,
because Sir Isaac Newton ate nothing at the first, and
threw the whole day's support upon the last?   No,
you will say, a rule is not defeated by one casual
deviation, nor by one person's constant deviation.

Everybody else was still dining at two, though Sir Isaac might not; and Sir Isaac himself on most days no more deferred his dinner beyond two, than he sat in public with one stocking off.   But what if everybody, Sir Isaac included, had deferred his substantial meal until night, and taken a slight refection only at two ? The question put does really represent the very case which has happened with us in England.   In 1700, a large part of London took a meal at two P. M., and another at seven or eight P. M.   At present, a large part of London is still doing the very same thing, tak-- ing one meal at two, and another at seven or eight. But the names are entirely changed : the two o'clock meal used to be called *dinner*, whereas at present it is called *luncheon ;* the seven o'clock meal used to be called *supper*, whereas at present it is called *dinner ;* and in both cases the difference is anything but *verbal :* it expresses a translation of that main meal, on which the day's support rested, from mid-day to evening.

Upon reviewing the idea of dinner, we soon perceive that time has little or no connection with it : since, both in England and France, dinner has travelled, like the hand of a clock, through *every* hour between ten A. M. and ten P. M.   We have a list, well attested, of every successive hour between these limits having been the known established hour for the royal dinner- table within the last three hundred and fifty years. Time, therefore, vanishes from the problem ; it is a quantity regularly exterminated.   The true elements of the idea are evidently these : — 1. That dinner is that meal, no matter when taken, which is the princi- pal meal ; *i. e.*, the meal on which the day's support is

thrown. 2. That it is *therefore* the meal of hospitality
3. That it is the meal (with reference to both Nos. 1
and 2) in which animal food predominate. 4. That it
is that meal which, upon a necessity arising for the
abolition of all *but* one, would naturally offer itself as
that one. Apply these four tests to *prandium:*—
How could that meal *prandium* answer to the first
test, as *the day's support,* which few people touched?
How could that meal *prandium* answer to the second
test, as the *meal of hospitality,* at which nobody sat
down? How could that meal *prandium* answer to the
third test, as the meal of animal food, which consisted
exclusively and notoriously of bread? Or answer to
the fourth test, as the privileged meal *entitled to survive the abolition of the rest,* which was itself abolished
at all times in practice?

Tried, therefore, by every test, *prandium* vanishes.
But I have something further to communicate about
this same *prandium.*

1. It came to pass, by a very natural association of
feeling, that *prandium* and *jentaculum,* in the latter
centuries of Rome, were generally confounded. This
result was inevitable. Both professed the same basis.
Both came in the morning. Both were fictions. Hence
they melted and collapsed into each other.

That fact speaks for itself — the modern breakfast
and luncheon never could have been confounded; but
who would be at the pains of distinguishing two
shadows? In a gambling-house of that class, where
you are at liberty to sit down to a splendid banquet,
anxiety probably prevents your sitting down at all;
but, if you do, the same cause prevents you noticing
what you eat. So of the two *pseudo* meals of Rome,

they came in the very midst of the Roman business —
viz., from nine A. M. to two P. M. Nobody could give
his mind to them, had they been of better quality.
There lay one cause of their vagueness — viz., in their
position. Another cause was, the common basis of
both. Bread was so notoriously the predominating
' feature ' in each of these prelusive banquets, that all
foreigners at Rome, who communicated with Romans
through the Greek language, knew both the one and
the other by the name of αρτοσιτος, or the *bread repast.*
Originally, this name had been restricted to the earlier
meal. But a distinction without a difference could not
sustain itself; and both alike disguised their emptiness
under this pompous quadrisyllable. All words are
suspicious, there is an odor of fraud about them, which
— being concerned with common things — are so base
as to stretch out to four syllables. What does an honest
word want with more than two ? In the identity of
substance, therefore, lay a second ground of confusion.
And then, thirdly, even as to the time, which had ever
been the sole real distinction, there arose from accident
a tendency to converge. For it happened that, while
some had *jentaculum* but no *prandium,* others had
*prandium* but no *jentaculum;* a third party had both ;
a fourth party, by much the largest, had neither. Out
of which four varieties (who would think that a non-
entity could cut up into so many somethings ?) arose a
fifth party of compromisers, who, because they could
not afford a regular *cœna,* and yet were hospitably disposed, fused the two ideas into one; and so, because
the usual time for the idea of a breakfast was nine to
ten, and for the idea of a luncheon twelve to one, compromised the rival pretensions by what diplomatists

call a *mezzo termine ;* bisecting the time at eleven, and melting the two ideas into one. But, by thus merging the separate times of each, they abolished the sole real difference that had ever divided them. Losing that, they lost all.

Perhaps, as two negatives make one affirmative, it may be thought that two layers of moonshine might coalesce into one pancake; and two Barmecide banquets might be the square root of one poached egg. Of that the company were the best judges. But, probably, as a rump and dozen, in our land of wagers, is construed with a very liberal latitude as to the materials, so Martial's invitation, ' to take bread with him at eleven,' might be understood by the συνετοι (the knowing ones) as significant of something better than ἀρτοσιτος. Otherwise, in good truth, ' moonshine and turn-out ' at eleven A. M. would be even worse than ' tea and turn-out ' at eight P. M., which the ' fervida juventus' of Young England so loudly deprecates. But, however that might be, in this convergement of the several frontiers, and the confusion that ensued, one cannot wonder that, whilst the two bladders collapsed into one idea, they actually expanded into four names — two Latin and two Greek, *gustus* and *gustatio,* γευσις and γευσμα — which all alike express the merely tentative or exploratory act of a *praegustator* or professional ' taster ' in a king's household : what, if applied to a fluid, we should denominate sipping.

At last, by so many steps all in one direction, things had come to such a pass — the two prelusive meals of the Roman morning, each for itself separately vague from the beginning, had so communicated and interfused their several and joint vaguenesses, that at last no man knew or cared to know what any other man included in his idea of either; how much or how little. And you might as well have hunted in the woods of Ethiopia for Prester John, or fixed the parish of the Everlasting Jew,[8] as have attempted to say what 'jentaculum' certainly *was*, or what 'prandium' certainly was *not*. Only one thing was clear, that neither was anything that people cared for. They were both empty shadows; but shadows as they were, we find from Cicero that they had a power of polluting and profaning better things than themselves.

We presume that no rational man will heceforth look for 'dinner'—that great idea according to Dr. Johnson — that sacred idea according to Cicero — in a bag of moonshine on one side, or a bag of pollution on the other. *Prandium*, so far from being what our foolish dictionaries pretend — dinner itself — never in its palmiest days was more or other than a miserable attempt at being *luncheon*. It was a *conatus*, what physiologists call a *nisus*, a struggle in a very ambitious spark, or *scintilla*, to kindle into a fire. This *nisus* went on for some centuries; but finally evaporated in smoke. If *prandium* had worked out its ambition, had 'the great stream of tendency' accomplished all its purposes, *prandium* never could have been more than a very indifferent luncheon. But now,

2. I have to offer another fact, ruinous to our dictionaries on another ground. Various circumstances have disguised the truth, but a truth it is, that 'prandium,' in its very origin and *incunabula*, never was a meal known to the Roman *culina*. In that court it was never recognized except as an alien. It had no

original domicile in the city of Rome.  It was a *vox
castrensis*, a word and an idea purely martial, and
pointing to martial necessities.  Amongst the new
ideas proclaimed to the recruit, this was one — 'Look
for no " *cœna*," no regular dinner, with us.  Resign
these unwarlike notions.  It is true that even war has
its respites; in these it would be possible to have our
Roman *cœna* with all its equipage of ministrations.
But luxury untunes the mind for doing and suffering.
Let us voluntarily renounce it ; that, when a necessity
of renouncing it arrives, we may not feel it among the
hardships of war.   From the day when you enter the
gates of the ·camp, reconcile yourself, tiro, to a new
fashion of meal, to what in camp dialect we call *prandium*.'  This *prandium*, this essentially military meal,
was taken standing, by way of symbolizing the necessity of being always ready for the enemy.  Hence
the posture in which it was taken at Rome, the very
counter-pole to the luxurious posture of dinner.  A
writer of the third century, a period from which the
Romans naturally looked back upon everything connected with their own early habits, with much the
same kind of interest as we extend to our Alfred (separated from us, as Romulus from them, by just a thousand years), in speaking of *prandium*, says, ' Quod
dictum est *parandium*, ab eo quod milites ad bellum
*paret*.'  Isidorus again says, ' Proprie apud veteres
prandium vocatum fuisse omnem militum cibum ante
pugnam : ' *i. e.*, ' that, properly speaking, amongst our
ancestors every military meal taken before battle was
termed *prandium*.'  According to Isidore, the proposition is reciprocating ; viz., that, as every *prandium*
was a military meal, so every military meal was called

*prandium.* But, in fact, the reason of that is apparent. Whether in the camp or the city, the early Romans had probably but one meal in a day. That is true of many a man amongst ourselves by choice; it is true also, to our knowledge, of some horse regiments in our service, and may be of all. This meal was called *cœna*, or dinner in the city — *prandium* in camps. In the city, it would always be tending to one fixed hour. In the camp, innumerable accidents of war would make it very uncertain. On this account it would be an established rule to celebrate the daily meal at noon, if nothing hindered; not that a later hour would not have been preferred, had the choice been free; but it was better to have a certainty at a bad hour, than by waiting for a better hour to make it an uncertainty. For it was a camp proverb — *Pransus, paratus;* armed with his daily meal, the soldier is ready for service. It was not, however, that all meals, as Isidore imagined, were indiscriminately called *prandium;* but that the one sole meal of the day, by accidents of war, might, and did, revolve through all hours of the day.

The first introduction of this military meal into Rome itself would be through the honorable pedantry of old centurions, &c., delighting (like the Commodore Trunnions of our navy) to keep up in peaceful life some image or memorial of their past experience, so wild, so full of peril, excitement, and romance, as Roman warfare must have been in those ages. Many non-military people for health's sake, many as an excuse for eating early, many by way of interposing some refreshment between the stages of forensic business, would adopt this hurried and informal meal. Many would wish to see their sons adopting such a

meal, as a training for foreign service in particular, **and**
for temperance in general. It would also be maintained by a solemn and very interesting commemoration of this camp repast in Rome.

This commemoration, because it has been grossly
misunderstood by Salmasius (whose error arose from
not marking the true point of a particular antithesis),
and still more, because it is a distinct confirmation of
all I have said as to the military nature of *prandium*,
I shall detach from the series of my illustrations, by
placing it in a separate paragraph.

On a set day the officers of the army were invited
by Cæsar to a banquet; it was a circumstance expressly noticed in the invitation, that the banquet was
not a 'cœna,' but a 'prandium.' What did *that* imply?
Why, that all the guests must present themselves
in full military accoutrement; whereas, observes the
historian, had it been a *cœna*, the officers would have
unbelted their swords; for he adds, even in Cæsar's
presence the officers are allowed to lay aside their
swords. The word *prandium*, in short, converted the
palace into the imperial tent; and Cæsar was no
longer a civil emperor and *princeps senātûs*, but
became a commander-in-chief amongst a council of
his staff, all belted and plumed, and in full military fig.

On this principle we come to understand why it is,
that, whenever the Latin poets speak of an army as
taking food, the word used is always *prandens* and
*pransus*; and when the word used is *prandens*, then
always it is an army that is concerned. Thus Juvenal
in a well-known passage : —

> ' Credimus altos
> Desiccasse amnes, epotaque flumina, Medo
> *Prandente* ' —

that rivers were drunk up, when the Mede [*i. e.*, the Median army under Xerxes] took his daily meal: *prandente*, observe, not *cœnante*: you might as well talk of an army taking tea and buttered toast, as taking *cœna*. Nor is that word ever applied to armies. It is true that the converse is not so rigorously observed; nor ought it, from the explanations already given. Though no soldier dined (*cœnabat*), yet the citizen sometimes adopted the camp usage, and took a *prandium*. But generally the poets use the word merely to mark the time of day. In that most humorous appeal of Perseus — 'Cur quis non prandeat, hoc est?' — is this a sufficient reason for losing one's *prandium*? — he was obliged to say *prandium*, because no exhibitions ever could cause a man to lose his *cœna*, since none were displayed at a time of day when nobody in Rome would have attended. Just as, in alluding to a parliamentary speech notoriously delivered at midnight, an English satirist might have said, Is this a speech to furnish an argument for leaving one's bed? — not as what stood foremost in his regard, but as the only thing that *could* be lost at that time of night.

On this principle, also — viz. by going back to the military origin of *prandium* — we gain the interpretation of all the peculiarities attached to it: viz. — 1, its early hour; 2, its being taken in a standing posture; 3, in the open air; 4, the humble quality of its materials — bread and biscuit (the main articles of military fare). In all these circumstances of the meal, we read most legibly written, the exotic (or non-civic) character of the meal, and its martial character.

Thus I have brought down our Roman friend to noonday, or even one hour later than noon, and to this moment the poor man has had nothing to eat. For supposing him to be not *impransus,* and supposing him *jentâsse* beside; yet it is evident (I hope) that neither one nor the other means more than what it was often called — viz., βαχχισμος, or, in plain English, a mouthful. How long do we intend to keep him waiting? Reader, he will dine at three, or (supposing dinner put off to the latest) at four. Dinner was never known to be later than the tenth hour at Rome, which in summer would be past five ; but for a far greater proportion of days would be near four in Rome. And so entirely was a Roman the creature of ceremonial usage, that a national mourning would probably have been celebrated, and the ' sad augurs ' would have been called in to expiate the prodigy, had the general dinner lingered beyond four.

But, meantime, what has our friend been about since perhaps six or seven in the morning? After paying his little homage to his *patronus,* in what way has he fought with the great enemy Time since then ? Why, reader, this illustrates one of the most interesting features in the Roman character. The Roman was the idlest of men. ' Man and boy,' he was ' an idler in the land.' He called himself and his pals, ' rerum dominos, gentemque togatam ' — ' *the gentry that wore the toga.*' Yes, a pretty set of *gentry* they were, and a pretty affair that ' toga ' was. Just figure to yourself, reader, the picture of a hard-working man, with horny hands, like our hedgers, ditchers, porters, &c., setting to work on the high road in that vast sweeping toga, filling with a strong gale like the mainsail of a frigate. Conceive the roars with which this magnificent figure would be received into the bosom of a

modern poor-house detachment sent out to attack the
stones on some line of road, or a fatigue party of dust-
men sent upon secret service. Had there been nothing
left as a memorial of the Romans but that one relic —
their immeasurable toga[9] — I should have known that
they were born and bred to idleness. In fact, except
in war, the Roman never did anything at all but sun
himself. *Uti se apricaret* was the final cause of peace
in his opinion; in literal truth, that he might make an
*apricot* of himself. The public rations at all times
supported the poorest inhabitant of Rome if he were a
citizen. Hence it was that Hadrian was so astonished
with the spectacle of Alexandria, '*civitas opulenta,
fæcunda, in quâ nemo vivat otiosus.*' Here first he
saw the spectacle of a vast city, second only to Rome,
where every man had something to do; *podagrosi
quod agant habent; habent cæci quod faciant; ne chi-
ragrici*' (those with gout in the fingers) '*apud eos
otiosi vivunt.*' No poor rates levied upon the rest of
the world for the benefit of their own paupers were
there distributed *gratis*. The prodigious spectacle
(such it seemed to Hadrian) was exhibited in Alexandria, of all men earning their bread in the sweat of
their brow. In Rome only (and at one time in some
of the Grecian states), it was the very meaning of *citizen* that he should vote and be idle. Precisely those
were the two things which the Roman, the *fæx Romuli*,
had to do — viz., sometimes to vote, and always to be
idle.

In these circumstances, where the whole sum of
life's duties amounted to voting, all the business a
man *could* have was to attend the public assemblies,
electioneering or factious. These, and any judicial

trial (public or private) that might happen to interest him for the persons concerned, or for the questions at stake, amused him through the morning; that is, from eight till one. He might also extract some diversion from the *columnæ*, or pillars of certain porticoes to which they pasted advertisements. These *affiches* must have been numerous; for all the girls in Rome who lost a trinket, or a pet bird, or a lap-dog, took this mode of angling in the great ocean of the public for the missing articles.

But all this time I take for granted that there were no shows in a course of exhibition, either the dreadful ones of the amphitheatre, or the bloodless ones of the circus. If there were, then that became the business of all Romans; and it was a business which would have occupied him from daylight until the light began to fail. Here we see another effect from the scarcity of artificial light amongst the ancients. These magnificent shows went on by daylight. But how incomparably more gorgeous would have been the splendor by lamp-light! What a gigantic conception! Two hundred and fifty thousand human faces all revealed under one blaze of lamp-light! Lord Bacon saw the mighty advantage of candle-light for the pomps and glories of this world. But the poverty of the earth was the original cause that the Pagan shows proceeded by day. Not that the masters of the world, who rained Arabian odors and perfumed waters of the most costly description from a thousand fountains, simply to cool the summer heats, would, in the *latter* centuries of Roman civilization, have regarded the expense of light; cedar and other odorous woods burning upon vast altars, together with every variety of fragrant torch, would have created light enough to shed a new day stretching over to the distant Adriatic. But precedents derived from early ages of poverty, ancient traditions, overruled the practical usage.

However, as there may happen to be no public spectacles, and the courts of political meetings (if not closed altogether by superstition) would at any rate be closed in the ordinary course by twelve or one o'clock, nothing remains for him to do, before returning home, except perhaps to attend the *palæstra*, or some public recitation of a poem written by a friend, but in any case to attend the public baths. For these the time varied; and many people have thought it tyrannical in some of the Cæsars that they imposed restraints on the time open for the baths; some, for instance, would not suffer them to open at all before two; and in any case, if you were later than four or five in summer, you would have to pay a fine, which most effectually cleaned out the baths of all raff, since it was a sum that *John Quires* could not have produced to save his life. But it should be considered that the emperor was the steward of the public resources for maintaining the baths in fuel, oil, attendance, repairs. And certain it is, that during the long peace of the first Cæsars, and after the *annonaria provisio* (that great pledge of popularity to a Roman prince) had been increased by the corn tribute from the Nile, the Roman population took a vast expansion ahead. The subsequent increase of baths, whilst no old ones were neglected, proves *that* decisively. And as citizenship expanded by means of the easy terms on which it could be had, so did the bathers multiply. The population of Rome in the century after Augustus, was far

greater than during that era; and this, still acting as
a vortex to the rest of the world, may have been one
great motive with Constantine for translating the capital eastwards; in reality, for breaking up one monster
capital into two of more manageable dimensions. Two
o'clock was sometimes the earliest hour at which the
public baths were opened. But in Martial's time a
man could go without blushing (*salvâ fronte*) at eleven;
though even then two o'clock was the meridian hour
for the great uproar of splashing, and swimming, and
'larking' in the endless baths of endless Rome.

And now, at last, bathing finished, and the exercises
of the *palæstra*, at half-past two, or three, our friend
finds his way home — not again to leave it for that
day. He is now a new man; refreshed, oiled with
perfumes, his dust washed off by hot water, and ready
for enjoyment. These were the things that determined the time for dinner. Had there been no other
proof that *cœna* was the Roman dinner, this is an ample one. Now first the Roman was fit for dinner, in a
condition of luxurious ease; business over — that day's
load of anxiety laid aside — his *cuticle*, as he delighted
to talk, cleansed and polished — nothing more to do
or to think of until the next morning: he might now
go and dine, and get drunk with a safe conscience.
Besides, if he does not get dinner now, when will he
get it? For most demonstrably he has taken nothing
yet which comes near in value to that basin of soup
which many of ourselves take at the Roman hour of
bathing. No; we have kept our man fasting as yet.
It is to be hoped, that something is coming at last.

Yes, something *is* coming; dinner is coming, the
great meal of 'cœna;' the meal sacred to hospitality

and genial pleasure comes now to fill up the rest of the day, until light fails altogether.

Many people are of opinion that the Romans only understood what the capabilities of dinner were. It is certain that they were the first great people that discovered the true secret and meaning of dinner, the great office which it fulfils, and which we in England are now so generally acting on. Barbarous nations — and none were, in that respect, more barbarous than our own ancestors — made this capital blunder: the brutes, if you asked them what was the use of dinner, what it was meant for, stared at you, and replied — as a horse would reply, if you put the same question about his provender — that it was to give him strength for finishing his work! Therefore, if you point your telescope back to antiquity about twelve or one o'clock in the daytime, you will descry our most worthy ancestors all eating for their very lives, eating as dogs eat — viz., in bodily fear that some other dog will come and take their dinner away. What swelling of the veins in the temples (see Boswell's natural history of Dr. Johnson at dinner)! what intense and rapid deglutition! what odious clatter of knives and plates! what silence of the human voice! what gravity! what fury in the libidinous eyes with which they contemplate the dishes! Positively it was an *indecent* spectacle to see Dr. Johnson at dinner. But, above all, what maniacal haste and hurry, as if the fiend were waiting with red-hot pincers to lay hold of the hindermost!

Oh, reader, do you recognize in this abominable picture your respected ancestors and ours? Excuse me for saying, 'What monsters!' I have a right to

call my own ancestors monsters ; and, if so, I must
have the same right over yours. For Southey has shown
plainly in the ' Doctor,' that every man having four
grandparents in the second stage of ascent, consequently (since each of those four will have had four
grandparents) sixteen in the third stage, consequently
sixty-four in the fourth, consequently two hundred
and fifty-six in the fifth, and so on, it follows that,
long before you get to the Conquest, every man and
woman then living in England will be wanted to make
up the sum of my separate ancestors ; consequently
you must take your ancestors out of the very same
fund, or (if you are too proud for that) you must go
without ancestors.   So that, your ancestors being
clearly mine, I have a right in law to call the whole
' kit' of them monsters. *Quod erat demonstrandum.*
Really and upon my honor, it makes one, for the moment, ashamed of one's descent ; one would wish to
disinherit one's-self backwards, and (as Sheridan says
in the ' Rivals ') to ' cut the connection.'  Wordsworth
has an admirable picture in ' Peter Bell ' of ' a snug
party in a parlor' removed into *limbus patrum* for their
offences in the flesh : —

> ' Cramming as they on earth were cramm'd ;
> All sipping wine, all sipping tea ;
> But, as you by their faces see,
> All *silent*, and all d——d.'

How well does that one word *silent* describe those
venerable ancestral dinners — ' All silent ! '  Contrast
this infernal silence of voice, and fury of eye, with the
' *risus ambilis*,' the festivity, the social kindness, the
music, the wine, the ' *dulcis insania*,' of a Roman
' *cœna*.'   I mentioned four tests for determining what

meal is, and what is not, dinner : we may now add **a**
fifth — viz., the spirit of festal joy and elegant enjoyment, of anxiety laid aside, and of honorable social
pleasure put on like a marriage garment.

And what caused the difference between our ancestors and the Romans ? Simply this — the error of interposing dinner in the middle of business, thus courting all the breezes of angry feeling that may happen to
blow from the business yet to come, instead of finishing, absolutely closing, the account with this world's
troubles before you sit down. That unhappy in-
terpolation ruined all. Dinner was an ugly little
parenthesis between two still uglier clauses of a tee-
totally ugly sentence. Whereas, with us, their enlightened posterity, to whom they have the honor to be
ancestors, dinner is a great re-action. There lies *my*
conception of the matter. It grew out of the very excess of the evil. When business was moderate, dinner
was allowed to divide and bisect it. When it swelled
into that vast strife and agony, as one may call it, that
boils along the tortured streets of modern London or
other capitals, men begin to see the necessity of an
adequate counter-force to push against this overwhelming torrent, and thus maintain the equilibrium. Were
it not for the soft relief of a six o'clock dinner, the
gentle demeanor succeeding to the boisterous hubbub
of the day, the soft glowing lights, the wine, the intellectual conversation, life in London is now come to
such a pass, that in two years all nerves would sink
before it. But for this periodic re-action, the modern
business which draws so cruelly on the brain, and so
little on the hands, would overthrow that organ in all
but those of coarse organization. Dinner it is —

meaning by dinner the whole complexity of attendant circumstances — which saves the modern brain-working man from going mad.

This revolution as to dinner was the greatest in virtue and value ever accomplished. In fact, those are always the most operative revolutions which are brought about through social or domestic changes. A nation must be barbarous, neither could it have much intellectual business, which dined in the morning. They could not be at ease in the morning. So much *must* be granted : every day has its separate *quantum*, its dose of anxiety, that could not be digested as soon noon. No man will say it. He, therefore, who dined at noon, showed himself willing to sit down squalid as he was, with his dress unchanged, his cares not washed off. And what follows from that? Why, that to him, to such a canine or cynical specimen of the genus *homo*, dinner existed only as a physical event, a mere animal relief, a purely carnal enjoyment. For in what, I demand, did this fleshly creature differ from the carrion crow, or the kite, or the vulture, or the cormorant? A French judge, in an action upon a wager, laid it down as law, that man only had a *bouche*, all other animals a *gueule* : only with regard to the horse, in consideration of his beauty, nobility, use, and in honor of the respect with which man regarded him, by the courtesy of Christendom, he might be allowed to have a *bouche*, and his reproach of brutality, if not taken away, might thus be hidden. But surely, of the rabid animal who is caught dining at noonday, the *homo ferus*, who affronts the meridian sun like Thyestes and Atreus, by his inhuman meals, we are, by parity of reason, entitled to say, that he has a ' maw ' (so has Milton's Death), but nothing resembling a stomach. And to this vile man a philosopher would say — 'Go away, sir, and come back to me two or three centuries hence, when you have learned to be a reasonable creature, and to make that physico-intellectual thing out of dinner which it was meant to be, and is capable of becoming.' In Henry VII.'s time the court dined at eleven in the forenoon. But even that hour was considered so shockingly late in the French court, that Louis XII. actually had his gray hairs brought down with sorrow to the grave, by changing his regular hour of half-past nine for eleven, in gallantry to his young English bride.[10] He fell a victim to late hours in the forenoon. In Cromwell's time they dined at one P. M. One century and a half had carried them on by two hours. Doubtless, old cooks and scullions wondered what the world would come to next. Our French neighbors were in the same predicament. But they far surpassed us in veneration for the meal. They actually dated from it. Dinner constituted the great era of the day. *L'apres diner* is almost the sole date which you find in Cardinal De Retz's memoirs of the *Fronde*. Dinner was their *Hegira* — dinner was their *line* in traversing the ocean of day : they crossed the equator when they dined. Our English Revolution came next ; it made some little difference, I have heard people say, in church and state ; I dare-say it did, like enough, but its great effects were perceived in dinner. People now dine at two. So dined Addison for his last thirty years ; so, through his entire life, dined Pope, whose birth was coeval with the Revolution. Precisely as the Rebellion of 1745 arose, did people (but observe, very great

people) advance to four P. M.   Philosophers, who watch
the 'semina rerum,' and the first symptoms of change,
had perceived this alteration singing in the upper air
like a coming storm some little time before.   About
the year 1740, Pope complains of Lady Suffolk's
dining so late as four.   Young people may bear those
things, he observed ; but as to himself, now turned of
fifty, if such things went on, if Lady Suffolk would
adopt such strange hours, he must really absent himself from Marble Hill.   Lady Suffolk had a right to
please herself; he himself loved her.   But, if she
would persist, all which remained for a decayed poet
was respectfully to cut his stick, and retire.   Whether
Pope ever put up with four o'clock dinners again, I
have vainly sought to fathom.   Some things advance
continuously, like a flood or a fire, which always make
an end of A, eat and digest it, before they go on to
B.   Other things advance *per saltum* — they do not
silently cancer their way onwards, but lie as still as a
snake after they have made some notable conquest,
then, when unobserved, they make themselves up ' for
mischief,' and take a flying bound onwards.   Thus
advanced Dinner, and by these fits got into the territory of evening.   And ever as it made a motion onwards, it found the nation more civilized (else the
change could not have been effected), and co-operated
in raising them to a still higher civilization.   The next
relay on that line of road, the next repeating frigate,
is Cowper in his poem on ' Conversation.'   He speaks
of four o'clock as still the elegant hour for dinner —
the hour for the *lautiores* and the *lepidi homines*.
Now this might be written about 1780, or a little
earlier ; perhaps, therefore, just one generation after

Pope's Lady Suffolk. But then Cowper was living amongst the rural gentry, not in high life; yet, again, Cowper was nearly connected by blood with the eminent Whig house of Cowper, and acknowledged as a kinsman. About twenty-five years after this, we may take Oxford as a good exponent of the national advance. As a magnificent body of 'foundations,' endowed by kings, nursed by queens, and resorted to by the flower of the national youth, Oxford ought to be elegant and even splendid in her habits. Yet, on the other hand, as a grave seat of learning, and feeling the weight of her position in the commonwealth, she is slow to move; she is inert as she should be, having the functions of *resistance* assigned to her against the popular instinct (surely active enough) of *movement*. Now, in Oxford, about 1804–5, there was a general move in the dinner hour. Those colleges who dined at three, of which there were still several, now began to dine at four: those who had dined at four, now translated their hour to five. These continued good general hours till about Waterloo. After that era, six, which had been somewhat of a gala hour, was promoted to the fixed station of dinner-time in ordinary; and there perhaps it will rest through centuries. For a more festal dinner, seven, eight, nine, ten, have all been in requisition since then; but I am not aware of any man's habitually dining later than ten P. M., except in that classical case recorded by Mr. Joseph Miller, of an Irishman who must have dined much later than ten, because his servant protested, when others were enforcing the dignity of their masters by the lateness of their dinner hours, that *his* master invariably dined 'to-morrow.'

20

Were the Romans not as barbarous as our own ancestors at one time? Most certainly they were; in
their primitive ages theey took their *cœna* at noon,[11]
*that* was before they had laid aside their barbarism;
before they shaved; it was during their barbarism,
and in consequence of their barbarism, that they timed
their *cœna* thus unseasonably. And this is made evident by the fact, that, so long as they erred in the
hour, they erred in the attending circumstances. At
this period they had no music at dinner, no festal
graces, and no reposing on sofas. They sat bolt upright in chairs, and were as grave as our áncestors, as
rabid, as libidinous in ogling the dishes, and doubtless
as furiously in haste.

With us the revolution has been equally complex.
We do not, indeed, adopt the luxurious attitude of
semi-recumbency; our climate makes that less requisite; and, moreover, the Romans had no knives and
forks, which could scarcely be used in that recumbent
posture; they ate with their fingers from dishes already
cut up — whence the peculiar force of Seneca's ' post
quod non sunt lavandæ manus.' But, exactly in proportion as our dinner has advanced towards evening, have
we and has *that* advanced in circumstances of elegance,
of taste, of intellectual value. This by itself would be
much. Infinite would be the gain for any people, that
it had ceased to be brutal, animal, fleshly; ceased to
regard the chief meal of the day as a ministration only
to an animal necessity; that they had raised it to a
higher office; associated it with social and humanizing
feelings, with manners, with graces moral and intellectual : moral in the self-restraint; intellectual in the
fact, notòrions to all men, that the chief arenas for the

*easy* display of intellectual power are at our dinner tables.   But dinner has *now* even a greater function than
this; as the fervor of our day's business increases,
dinner is continually more needed in its office of a
great *re-action*.   I repeat that, at this moment, but for
the daily relief of dinner, the brain of all men who
mix in the strife of capitals would be unhinged and
thrown off its centre.

If we should suppose the case of a nation taking
three equidistant meals, all of the same material and
the same quantity — all milk, for instance, all bread,
or all rice — it would be impossible for Thomas
Aquinas himself to say which was or was not dinner.
The case would be that of the Roman *ancile* which
dropped from the skies; tò prevent its ever being
stolen, the priests made eleven *fac-similes* of it, in
order that a thief, seeing the hopelessness of distinguishing the true one, might let all alone.   And the
result was, that, in the next generation, nobody could
point to the true one.   But our dinner, the Roman
*cœna*, is distinguished from the rest by far more than
the hour; it is distinguished by great functions, and
by still greater capacities.   It is already most beneficial; *if it* saves (as I say it does) the nation from
madness, it may become more so.

In saying this, I point to the lighter graces of music,
and conversation *more varied*, by which the Roman
*cœna* was chiefly distinguished from our dinner.   I am
far from agreeing with Mr. Croly, that the Roman
meal was more 'intellectual' than ours.   On the contrary, ours is the more intellectual by much; we have
far greater knowledge, far greater means for making it
such.   In fact, the fault of our meal is - - that it is *too*

intellectual ; of too severe a character ; too political ; too much tending, in many hands, to disquisition. Reciprocation of question and answer, variety of topics, shifting of topics, are points not sufficiently cultivated. In all else I assent to the following passage from Mr. Croly's eloquent 'Salathiel : ' —

'If an ancient Roman could start from his slumber into the midst of European life, he must look with scorn on its absence of grace, elegance, and fancy. But it is in its festivity, and most of all in its banquets, that he would feel the incurable barbarism of the Gothic blood. Contrasted with the fine displays that made the table of the Roman noble a picture, and threw over the indulgence of appetite the colors of the imagination, with what eyes must he contemplate the tasteless and commonplace dress, the coarse attendants, the meagre ornament, the want of mirth, music, and intellectual interest — the whole heavy machinery that converts the feast into the mere drudgery of devouring !'

Thus far the reader knows already that I dissent violently ; and by looking back he will see a picture of our ancestors at dinner, in which they rehearse the very part in relation to ourselves, that Mr. Croly supposes all moderns to rehearse in relation to the Romans ; but in the rest of the beautiful description, the positive, though not the comparative part, we must all concur : —

' The guests before me were fifty or sixty splendidly dressed men' (they were in fact Titus and his staff, then occupied with the siege of Jerusalem), 'attended by a crowd of domestics, attired with scarcely less splendor ; for no man thought of coming to the banquet in the robes of ordinary life. The embroidered couches, themselves striking objects, allowed the ease of position at once delightful in the relaxing climates of the south, and capable of combining with every grace of the human figure. At a slight distance, the table loaded with plate glittering under a profusion of lamps, and surrounded by couches thus covered by rich draperies, was like a central source of light radiating in broad shafts of every brilliant hue. The wealth of the patricians, and their intercourse with the Greeks, made them masters of the first performances of the arts. Copies of the most famous statues, and groups of sculpture in the precious metals; trophies of victories; models of temples, were mingled with vases of flowers and lighted perfumes. Finally, covering and closing all, was a vast scarlet canopy, which combined the groups beneath to the eye, and threw the whole into the form that a painter would love.'

Mr. Croly then goes on to insist on the intellectual embellishments of the Roman dinner; their variety, their grace, their adaptation to a festive purpose. The truth is, our English imagination, more profound than the Roman, is also more gloomy, less gay, less *riante*. That accounts for our want of the gorgeous *triclinium*, with its scarlet draperies, and for many other differences both to the eye and to the understanding. But both we and the Romans agree in the main point: we both discovered the true purpose which dinner might serve — 1, to throw the grace of intellectual enjoyment over an animal necessity; 2, to relieve and to meet by a benign antagonism the toil of brain incident to high forms of social life.

My object has been to point the eye to this fact; to

show uses imperfectly suspected in a recurring accident
of life ; to show a steady tendency to that consummation, by holding up, as in a mirror, a series of changes,
corresponding to our own series with regard to the
same chief meal, silently going on in a great people of
antiquity.

# NOTES.

### Note 1.    Page 198.

' *In pro:inct :* ' — Milton's translation (somewhere in the
' Paradise Regained ') of the technical phrase ' in procinctu.'

### Note 2.    Page 199.

' *Geologists know not :* ' — In man the sixtieth part of six thousand years is a very venerable age.    But as to a planet, as to our
little earth, instead of arguing dotage, six thousand years may
have scarcely carried her beyond babyhood.    Some people think
she is cutting her first teeth; some think her in her teens.    But,
seriously, it is a very interesting problem.    Do the sixty centuries of our earth imply youth, maturity, or dotage ?

### Note 3.    Page 200.

' *Everywhere the ancients went to bed, like good boys, from
seven to nine o'clock :* ' — As I am perfectly serious, I must beg
the reader, who fancies any joke in all this, to consider what an
immense difference it must have made to the earth, considered as
a steward of her own resources — whether great nations, in a period when their resources were so feebly developed, did, or did
not, for many centuries, require candles; and, I may add, fire.
The five heads of human expenditure are — 1. Food; 2. Shelter;
3. Clothing; 4. Fuel; 5. Light.    All were pitched on a lower scale
in the Pagan era; and the two last were almost banished from
ancient housekeeping.    What a great relief this must have been
to our good mother the earth ! who at *first* was obliged to request
of her children that they would settle round the Mediterranean.
She could not even afford them water, unless they would come
and fetch it themselves out of a common tank or cistern.

### Note 4.  Page 201.

' *The manè salutantes :* ' — There can be no doubt that the *levees* of modern princes and ministers have been inherited from this ancient usage of Rome; one which belonged to Rome republican, as well as Rome imperial.  The fiction in our modern practice is — that we wait upon the *lever*, or rising of the prince.  In France, at one era, this fiction was realized : the courtiers did really attend the king's dressing.  And, as to the queen, even up to the Revolution, Marie Antoinette gave audience at her toilette.

### Note 5.  Page 204.

' *Or again, "siccum pro biscocto, ut hodie vocamus, sumemus ? "* ' — It is odd enough that a scholar so complete as Salmasius, whom nothing ever escapes, should have overlooked so obvious an alternative as that of *siccus* in the sense of being without *opsonium* — *Scoticè*, without ' kitchen.'

### Note 6.  Page 206.

' *The whole amount of relief:* ' — From which it appears how grossly Locke (see his ' Education ') was deceived in fancying that Augustus practised any remarkable abstinence in taking only a bit of bread and a raisin or two, by way of luncheon.  Augustus did no more than most people did; secondly, he abstained only upon principles of luxury with a view to dinner ; and thirdly, for this dinner he never waited longer than up to four o'clock.

### Note 7.  Page 212.

' *Mansiones :* ' — The halts of the Roman legions, the stationary places of repose which divided the marches, were so called.

### Note 8.  Page 217.

' *The Everlasting Jew :* ' — The German name for what we English call the Wandering Jew.  The German imagination has been most struck by the duration of the man's life, and his unhappy sanctity from death; the English, by the unrestingness of the man's life, his incapacity of repose.

### Note 9.   Page 223.

' *Immeasurable toga :* ' — It is very true that in the time of Augustus the *toga* had disappeared amongst the lowest plebs, and greatly Augustus was shocked at that spectacle.   It is a very curious fact in itself, especially as expounding the main cause of the civil wars.   Mere poverty, and the absence of bribery from Rome, whilst all popular competition for offices drooped, can alone explain this remarkable revolution of dress.

### Note 10.   Page 231.

' *His young English Bride :* ' — The case of an old man, or one reputed old, marrying a very girlish wife, is always too much for the gravity of history; and, rather than lose the joke, the historian prudently disguises the age, which, after all, in this case was not above fifty-four.   And the very persons who insist on the late dinner as the proximate cause of death, elsewhere insinuate something more plausible, but not so decorously expressed. It is odd that this amiable prince, so memorable as having been a martyr to late dining at eleven A. M., was the same person who is so equally memorable for the noble, almost the sublime, answer about a King of France not remembering the wrongs of a Duke of Orleans.

### Note 11.   Page 234.

' *Took their cœna at noon:* ' — And, by the way, in order to show how little *cœna* had to do with any evening hour (though, in any age but that of our fathers, four in the afternoon would never have been thought an evening hour), the Roman *gourmands* and *bons vivants* continued through the very last ages of Rome to take their *cœna*, when more than usually sumptuous, at noon.   This, indeed, all people did occasionally, just as we sometimes give a dinner even now so early as four P. M., under the name of a breakfast.   Those who took their *cœna* so early as this, were said *de die cœnare* — to begin dining from high day. That line in Horace — ' Ut jugulent homines, surgunt *de nocte* latrones ' — does not mean that the robbers rise when others are going to bed, viz., at nightfall, but at midnight.   For, says one of the three best scholars of this earth, *de die, de nocte,* mean from that hour which was most fully, most intensely day or night, viz., the centre, the meridian. This one fact is surely a clincher as to the question whether *cœna* meant dinner or supper.

# ORTHOGRAPHIC MUTINEERS.

WITH A SPECIAL REFERENCE TO THE WORKS OF WALTER
SAVAGE LANDOR.

As we are all of us crazy when the wind sets in
some particular quarter, let not Mr. Landor be angry
with me for suggesting that he is outrageously crazy
upon one solitary subject of spelling. It occurs to
me, as a plausible solution of his fury upon this point,
that perhaps in his earliest school-days, when it is
understood that he was exceedingly pugnacious, he
may have detested spelling, and (like Roberte the
Deville[1]) have found it more satisfactory for all parties, that when the presumptuous schoolmaster differed
from him on the spelling of a word, the question
between them should be settled by a stand-up fight.
Both parties would have the victory at times: and
if, according to Pope's expression, 'justice rul'd the
ball,' the schoolmaster (who is always a villain) would
be floored three times out of four; no great matter
whether wrong or not upon the immediate point of
spelling discussed. It is in this way, viz., from the
irregular adjudications upon litigated spelling, which
must have arisen under such a mode of investigating
the matter, that we account for Mr. Landor's being
sometimes in the right, but too often (with regard to

[243]

long words) egregiously in the wrong.  As he grew
stronger and taller, he would be coming more and
more amongst polysyllables, and more and more
would be getting the upper hand of the schoolmaster;
so that at length he would have it all his own way;
one round would decide the turn-up; and thencefor-
wards his spelling would become frightful.  Now, I
myself detested spelling as much as all people ought
to do, except Continental compositors, who have extra
fees for doctoring the lame spelling of ladies and gentlemen.  But, unhappily, I had no power to thump the
schoolmaster into a conviction of his own absurdities;
which, however, I greatly desired to do.  Still, my
nature, powerless at that time for any active recusancy,
was strong for passive resistance; and *that* is the
hardest to conquer.  I took one lesson of this infernal
art, and then declined ever to take a second; and in
fact, I never *did*.  Well I remember that unique morning's experience.  It was the first page of Entick's
Dictionary that I had to get by heart; a sweet sentimental task; and not, as may be fancied, the spelling
only, but the horrid attempts of this depraved Entick
to explain the supposed meaning of words that probably had none; many of these, it is my belief, Entick
himself forged.  Among the strange, grim-looking
words, to whose acquaintance I was introduced on that
unhappy morning, were *abalienate* and *ablaqueation* —
most respectable words, I am fully persuaded, but so
exceedingly retired in their habits, that I never once
had the honor of meeting either of them in any book,
pamphlet, journal, whether in prose or numerous
verse, though haunting such society myself all my
life.  I also formed the acquaintance, at that time, of

the word *abacus*, which, as a Latin word, I have often used, but, as an English one, I really never had occasion to spell, until this very moment. Yet, after all, what harm comes of such obstinate recusancy against orthography? I was an ' occasional conformist ; ' I conformed for one morning, and never more. But, for all that, I spell as well as my neighbors; and I can spell *ablaqueation* besides, which I suspect that some of them can *not*.

My own spelling, therefore, went right, because I was left to nature, with strict neutrality on the part of the authorities. Mr. Landor's too often went wrong, because he was thrown into a perverse channel by his continued triumphs over the prostrate schoolmaster. To toss up, as it were, for the spelling of a word, by the best of nine rounds, inevitably left the impression that chance governed all; and this accounts for the extreme capriciousness of Landor.

It is a work for a separate dictionary in quarto to record *all* the proposed revolutions in spelling through which our English blood, either at home or in America, has thrown off, at times, the surplus energy that consumed it. I conceive this to be a sort of cutaneous affection, like nettle-rash, or ringworm, through which the patient gains relief for his own nervous distraction, whilst, in fact, he does no harm to anybody : for usually he forgets his own reforms, and if *he* should not, everybody else *does*. Not to travel back into the seventeenth century, and the noble army of short-hand writers who have all made war upon orthography, for secret purposes of their own, even in the last century, and in the present, what a list of eminent rebels against the spelling-book might be called up to answer for

their wickedness at the bar of the Old Bailey, if anybody would be kind enough to make it a felony!
Cowper, for instance, too modest and too pensive to
raise upon any subject an open standard of rebellion,
yet, in quiet Olney, made a small *émeute* as to the
word 'Grecian.'    Everybody else was content with
one '*e;*' but he recollecting the cornucopia of *e's,*
which Providence had thought fit to empty upon the
mother word *Greece,* deemed it shocking to disinherit
the poor child of its hereditary wealth, and wrote it,
therefore, *Greecian* throughout his Homer.   Such a
modest reform the sternest old Tory could not find in
his heart to denounce.   But some contagion must have
collected about this word *Greece;* for the next man,
who had much occasion to use it — viz., Mitford [2] —
who wrote that 'History of Greece' so eccentric, and
so eccentrically praised by Lord Byron, absolutely
took to spelling like a heathen, slashed right and left
against decent old English words, until, in fact, the
whole of Entick's Dictionary (*ablaqueation* and all)
was ready to swear the peace against him.   Mitford,
in course of time, slept with his fathers; his grave, I
trust, not haunted by the injured words whom he had
tomahawked; and, at this present moment, the Bishop
of St. David's reigneth in his stead.   His Lordship,
bound over to episcopal decorum, has hitherto been
sparing in his assaults upon pure old English words:
but one may trace the insurrectionary taint, passing
down from Cowper through the word *Grecian,* in
many of his Anglo-Hellenic forms.   For instance, he
insists on our saying — not *Heracleidæ* and *Pelopidæ,*
as we all used to do — but *Heracleids* and *Pelopids.*
A list of my Lord's barbarities, in many other cases,

upon unprotected words, poor shivering aliens that fall
into his power, when thrown upon the coast of his diocese, I had — *had*, I say, for, alas! *fuit Ilium.*

Yet, really, one is ashamed to linger on cases so
mild as those, coming, as one does, in the order of
atrocity, to Elphinstone, to Noah Webster, a Yankee
— which word means, not an American, but that
separate order of Americans, growing in Massachu-
setts, Rhode Island, or Connecticut, in fact, a New
Englander [3] — and to the rabid Ritson. Noah would
naturally have reduced us all to an antediluvian simplicity. Shem, Ham, and Japheth, probably separated
in consequence of perverse varieties in spelling ; so
that orthographical unity might seem to him one condition for preventing national schisms. But as to the
rabid Ritson, who can describe his vagaries ? What
great arithmetician can furnish an index to his absurdities, or what great decipherer furnish a key to the
principles of these absurdities ? In his very title-
pages, nay, in the most obstinate of ancient techni-
calities, he showed his cloven foot to the astonished
reader. Some of his many works were printed in
*Pall-Mall ;* now, as the world is pleased to pronounce
that word *Pel-Mel,* thus and no otherwise (said Ritson) it shall be spelled for ever. Whereas, on the
contrary, some men would have said : The spelling is
well enough, it is the public pronunciation which is
wrong. This ought to be *Paul-Maul ;* or, perhaps —
agreeably to the sound which we give to the *a* in such
words as *what, quantity, want* — still better, and with
more gallantry, *Poll-Moll.* The word Mr., again, in
Ritson's reformation, must have astonished the Post-
office. He insisted that this cabalistical-looking form,

which might as reasonably be translated into *monster*,
was a direct fraud on the national language, quite as
bad as clipping the Queen's coinage. How, then,
*should* it be written? Reader! reader! that you will
ask such a question! *mister*, of course; and mind that
you put no capital *m*; unless, indeed, you are speaking of some great gun, some mister of misters, such as
Mr. Pitt of old, or perhaps a reformer of spelling.
The plural, again, of such words as *romance*, *age*,
*horse*, he wrote *romanceës, ageës, horseës*; and upon
the following equitable consideration, that, inasmuch
as the *e* final in the singular is mute, that is, by a
general vote of the nation has been allowed to retire
upon a superannuation allowance, it is abominable to
call it back upon active service — like the modern
Chelsea pensioners — as must be done, if it is to bear
the whole weight of a separate syllable like *ces*. Consequently, if the nation and Parliament mean to keep
faith, they are bound to hire a stout young *e* to run in
the traces with the old original *e*, taking the whole
work off his aged shoulders. Volumes would not suffice to exhaust the madness of Ritson upon this sub-
jcet. And there was this peculiarity in his madness,
over and above its clamorous ferocity, that being no
classical scholar (a meagre self-taught Latinist, and
no Grecian at all), though profound as a black-letter
scholar, he cared not one straw for ethnographic relations of the words, nor unity of analogy, which are the
principles that generally have governed reformers of
spelling. He was an attorney, and moved constantly
under the *monomaniac* idea that an action lay on behalf of the misused letters; mutes, liquids, vowels, and
diphthongs, against somebody or other (John Doe, was

it, or Richard Roe ?) for trespass on any rights of theirs which an attorney might trace, and of course for any direct outrage upon their persons. Yet no man was more systematically an offender in both ways than himself; tying up one leg of a quadruped word, and forcing it to run upon three; cutting off noses and ears, if he fancied that equity required it: and living in eternal hot water with a language which he pretended eternally to protect.

And yet all these fellows were nothing in comparison of Mr. [4] Pinkerton. The most of these men did but ruin the national *spelling;* but Pinkerton — the monster Pinkerton — proposed a revolution which would have left us nothing to spell. It is almost incredible — if a book regularly printed and published, bought and sold, did not remain to attest the fact — that this horrid barbarian seriously proposed, as a glorious discovery for refining our language, the following plan. All people were content with the compass of the English language: its range of expression was equal to anything; but, unfortunately, as compared with the sweet, orchestral languages of the south — Spanish the stately, and Italian the lovely — it wanted rhythmus and melody. Clearly, then, the one supplementary grace, which it remained for modern art to give, is that every one should add at discretion *o* and *a, ino* and *ano,* to the end of the English words. The language, in its old days, should be taught *struttare struttissimamente.* As a specimen, Mr. Pinkerton favored us with his own version of a famous passage in Addison, viz., 'The Vision of Mirza.' The passage, which begins thus, 'As I sat on the top of a rock,' being translated into, 'As I satto on the toppino of a rocko,' &c. But *luckilissime* this *proposalio* of the *absurdissimo Pinkertonio* [5] was not *adoptado* by *anybody-ini whatever-ano.*

Mr. Landor is more learned, and probably more consistent in his assaults upon the established spelling than most of these elder reformers. But *that* does not. make him either learned enough or consistent enough. He never ascends into Anglo-Saxon, or the many cognate languages of the Teutonic family, which is indispensable to a searching inquest upon our language; he does not put forward in this direction even the slender qualifications of Horne Tooke. But Greek and Latin are quite unequal, when disjoined from the elder wheels in our etymological system, to the working of the total machinery of the English language. Mr. Landor proceeds upon no fixed principles in his changes. Sometimes it is on the principle of internal analogy within itself, that he would distort or retrotort the language; sometimes on the principle of external analogy with its roots; sometimes on the principle of euphony, or of metrical convenience. Even within such principles he is not uniform. All well-built English scholars, for instance, know that the word *feälty* cannot be made into a dissyllable: trisyllabic it ever was [6] with the elder poets — Spenser, Milton, &c.; and so it is amongst all the modern poets who have taken any pains with their English studies: *e. g.*

> 'The eagle, lord of land and sea,
> Stoop'd — down to pay him fe-al-ty.'

It is dreadful to hear a man say *feal-ty* in any case; but here it is luckily impossible. Now, Mr. Landor generally is correct, and trisects the word; but once,

at least, he bisects it. I complain, besides, that Mr.
Landor, in urging the authority of Milton for ortho-
graphic innovations, does not always distinguish as to
Milton's motives. It is true, as he contends, that, in
some instances, Milton reformed the spelling in obedience to the Italian precedent: and certainly without
blame; as in *sovran, sdeign,* which ought not to be
printed (as it is) with an elision before the *s*, as if
short for disdain; but in other instances Milton's motive had no reference to etymology. Sometimes it was
this. In Milton's day the modern use of italics was
nearly unknown. Everybody is aware that, in our
authorized version of the Bible, published in Milton's
infancy, italics are never once used for the purpose of
emphasis — but exclusively to indicate such words or
auxiliary forms as, though implied and *virtually* present in the original, are not textually expressed, but
must be so in English, from the different genius of
the language.[7] Now, this want of a proper technical
resource amongst the compositors of the age, for indicating a peculiar stress upon the word, evidently drove
Milton into some perplexity for a compensatory contrivance. It was unusually requisite for *him*, with his
elaborate metrical system and his divine ear, to have
an art for throwing attention upon his accents, and
upon his muffling of accents. When, for instance, he
wishes to direct a bright jet of emphasis upon the pos-
sessive pronoun *their*, he writes it as we now write it.
But, when he wishes to take off the accent, he writes
it *thir*.[8] Like Ritson, he writes *therefor* and *wherefor*
without the final *e*; not regarding the analogy, but
singly the metrical quantity: for it was shocking to
his classical feeling that a sound so short to the ear

should be represented to the eye by so long a combination as *fore;* and the more so, because uneducated
people did then, and do now, often equilibrate the
accent between the two syllables, or rather make the
*quantity* long in both syllables, whilst giving an over-
balance of the *accent* to the last. The 'Paradise Lost,'
being printed during Milton's blindness, did not receive
the full and consistent benefit of his spelling reforms,
which (as I have contended) certainly arose partly in
the imperfections of typography at that æra; but such
changes as had happened most to impress his ear with
a sense of their importance, he took a special trouble,
even under all the disadvantages of his darkness, to
have rigorously adopted.   He must have astonished
the compositors, though not quite so much as the
tiger-cat Ritson or the Mr. (viz. monster) Pinkerton —
each after *his* kind — astonished *their* compositors.

But the caprice of Mr. Landor is shown most of all
upon Greek names. *Nous autres* say ' Aristotle,' and
are quite content with it until we migrate into some
extra-superfine world; but this title will not do for
*him :* 'Aristotles' it must be.   And why so?   Because, answers the Landor, if once I consent to say
Aristotle, then I am pledged to go the whole hog;
and perhaps the next man I meet is Empedocles,
whom, in that case, I must call Empedocle.   Well, do
so.   *Call* him Empedocle; it will not break his back,
which seems broad enough.   But, now, mark the con-
tradictions in which Mr. Landor is soon landed.   He
says, as everybody says, Terence, and not Terentius,
Horace, and not Horatius; but he must leave off such
horrid practices, because he dares not call Lucretius by
the analogous name of Lucrece, since *that* would be

putting a she instead of a he; nor Propertius by the
name of Properce, because *that* would be speaking
French instead of English. Next he says, and continually he says, Virgil for Virgilius. But, on that
principle, he ought to say Valer for Valerius; and yet
again he ought not: because as he says Tully and not
Tull for Tullius, so also is he bound, in Christian
equity, to say Valery for Valer; but he cannot say
either Valer or Valery. So here we are in a mess.
Thirdly, I charge him with saying Ovid for Ovidius:
which *I* do, which everybody does, but which *he* must
not do: for if he means to persist in *that*, then, upon
his own argument from analogy, he must call Didius
Julianus by the shocking name of *Did*, which is the
same thing as Tit — since T is D soft. Did was a
very great man indeed, and for a very short time
indeed. Probably Did was the only man that ever
bade for an empire, and no mistake, at a public auc-
tion. Think of Did's bidding for the Roman empire;
nay, think also of Did's having the lot actually
knocked down to him; and of Did's going home to
dinner with the lot in his pocket. It makes one per-
spire to think that, if the reader or myself had been
living at that time, and had been prompted by some
whim within us to bid against him — that is, he or I
— should actually have come down to posterity by the
abominable name of Anti-Did. All of us in England
say Livy when speaking of the great historian, not
Livius. Yet Livius Andronicus it would be impossible to indulge with that brotherly name of Livy.
Marcus Antonius is called — not by Shakspeare only,
but by all the world — Mark Antony; but who is it
that ever called Marcus Brutus by the affectionate

name of Mark Brute? 'Keep your distance,' we say
to that very doubtful brute, ' and expect no pet names
from us.' Finally, apply the principle of abbreviation,
involved in the names of Pliny, Livy, Tully, all substituting *y* for *ius*, to Marius — that grimmest of grim
visions that rises up to us from the phantasmagoria of
Roman history. Figure to yourself, reader, that truculent face, trenched and scarred with hostile swords,
carrying thunder in its ominous eye-brows, and fright-
ening armies a mile off with its scowl, being saluted
by the tenderest of feminine names, as ' My Mary.'

Not only, therefore, is Mr. Landor inconsistent in
these innovations, but the innovations themselves, supposing them all harmonized and established, would
but plough up the landmarks of old hereditary feelings. We learn oftentimes, by a man's bearing a
good-natured sobriquet amongst his comrades, that he
is a kind-hearted, social creature, popular with them
all! And it is an illustration of the same tendency,
that the scale of popularity for the classical authors
amongst our fathers, is registered tolerably well, in a
gross general way, by the difference between having
and *not* having a familiar name. If we except the first
Cæsar, the mighty Caius Julius, who was too majestic
to invite familiarity, though too gracious to have
repelled it, there is no author whom our forefathers
loved, but has won a sort of Christian name in the
land. Homer, and Hesiod, and Pindar, we all say;
we cancel the alien *us* ; but we never say Theocrit for
Theocritus. Anacreon remains rigidly Grecian marble;
but *that* is only because his name is not of a plastic
form — else everybody loves the sad old fellow. The
same bar to familiarity existed in the names of the

tragic poets, except perhaps for Æschylus; who, however, like Cæsar, is too awful for a caressing name. But Roman names were, generally, more flexible. Livy and Sallust have ever been favorites with men; Livy with everybody; Sallust, in a degree that may be called extravagant, with many celebrated Frenchmen, as the President des Brosses, and in our own days with M. Lerminier, a most eloquent and original writer (' *Etudes Historiques* '); and two centuries ago, with the greatest of men, John Milton, in a degree that seems to me absolutely mysterious. These writers are baptized into our society — have gained a settlement in our parish: when you call a man Jack, and not Mr. John, it's plain you like him. But, as to the gloomy Tacitus, our fathers liked him not. He was too vinegar a fellow for them; nothing hearty or genial about him; he thought ill of everybody; and we all suspect that, for those times, he was perhaps the worst of the bunch himself. Accordingly, this Tacitus, because he remained so perfectly tacit for our jolly old forefathers' ears, never slipped into the name Tacit for their mouths; nor ever will, I predict, for the mouths of posterity. Coming to the Roman poets, I must grant that three great ones, viz., Lucretius, Statius, and Valerius Flaccus, have not been complimented with the freedom of our city, as they should have been, in a gold box. I regret, also, the ill fortune, in this respect, of Catullus, if he was really the author of that grand headlong dithyrambic, the Atys: he certainly ought to have been ennobled by the title of Catull. Looking to very much of his writings, much more I regret the case of Plautus; and I am sure that if her Majesty would warrant his bearing the name and arms of *Plaut* in all time coming, **it** would gratify many of us. As to the rest, or those that anybody cares about, Horace, Virgil, Ovid, Lucan, Martial, Claudian, all have been raised to the peerage. Ovid was the great poetic favorite of Milton; and not without a philosophic ground: his festal gayety, and the brilliant velocity of his *aurora borealis* intellect, forming a deep natural equipoise to the mighty gloom and solemn planetary movement in the mind of the other; like the wedding of male and female counterparts. Ovid was, therefore, rightly Milton's favorite. But the favorite of all the world is Horace. Were there ten peerages, were there three blue ribbons, vacant, he ought to have them all.

Besides, if Mr. Landor could issue decrees, and even harmonize his decrees for reforming our Anglo-Grecian spelling — decrees which no Council of Trent could execute, without first rebuilding the Holy Office of the Inquisition — still there would be little accomplished. The names of all continental Europe are often in confusion, from different causes, when Anglicized: German names are rarely spelled rightly by the *laity* of our isle: Polish and Hungarian never. Many foreign towns have in England what botanists would call *trivial* names; Leghorn, for instance, Florence, Madrid, Lisbon, Vienna, Munich, Antwerp, Brussels, the Hague, — all unintelligible names to the savage Continental native. Then, if Mr. Landor reads as much of Anglo-Indian books as I do, he must be aware that, for many years back, they have all been at sixes and sevens; so that now most Hindoo words are in masquerade, and we shall soon require *English* pundits in Leadenhall Street.[9] How does he like, for instance, *Sipahee,* the

modern form for *Sepoy*? or *Tepheen* for *Tiffin*? At
this rate of metamorphosis, absorbing even the consecrated names of social meals, we shall soon cease to
understand what that *disjune* was which his sacred
Majesty graciously accepted at Tillietudlem. But even
elder forms of oriental speech are as little harmonized
in Christendom. A few leagues of travelling make
the Hebrew unintelligible to us; and the Bible becomes a Delphic mystery to Englishmen amongst the
countrymen of Luther. Solomon is there called Sala-
mo; Samson is called Simson, though probably he
never published an edition of Euclid. Nay, even in
this native isle of ours, you may be at cross purposes
on the Bible with your own brother. I am, myself,
next door neighbor to Westmoreland, being a Lancashire man; and, one day, I was talking with a
Westmoreland farmer, whom, of course, I ought to
have understood very well; but I had no chance with
him: for I could not make out who that *No* was, concerning *whom* or concerning *which*, he persisted in
talking. It seemed to me, from the context, that *No*
must be a man, and by no means a chair; but so very
negative a name, you perceive, furnished no positive
hints for solving the problem. I said as much to the
farmer, who stared in stupefaction. 'What,' cried
he, 'did a far-larn'd man, like you, fresh from Oxford,
never hear of *No*, an old gentleman that should have been
been drowned, but was *not*, when all his folk were
drowned?' 'Never, so help me Jupiter,' was my
reply: 'never heard of him to this hour, any more
than of *Yes*, an old gentleman that should have been
hanged, but was *not*, when all his folk were hanged.
*Populous No* — I had read of in the Prophets; but
22

that was *not* an old gentleman.' It turned out that
the farmer and all his compatriots in bonny Martindale
had been taught at the parish school to rob the Patri-
arch Noah of one clear moiety appertaining in fee
simple to that ancient name. But afterwards I found
that the farmer was not so entirely absurd as he had
seemed. The Septuagint, indeed, is clearly against
him; for *there*, as plain as a pikestaff, the farmer
might have read *Nωἐ*. But, on the other hand, Pope,
not quite so great a scholar as he was a poet, yet still
a fair one, *always* made Noah into a monosyllable;
and that seems to argue an old English usage; though
I really believe Pope's reason for adhering to such an
absurdity was with a prospective view to the rhymes
*blow*, or *row*, or *stow* (an important idea to the Ark),
which struck him as *likely* words, in case of any call
for writing about Noah.

The long and the short of it is — that the whole
world lies in heresy or schism on the subject of orthography. All climates alike groan under heterography.
It is absolutely of no use to begin with one's own
grandmother in such labors of reformation. It is toil
thrown away : and as nearly hopeless a task as the
proverb insinuates that it is to attempt a reformation in
that old lady's mode of eating eggs. She laughs at
one. She has a vain conceit that she is able, out of
her own proper resources, to do both, viz., the spelling
and the eating of the eggs. And all that remains for
philosophers, like Mr. Landor and myself, is — to turn
away in sorrow rather than in anger, dropping a silent
tear for the poor old lady's infatuation.

# NOTES.

## Note 1.    Page 243.

' *Roberte the Deville :* ' — See the old metrical romance of that name : it belongs to the fourteenth century, and was printed some thirty years ago, with wood engravings of the illuminations. Roberte, however, took the liberty of murdering *his* schoolmaster. But could he well do less ?    Being a reigning Duke's son, and after the rebellious schoolmaster had said —

> ' *Sir, ye bee too bolde :*
> *And therewith tooke a rodde hym for to chaste.*'

Upon which the meek Robin, without using any bad language as the schoolmaster had done, simply took out a long dagger ' *hym for to chaste,*' which he did effectually.    The schoolmaster gave no bad language after that.

## Note 2.    Page 246.

Mitford, who was the brother of a man better known than himself to the public eye, viz., Lord Redesdale, may be considered a very unfortunate author.    His work upon Greece, which Lord Byron celebrated for its ' wrath and its partiality, really had those merits : choleric it was in excess, and as entirely partial, as nearly perfect in its injustice, as human infirmity would allow.    Nothing is truly perfect in this shocking world; absolute injustice, alas ! the perfection of wrong, must not be looked for until we reach some high Platonic form of polity.    Then shall we revel and bask in a vertical sun of iniquity.    Meantime, I *will* say — that to satisfy all bilious and unreasonable men, a better historian of Greece, than Mitford, could not be fancied.    And yet, at the very moment when he was stepping into his harvest of popularity, down comes one of those omnivorous Germans that, by reading everything and a trifle besides, contrive to throw really learned men — and perhaps better thinkers than themseves — into the shade.  Ottfried Mueller, with other archæologists and travellers into Hellas, gave new aspects to the very purposes of Grecian history.  Do you hear, reader ? not new answers, but new questions  And Mitford, that was gradually displacing the unlearned Gillies, &c., was himself displaced by those who intrigued with Germany.  His other work on 'the Harmony of Language,' though one of the many that attempted, and the few that accomplished, the distinction between accent and quantity, or learnedly appreciated the metrical science of Milton, was yet, in my hearing, pronounced utterly intelligible by the best *practical* commentator on Milton, viz., the best reproducer of his exquisite effects in blank verse, that any generation since Milton has been able to show.  Mr. Mitford was one of the many accomplished scholars that are ill-used.  Had he possessed the splendid powers of the Landor, he would have raised a clatter on the armor of modern society, such as Samson threatened to the giant Harapha.  For, in many respects, he resembled the Landor : he had much of his learning — he had the same extensive access to books and influential circles in great cities — the same gloomy disdain of popular falsehoods or commonplaces — and the same disposition to run a-muck against all nations, languages, and spelling-books.

## Note 3.   Page 247.

' *In fact, a New Englander.*' — This explanation, upon a matter familiar to the well-informed, it is proper to repeat occasionally, because we English exceedingly perplex and confound the Americans by calling, for instance, a Virginian or a Kentuck by the name of Yankee, whilst that term was originally intro duced as antithetic to these more southern States.

## Note 4.   Page 249.

Pinkerton published one of his earliest volumes, under this title — ' Rimes, by Mr. Pinkerton,' not having the fear of Ritson before his eyes.  And, for once, we have reason to thank Ritson for his remark — that the form Mr. might just as well be read

*Monster.* Pinkerton in this point was a perfect monster. As to the word *Rimes*, instead of *Rhymes*, he had something to stand upon; the Greek *rythmos* was certainly the remote fountain; but the proximate fountain must have been the Italian *rima.*

### Note 5. Page 250.

The most extravagant of all experiments on language is brought forward in the ' *Letters of Literature*, by Robert Heron.' But Robert Heron is a *pseudonyme* for John Pinkerton ; and I have been told that Pinkerton's motive for assuming it was — because *Heron* had been the maiden name of his mother. Poor lady, she would have stared to find herself, in old age, transformed into Mistressina Heronilla. What most amuses one in pursuing the steps of such an attempt at refinement, is its reception by ' Jack ' in the navy.

### Note 6. Page 250.

' *It ever was* ' — and, of course, being (as there is no need to tell Mr. Landor) a form obtained by contraction from *fidelitas.*

### Note 7. Page 251.

Of this a ludicrous illustration is mentioned by the writer once known to the public as *Trinity Jones.* Some young clergyman, unacquainted with the technical use of italics by the original compositors of James the First's Bible, on coming to the 27th verse, chap. xiii. of 1st Kings, ' And he' (viz., the old prophet of Bethel) ' spake to his sons, saying, Saddle me the ass. And they saddled *him;* ' (where the italic *him* simply meant that this word was involved, but not expressed, in the original,) read it, ' And they saddled ᴴᴵᴹ ; ' as though these undutiful sons, instead of saddling the donkey, had saddled the old prophet. In fact, the old gentleman's directions are not quite without an opening for a filial misconception, if the reader examines them as closely as *I* examine words.

### Note 8. Page 251.

He uses this and similar artifices, in fact, as the damper in a modern piano-forte, for modyfying the swell of the intonation.

Note 9.    Page 256.

The reasons for this anarchy in the naturalization of Eastern words are to be sought in three causes : 1. In national rivalships : French travellers in India, like Jacquemont, &c., as they will not adopt our English First Meridian, will not, of course, adopt our English spelling.   In one of Paul Richter's novels a man assumes the First Meridian to lie generally, not through Greenwich, but through his own skull, and always through his own study.   I have myself long suspected the Magnetic Pole to lie under a friend's wine-cellar, from the vibrating movement which I have remarked constantly going on in his cluster of keys towards that particular point.   Really, the French, like Sir Anthony Absolute, must ' get an atmosphere of their own,' such is their hatred to holding anything in common with us.   2. They are to be sought in local *Indian* differences of pronunciation.   3. In the variety of our own British population — soldiers, missionaries, merchants, who are unlearned or half-learned — scholars, really learned, but often fantastically learned, and lastly (as you may swear) young ladies — anxious, above all things, to mystify us outside barbarians.

# SORTILEGE ON BEHALF OF THE GLAS-GOW ATHENÆUM.

SUDDENLY, about the middle of February, I received a request for some contribution of my own proper writing to a meditated ALBUM of the Glasgow Athenæum. What was to be done? The 13th of the month had already dawned before the request reached me; 'return of post' was the sharp limitation notified within which my communication must revolve; whilst the request itself was dated Feb. 10: so that already three 'returns of post' had finished their brief career on earth. I am not one of those people who, in respect to bread, insist on the discretionary allowance of Paris; but, in respect to time, I *do*. Positively, for all efforts of thought I must have time *à discrétion*. In this case, now, all *discretion* was out of the question; a mounted jockey, in the *melée* of a Newmarket start, might as well demand time for meditation on the philosophy of racing. There was clearly no resource available but one; and it was this: — In my study I have a bath, large enough to swim in, provided the swimmer, not being an ambitious man, is content with going a-head to the extent of six inches at the utmost. This bath, having been superseded (as regards its original purpose) by another mode of bathing, has yielded a secondary service to me as a reservoir for my

MSS. Filled to the brim it is by papers of all sorts and sizes. Every paper written *by* me, *to* me, *for* me, *of* or *concerning* me, and, finally, *against* me, is to be found, after an impossible search, in this capacious repertory. Those papers, by the way, that come under the last (or hostile) subdivision, are chiefly composed by shoemakers and tailors — an affectionate class of men, who stick by one to the last like pitch-plasters. One admires this fidelity; but it shows itself too often in waspishness, and all the little nervous irritabilities of attachment too ardent. They are wretched if they do not continually hear what one is 'about,' what one is 'up to,' and which way one is going to travel. Me, because I am a political economist, they plague for my private opinions on the currency, especially on that part of it which consists in bills at two years after date; and they always want an answer by return of post. What the deuce! one can't answer *every*body by return of post. Now, from this reservoir I resolved to draw some paper for the use of the Athenæum. It was my fixed determination that this Institution should receive full justice, so far as human precautions could secure it. Four dips into the bath I decreed that the Athenæum should have; whereas an individual man, however hyperbolically illustrious, could have had but one. On the other hand, the Athenæum must really content itself with what fortune might send, and not murmur at me as if I had been playing with loaded dice. To cut off all pretence for this allegation, I requested the presence of three young ladies, haters of everything unfair, as female attorneys, to watch the proceedings on behalf of the Athenæum, to see that the dipping went on correctly, and also to advise the court in case of any difficulties arising. At 6 P. M. all was reported right for starting in my study. The bath had been brilliantly illuminated from above, so that no tricks *could* be played in that quarter; and the young man who was to execute the dips had finished dressing in a new potato sack, with holes cut through the bottom for his legs. Now, as the sack was tied with distressing tightness about his throat, leaving only a loop-hole for his right arm to play freely, it is clear that, however sincerely fraudulent in his intentions, and in possible collusion with myself, he could not assist me by secreting any papers about his person, or by any other knavery that we might wish to perpetrate. The young ladies having taken their seats in stations admirably chosen for overlooking the movements of the young man and myself, the proceedings opened. The inaugural step was made in a neat speech from myself, complaining that I was the object of unjust suspicions, and endeavoring to re-establish my character for absolute purity of intentions; but, I regret to say, ineffectually. This angered me, and I declared with some warmth, that in the bath, but whereabouts I could not guess, there lay a particular paper which I valued as equal to the half of my kingdom; 'but for all that,' I went on, 'if our hon. friend in the potato sack should chance to haul up this very paper, I am resolved to stand by the event, yes, in that case, to the half of my kingdom I will express my interest in the Institution. Should even *that* prize be drawn, out of this house it shall pack off to Glasgow this very night.' Upon this, the leader of the attorneys, whom, out of honor to Shakspeare, I may as well call Portia, chilled my enthusiasm disagreeably by

23

saying — 'There was no occasion for any extra zeal on *my* part in such an event, since, as to packing out of this house to Glasgow, she and her learned sisters would take good care that it *did;*' — in fact, *I* was to have no merit whatever I did. Upon this, by way of driving away the melancholy caused by the obstinate prejudice of the attorneys, I called for a glass of wine, and, turning to the west, I drank the health of the Athenæum, under the allegoric idea of a young lady about to come of age and enter upon the enjoyment of her estates. 'Here's to your prosperity, my dear lass,' I said; 'you're very young — but that's a fault which, according to the old Greek adage, is mending every day; and I'm sure you'll always continue as amiable as you are now towards strangers in distress for books and journals. Never grow churlish, my dear, as some of your sex are' (saying which, I looked savagely at Portia). And then, I made the signal to the young man for getting to work — Portia's eyes, as I noticed privately, brightening like a hawk's. '*Prepare to dip!*' I called aloud; and soon after — '*Dip!*' At the '*prepare,*' Potato-sack went on his right knee (his face being at right angles to the bath); at the '*Dip!*' he plunged his right arm into the billowy ocean of papers. For one minute he worked amongst them as if he had been pulling an oar; and then, at the peremptory order '*Haul up!*' he raised aloft in air, like Brutus refulgent from the stroke of Cæsar, his booty. It was handed, of course, to the attorneys, who showed a little female curiosity at first, for it was a letter with the seal as yet unbroken, and might prove to be some old love-letter of my writing, recently sent back to me by the Dead-Letter Office.

It still looked fresh and blooming. So, if there was no prize for Glasgow, there might still be an interesting secret for the benefit of the attorneys. What it was, and what each successive haul netted, I will register under the corresponding numbers.

No. 1. — This was a dinner invitation for the 15th of February, which I had neglected to open. It was, as bill-brokers say, 'coming to maturity,' but luckily not *past due* (in which case you have but a poor remedy), for, though twenty days after date, it had still two days to run before it could be presented for payment. A debate arose with the attorneys — Whether this might not do for the *Album*, in default of any better haul? I argued, for the affirmative, — that, although a dinner invitation cannot in reason be looked to for very showy writing, its motto being *Esse quam videri* (which is good Latin for — *To eat rather than make believe to eat*, as at ball suppers or Barmecide banquets), yet, put the case that I should send this invitation to the Athenæum, accompanied with a power-of-attorney to eat the dinner in my stead — might not *that* solid bonus as an enclosure weigh down the levity of the letter considered as a contribution to the *Album*, and take off the edge of the Athenæum's displeasure? Portia argued *contra* — that such a thing was impossible; because the Athenæum had two thousand mouths, and would therefore require two thousand dinners; — an argument which I admitted to be showy, but, legally speaking, hardly tenable: because the Athenæum had power to appoint a plenipotentiary — some man of immense calibre — to eat the dinner, as representative of the collective two thousand. Portia parried this objection by replying, that if the invita-

tion had been to a ball there might be something in
what I said; but as to a mere dinner, and full fifty
miles·to travel for it from Glasgow, the plenipotentiary (whatever might be his calibre) would decline to
work so hard for such a trifle. 'Trifle!' I replied —
'But, with submission, a dinner twenty-two days after
date of invitation is not likely to prove a trifle. This,
however is, always the way in which young ladies,
whether attorneys or not, treat the subject of dinner.
And as to the fifty miles, the plenipotentiary could go
in an hour.' 'How?' said Portia, sternly. 'Per
rail,' I replied with equal sternness. What there was
to laugh at, I don't see; but at this hot skirmish between me and Portia concerning that rather visionary
person the plenipotentiary, and what he might choose
to do in certain remote contingencies, and especially
when the gross reality of '*per rail*' came into collision
with his aerial essence, Potato-sack began to laugh so
immoderately, that I was obliged to pull him up by
giving the word rather imperiously — '*Prepare to
dip!*' Before he could obey, I was myself pulled up
by Portia, with a triumph in her eye that alarmed me.
She and her sister attorneys had been examining the
dinner invitation — 'and,' said Portia maliciously to
me, 'it's quite correct — as you observe there are two
days good to the dinner hour on the 15th; "*Prepare
to dine!*" is the signal that *should* be flying at this
moment, and in two days more "*Dine!*" — only, by
misfortune, the letter is in the wrong year — it is four
years old!' Oh! fancy the horror of this; since,
besides the mortification from Portia's victory, I had
perhaps narrowly escaped an indictment from the
plenipotentiary for sending him what might *now* be

considered a swindle. I hurried to cover my confusion, by issuing the two orders ' *Prepare to dip !* ' and '*Dip !* ' almost in the same breath. No. 1, after all the waste of legal learning upon it, had suddenly burst like an air-bubble; and the greater stress of expectation, therefore, had now settled on No. 2. With considerable trepidation of voice, I gave the final order — '*Haul up !* '

No. 2. — It is disagreeable to mention that this haul brought up — ' a dun.' Disgust was written upon every countenance; and I fear that suspicion began to thicken upon myself — as having possibly (from my personal experience in these waters) indicated to our young friend where to dredge for duns with most chance of success. But I protest fervently my innocence. It is true that I had myself long remarked that part of the channel to be dangerously infested with duns. In searching for literary or philosophic papers, it would often happen for an hour together that I brought up little else than variegated specimens of the dun. And one vast bank there was, which I called the Goodwin Sands, because nothing within the memory of man was ever known to be hauled up from it except eternal specimens of the dun — some gray with antiquity, some of a neutral tint, some green and lively. With grief it was that I had seen our dipper shoaling his water towards that dangerous neighborhood. But what could I do? If I had warned him off, Portia would have been sure to fancy that there was some great oyster-bed or pearl-fishery in that region; and all I should have effected by my honesty would have been a general conviction of my treachery. I therefore became as anxious as everybody else for

No. 3, which might set all to rights — *might*, **but**
slight were my hopes that it *would*, when I saw in
what direction the dipper's arm was working. Exactly below that very spot where he had dipped, lay,
as stationary as if he had been anchored, a huge and
ferocious dun of great antiquity. Age had not at all
softened the atrocious expression of his countenance,
but rather aided it by endowing him with a tawny
hue. The size of this monster was enormous, nearly
two square feet; and I fancied at times that, in spite
of his extreme old age, he had not done growing. I
knew him but too well; because whenever I happened
to search in that region of the bath, let me be seeking
what I would, and let me miss what I might, always I
was sure to haul up *him* whom I never wanted to see
again. Sometimes I even found him basking on the
very summit of the papers; and I conceived an idea,
which may be a mere fancy, that he came up for air in
particular states of the atmosphere. At present he
was *not* basking on the surface: better for the Athenæum if he *had:* for then the young man would have
been cautious. Not being above, he was certainly
below, and underneath the very centre of the dipper's
plunge. Unable to control my feelings, I cried out —
' Bear away to the right!' But Portia protested with
energy against this intermeddling of mine, as perfidy
too obvious. ' Well,' I said, ' have it your own way:
you'll see what will happen.'

No. 3. — This, it is needless to say, turned out the
horrid old shark, as I had long christened him: I knew
his vast proportions, and his bilious aspect, the moment that the hauling up commenced, which in *his*
case occupied some time. Portia was the more angry,

because she had thrown away her right to *express* any anger by neutralizing my judicious interference. She grew even more angry, because I, though sorry for the Athenæum, really could not help laughing when I saw the truculent old wretch expanding his huge dimensions — all umbered by time and ill-temper — under the eyes of the wondering young ladies; so mighty was the contrast between this sallow behemoth and a rose-colored little billet of their own. By the way, No. 2 had been a specimen of the dulcet dun, breathing only zephyrs of request and persuasion; but this No. 3 was a specimen of the polar opposite — the dun horrific and Gorgonian — blowing great guns of menace. As ideal specimens in their several classes, might they not have a value for the *museum* of the Athenæum, if it *has* one, or even for the *Album*? This was *my* suggestion, but overruled, like everything else that I proposed; and on the ground that Glasgow had too vast a conservatory of duns, native and indigenous, to need any exotic specimens. This settled, we hurried to the next dip, which, being by contract the last, made us all nervous.

No. 4. — This, alas! turned out a lecture addressed to myself by an ultra-moral friend; a lecture on procrastination; and not badly written. I feared that something of the sort was coming; for, at the moment of dipping, I called out to the dipper — 'Starboard your helm! you're going smack upon the Goodwins: in thirty seconds you'll founder.' Upon this, in an agony of fright, the dipper forged off, but evidently quite unaware that vast spurs stretched off from the Goodwins — shoals and sand-banks — where it was mere destruction to sail without a special knowledge

of the soundings.   He had run upon an ethical sand-
bank.   ' Yet, after all, since this is to be the last dip,'
said Portia, ' if the lecture is well written, might it
not be acceptable to the Athenæum ? '   ' Possibly,' 1
replied ; ' but it is too personal, besides being founded
in error from first to last.   I could not allow myself
to be advertised in a book as a procrastinator on principle, unless the Athenæum would add a postscript
under its official seal, expressing entire disbelief of the
accusation ; which I have  private reasons for thinking
that the Athenæum may decline to do.'

' Well, then,' said Portia, ' as you wilfully rob the
Athenæum of No. 4, which by contract is the undoubted property of that body, in fee simple and not
in fee conditional,' (mark Portia's learning as an attorney,) ' then you are bound to give us a 5th dip ;
particularly as you've been so treacherous all along.'
Tears rushed to my eyes at this most unjust assumption.   In agonizing tones I cried out, ' Potato-sack !
my friend Potato-sack ! will you quietly listen to this
charge upon me, that am as innocent as the child un-
born ?   If it is a crime in me to know, and in you *not*
to know, where the Goodwins lie, why then, let you
and me sheer off to the other side of the room, and
let Portia try if *she* can do better.   I allow her motion
for a fresh trial.   I grant a 5th dip : and the more
readily, because it is an old saying — that there is
luck in odd numbers : *numero dues impare gaudet ;* —
only I must request of Portio to be the dipper on this
final occasion.'   All the three attorneys blushed a
rosy red on this unexpected summons.   It was one
thing to criticize, but quite another thing to undertake
the performance ; and the fair attorneys trembled for

their professional reputation. Secretly, however, I whispered to Potato-sack, 'You'll see now, such is female address, that whatever sort of monster they haul up, they'll swear it's a great prize, and contrive to extract some use from it that may seem to justify this application for a new trial.'

No. 5. — Awful and thrilling were the doubts, fears, expectations of us all, when Portia 'prepared to dip,' and secondly 'dipped.' She shifted her hand, and 'ploitered' amongst the papers for full five minutes. I winked at this in consideration of past misfortunes; but, strictly speaking, she had no right to 'ploiter' for more than one minute. She contended that she knew, by intuition, the sort of paper upon which 'duns' were written; and whatever else might come up, she was resolved it should not be a dun. 'Don't be too sure,' I said; and, at last, when she seemed to have settled her choice, I called out the usual word of command, '*Haul up.*'

'What is it?' we said; 'what's the prize?' we demanded, all rushing up to Portia. Guess, reader; — it was a sheet of blank paper!

I, for my part, was afraid either to laugh or to cry. I really felt for Portia, and, at the same time, for the Athenæum. Yet I had a monstrous desire to laugh horribly. But, bless you, reader! there was no call for pity to Portia. With the utmost coolness she said, 'Oh! here is *carte blanche* for receiving your latest thoughts. This is the paper on which you are to write an essay for the Athenæum; and thus we are providentially enabled to assure our client the Athenæum of something expressly manufactured for the occasion, and not an old wreck from the Goodwins.

Fortune loves the Athenæum; and her four blanks **at** starting were only meant to tease that Institution, and to enhance the value of her final favor.' ' Ah, in-- deed!' I said in an under tone, ' *meant to tease !* there are other ladies who understand that little science be- side Fortune !'   However, there is no disobeying the commands of Portia; so I sate down to write a paper on ASTROLOGY.   But, before beginning, I looked at Potato-sack, saying only, ' You see : I told you what would happen.'

## ASTROLOGY.

As my contribution to their *Album*, I will beg the Athenæum to accept a single thought on this much- injured subject.   Astrology I greatly respect; but it is singular that my respect for the science arose out of my contempt for its professors, — not exactly as **a** direct logical consequence, but as **a** casual suggestion from that contempt.   I believe in astrology, but not in astrologers; as to *them* I am an incorrigible infidel. First, let me state the occasion upon which my astrological thought arose ; and then, secondly, the thought itself..

When about seventeen years old, I was wandering as a pedestrian tourist in North Wales.   For some little time, the centre of my ramblings (upon which I still revolved from all my excursions, whether ellip- tical, circular, or zig-zag) was Llangollen in Denbigh- shire, or else Rhuabon, not more than a few miles distant.   One morning I was told by a young married woman, at whose cottage I had received some kind

hospitalities, that an astrologer lived in the neighborhood. 'What might be his name?' Very good English it was that my young hostess had hitherto spoken;
and yet, in this instance, she chose to answer me in
Welsh. *Mochinahante*, was her brief reply. I dare
say that my spelling of the word will not stand Welsh
criticism; but what can you expect from a man's first
attempt at Welsh orthography? I am sure that my
*written* word reflects the *vocal* word which I heard —
provided you pronounce the *ch* as a Celtic guttural;
and I can swear to three letters out of the twelve, viz.
the first, the tenth, and the eleventh, as rigorously correct. Pretty well, I think, *that*, for a mere beginner
— only seventy-five per cent. by possibility wrong!
But what did *Mochinahante* mean? For a man might
as well be anonymous, or call himself X Y Z, as offer
one his visiting card indorsed with a name so frightful
to look at — so shocking to utter — so agonizing to
spell — as *Mochinahante*. And that it had a trans-
latable meaning — that it was not a proper name but
an appellative, in fact some playful *sobriquet*, I felt
certain, from observing the young woman to smile
whilst she uttered it. My next question drew from
her — that this Pagan-looking monster of a name
meant *Pig-in-the-dingle*. But really, now, between
the original monster and this English interpretation,
there was very little to choose; in fact the interpretation, as often happens, strikes one as the harder to
understand of the two. 'To be sure it does,' says a
lady sitting at my elbow, and tormented by a passion
so totally unfeminine as curiosity — ' to be sure — very
much harder; for *Mochina — what-do-you-call-it?*
might, you know, mean something or other, for any-

thing that you or I could say to the contrary; but as
to *Pig-in-the-dingle* — what dreadful nonsense! what
impossible description of an astrologer! A man that
— let me see — does something or other about the
stars : how can *he* be described as a pig? pig in *any*
sense, you know — pig in *any* place? But *Pig-in-a-
dingle!* — why, if he's a pig at all, he must be *Pig-
on-a-steeple*, or *Pig-on-the-top-of-a-hill*, that he may
rise above the mists and vapors. Now I insist, my
dear creature, on your explaining all this riddle on the
spot. *You* know it — you came to the end of the
mystery; but none of *us* that are sitting here can
guess at the meaning; we shall all be ill, if you keep
us waiting — I've a headach beginning already — so
say the thing at once, and put us out of torment!'

What's to be done? I *must* explain the thing to
the Athenæum; and if I stop to premise an oral explanation for the lady's separate use, there will be no
time to save the Glasgow post, which waits for no
man, and is deaf even to female outcries. By way of
compromise, therefore, I request of the lady that she
will follow my pen with her radiant eyes, by which
means she will obtain the earliest intelligence, and the
speediest relief to her headach. I, on my part, will
not loiter, but will make my answer as near to a tele-
graphic answer, in point of speed, as a rigid metallic
pen will allow: —— I divide this answer into two
heads : the first concerning ' *in the dingle*,' the second
concerning '*pig*.' My philosophic researches, and a
visit to the astrologer, ascertained a profound reason
for describing him as *in-the-dingle*; viz. because he
*was* in a dingle. He was the sole occupant of a little
cove amongst the hills — the sole householder; and

so absolutely such, that if ever any treason should be hatched in the dingle, clear it was to my mind that *Mochinahante* would be found at the bottom of it; if ever war should be levied in this dingle, *Mochinahante* must be the sole belligerent; and if a forced contribution were ever imposed upon this dingle, *Mochinahante* (poor man!) must pay it all out of his own pocket. The lady interrupts me at this point to say — ' Well, I understand all *that* — that's all very clear. But what I want to know about is — *Pig*. Come to *Pig*. Why *Pig*? How *Pig*? In what sense *Pig*? You can't have any profound reason, you know, for *that*.'

Yes I have; a *very* profound reason; and satisfactory to the most sceptical of philosophers, viz. that he *was* a Pig. I was presented by my fair hostess to the great interpreter of the stars, in person; for I was anxious to make the acquaintance of an astrologer, and especially of one who, whilst owning to so rare a profession, owned also to the soft impeachment of so very significant a name. Having myself enjoyed so favorable an opportunity for investigating the reasonableness of that name, *Mochinahante*, as applied to the Denbighshire astrologer, I venture to pronounce it unimpeachable. About his dress there was a forlornness, and an ancient tarnish or *œrugo*, which went far to justify the name; and upon his face there sate that lugubrious rust (or what medallists technically call *patina*) which bears so costly a value when it is found on the *coined* face of a Syro-Macedonian prince long since compounded with dust, but, alas! bears no value at all if found upon the flesh-and-blood face of a living philosopher. Speaking humanly, one would have insinuated that the star-gazer wanted much washing and

scouring ; but, astrologically speaking, perhaps he
would have been spoiled by earthly waters for his
celestial vigils.

*Mochinahante* was civil enough ; a pig is not necessarily rude ; and, after seating me in his chair of state,
he prepared for his learned labors by cross-examina-
tions as to the day and hour of my birth.  The *day* I
knew to a certainty ; and even about the *hour* I could
tell quite as much as ought in reason to be expected·
from one who certainly had not been studying a chro-
nometer when that event occurred.  These points settled, the astrologer withdrew into an adjoining room,
for the purpose (as he assured me) of scientifically con-
structing my horoscope ; but unless the drawing of
corks is a part of that process, I should myself incline
to think that the great man, instead of minding my
interests amongst the stars and investigating my horoscope, had been seeking consolation for himself in
bottled porter.  Within half-an-hour he returned ;
looking more lugubrious than ever ; more grim ;
more grimy (if *grime* yields any such adjective) ; a
little more rusty ; rather more *patinous*, if numisma-
tists will lend me that word ; and a great deal more in
want of scouring.  He had a paper of diagrams in his
hand, which of course contained some short-hand
memoranda upon my horoscope ; but, from its smoki-
ness, a malicious visitor might have argued a possibility
that it had served for more customers than myself.  Under his arm he carried a folio book, which (he said) was
a manuscript of unspeakable antiquity.  This he was
jealous of my seeing ; and before he would open it, as
if I and the book had been two prisoners at the bar
suspected of meditating some collusive mischief (such

as tying a cracker to the judge's wig), he separated us as widely from each other as the dimensions of the room allowed. These solemnities finished, we were all ready — I, and the folio volume, and Pig-in-the-dingle — for our several parts in the play. *Mochinahante* began : — He opened the pleadings in a deprecatory tone, protesting, almost with tears, that if anything should turn out amiss in the forthcoming revelations, it was much against his will ; that *he* was power-less, and could not justly be held responsible for any part of the disagreeable message which it might be his unhappiness to deliver. I hastened to assure him that I was incapable of such injustice ; that I should hold the stars responsible for the whole ; by nature, that I was very forgiving ; that any little mal-ice, which I might harbor for a year or so, should all be reserved for the use of the particular constellations concerned in the plot against myself ; and, lastly, that I was now quite ready to stand the worst of their thunders. Pig was pleased with this reasonableness ; he saw that he had to deal with a philosopher ; and, in a more cheerful tone, he now explained that my case was msystically contained in the diagrams ; these smoke-dried documents submitted, as it were, a series of questions to the book ; which book it was — a book of unspeakable antiquity — that gave the inflexible answers, like the gloomy oracle that it was. But I was not to be angry with the book, any more than with himself, since —— ' Of course not,' I replied, in-terrupting him, ' the book did but utter the sounds which were predetermined by the white and black keys struck in the smoky diagrams ; and I could no more be angry with the book for speaking what it conscientiously believed to be the truth than with a decanter of port wine, or a bottle of porter, for declining to yield more than one or two wine-glasses of the precious liquor at the moment when I was looking for a dozen, under a transient forgetfulness, incident to the greatest minds, that I myself, ten minutes before, had nearly drunk up the whole.' This comparison, though to a critic wide awake it might have seemed slightly personal, met with the entire approbation of *Pig-in-the-dingle*. A better frame of mind for receiving disastrous news, he evidently conceived, could not exist or be fancied by the mind of man than existed at that moment in myself. *He* was in a state of intense pathos from the bottled porter. *I* was in a state of intense excitement (pathos combined with horror) at the prospect of a dreadful lecture on my future life, now ready to be thundered into my ears from that huge folio of unspeakable antiquity, prompted by those wretched smoke-dried diagrams. I believe we were in magnetical rapport. Think of *that*, reader! — Pig and I in magnetical rapport! Both making passes at each other! What in the world would have become of us if suddenly we should have taken to somnambulizing? Pig would have abandoned his dingle to me; and I should have dismissed Pig to that life of wandering which must have betrayed the unscoured patinous condition of the astrologer to the astonished eyes of Cambria : —

' Stout Glos'ter stood aghast [or *might* have stood] in speechless trance.
*To arms!* cried Mortimer [or at least *might* have cried], and couch'd his quivering lance.'

But Pig was-a greater man than he seemed. He

yielded neither to magnetism nor to bottled porter, but commenced reading from the black book in the most awful tone of voice, and, generally speaking, most correctly. Certainly he made one dreadful mistake; he started from the very middle of a sentence, instead of the beginning; but then *that* had a truly lyrical effect, and also it was excused by the bottled porter. The words of the prophetic denunciation, from which he started, were these — 'also *he* [that was myself, you understand] shall have red hair.' ' *There* goes a bounce,' I said in an under tone; ' the stars it seems, can tell falsehoods as well as other people.' 'Also,' for Pig went on without stopping, ' he shall have seven-and-twenty-children.' Too horror-struck I was by this news to utter one word of protest against it. 'Also,' Pig yelled out at the top of his voice, ' he shall desert them.' Anger restored my voice, and I cried out, ' That's not only a lie in the stars, but a libel; and, if an action lay against a constellation, I should recover damages.' Vain it would be to trouble the reader with all the monstrous prophecies that Pig read against me. He read with a steady Pythian fury. Dreadful was his voice: dreadful were the starry charges against myself — things that I *was* to do, things that I *must* do: dreadful was the wrath with which secretly I denounced all participation in the acts which these wicked stars laid to my charge. But this infirmity of good nature besets me, that, if a man shows trust and absolute faith in any agent or agency whatever, heart there is not in me to resist him, or to expose his folly. Pig trusted — oh how profoundly! — in his black book of unspeakable antiquity. It would have killed him on the spot to

prove that the black book was a hoax, and that **he**
himself was another.   Consequently, I submitted in
silence to pass for the monster that Pig, under coer ·
cion of the stars, had pronounced me, rather than part
in anger from the solitary man, who after all was not
to blame, acting only in a ministerial capacity, and
reading only what the stars obliged him to read.   I
rose without saying one word, advanced to the table,
and paid my fees ; . for it is a disagreeable fact · to
record, that astrologers grant no credit, nor even dis-
count upon prompt payment. ' I shook hands with
*Mochinahante ;* we exchanged kind farewells — he
smiling benignly upon me, in total forgetfulness that
he had just dismissed me to a life of storms and
crimes ; I, in return, as the very best benediction that
I could think of, saying secretly, 'Oh Pig, may the
heavens rain their choicest soap-suds upon thee ! '

Emerging into the open air, I told my fair hostess
of the red hair which the purblind astrologer had
obtained for me from the stars, and which, with *their*
permission, I would make over to *Mochinahante* for a
reversionary wig in his days of approaching baldness.
But I said not one word upon · that too bountiful
allowance of children with which *Moch.* had endowed
me. . I retreated by nervous anticipation ; from that
inextinguishable laughter 'which, 'I was too 'certain,
would follow · upon' *her* part ;  and yet, when 'we
reached the outlet of the dingle, and turned round to
take a ̄ parting look of the astrological dwelling, I
myself was overtaken by fits of laughter ;  for suddenly I figured in vision my own future return to this
mountain recess, with the young legion of twenty-
seven children.  ' *I* desert them, the darlings ! ' I

exclaimed, 'far from it! Backed by this filial army, I shall feel myself equal to the task of taking vengeance on the stars for the affronts they have put upon me through Pig their servant. It will be like the return of the Heracleidæ to the Peloponnesus. The sacred legion will storm the " dingle," whilst *I* storm Pig; the rising generation will take military possession of "*-inahante*," whilst I deal with " *Moch* " (which I presume to be the part in the long word answering to Pig).' My hostess laughed in sympathy with *my* laughter; but I was cautious of letting her have a look into my vision of the sacred legion. We quitted the dingle for ever; and so ended my first visit, being also my last, to an astrologer.

This, reader, was the true general occasion of my one thought upon astrology; and, before I mention it, I may add that the immediate impulse drawing my mind in any such direction was this : — On walking to the table where the astrologer sat, in order to pay my fees, naturally I came nearer to the folio book than astrological prudence would generally have allowed. But Pig's attention was diverted for the moment to the silver coins laid before him; these he reviewed with the care reasonable in one so poor, and in a state of the coinage so neglected as it then was. By this moment of avarice in Pig, I profited so far as to look over the astrologer's person, sitting and bending forward full upon the book. It was spread open, and at a glance I saw that it was no MS. but a printed book, printed in black-letter types. The month of August stood as a rubric at the head of the broad margin; and below it stood some days of that month in orderly succession. ' So then, Pig,' said I in my thoughts, ' it seems that any person whatever, born on any particular day and hour of August, is to have the same exact fate as myself. But a king and a beggar may chance thus far to agree. And be you assured, Pig, that all the infinite variety of cases lying between these two *termini* differ from each other in fortunes and incidents of life as much, though not so notoriously, as king and beggar.'

Hence arose a confirmation of my contempt for astrology. It seemed as if *necessarily* false — false by an *à priori* principle, viz. that the possible differences in human fortunes, which are infinite, cannot be measured by the possible differences in the particular moments of birth, which are too strikingly finite. It strengthened me in this way of thinking, that subsequently I found the very same objection in Macrobius. Macrobius may have stolen the idea; but certainly not from me — *as* certainly I did not steal it from him; so that here is a concurrence of two people independently, *one* of them a great philosopher, in the very same annihilating objection.

Now comes my one thought. Both of us were wrong, Macrobius and myself. Even the great philosopher is obliged to confess it. The objection truly valued is — to astrologers, not to astrology. No two events ever *did* coincide in point of time. Every event has, and must have, a certain duration; this you may call its *breadth;* and the true *locus* of the event in time is the central point of that breadth, which never was or will be the same for any two separate events, though grossly held to be contemporaneous. It is the mere imperfection of our human means for chasing the infinite subdivisibilities of time which causes us to regard two events as even by possibility concurring in their central moments. This imperfection is crushing to the pretensions of astrologers; but astrology laughs at it in the heavens; and astrology, armed with celestial chronometers, is true!

Suffer me to illustrate the case a little:— It is rare that a metaphysical difficulty can be made as clear as a pikestaff. This can. Suppose two events to occur in the same quarter of a minute—that is, in the same fifteen seconds; then, if they started precisely together, and ended precisely together, they would not only have the same breadth, but this breadth would accurately coincide in all its parts or fluxions; consequently, the central moment, viz., the 8th, would coincide rigorously with the centre of each event. But, suppose that one of the two events, A for instance, commenced a single second before B the other, then, as we are still supposing them to have the same breadth or extension, A will have ended in the second before B ends; and, consequently, the centres will be different, for the 8th second of A will be the 7th of B. The disks of the two events will overlap—A will overlap B at the beginning; B will overlap A at the end. Now, go on to assume that, in a particular case, this overlapping does not take place, but that the two events eclipse each other, lying as truly surface to surface as two sovereigns in a tight *rouleau* of sovereigns, or one dessert-spoon nestling in the bosom of another; in that case, the 8th or central second will be the centre for both. But even here a question will arise as to the degree of rigor in the coincidence; for divide that 8th second into a thousand parts or sub-moments, and perhaps the centre of A will be found to hit the 450th sub-moment, whilst that of B may hit the 600th. Or suppose, again, even this trial surmounted: the two harmonious creatures, A and B, running neck and neck together, have both hit simultaneously the true centre of the thousand sub-moments which lies half-way between the 500th and the 501st. All is right so far — 'all right behind;' but go on, if you please; subdivide this last centre, which we will call X, into a thousand lesser fractions. Take, in fact, a railway express-train of decimal fractions, and give chase to A and B; my word for it that you will come up with them in some stage or other of the journey, and arrest them in the very act of separating their centres — which is a dreadful crime in the eye of astrology; for, it is utterly impossible that the initial moment, or *sub-moment*, or *sub-sub*-moment of A and B should absolutely coincide. Such a thing as a perfect start was never heard of at Doncaster. Now, this severe accuracy is not wanted on earth. Archimedes, it is well known, never saw a perfect circle, nor even, with his leave, a decent circle; for, doubtless, the reader knows the following fact, viz., that, if you take the most perfect Vandyking ever cut out of paper or silk, by the most delicate of female fingers, with the most exquisite of Salisbury scissors, upon viewing it through a microscope you will find the edges frightfully ragged; but, if you apply the same microscope to one of God's Vandyking on the corolla or calyx of a flower, you will find it as truly cut and as smooth as a moonbeam. We on earth, I repeat, need no such rigorous truth. For instance, you and I, my reader, want little perhaps with circles, except now and then to bore one with an augre in a ship's bottom, when we wish to sink her and to cheat the underwriters; or, by way of variety, to cut one with a centre-bit through shop-shutters, in order to rob a jeweller;—so *we* don't care much whether the circumference is ragged or not. But that won't do for a constellation! The stars *n'entendent pas la raillerie* on the subject of geometry. The pendulum of the starry heavens oscillates truly; and if the Greenwich time of the *Empyreum* can't be repeated upon earth, without an error, a horoscope is as much a chimera as the perpetual motion, or as an agreeable income-tax. · In fact, in casting a nativity, to swerve from the true centre by the trillionth of a centillionth is as fatal as to leave room for a coach and six to turn between your pistol shot and the bull's eye. If you haven't done the trick, no matter how near you've come to it. And to overlook this, is as absurd as was the answer of that Lieutenant M., who, being asked whether he had any connection with another officer of the same name, replied — 'Oh yes! a very close one.' 'But in what way?' 'Why, you see, I'm in the 50th regiment of foot, and he's in the 49th:' walking, in fact, just behind him! Yet, for all this, horoscopes may be calculated very truly by the stars amongst themselves; and my conviction is — that they are. They are perhaps even printed hieroglyphically, and published as regularly as a nautical almanac; only, they cannot be re-published upon earth by any mode of piracy yet discovered amongst sublunary booksellers. Astrology, in fact, is a very profound, or at least a very lofty science; but astrologers are humbugs.

I have finished, and I am vain of my work; for I have accomplished three considerable things: — I have floored Macrobius; I have cured a lady of her

headache; and lastly, which is best of all, I have expressed my sincere interest in the prosperity of the
Glasgow Athenæum.

But the Glasgow post is mounting, and this paper
will be lost; a fact which, amongst all the dangers
besetting me in this life, the wretched Pig forgot to
warn me of.

Feb. 24, 1848.

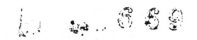

Lightning Source UK Ltd.
Milton Keynes UK
UKHW020819241218
334505UK00012B/980/P

9 781330 878606